THE STRONGEST SAGE
WITH THE WEAKEST CREST

Story | Shinkoshoto

Art | Liver Jam & POPO (Friendly Land)

Character Design | Huuka Kazabana

Translation: Caleb D. Cook
Lettering: Ken Kamura
Cover Design: Phil Balsman
Editor: Tania Biswas

SHIKKAKUMON NO SAIKYOKENJA Volume 3
©Shinkoshoto/SB Creative Corp.
Original Character Designs:©Huuka Kazabana/SB Creative Corp.
©Friendly Land/SQUARE ENIX CO., LTD.
First published in Japan in 2018 by SQUARE ENIX CO., LTD.
English translation rights arranged with SQUARE ENIX
CO., LTD. and SQUARE ENIX, INC.
English translation © 2021 by SQUARE ENIX CO., LTD.

ISBN: 978-1-64609-045-7

Library of Congress Cataloging-in-Publication
Data is on file with the publisher.

Printed in the U.S.A.
First printing, January 2021
10 9 8 7 6 5 4 3 2 1

SQUARE ENIX
MANGA & BOOKS
www.square-enix-books.com

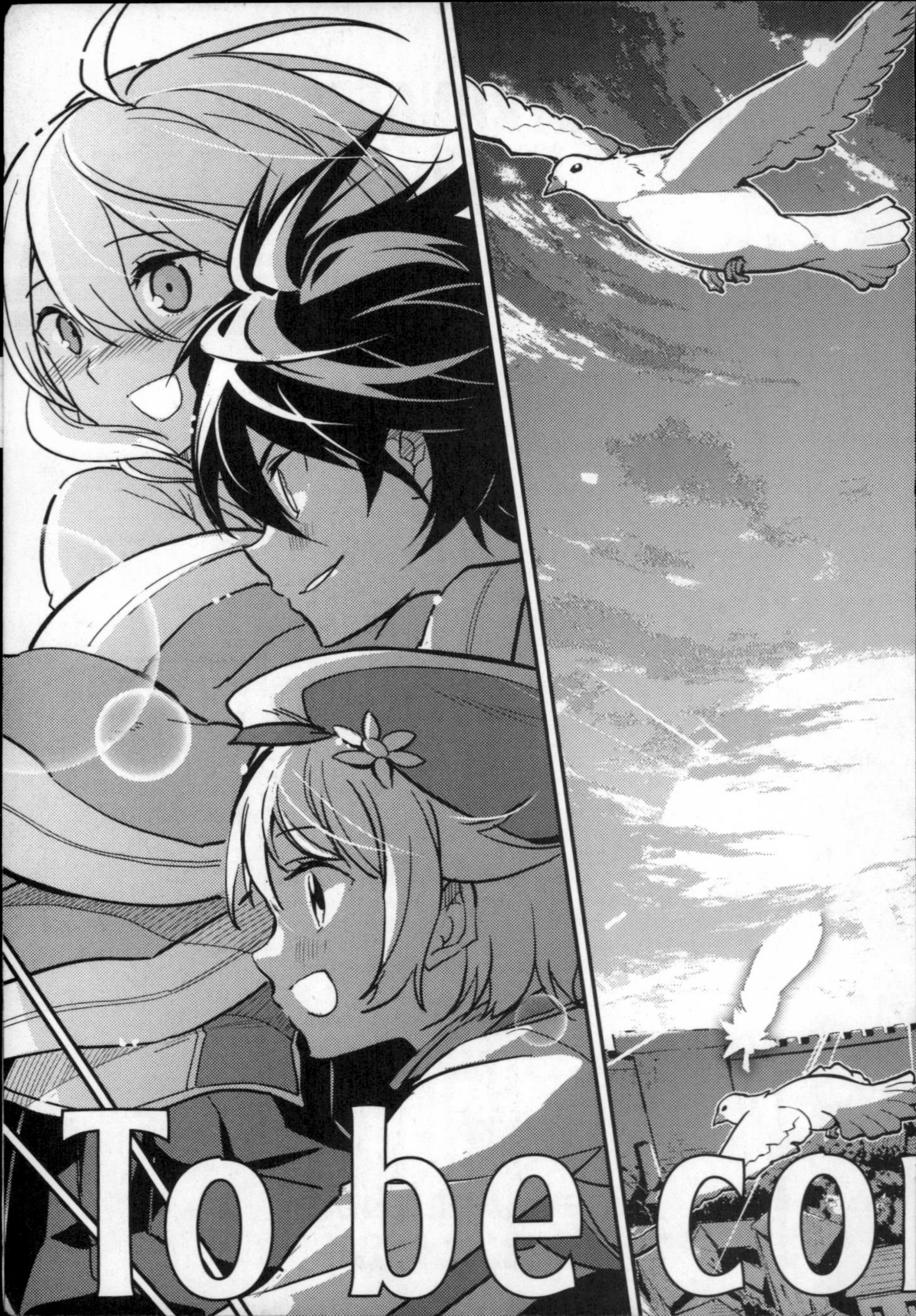
To be co

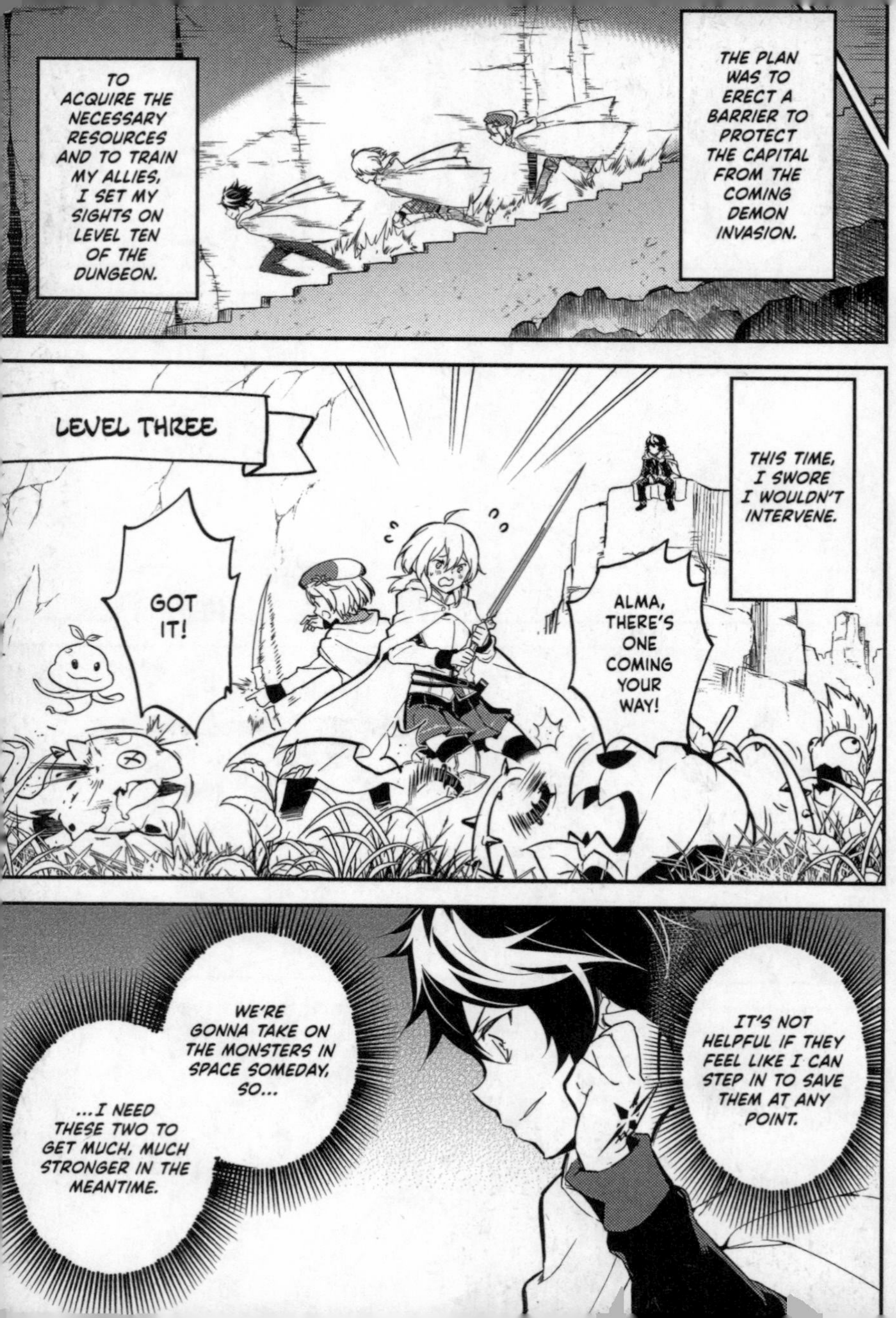
THE PLAN WAS TO ERECT A BARRIER TO PROTECT THE CAPITAL FROM THE COMING DEMON INVASION.
TO ACQUIRE THE NECESSARY RESOURCES AND TO TRAIN MY ALLIES, I SET MY SIGHTS ON LEVEL TEN OF THE DUNGEON.
THIS TIME, I SWORE I WOULDN'T INTERVENE.
LEVEL THREE
ALMA, THERE'S ONE COMING YOUR WAY!
GOT IT!
IT'S NOT HELPFUL IF THEY FEEL LIKE I CAN STEP IN TO SAVE THEM AT ANY POINT.
WE'RE GONNA TAKE ON THE MONSTERS IN SPACE SOMEDAY, SO...
...I NEED THESE TWO TO GET MUCH, MUCH STRONGER IN THE MEANTIME.

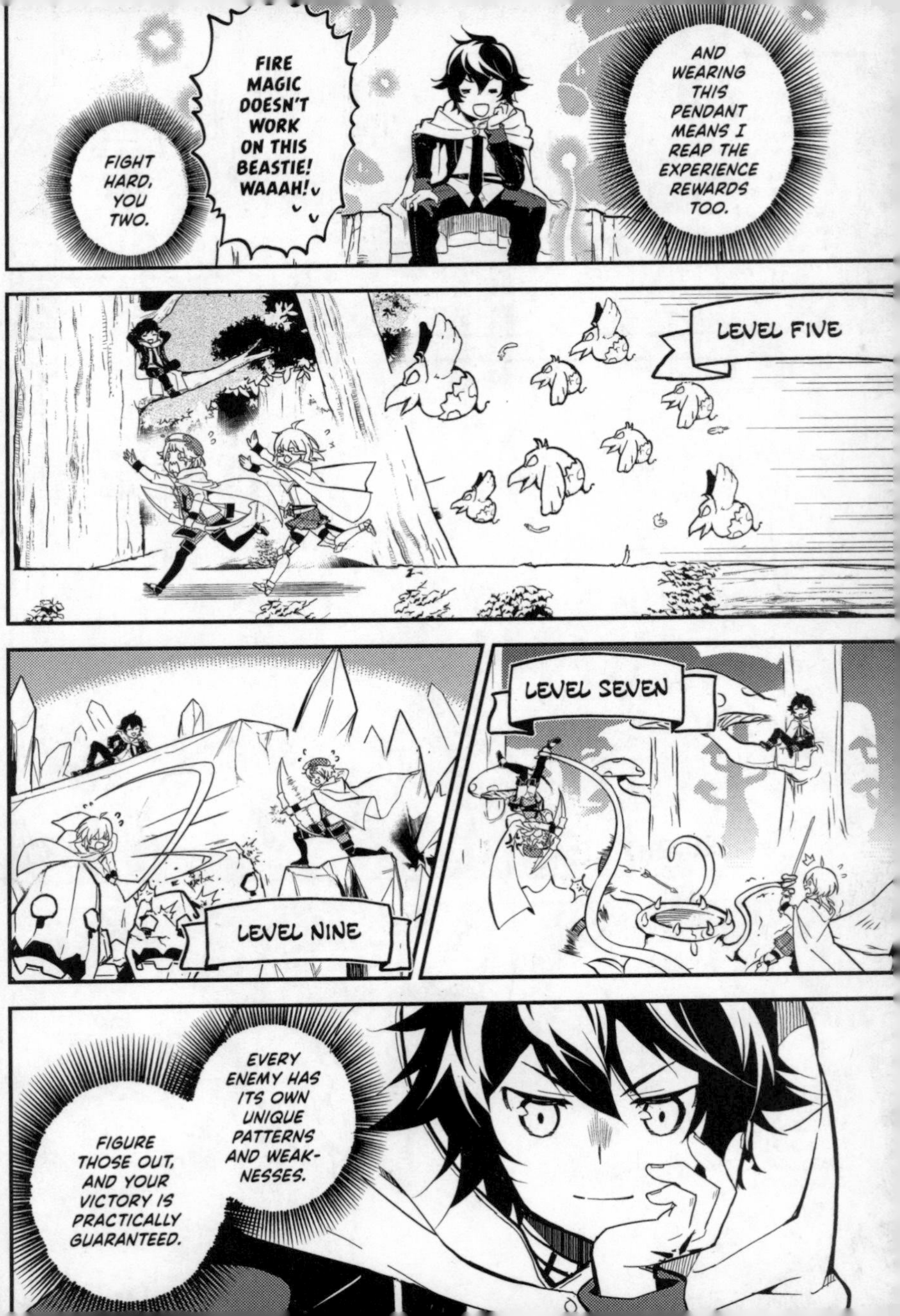
AND WEARING THIS PENDANT MEANS I REAP THE EXPERIENCE REWARDS TOO.
FIRE MAGIC DOESN'T WORK ON THIS BEASTIE! WAAAH!
FIGHT HARD, YOU TWO.
LEVEL FIVE
LEVEL SEVEN
LEVEL NINE
EVERY ENEMY HAS ITS OWN UNIQUE PATTERNS AND WEAK-NESSES.
FIGURE THOSE OUT, AND YOUR VICTORY IS PRACTICALLY GUARANTEED.

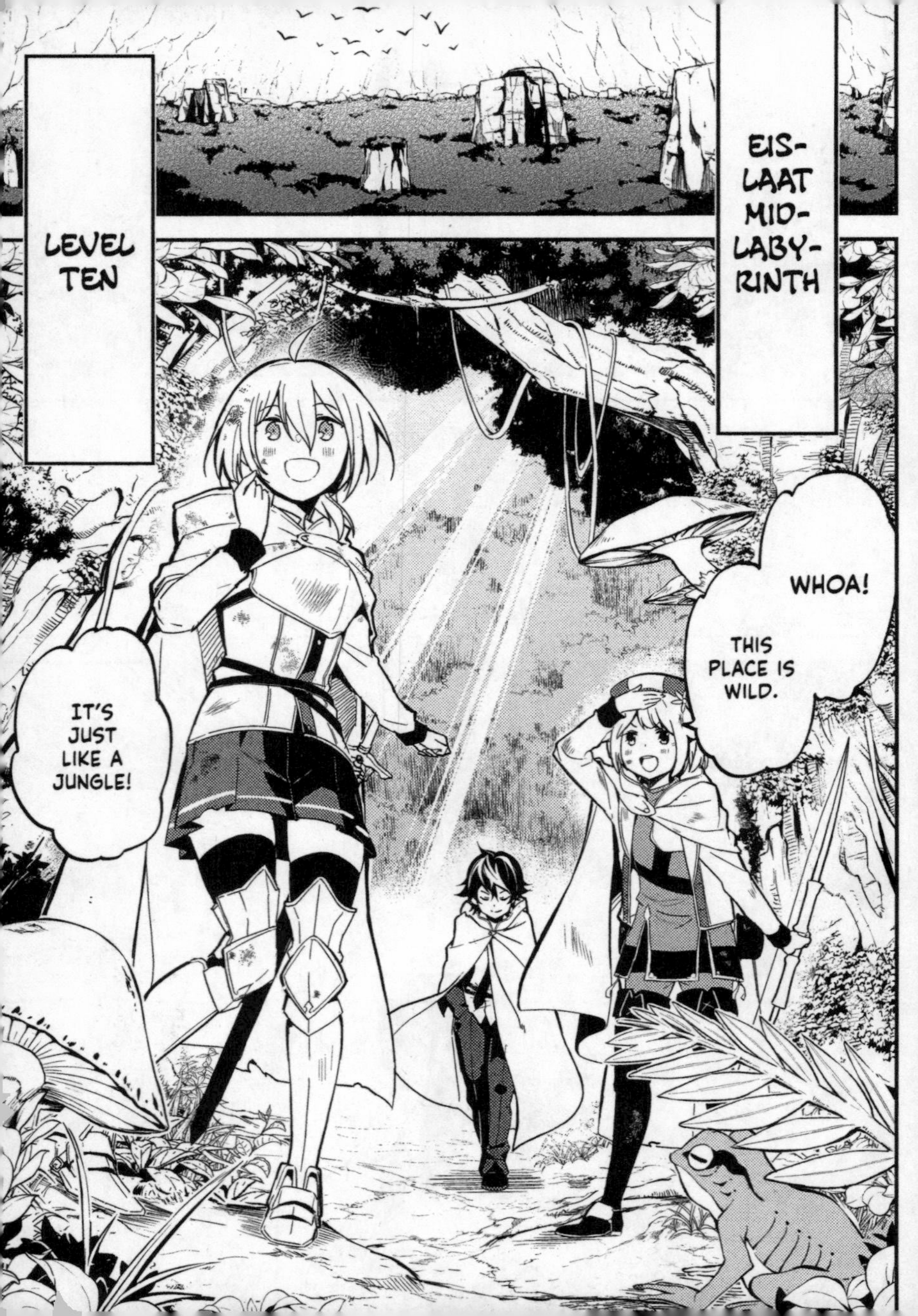
EIS-LAAT MID-LABYRINTH
LEVEL TEN
WHOA!
THIS PLACE IS WILD.
IT'S JUST LIKE A JUNGLE!

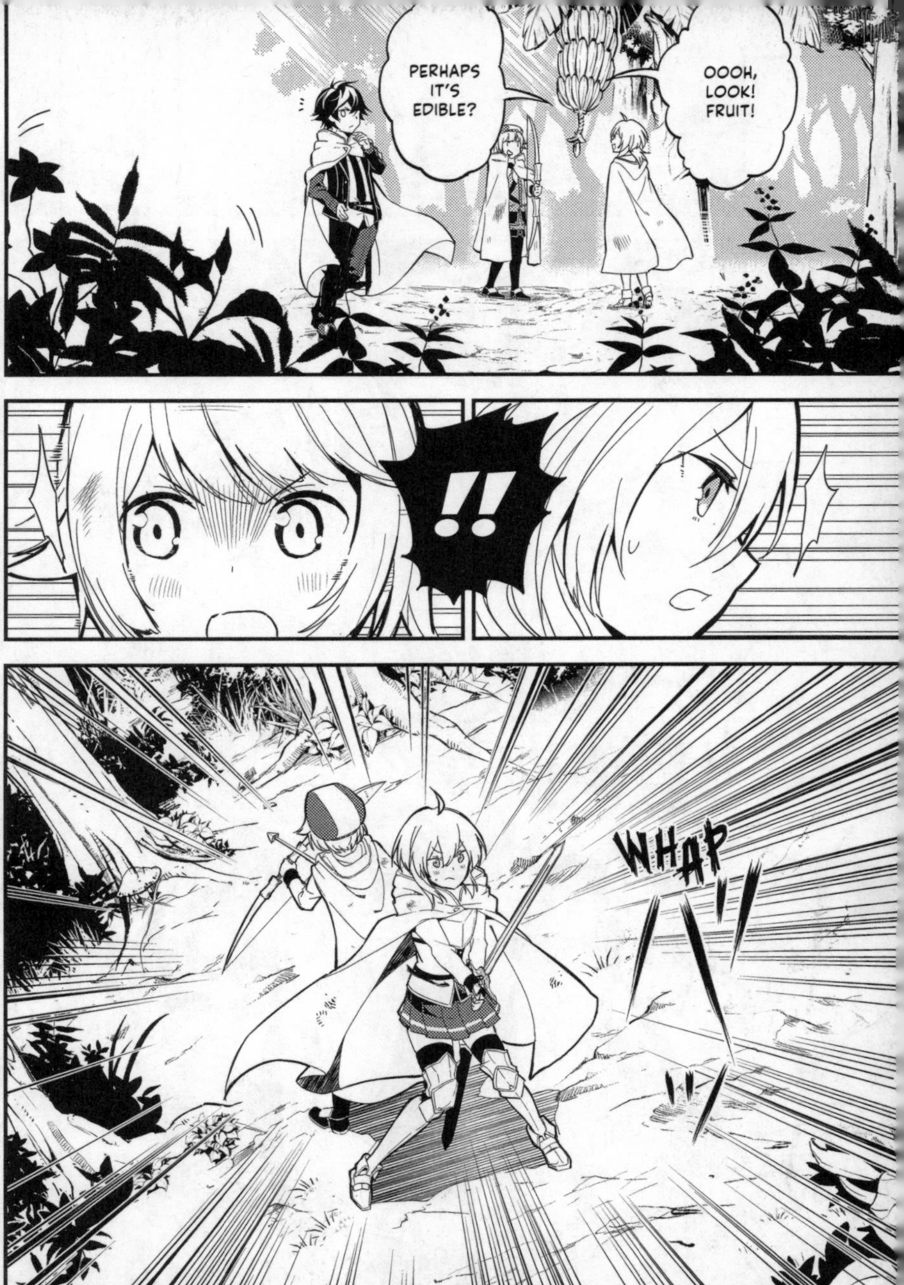
OOOH, LOOK! FRUIT!
PERHAPS IT'S EDIBLE?
!!
WHAP

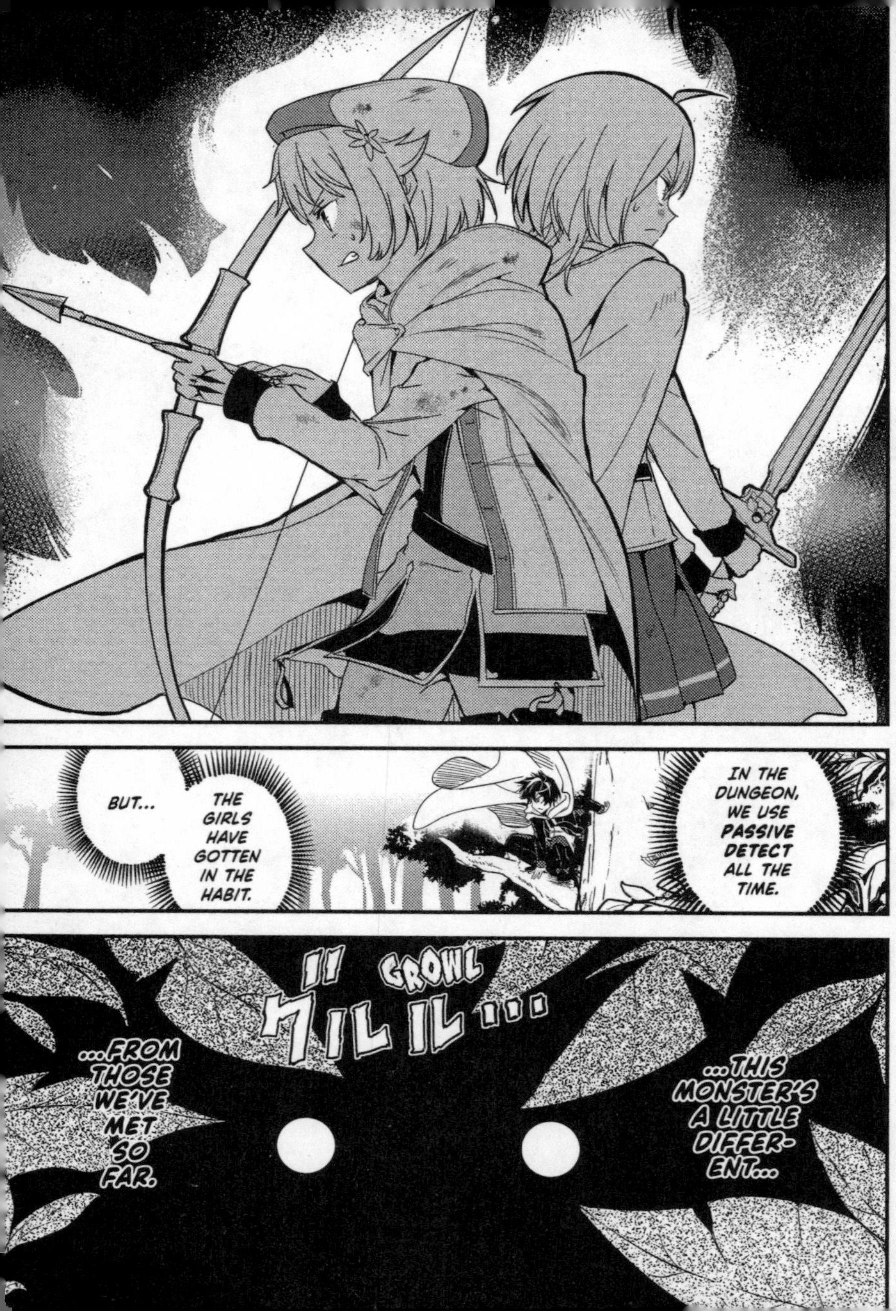
IN THE DUNGEON, WE USE PASSIVE DETECT ALL THE TIME.
THE GIRLS HAVE GOTTEN IN THE HABIT.
BUT...
GROWL
...THIS MONSTER'S A LITTLE DIFFER-ENT...
...FROM THOSE WE'VE MET SO FAR.

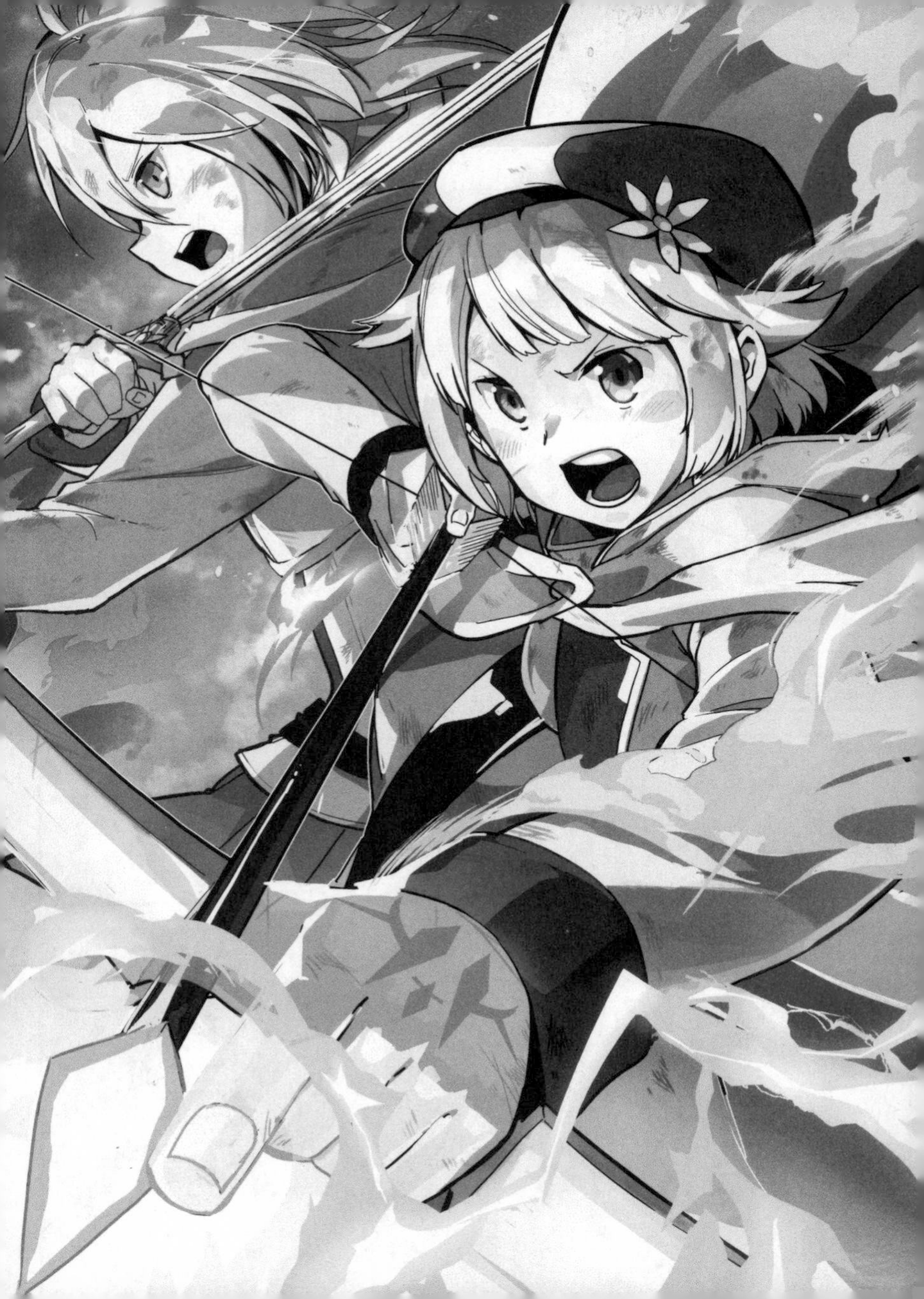

CHAPTER 9 ◆ The Strongest Sage Struts His Stuff

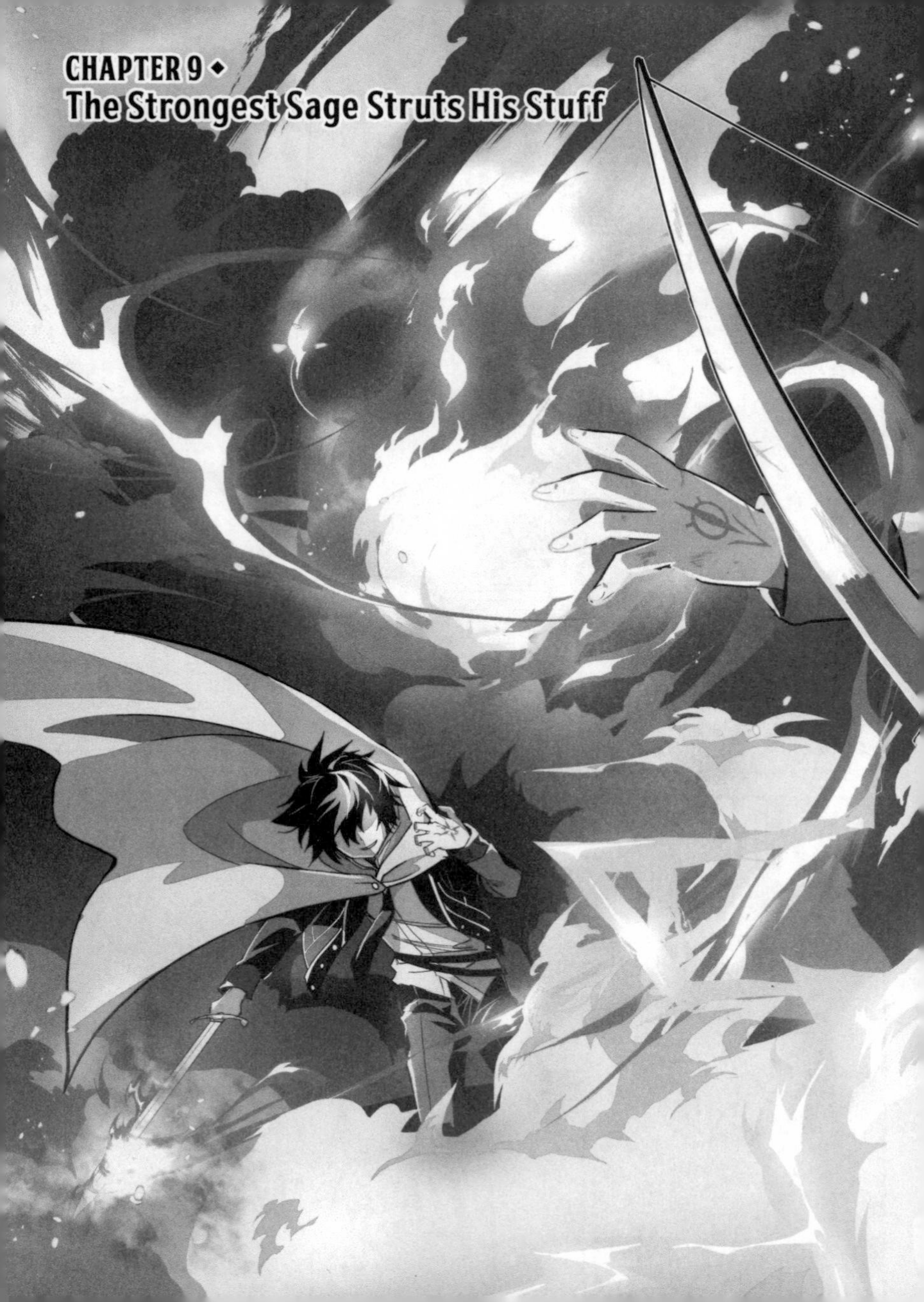

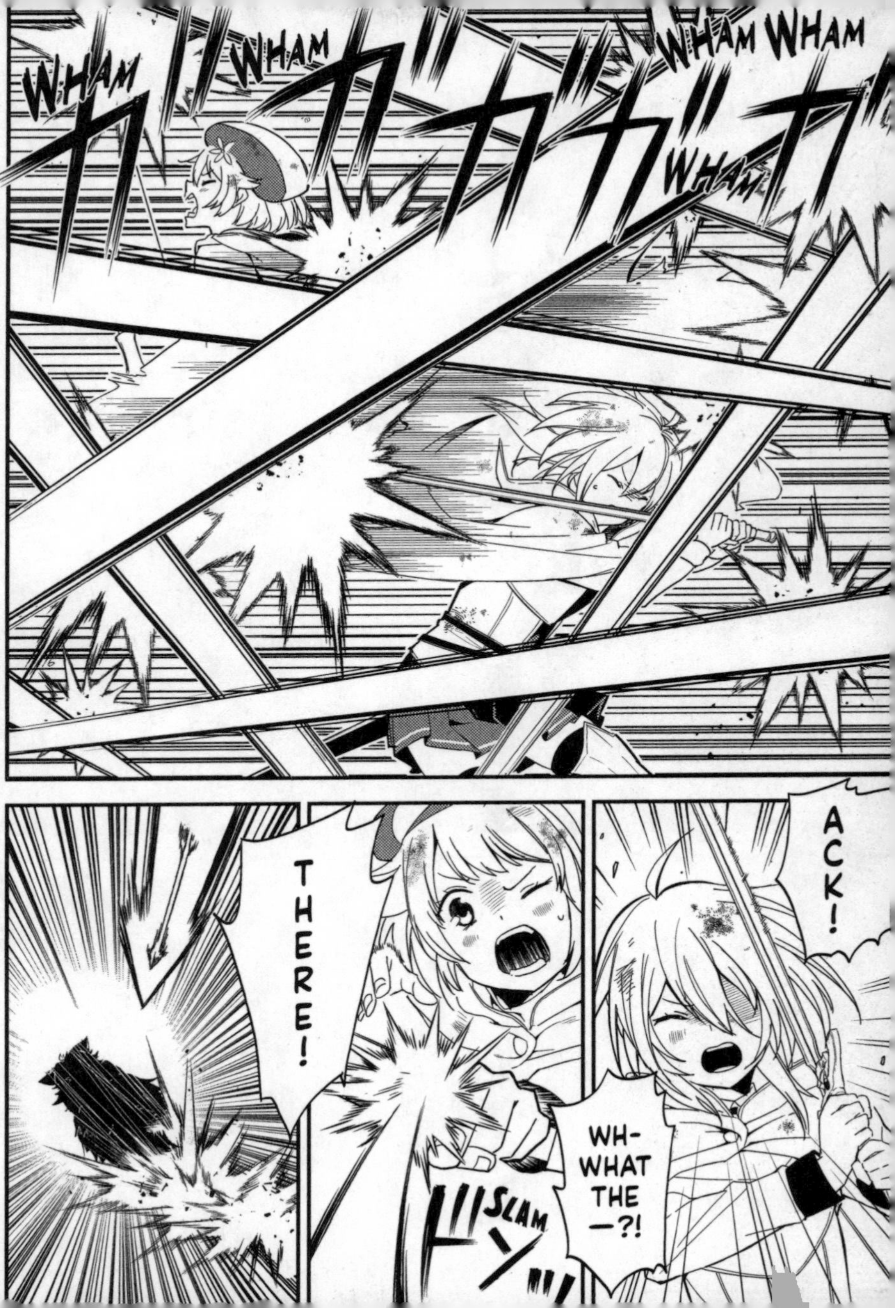
WHAM WHAM
WHAM
WHAM
WHAM
ACK!
WH- WHAT THE —?!
THERE!
SLAM

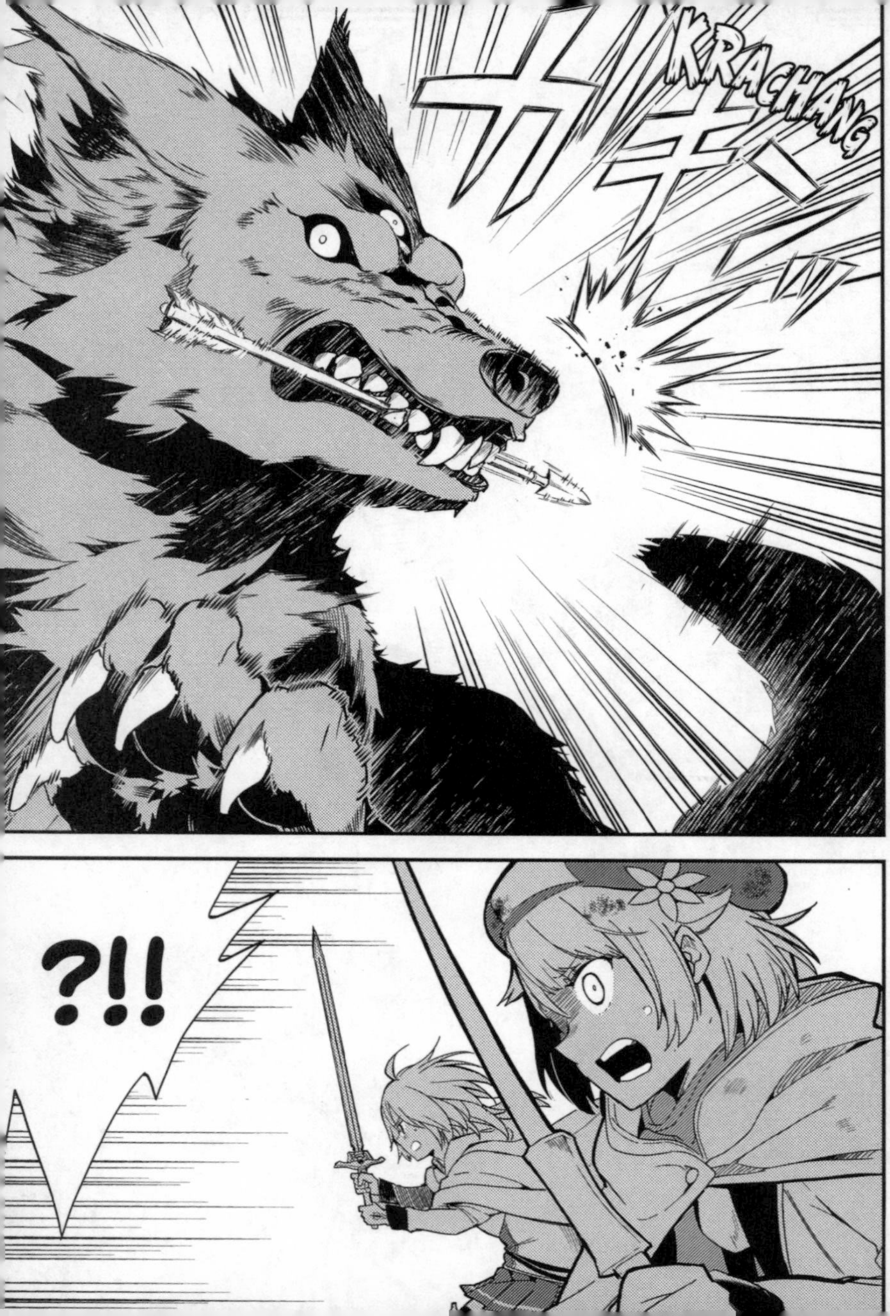
KRACHANG
?!!

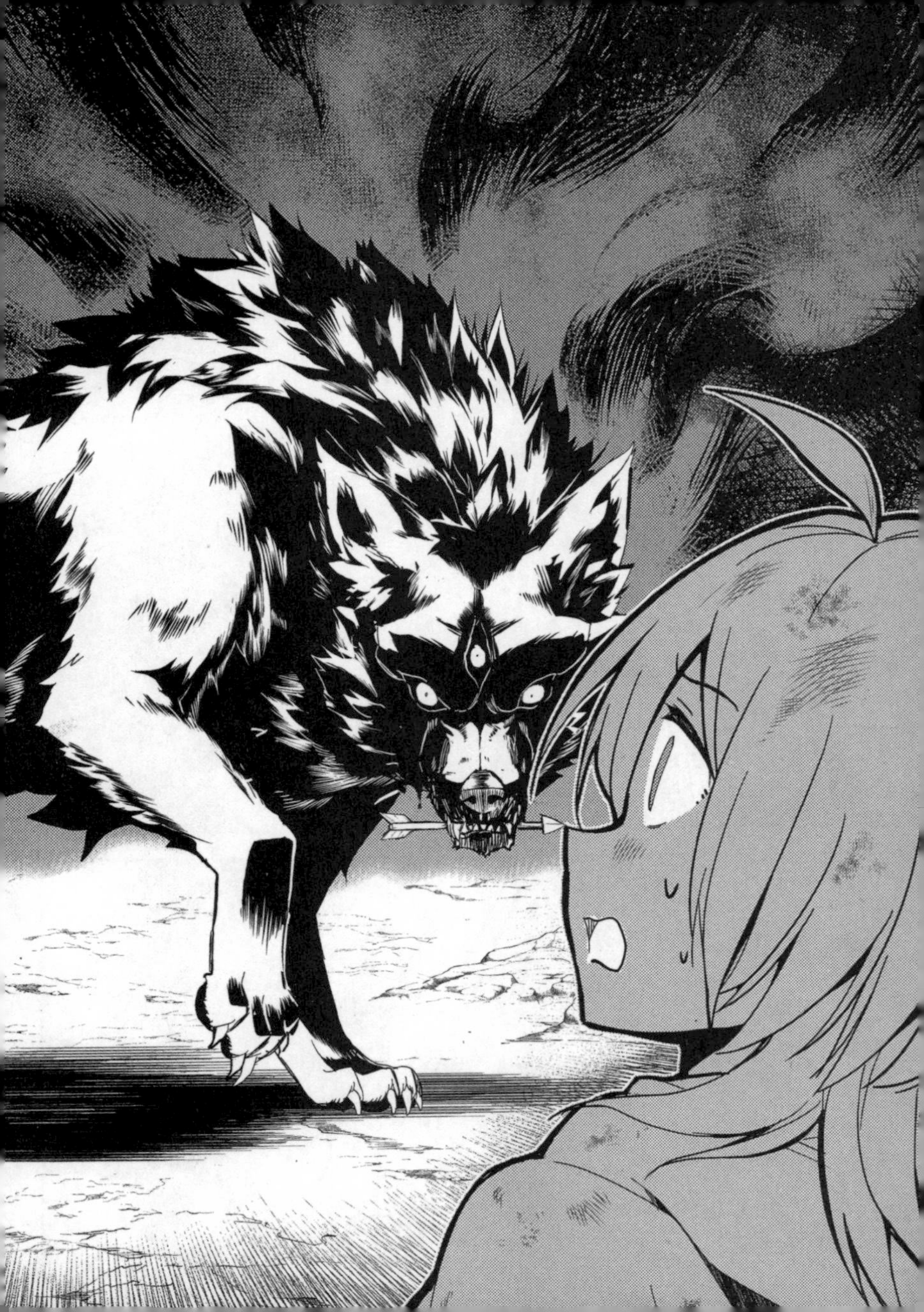

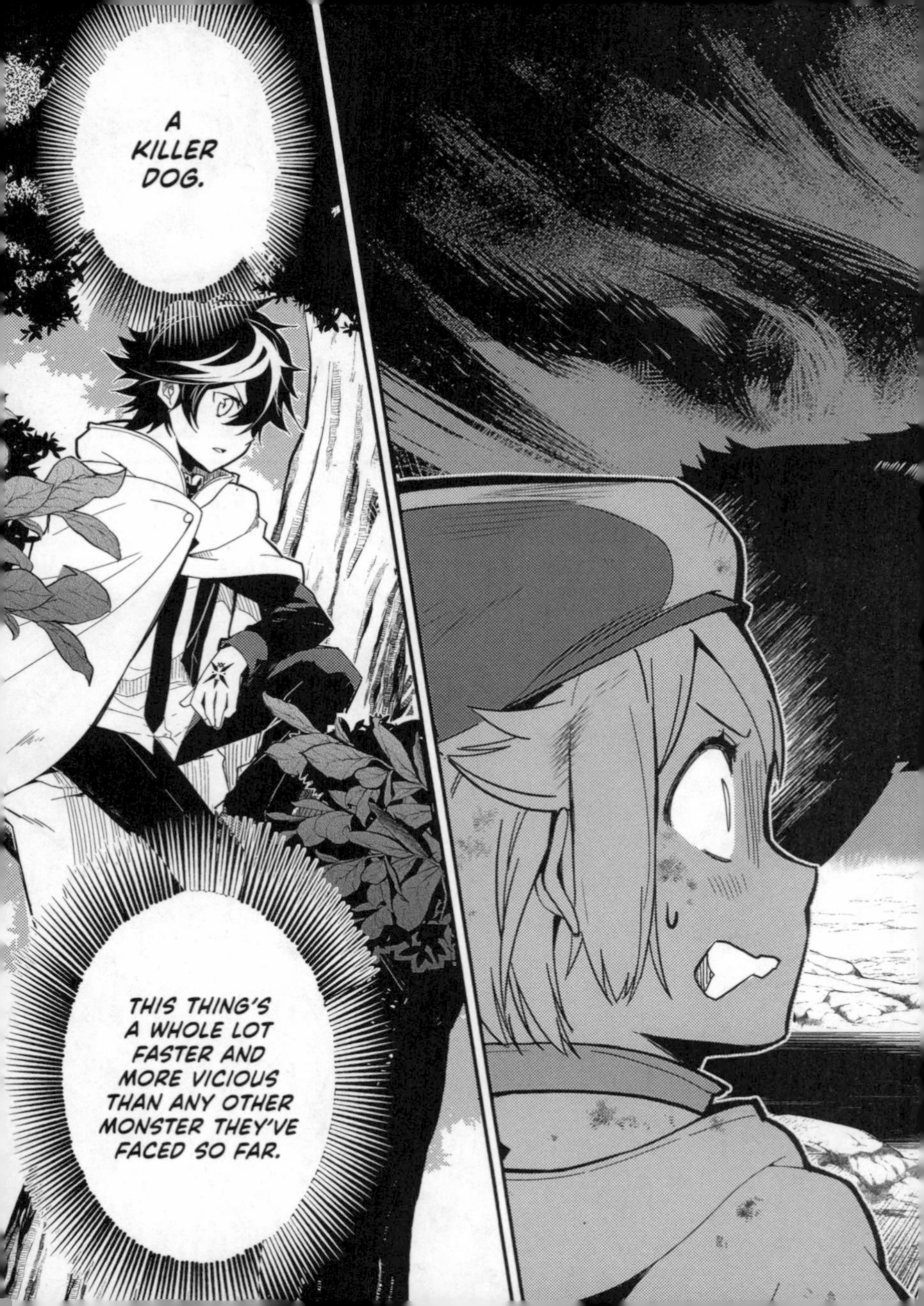
A KILLER DOG.
THIS THING'S A WHOLE LOT FASTER AND MORE VICIOUS THAN ANY OTHER MONSTER THEY'VE FACED SO FAR.

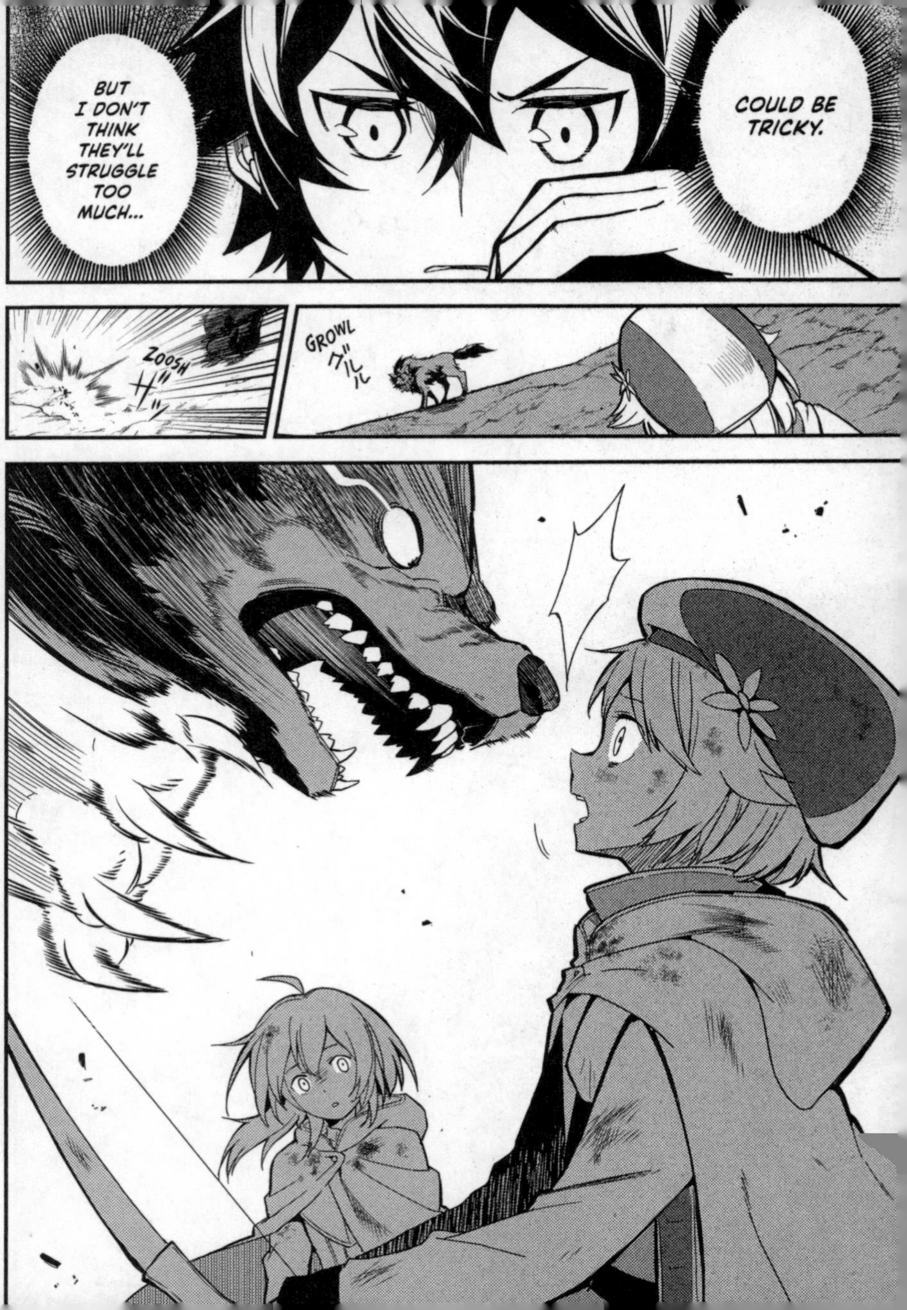
COULD BE TRICKY.
BUT I DON'T THINK THEY'LL STRUGGLE TOO MUCH...
GROWL
グルル
ZOOSH

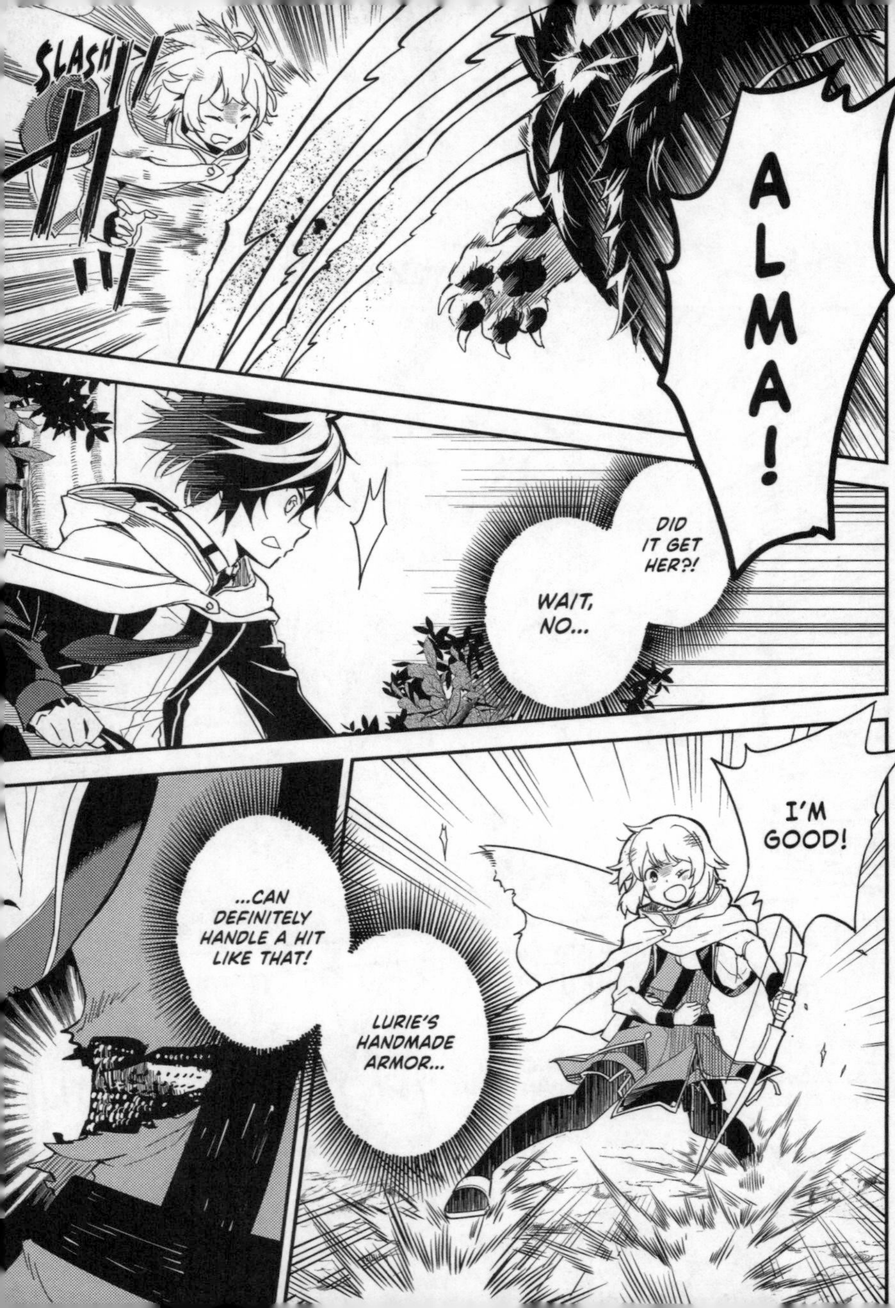
ALMA!
SLASH
DID IT GET HER?!
WAIT, NO...
I'M GOOD!
LURIE'S HANDMADE ARMOR...
...CAN DEFINITELY HANDLE A HIT LIKE THAT!

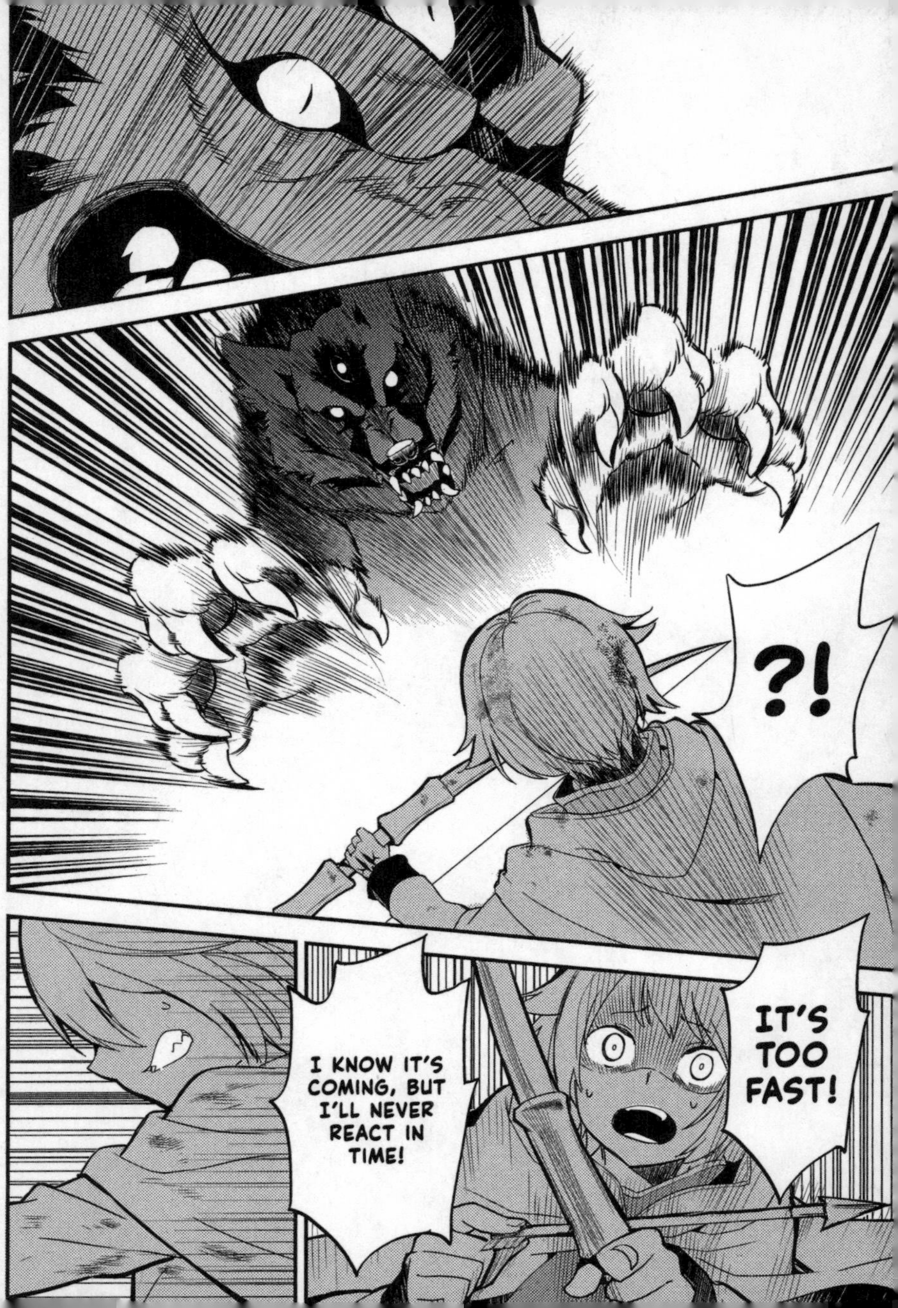
?!
IT'S TOO FAST!
I KNOW IT'S COMING, BUT I'LL NEVER REACT IN TIME!

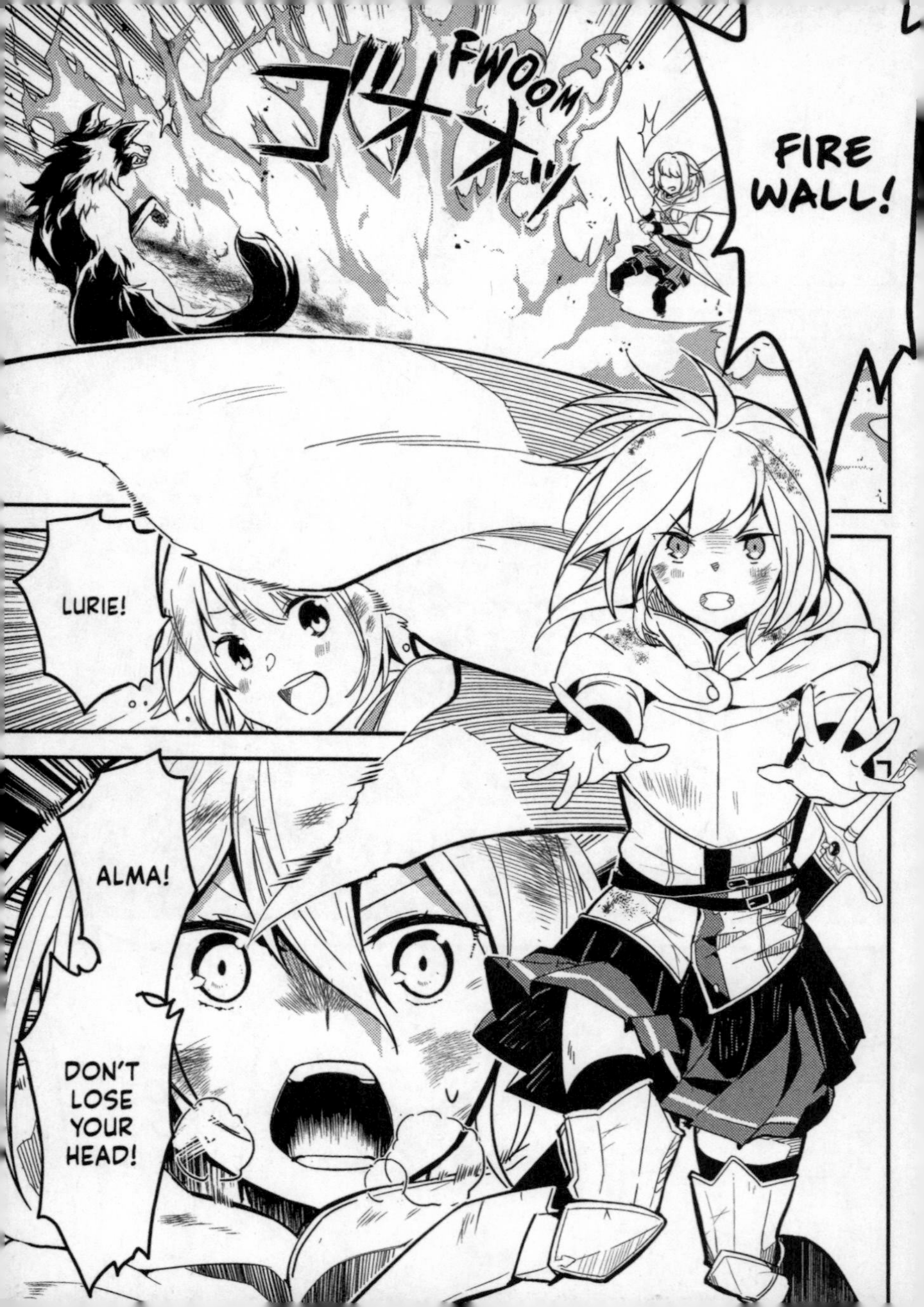
FIRE WALL!
FWOOM
ゴオオッ
LURIE!
ALMA!
DON'T LOSE YOUR HEAD!

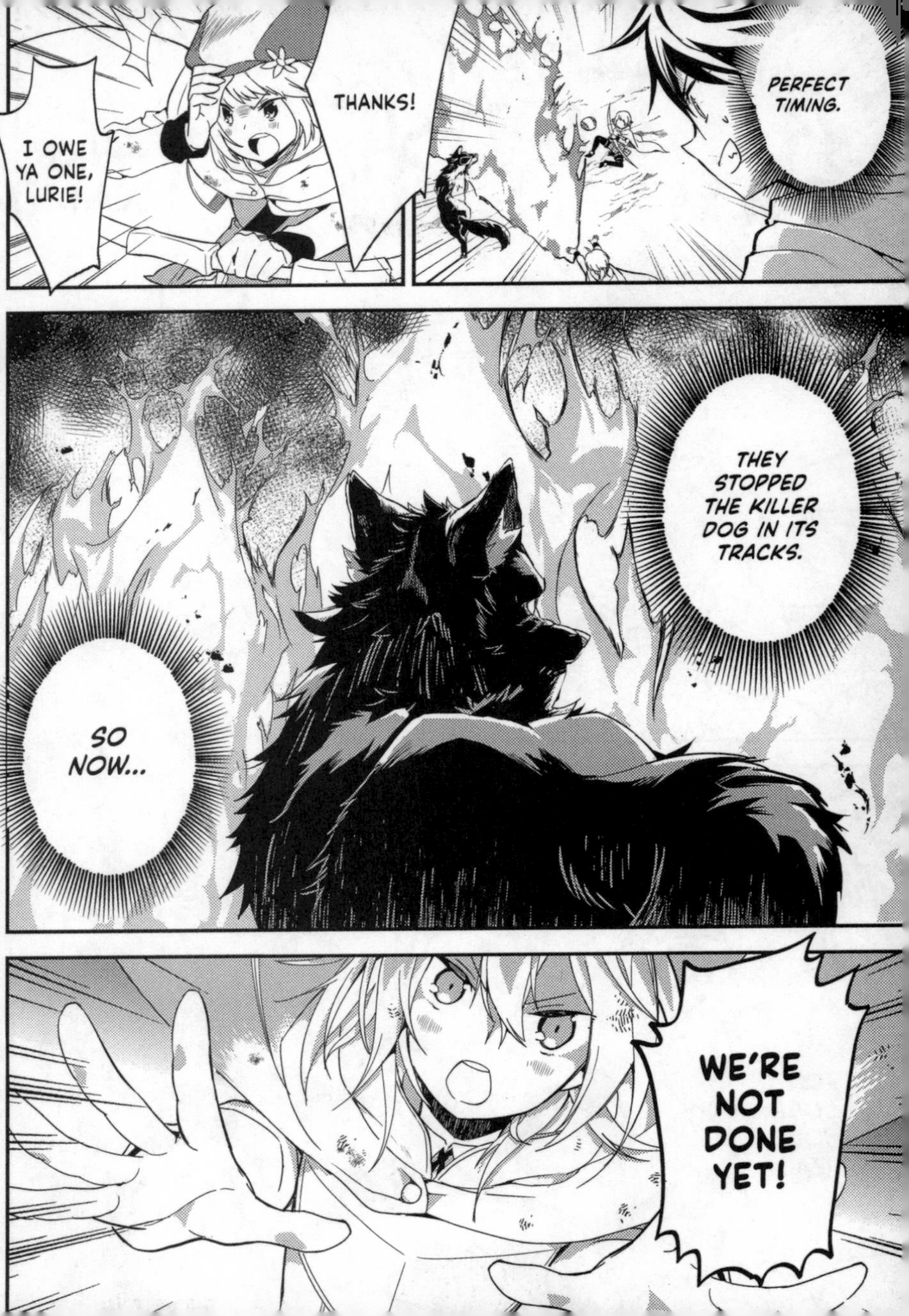
PERFECT TIMING.
THANKS!
I OWE YA ONE, LURIE!
THEY STOPPED THE KILLER DOG IN ITS TRACKS.
SO NOW...
WE'RE NOT DONE YET!

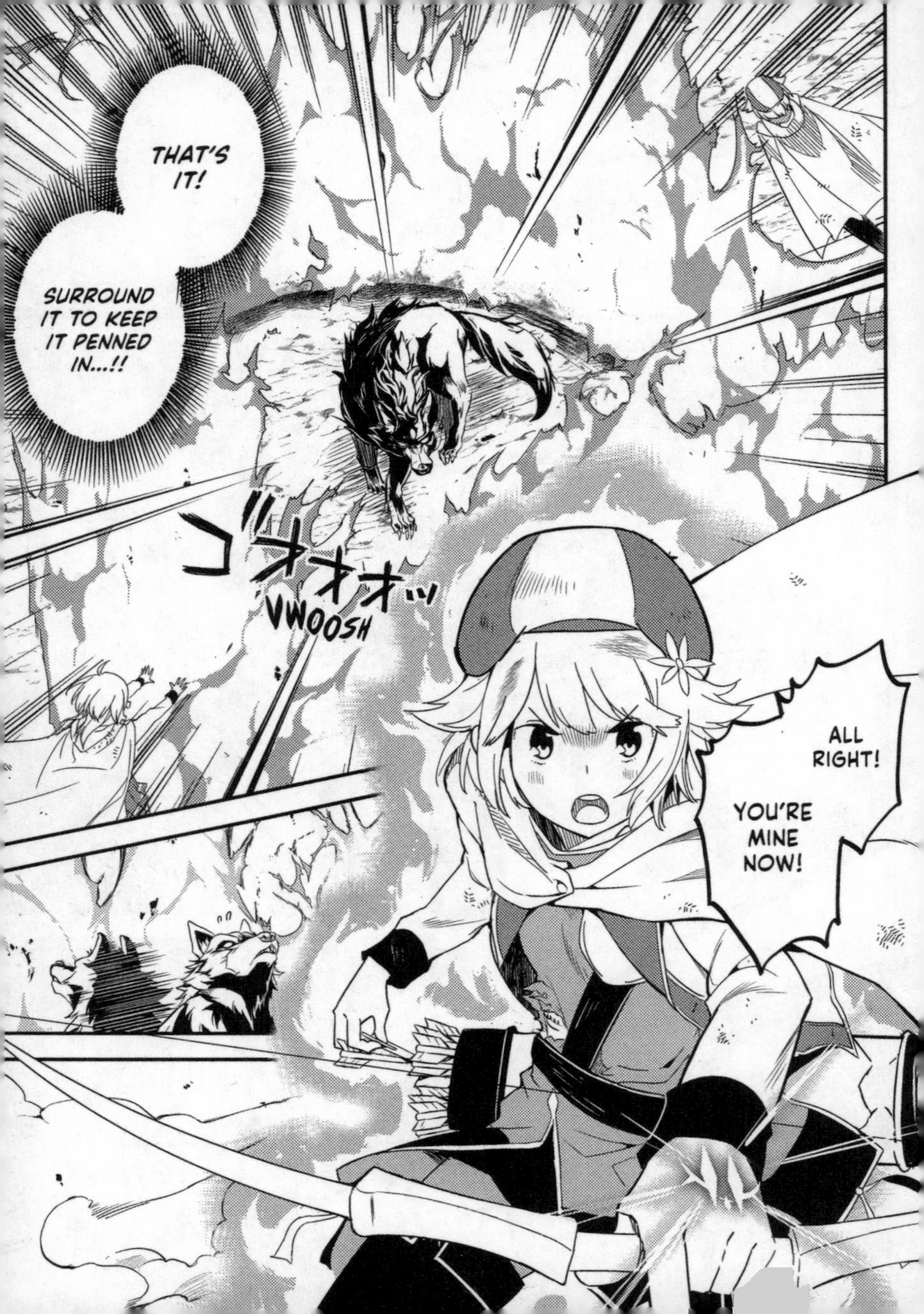
THAT'S IT!
SURROUND IT TO KEEP IT PENNED IN...!!
ゴオオオッ
VWOOSH
ALL RIGHT!
YOU'RE MINE NOW!

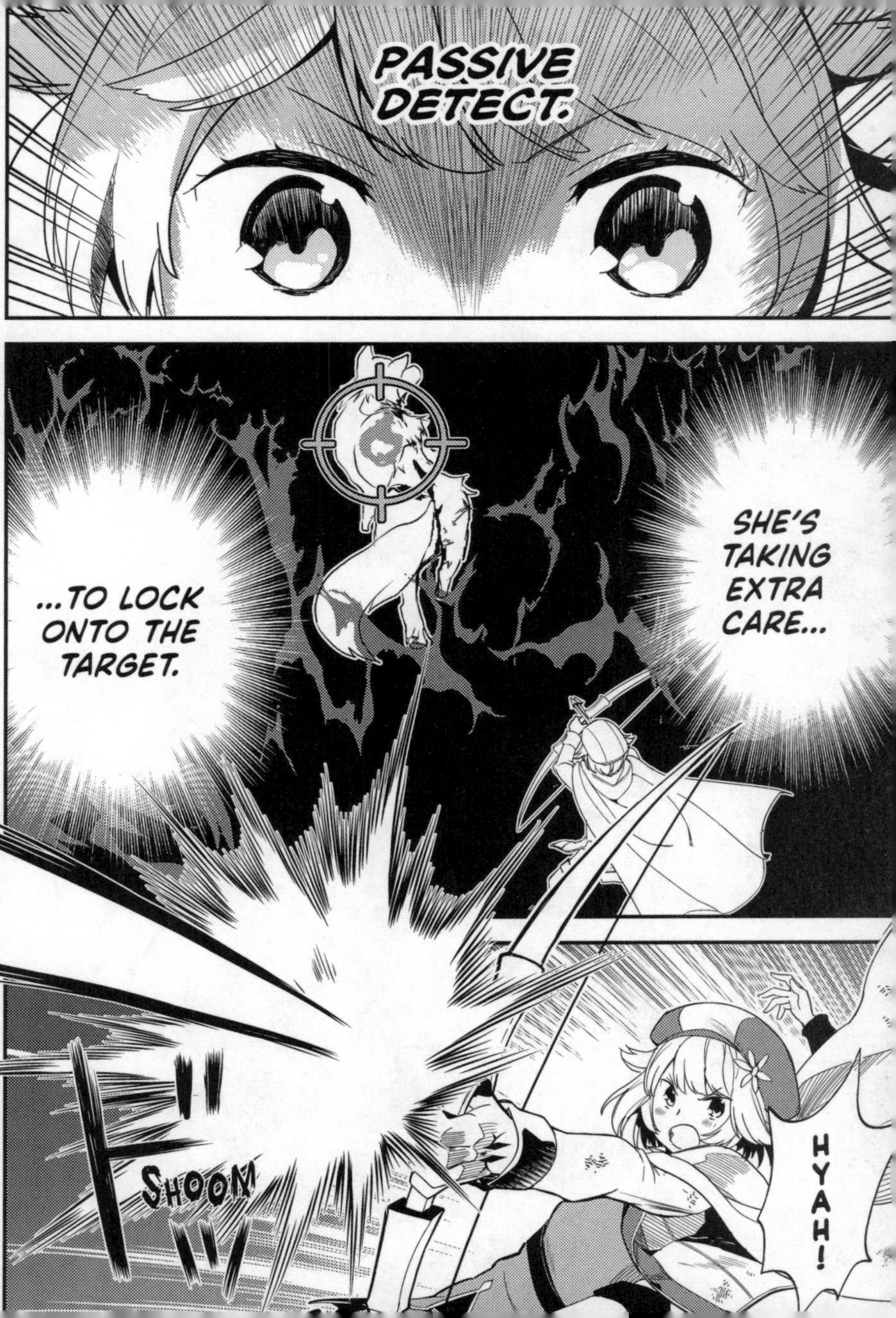
PASSIVE DETECT.
SHE'S TAKING EXTRA CARE...
...TO LOCK ONTO THE TARGET.
HYAH!
SHOOM

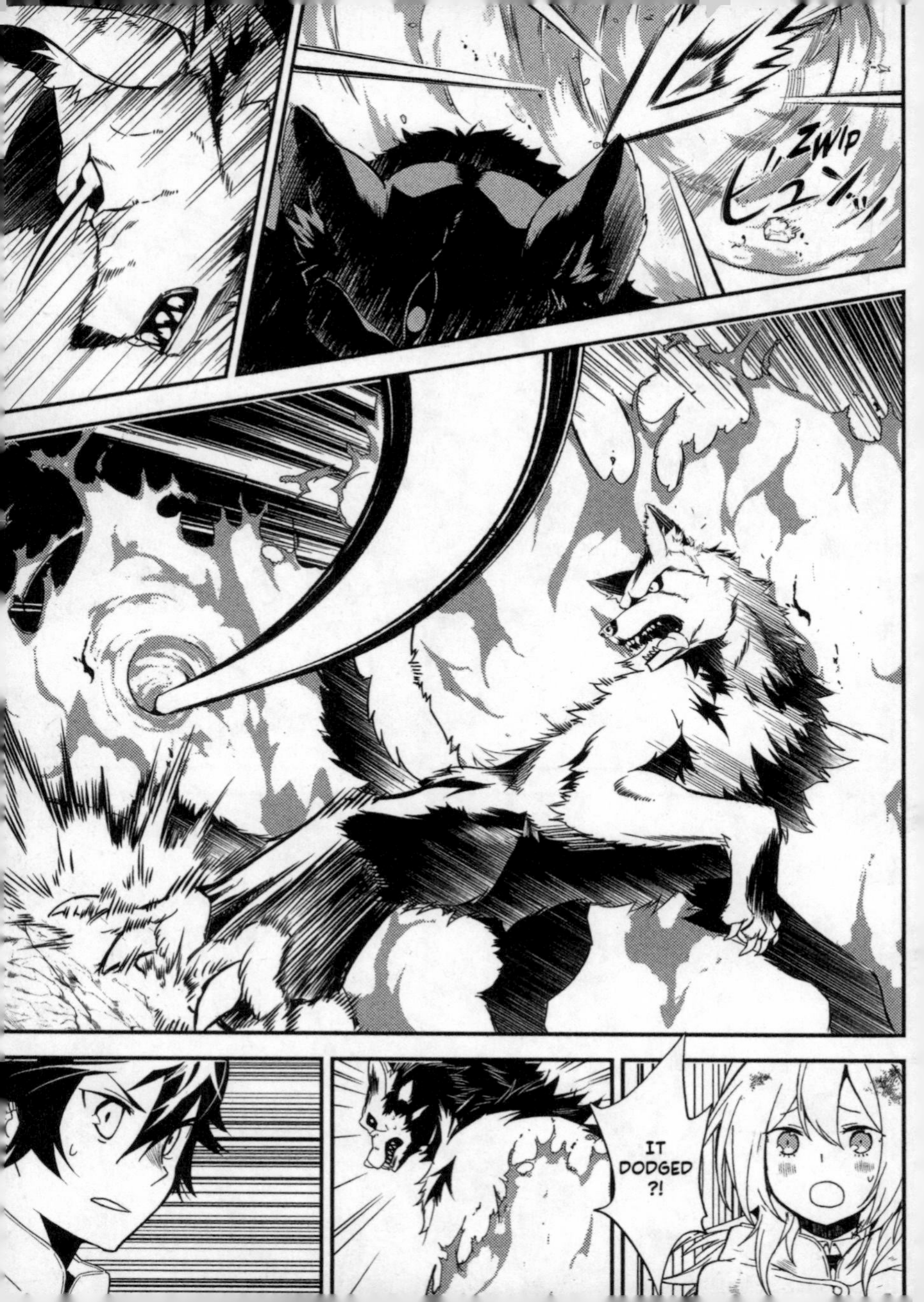
ZWIP
ビュンッ
IT DODGED ?!

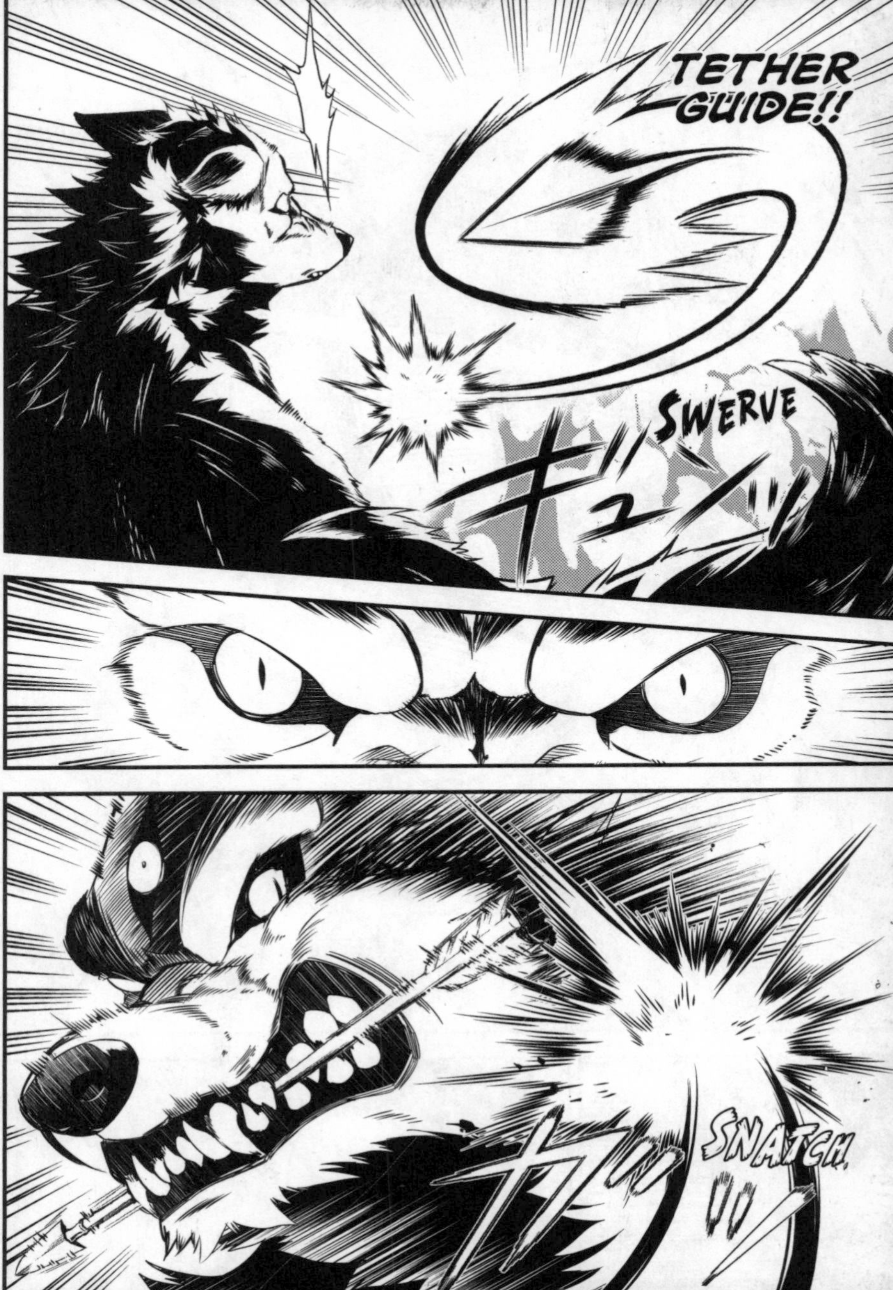
TETHER GUIDE!!
SWERVE
SNATCH

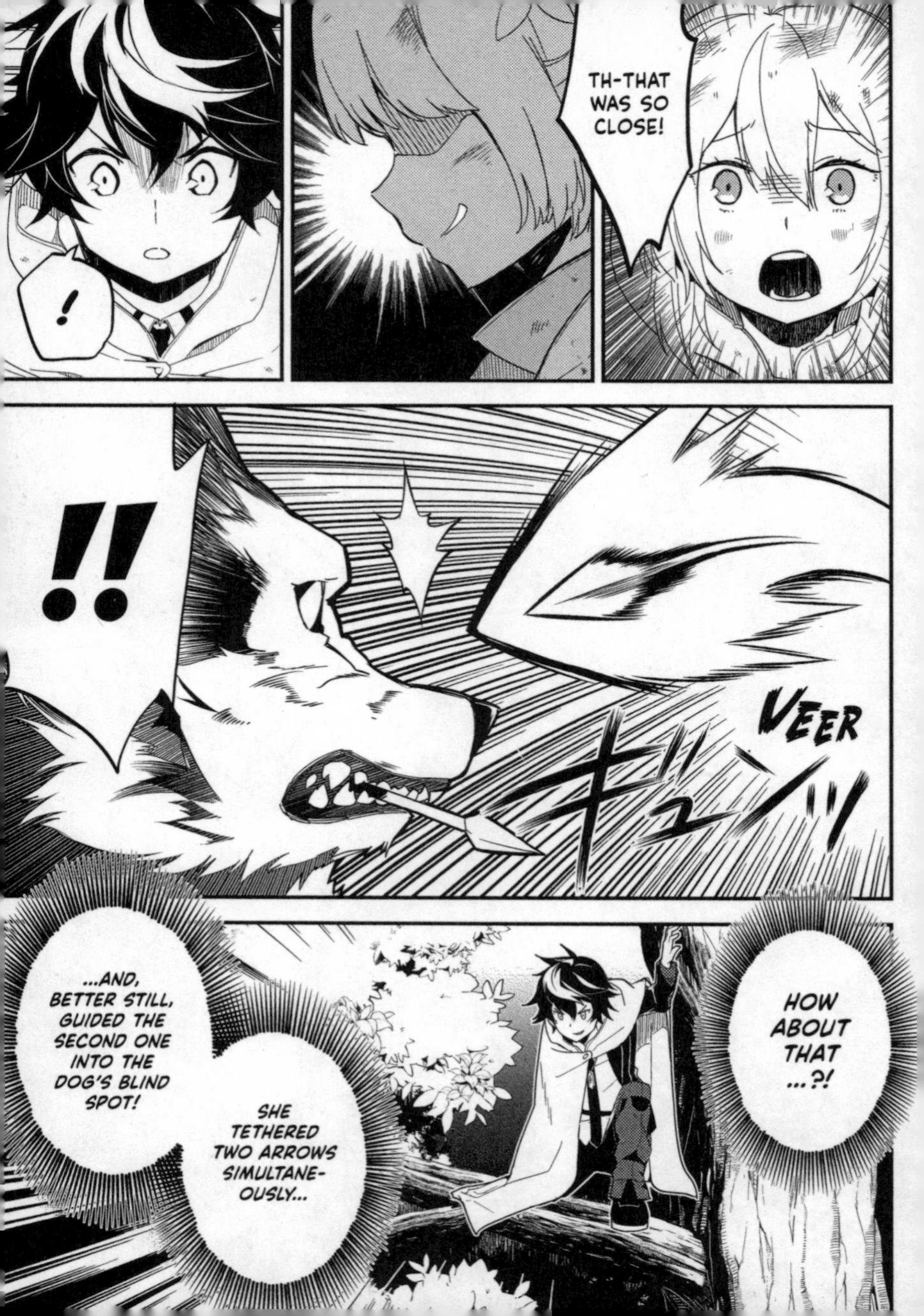
TH-THAT WAS SO CLOSE!
!
!!
VEER
ギュンッ
HOW ABOUT THAT ...?!
SHE TETHERED TWO ARROWS SIMULTANE-OUSLY...
...AND, BETTER STILL, GUIDED THE SECOND ONE INTO THE DOG'S BLIND SPOT!

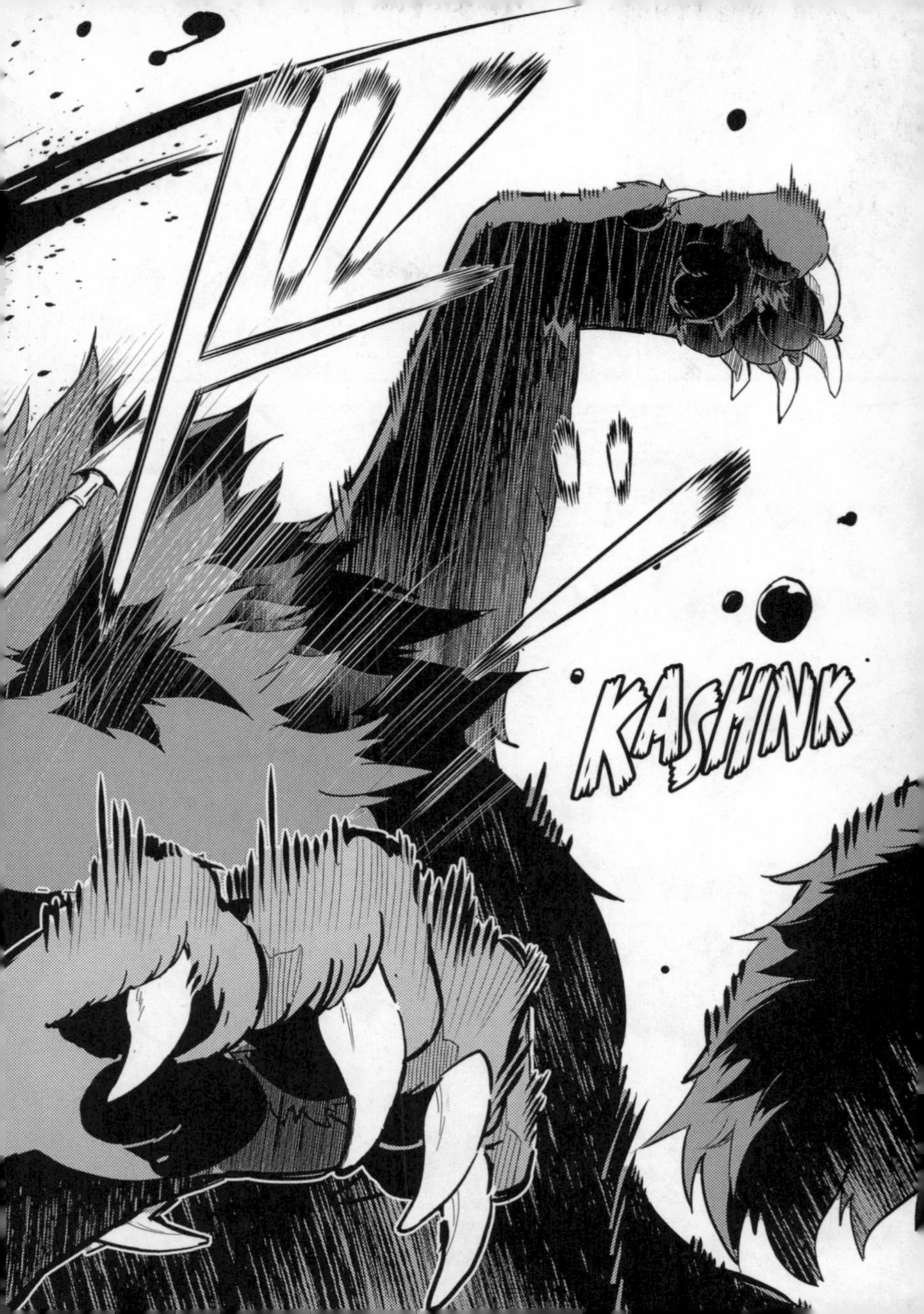
KASHINK

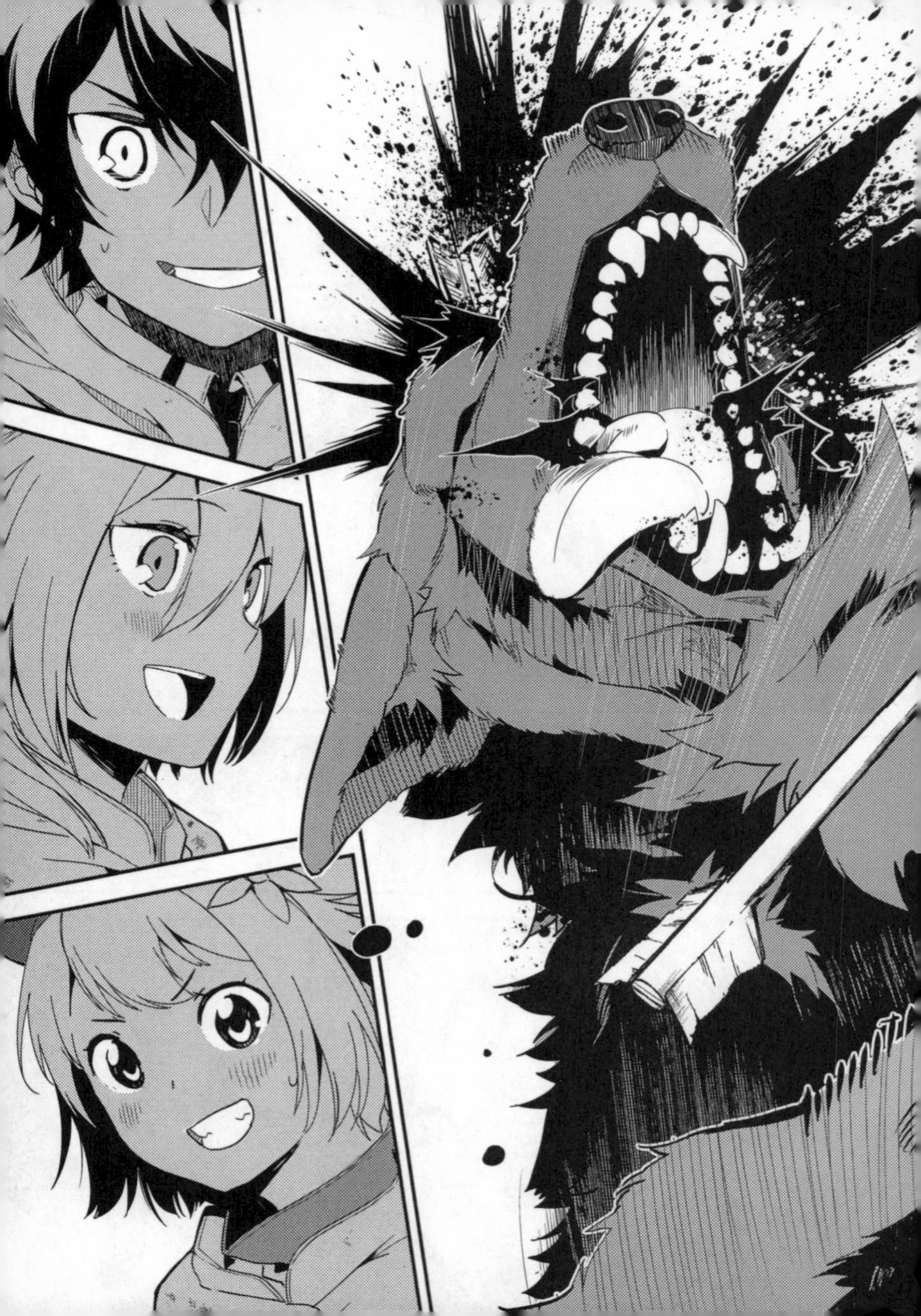

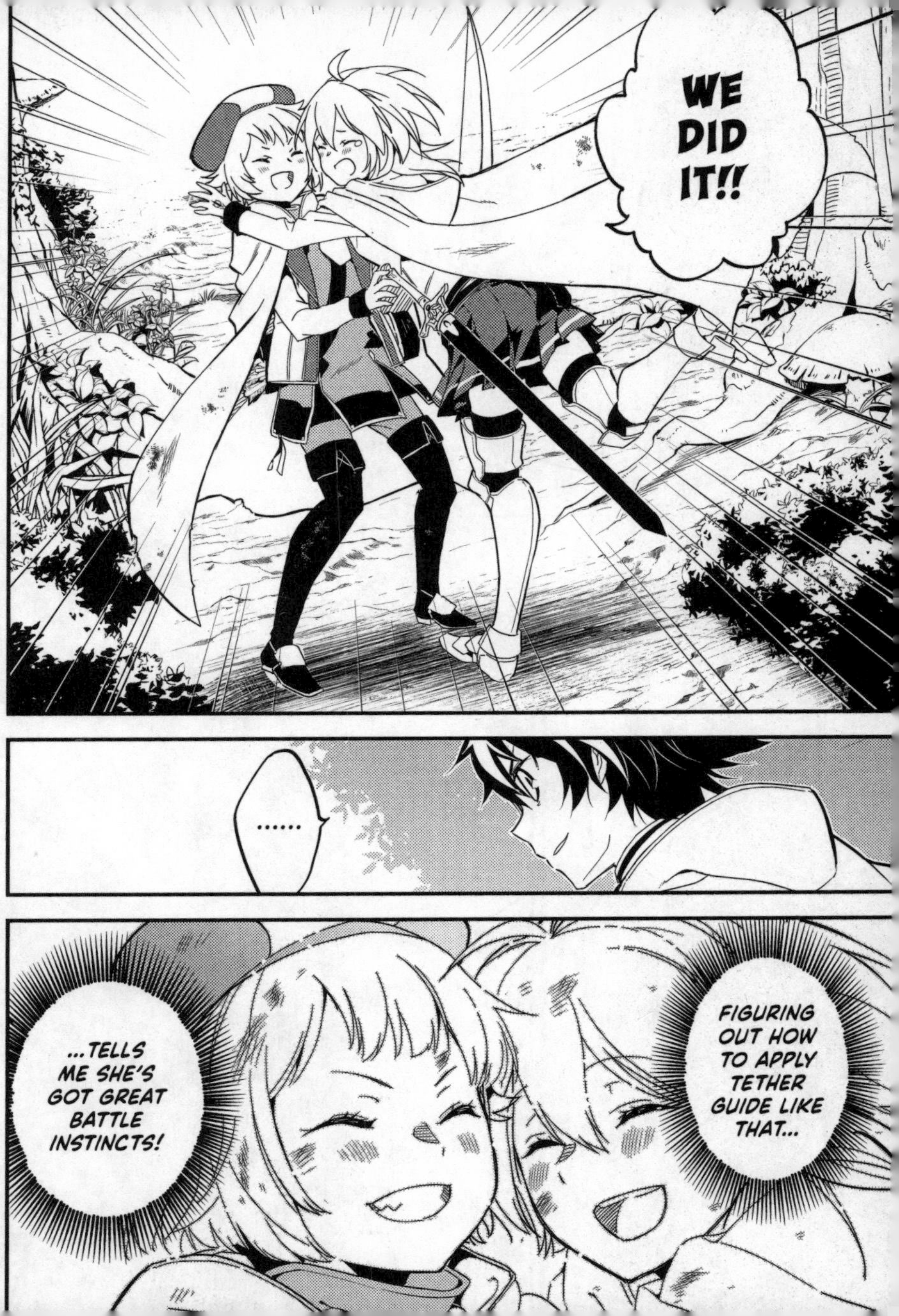
WE DID IT!!
......
FIGURING OUT HOW TO APPLY TETHER GUIDE LIKE THAT...
...TELLS ME SHE'S GOT GREAT BATTLE INSTINCTS!

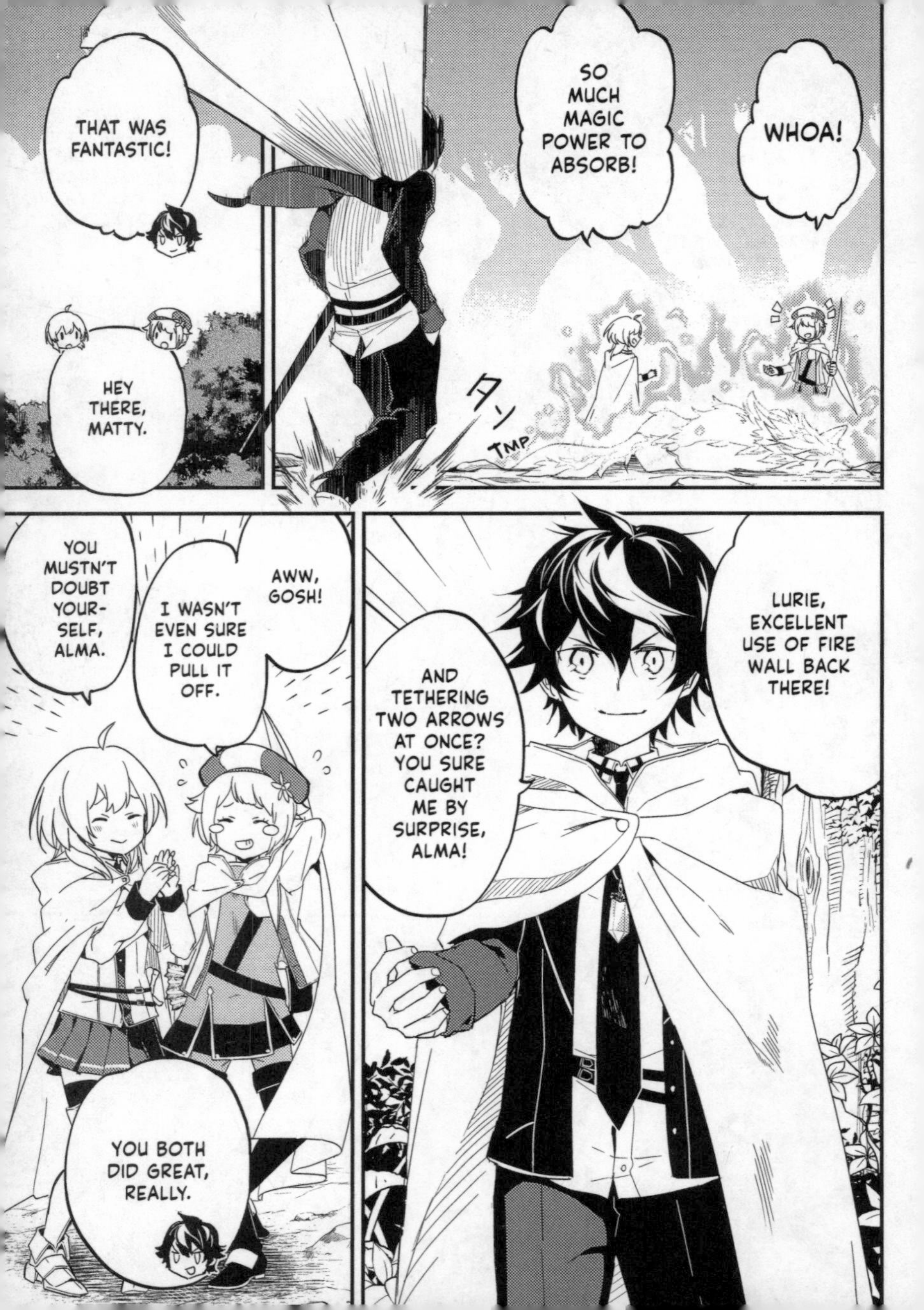
WHOA!
SO MUCH MAGIC POWER TO ABSORB!
タン
TMP
THAT WAS FANTASTIC!
HEY THERE, MATTY.
LURIE, EXCELLENT USE OF FIRE WALL BACK THERE!
AND TETHERING TWO ARROWS AT ONCE? YOU SURE CAUGHT ME BY SURPRISE, ALMA!
AWW, GOSH!
I WASN'T EVEN SURE I COULD PULL IT OFF.
YOU MUSTN'T DOUBT YOUR-SELF, ALMA.
YOU BOTH DID GREAT, REALLY.

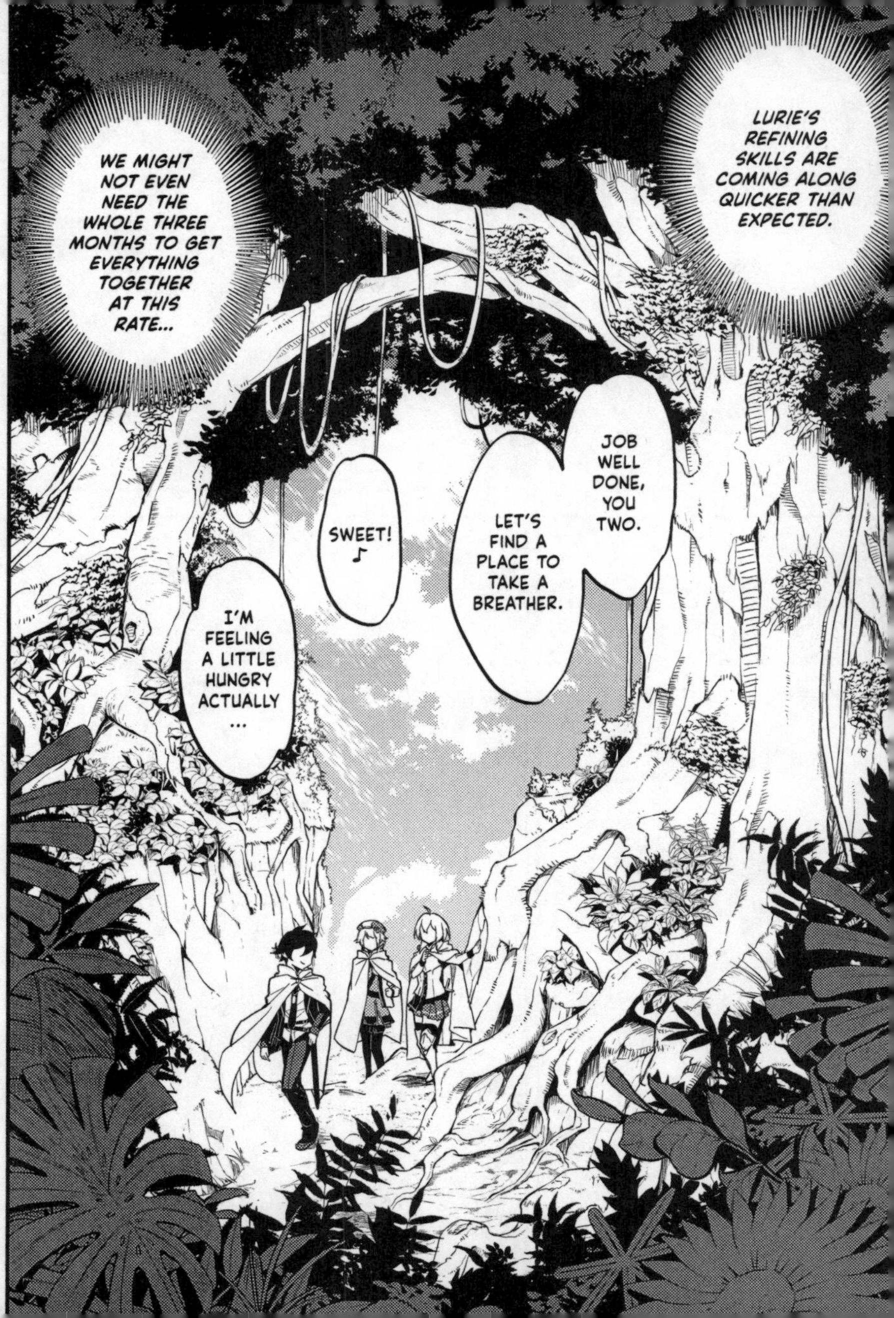
LURIE'S REFINING SKILLS ARE COMING ALONG QUICKER THAN EXPECTED.
WE MIGHT NOT EVEN NEED THE WHOLE THREE MONTHS TO GET EVERYTHING TOGETHER AT THIS RATE...
JOB WELL DONE, YOU TWO.
LET'S FIND A PLACE TO TAKE A BREATHER.
SWEET! ♪
I'M FEELING A LITTLE HUNGRY ACTUALLY ...

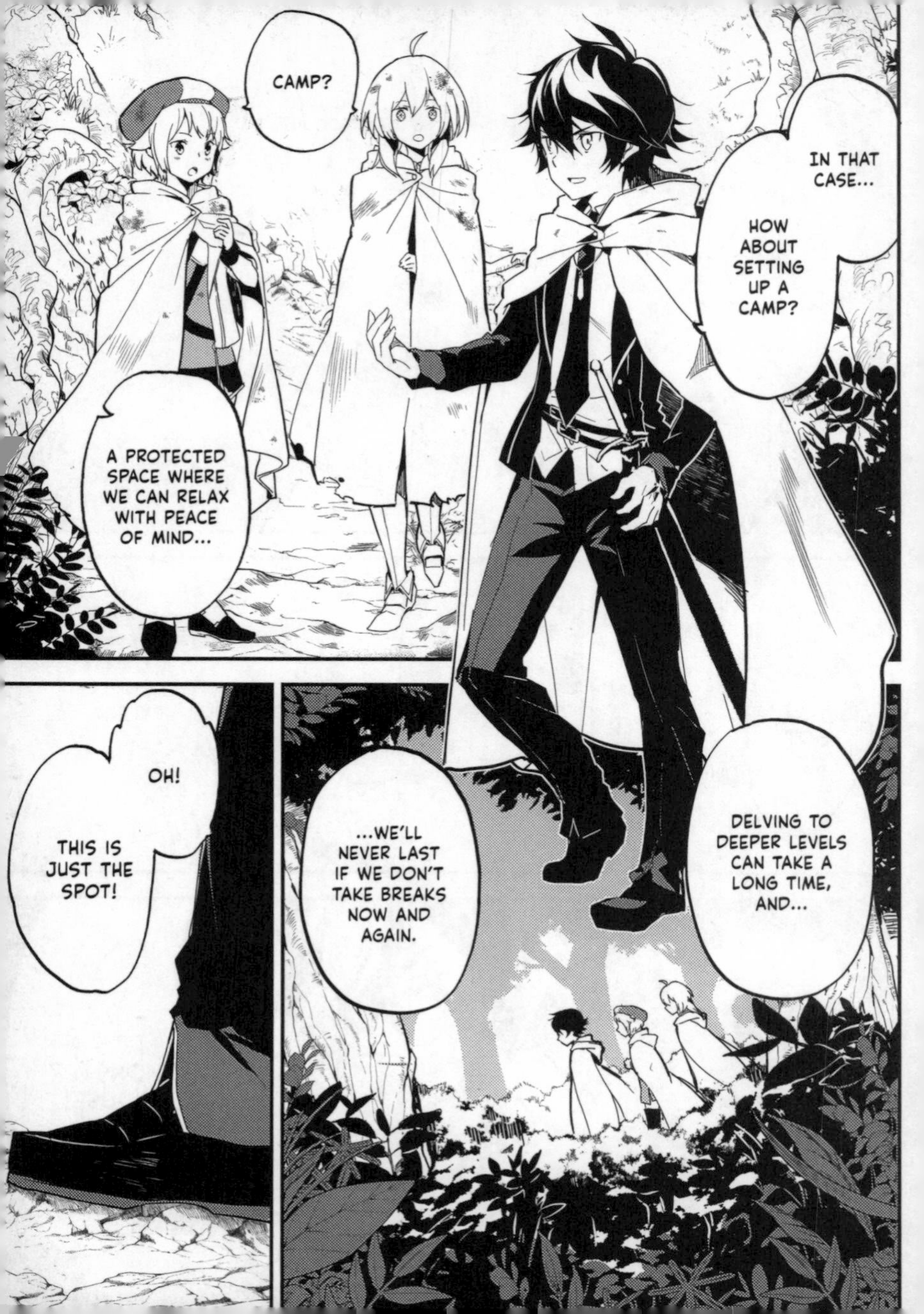
IN THAT CASE... HOW ABOUT SETTING UP A CAMP?
CAMP?
A PROTECTED SPACE WHERE WE CAN RELAX WITH PEACE OF MIND...
DELVING TO DEEPER LEVELS CAN TAKE A LONG TIME, AND...
...WE'LL NEVER LAST IF WE DON'T TAKE BREAKS NOW AND AGAIN.
OH! THIS IS JUST THE SPOT!

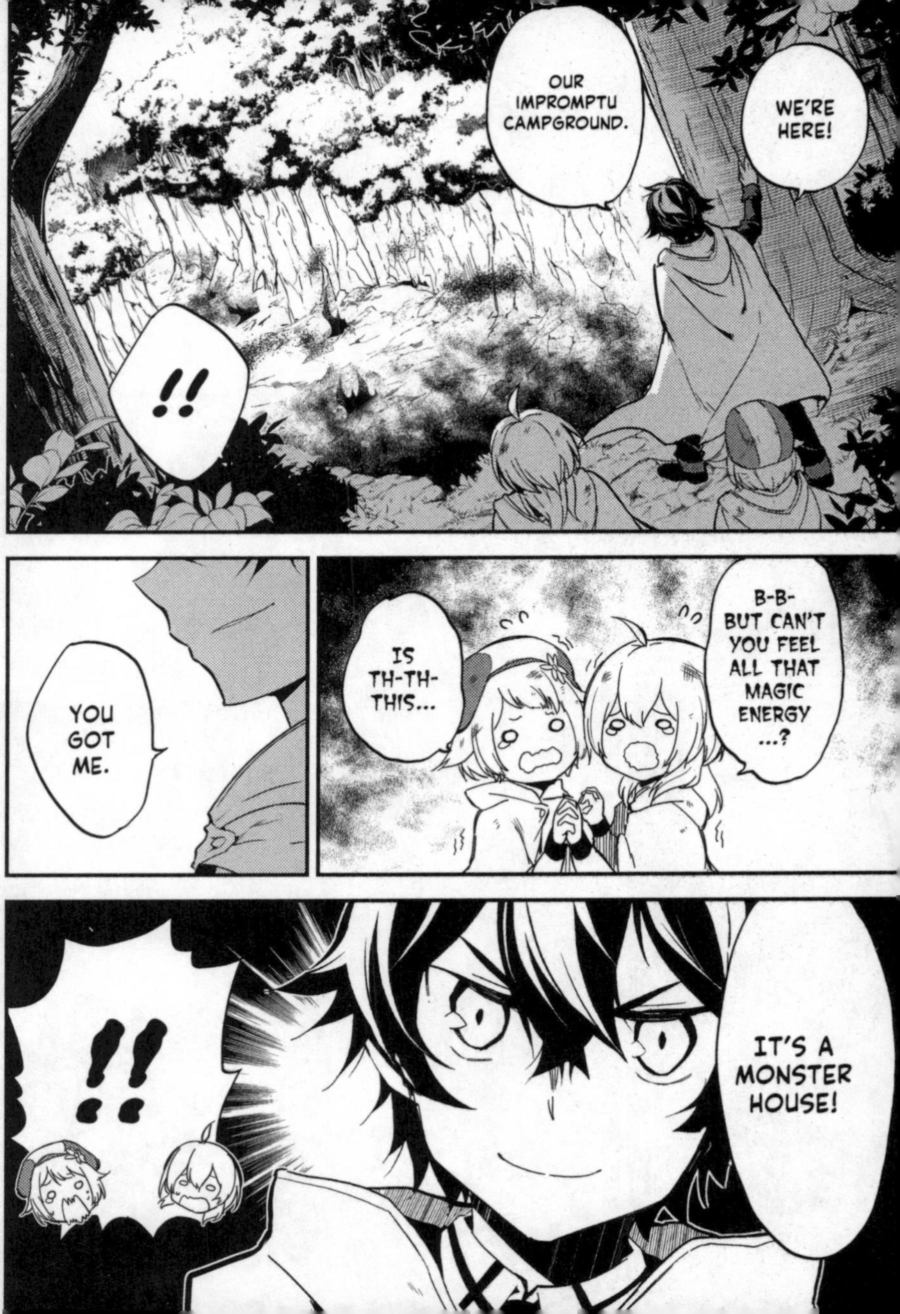
WE'RE HERE!
OUR IMPROMPTU CAMPGROUND.
!!
B-B-BUT CAN'T YOU FEEL ALL THAT MAGIC ENERGY ...?
IS TH-TH-THIS...
YOU GOT ME.
IT'S A MONSTER HOUSE!
!!

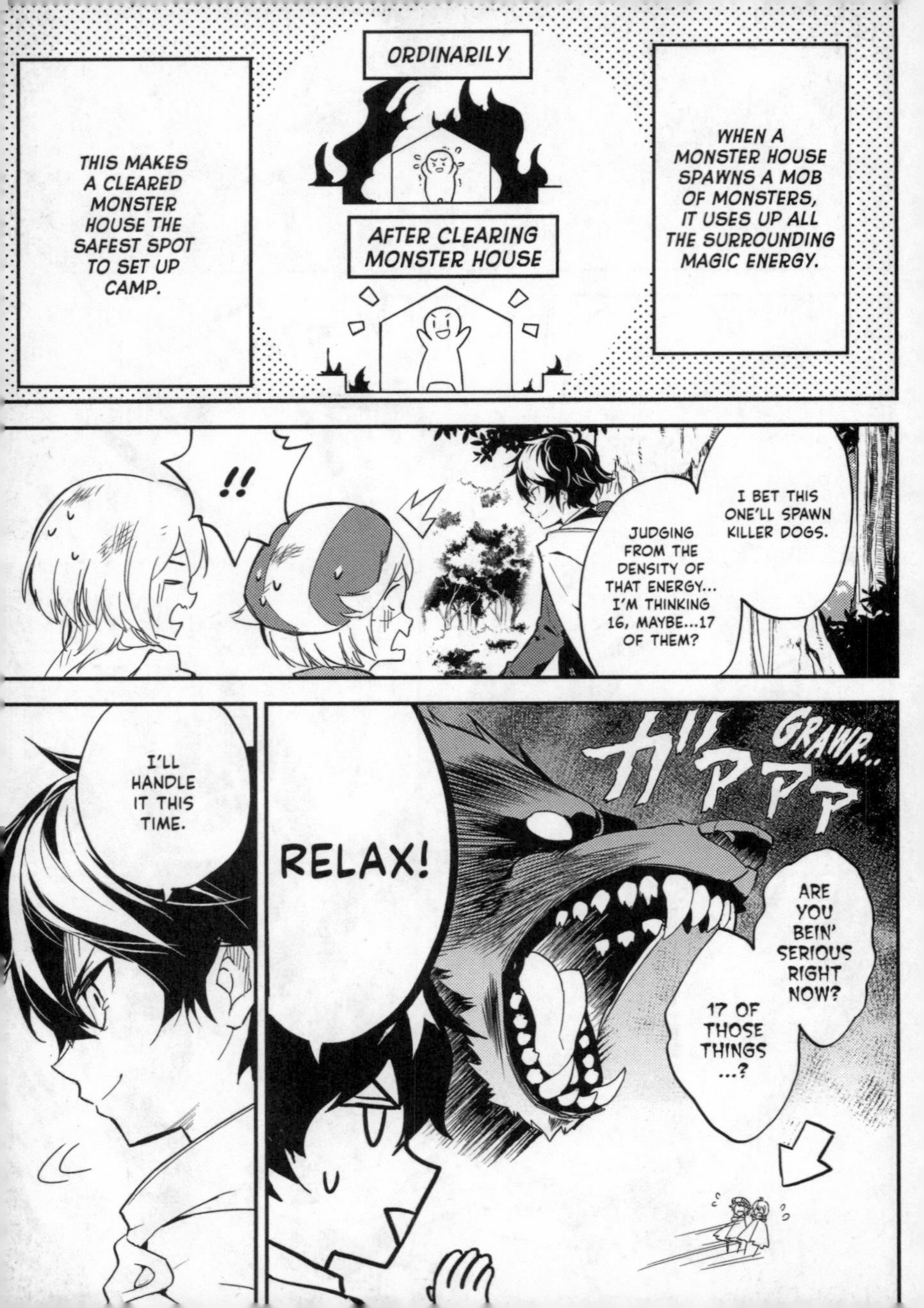
WHEN A MONSTER HOUSE SPAWNS A MOB OF MONSTERS, IT USES UP ALL THE SURROUNDING MAGIC ENERGY.
ORDINARILY
AFTER CLEARING MONSTER HOUSE
THIS MAKES A CLEARED MONSTER HOUSE THE SAFEST SPOT TO SET UP CAMP.
I BET THIS ONE'LL SPAWN KILLER DOGS.
JUDGING FROM THE DENSITY OF THAT ENERGY... I'M THINKING 16, MAYBE...17 OF THEM?
!!
ガアアア
GRAWR...
ARE YOU BEIN' SERIOUS RIGHT NOW?
17 OF THOSE THINGS ...?
RELAX!
I'LL HANDLE IT THIS TIME.

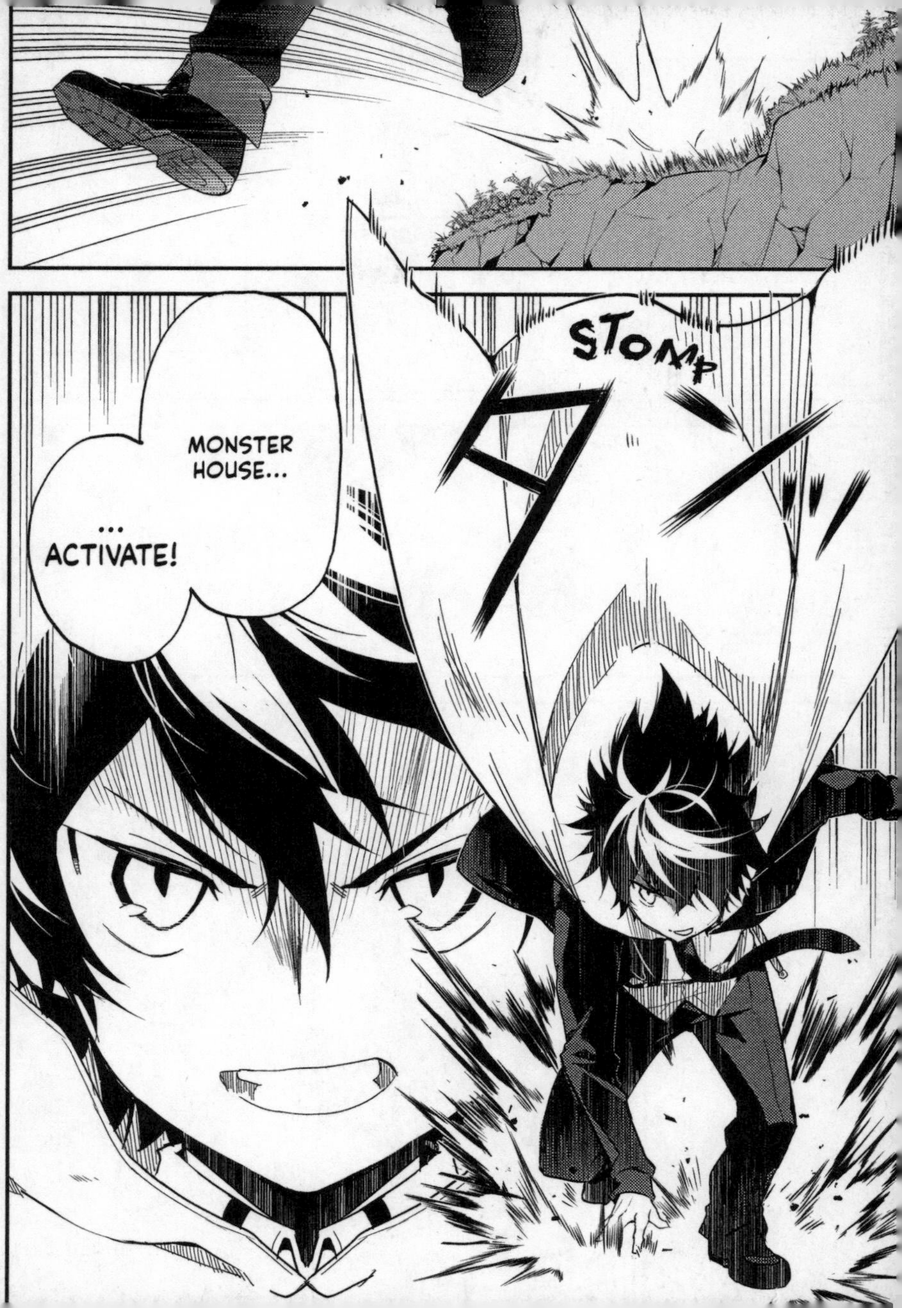
STOMP
MONSTER HOUSE...
... ACTIVATE!

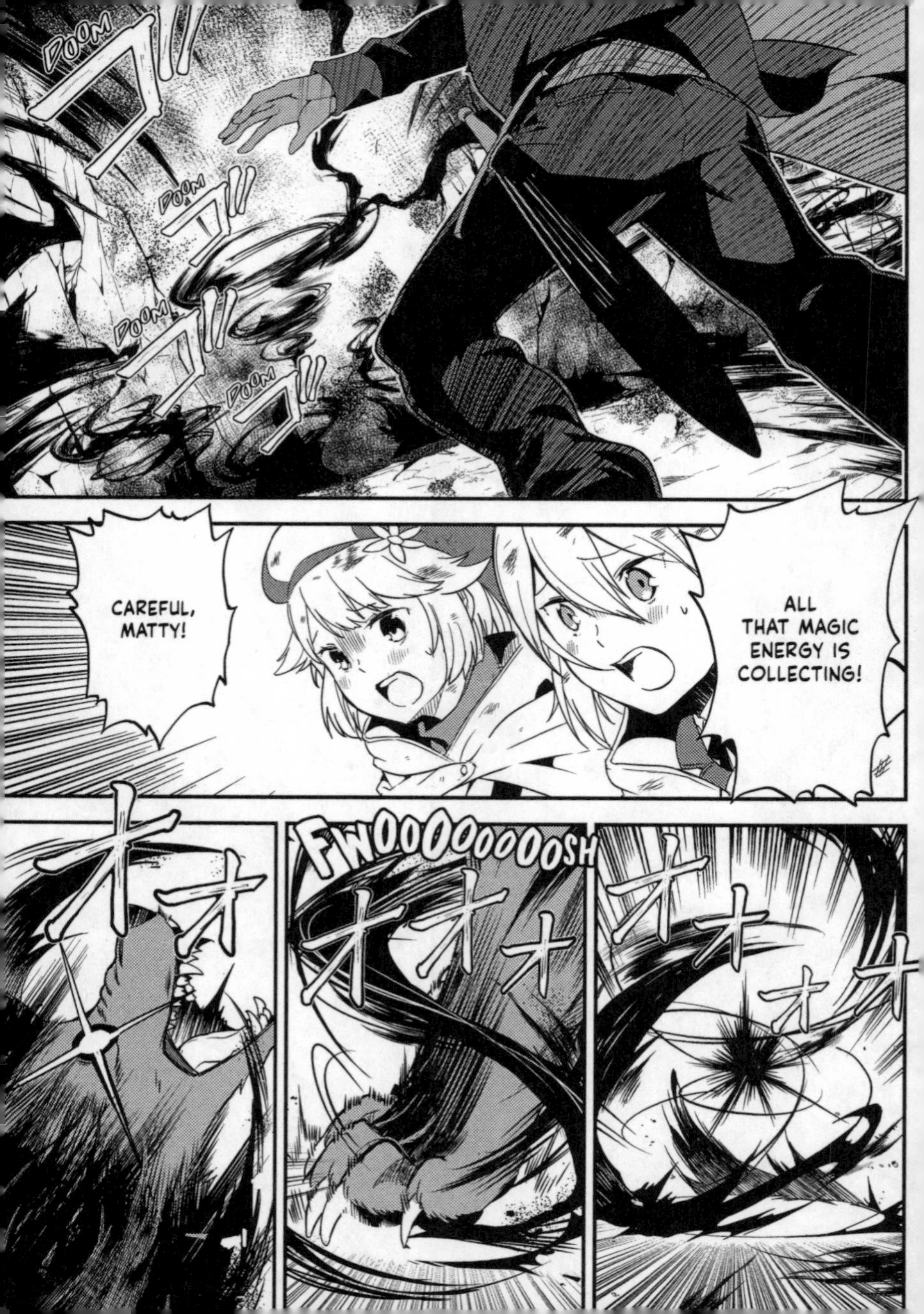
DOOM
DOOM
DOOM
DOOM
ALL THAT MAGIC ENERGY IS COLLECTING!
CAREFUL, MATTY!
FWOOOOOOOOOSH

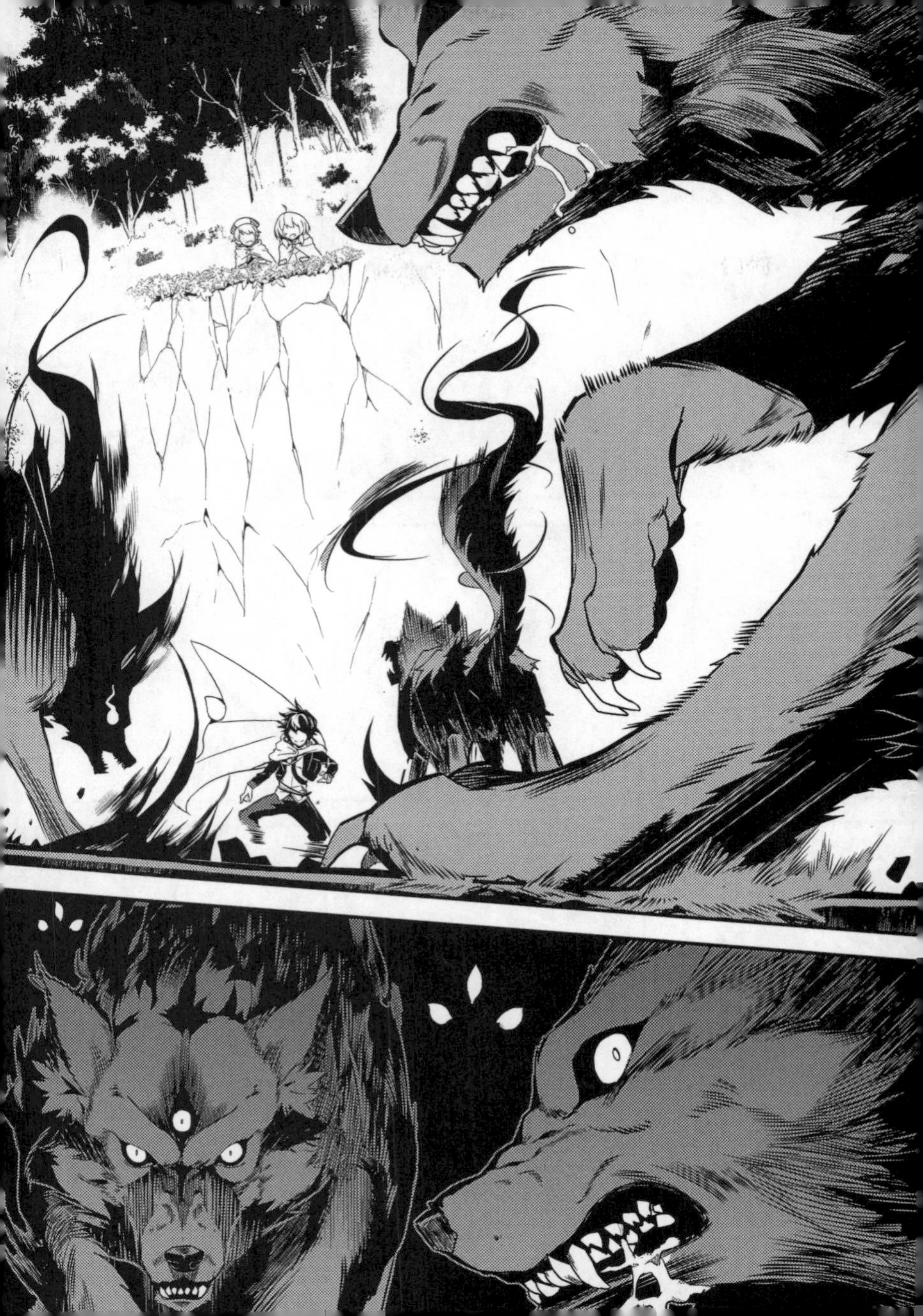

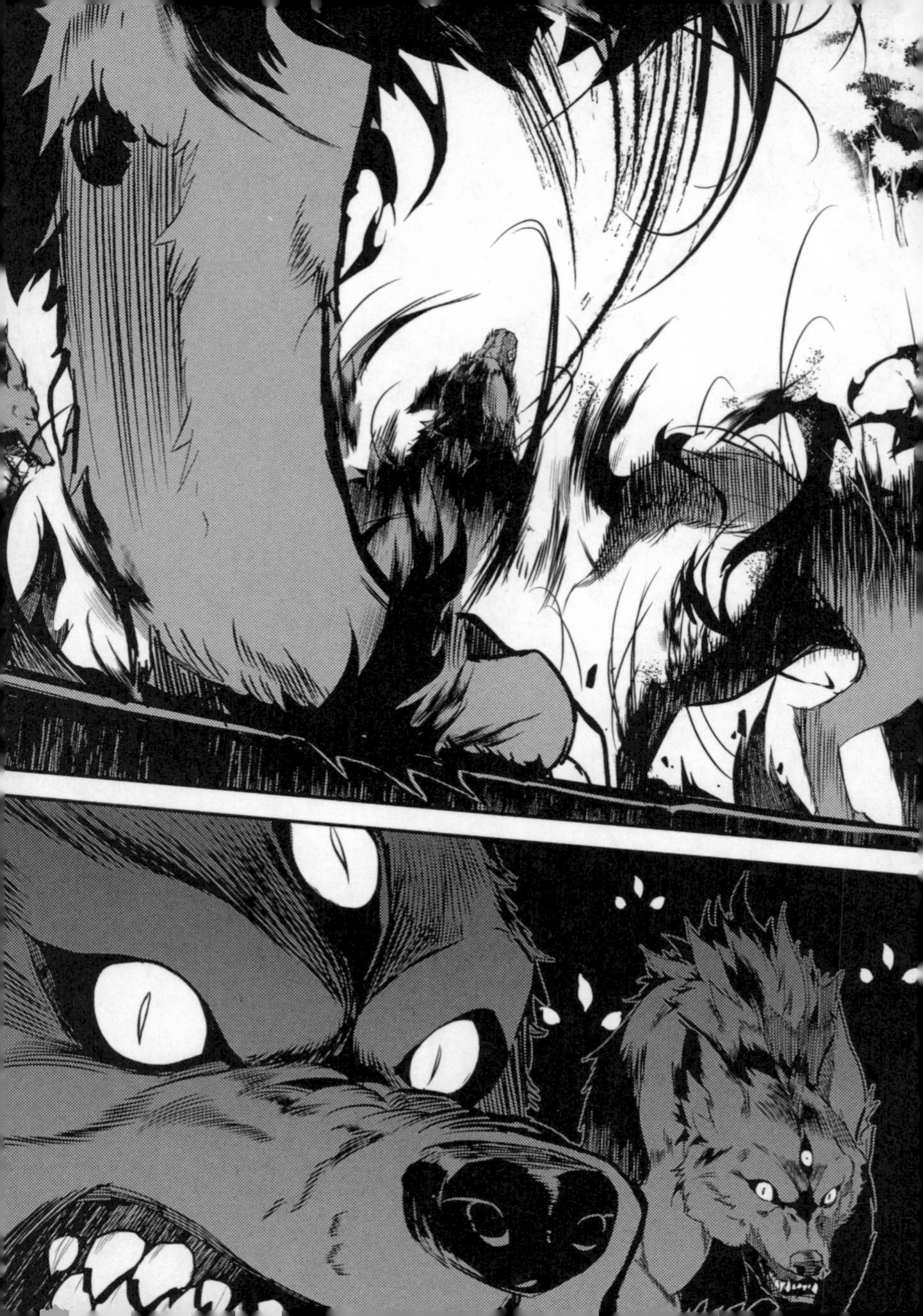

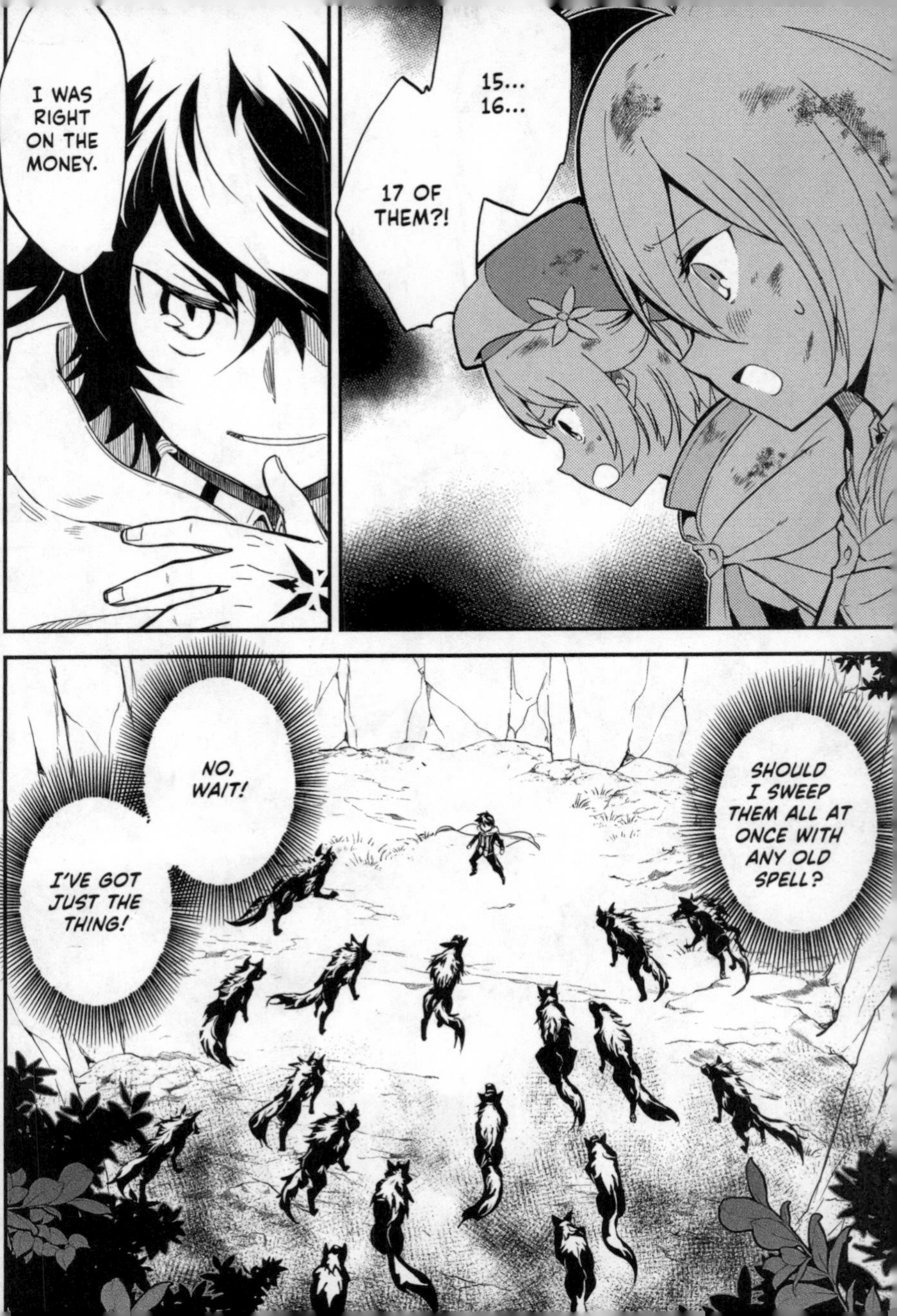
15... 16...
17 OF THEM?!
I WAS RIGHT ON THE MONEY.
SHOULD I SWEEP THEM ALL AT ONCE WITH ANY OLD SPELL?
NO, WAIT!
I'VE GOT JUST THE THING!

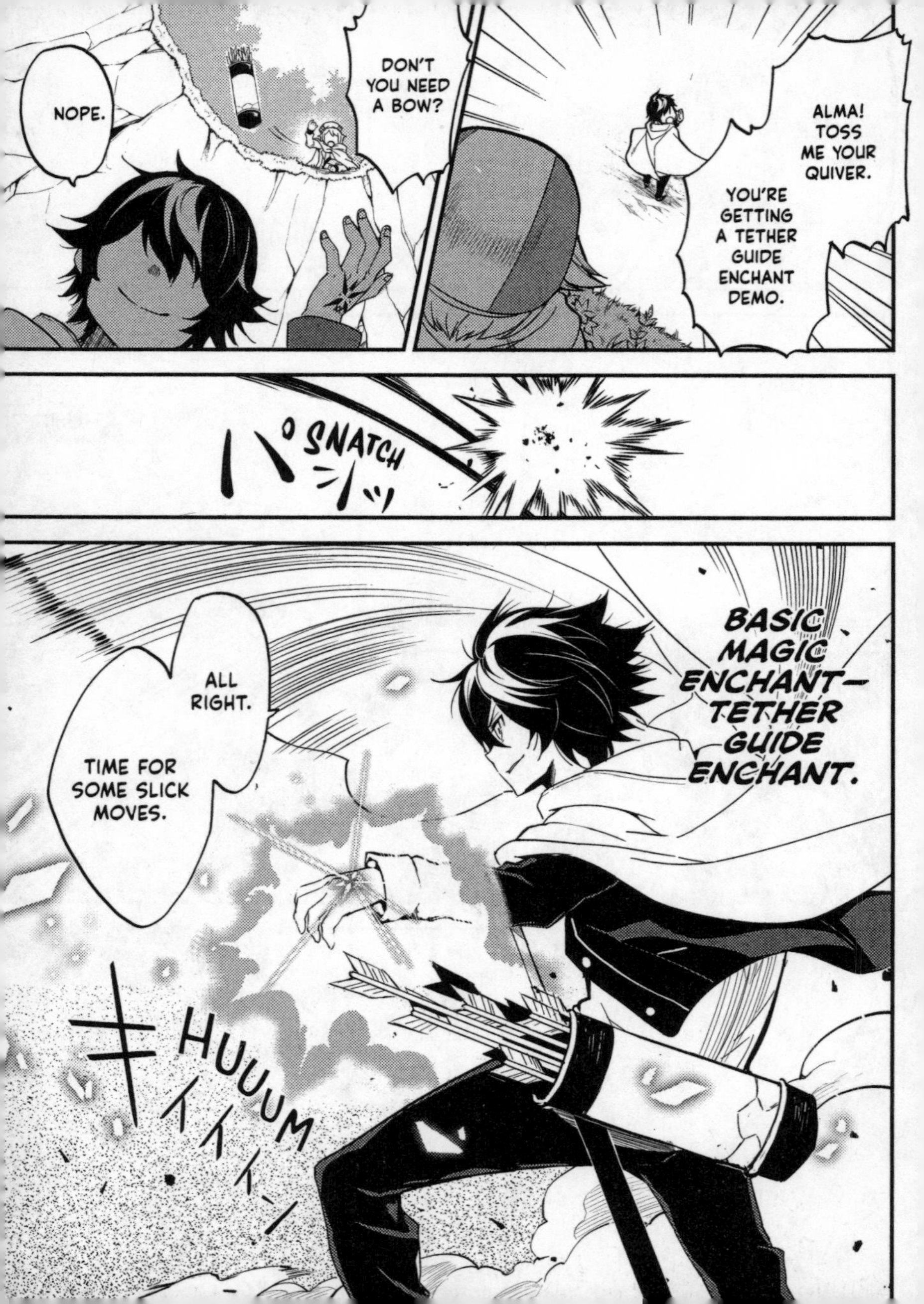
ALMA! TOSS ME YOUR QUIVER.
YOU'RE GETTING A TETHER GUIDE ENCHANT DEMO.
DON'T YOU NEED A BOW?
NOPE.
パッ
SNATCH
BASIC MAGIC ENCHANT— TETHER GUIDE ENCHANT.
ALL RIGHT.
TIME FOR SOME SLICK MOVES.
キイイイン
HUUUUM

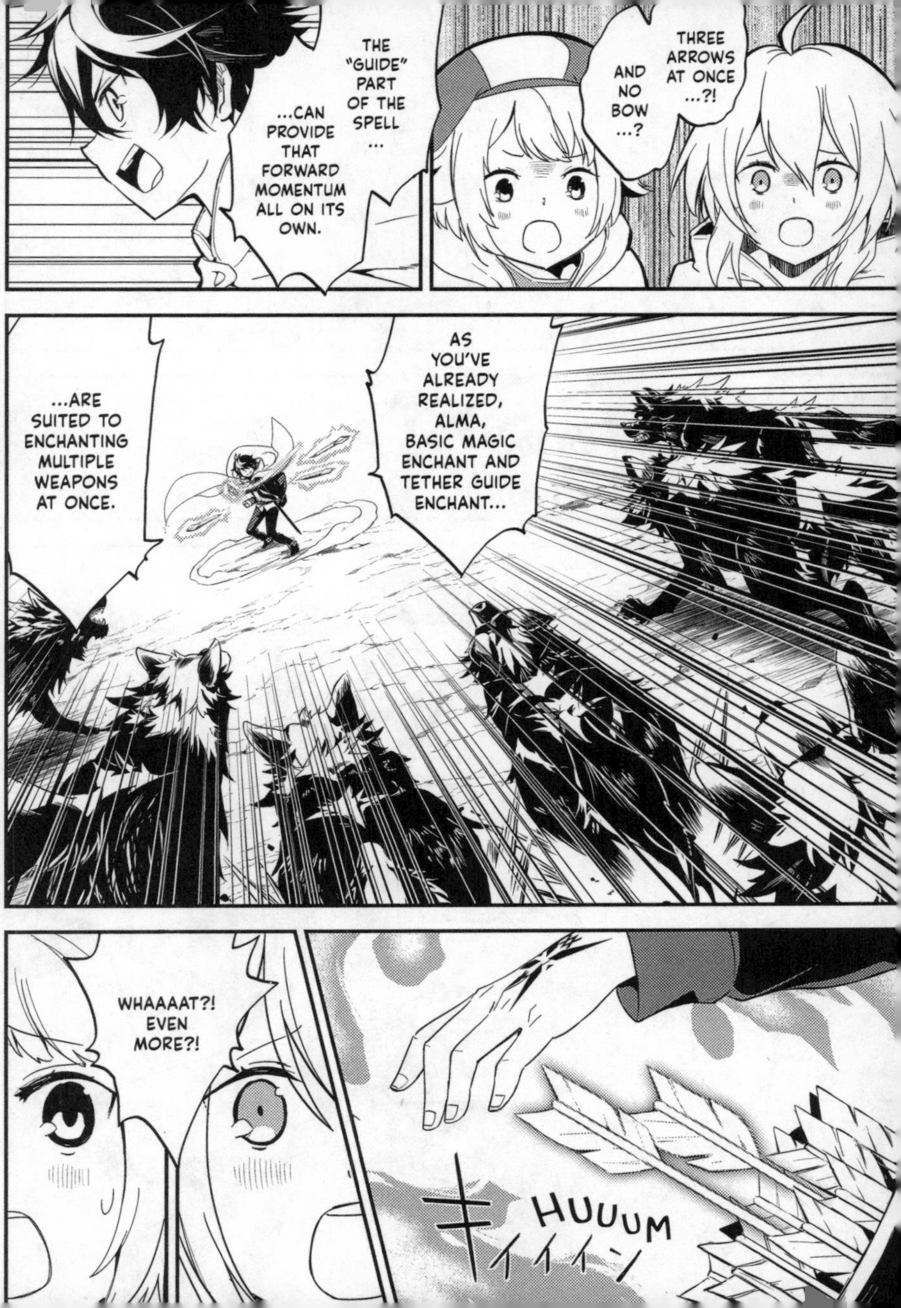
THREE ARROWS AT ONCE ...?!
AND NO BOW ...?
THE "GUIDE" PART OF THE SPELL ...
...CAN PROVIDE THAT FORWARD MOMENTUM ALL ON ITS OWN.
AS YOU'VE ALREADY REALIZED, ALMA, BASIC MAGIC ENCHANT AND TETHER GUIDE ENCHANT...
...ARE SUITED TO ENCHANTING MULTIPLE WEAPONS AT ONCE.
HUUUM
キイイン
WHAAAAT?! EVEN MORE?!

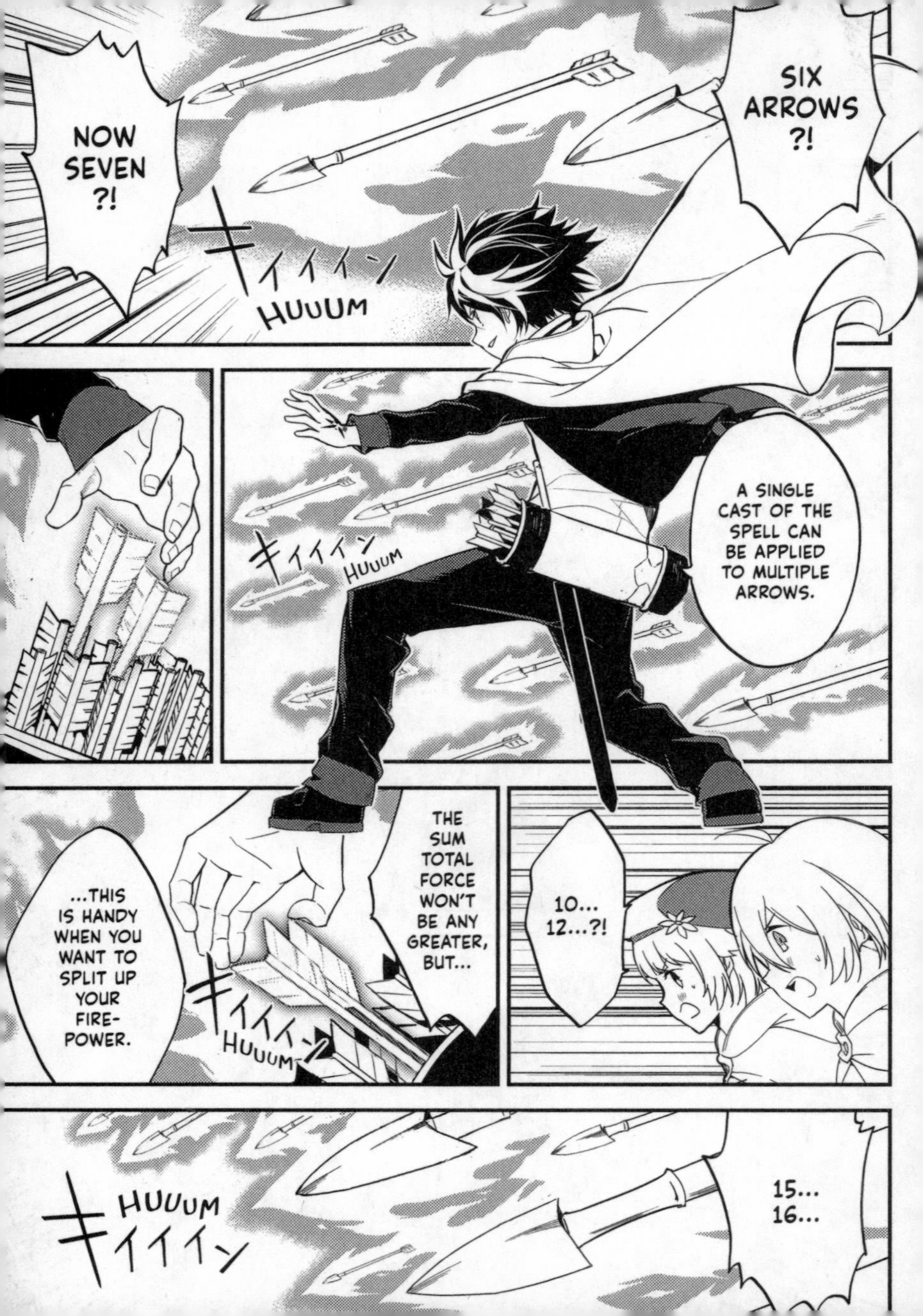
SIX ARROWS ?!
NOW SEVEN ?!
キイイイン
HUUUM
A SINGLE CAST OF THE SPELL CAN BE APPLIED TO MULTIPLE ARROWS.
キイイイン
HUUUM
10... 12...?!
THE SUM TOTAL FORCE WON'T BE ANY GREATER, BUT...
...THIS IS HANDY WHEN YOU WANT TO SPLIT UP YOUR FIRE-POWER.
キイイイーン
HUUUM-
15... 16...
HUUUM
キイイイン

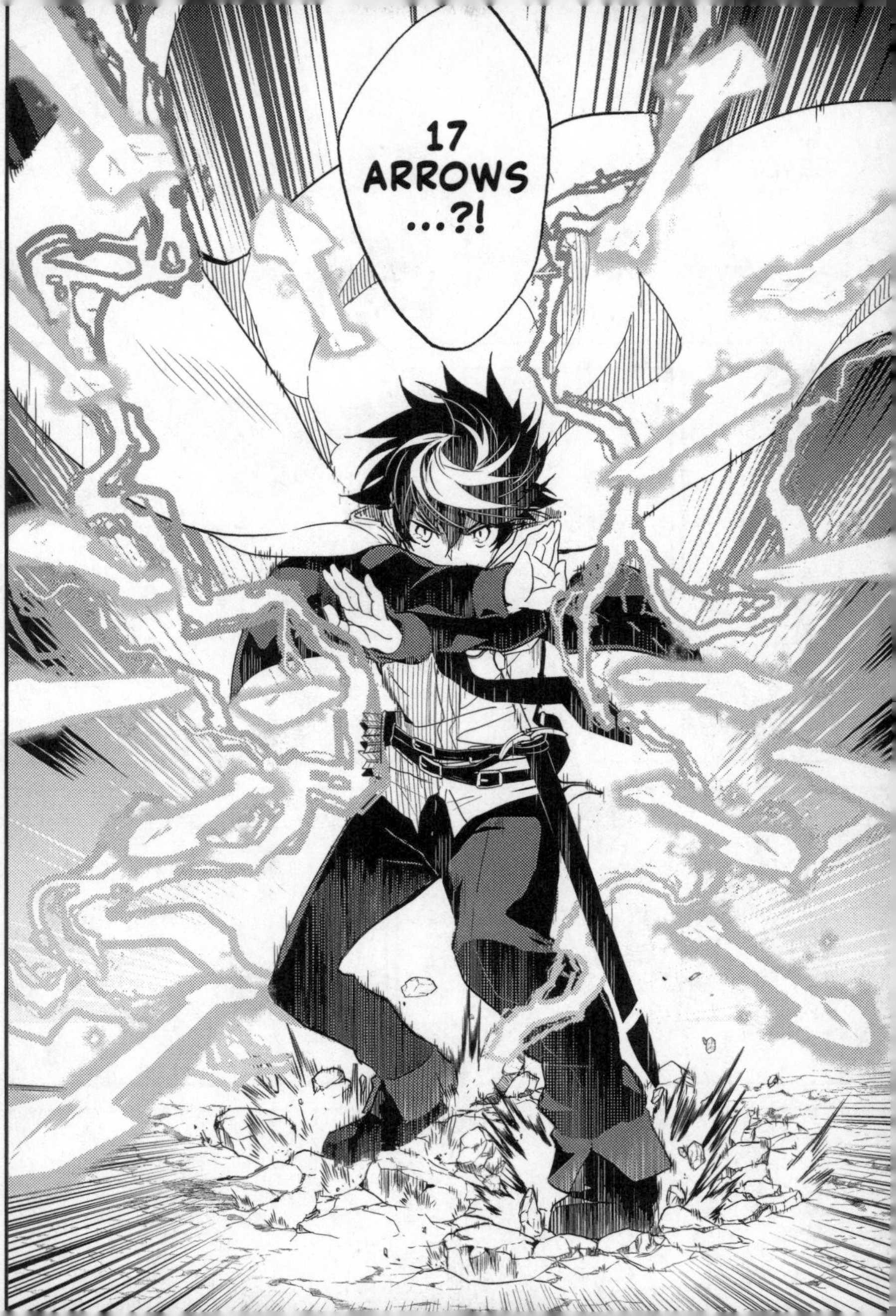
17 ARROWS ...?!

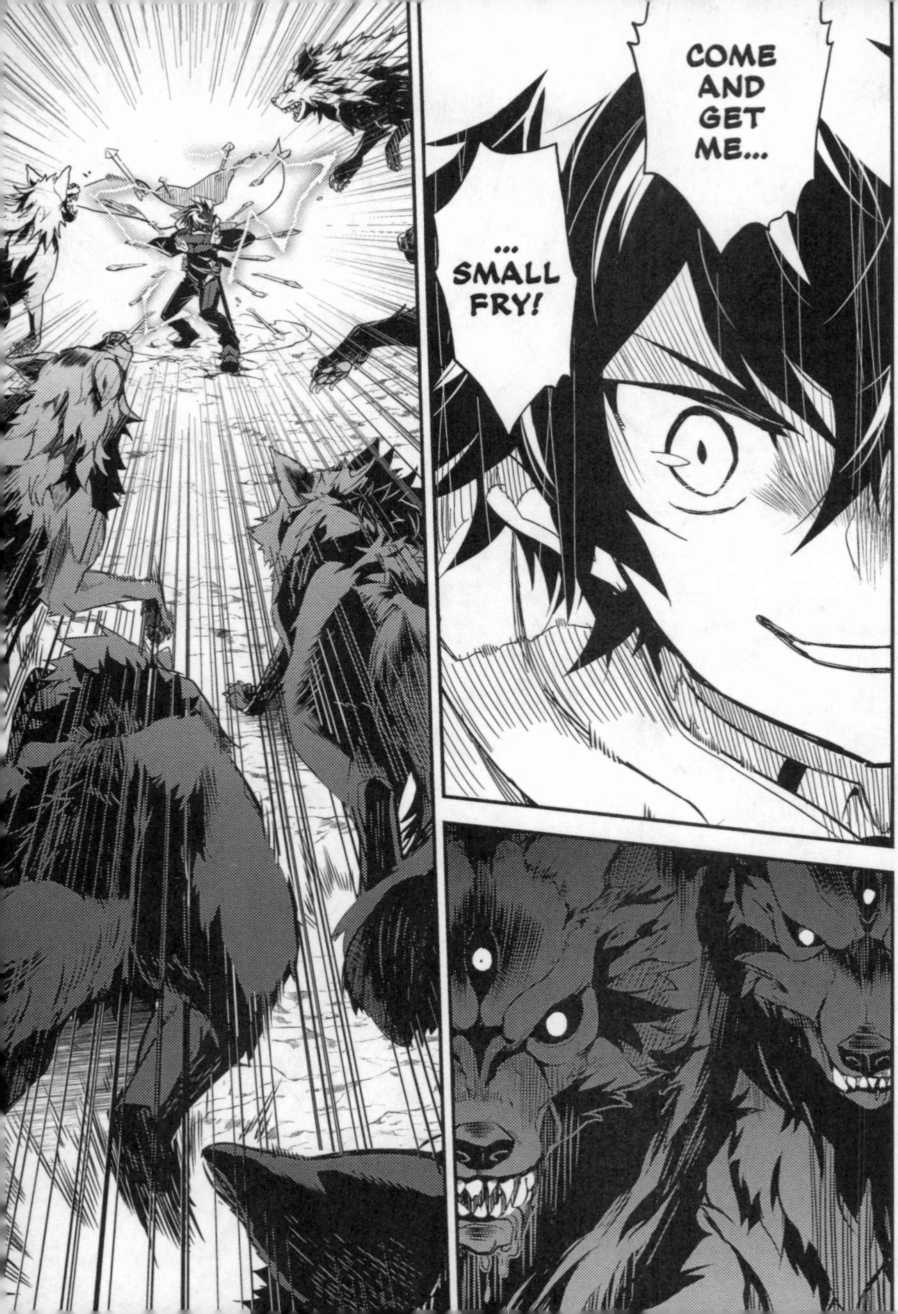
COME AND GET ME...
... SMALL FRY!

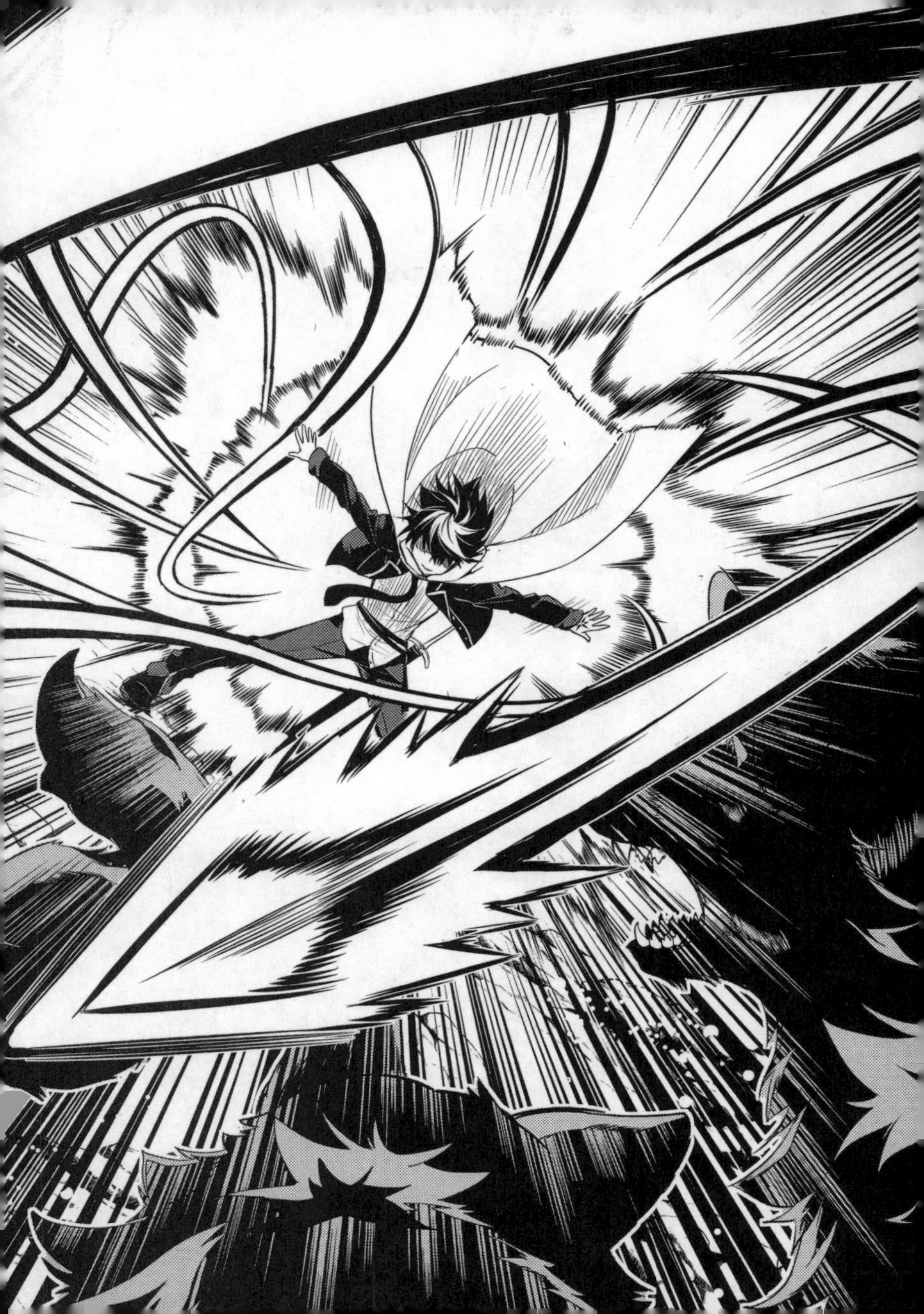

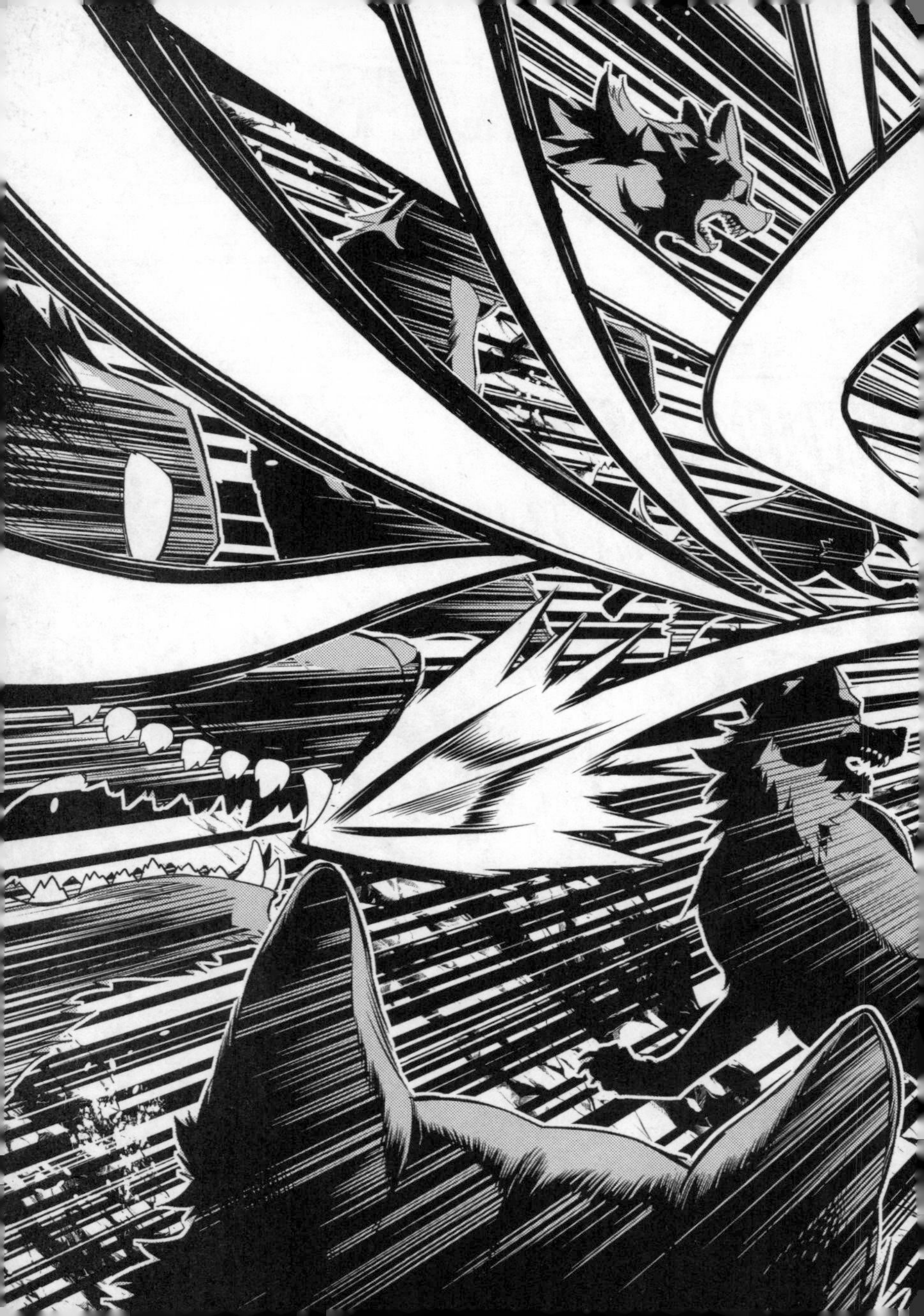

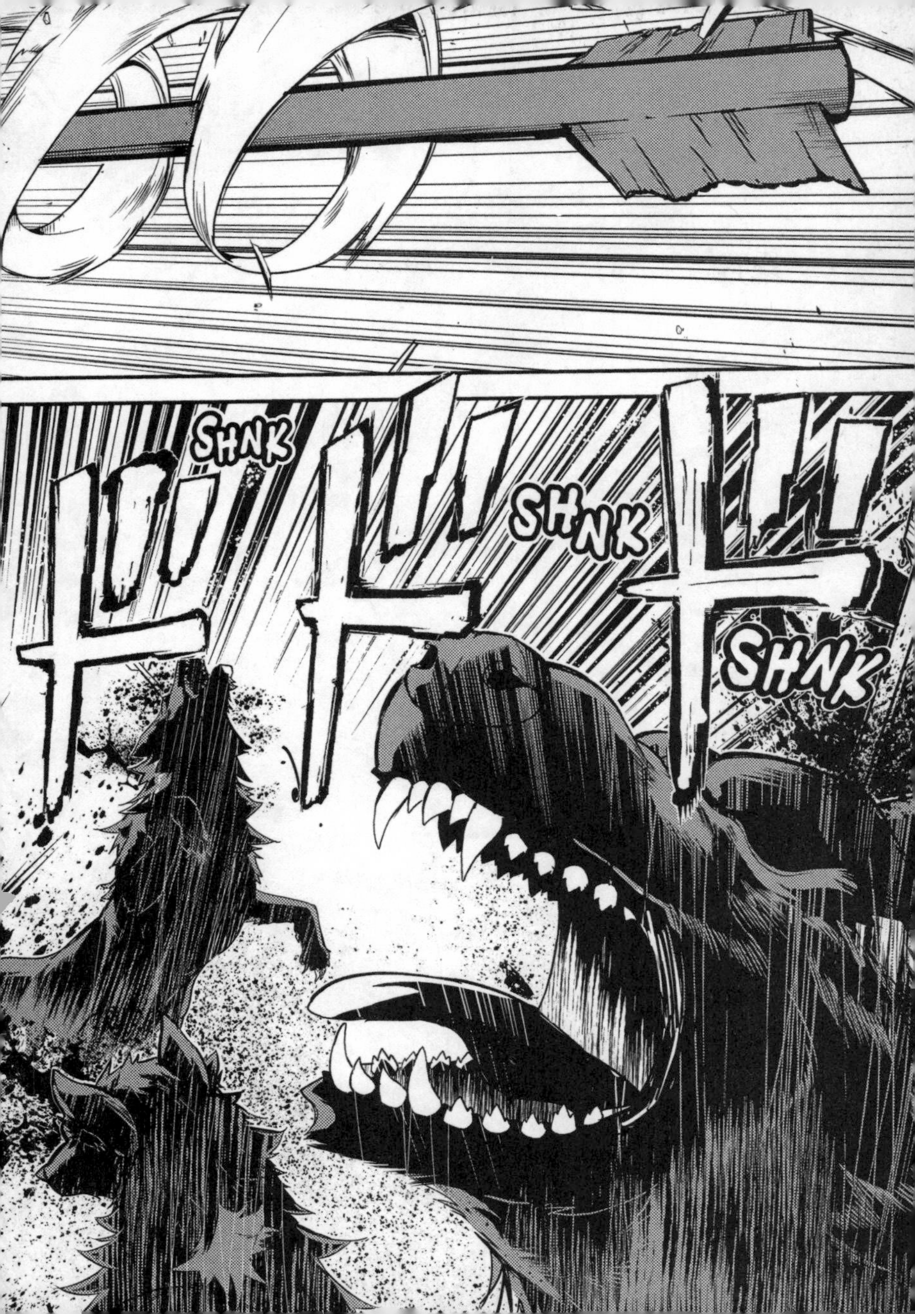
SHNK
SHNK
SHNK

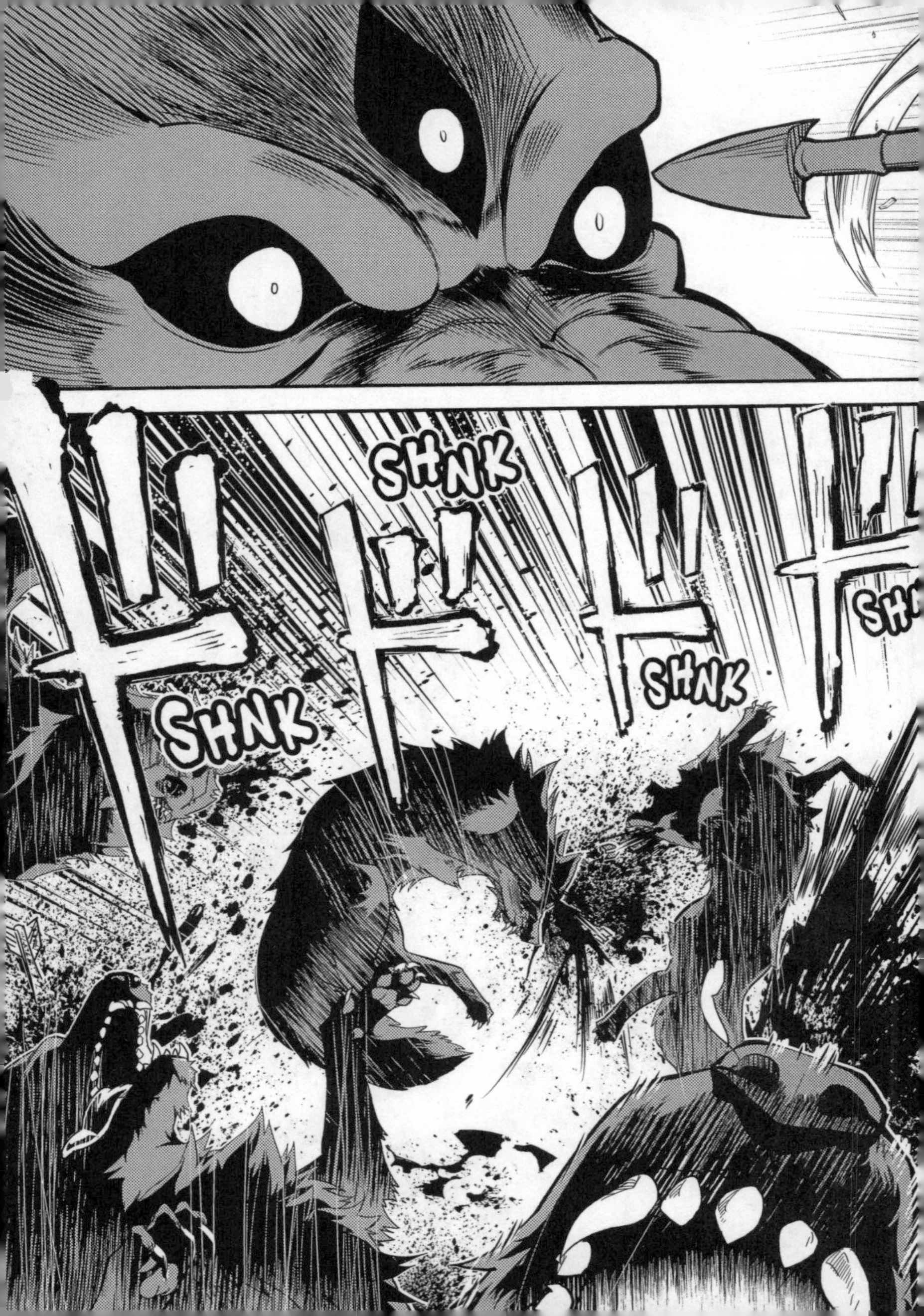

SHNK
SHNK
SHNK

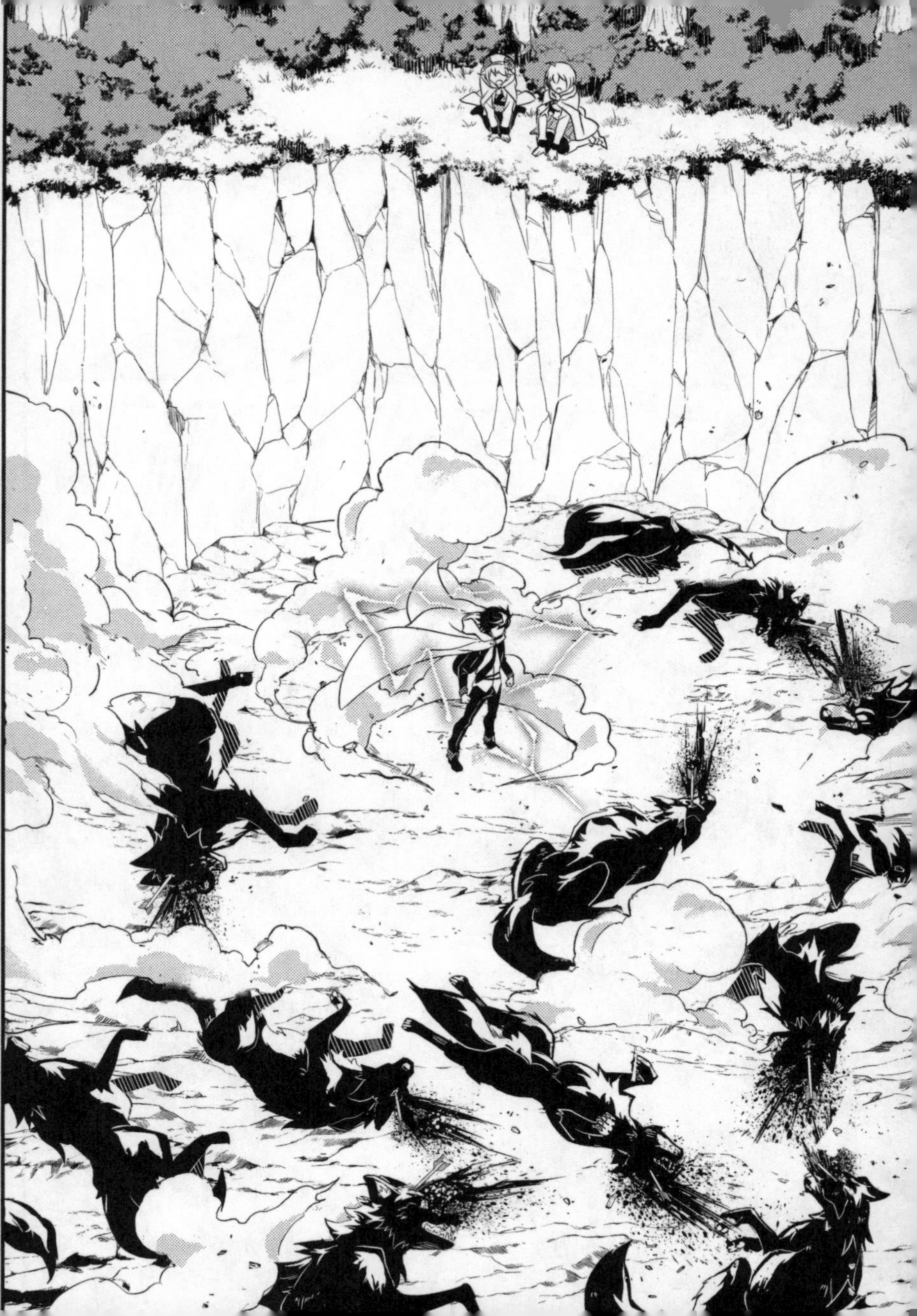

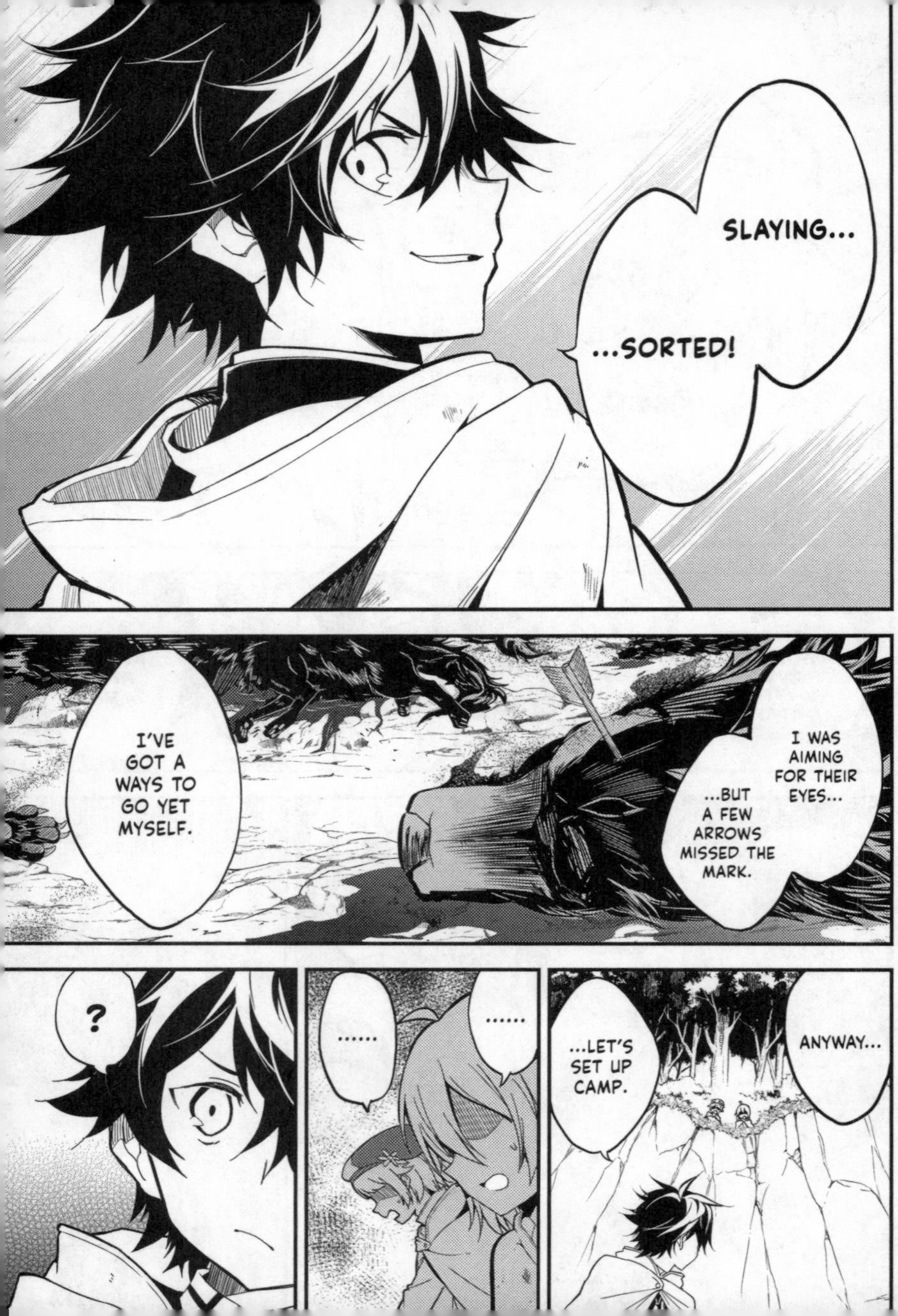
SLAYING...
...SORTED!
I WAS AIMING FOR THEIR EYES...
...BUT A FEW ARROWS MISSED THE MARK.
I'VE GOT A WAYS TO GO YET MYSELF.
ANYWAY...
...LET'S SET UP CAMP.
......
......
?

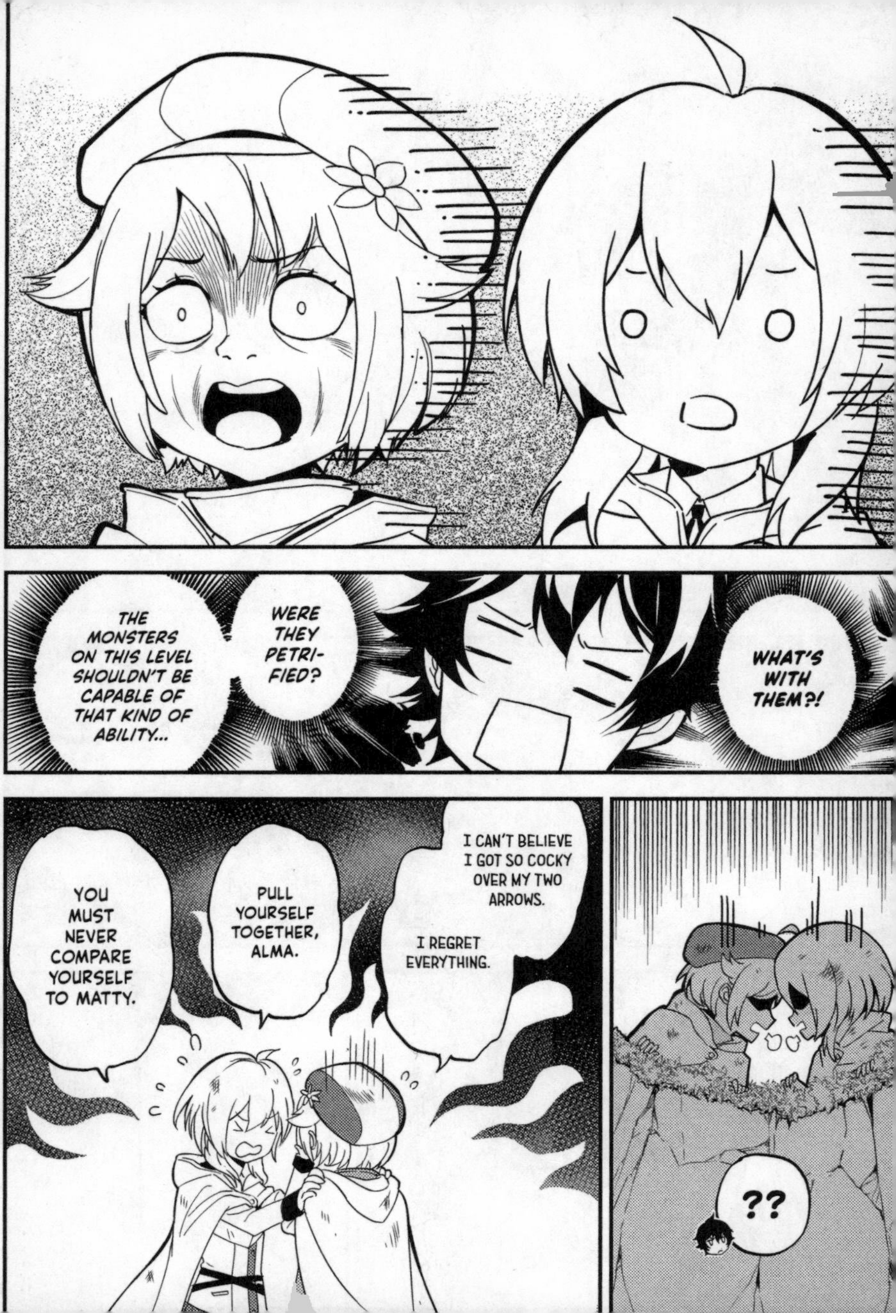
WHAT'S WITH THEM?!
WERE THEY PETRIFIED?
THE MONSTERS ON THIS LEVEL SHOULDN'T BE CAPABLE OF THAT KIND OF ABILITY...
??
I CAN'T BELIEVE I GOT SO COCKY OVER MY TWO ARROWS.
I REGRET EVERYTHING.
PULL YOURSELF TOGETHER, ALMA.
YOU MUST NEVER COMPARE YOURSELF TO MATTY.

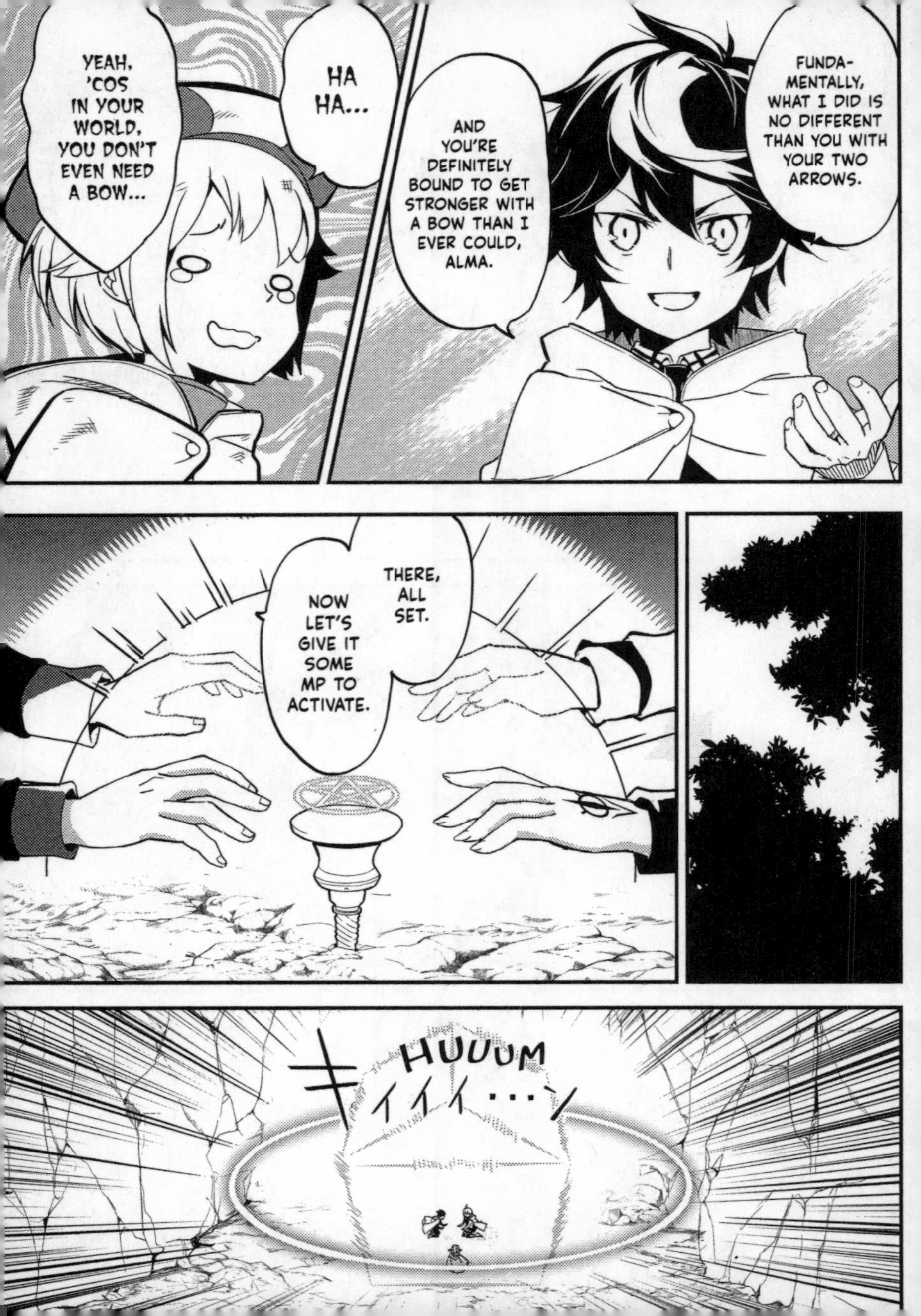
FUNDA-MENTALLY, WHAT I DID IS NO DIFFERENT THAN YOU WITH YOUR TWO ARROWS.
AND YOU'RE DEFINITELY BOUND TO GET STRONGER WITH A BOW THAN I EVER COULD, ALMA.
HA HA...
YEAH, 'COS IN YOUR WORLD, YOU DON'T EVEN NEED A BOW...
THERE, ALL SET.
NOW LET'S GIVE IT SOME MP TO ACTIVATE.
HUUUM
キイイイ…ン

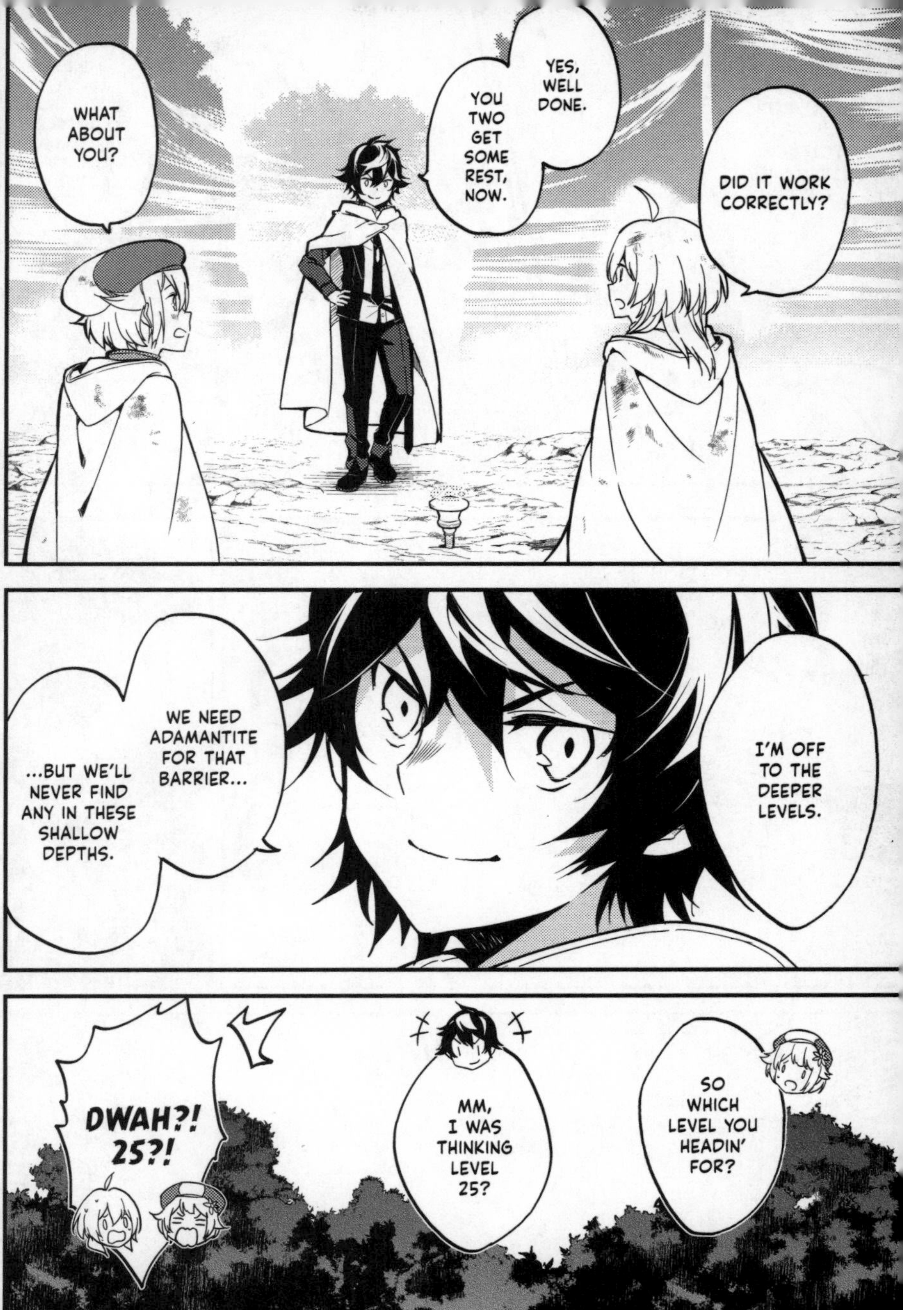
DID IT WORK CORRECTLY?
YES, WELL DONE.
YOU TWO GET SOME REST, NOW.
WHAT ABOUT YOU?
I'M OFF TO THE DEEPER LEVELS.
WE NEED ADAMANTITE FOR THAT BARRIER...
...BUT WE'LL NEVER FIND ANY IN THESE SHALLOW DEPTHS.
SO WHICH LEVEL YOU HEADIN' FOR?
MM, I WAS THINKING LEVEL 25?
DWAH?! 25?!

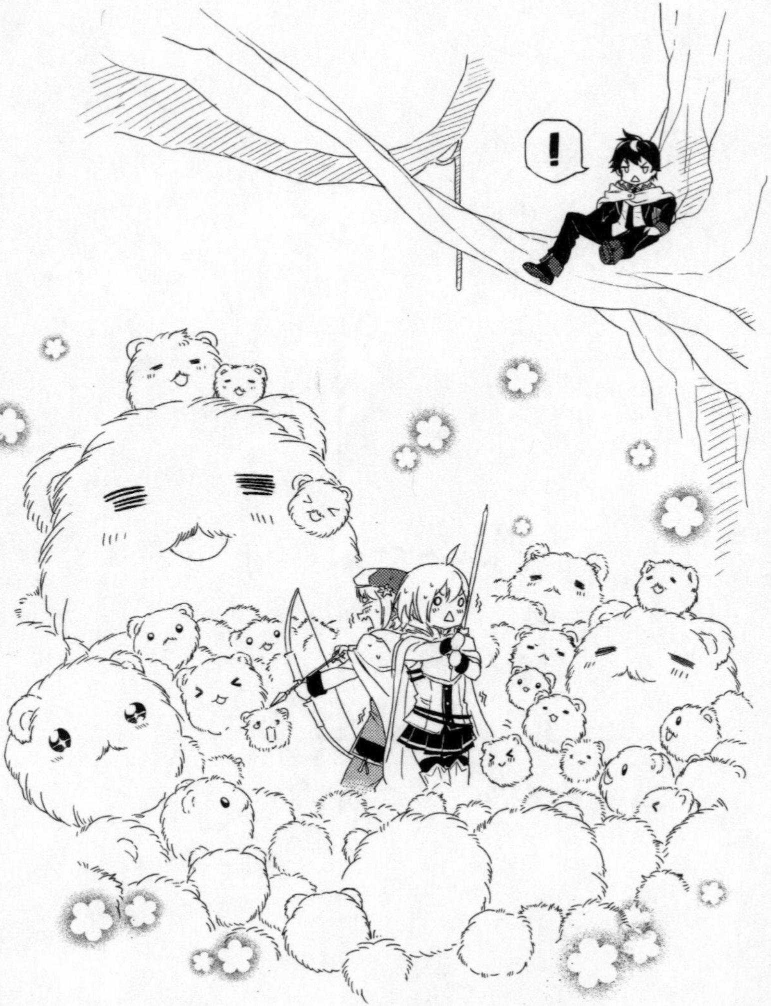
!

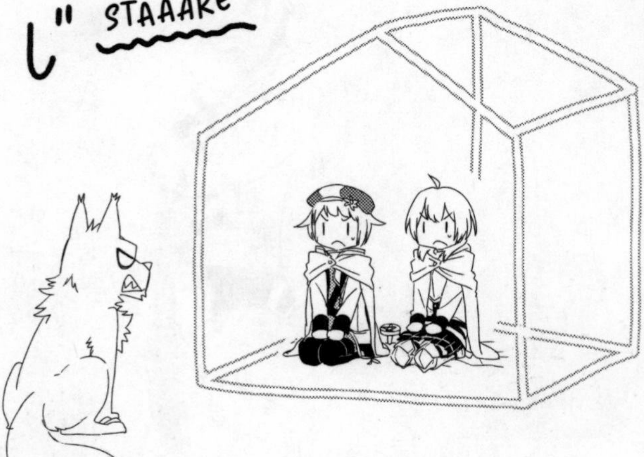
じ" STAAARE

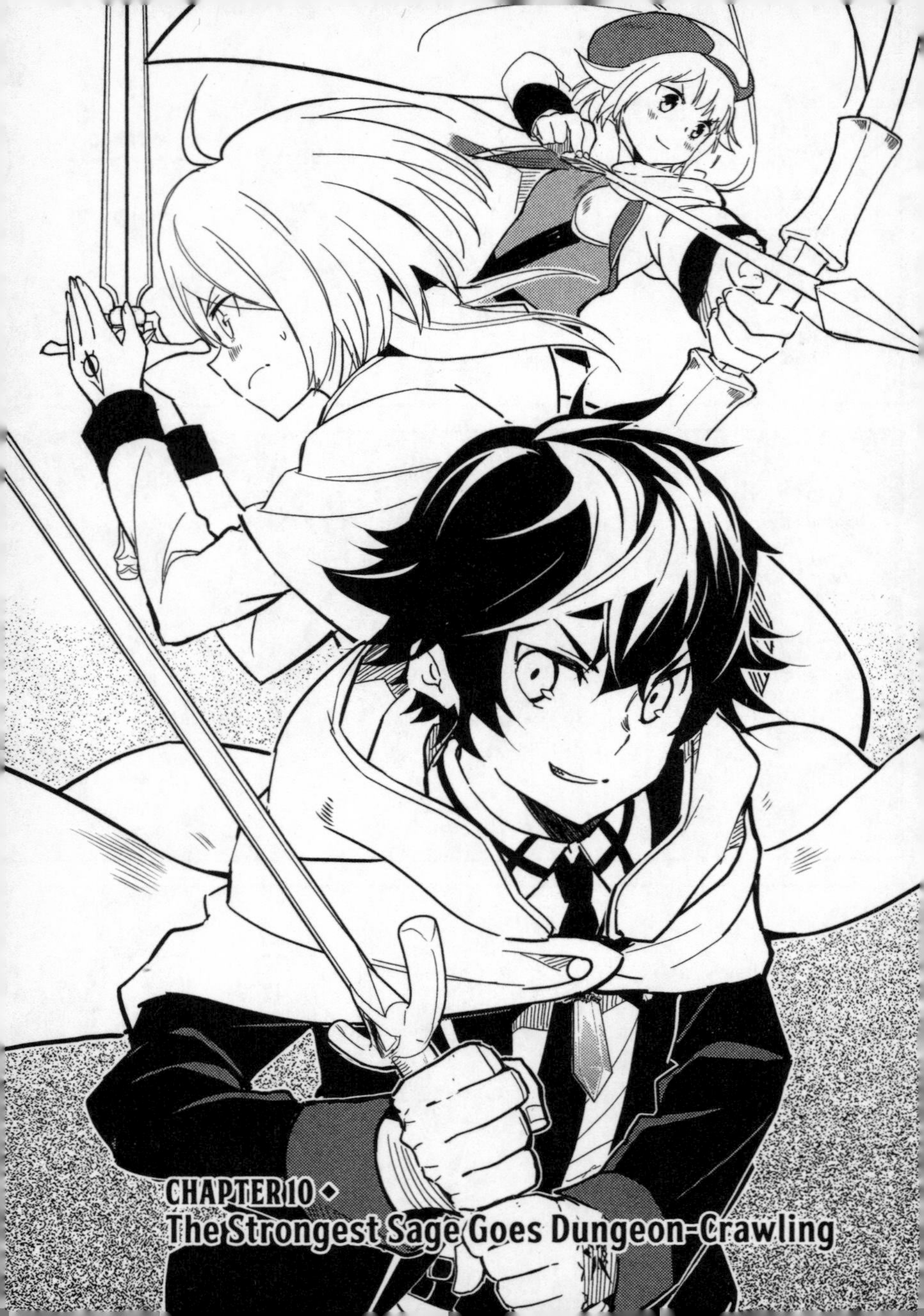
CHAPTER 10 ◆
The Strongest Sage Goes Dungeon-Crawling

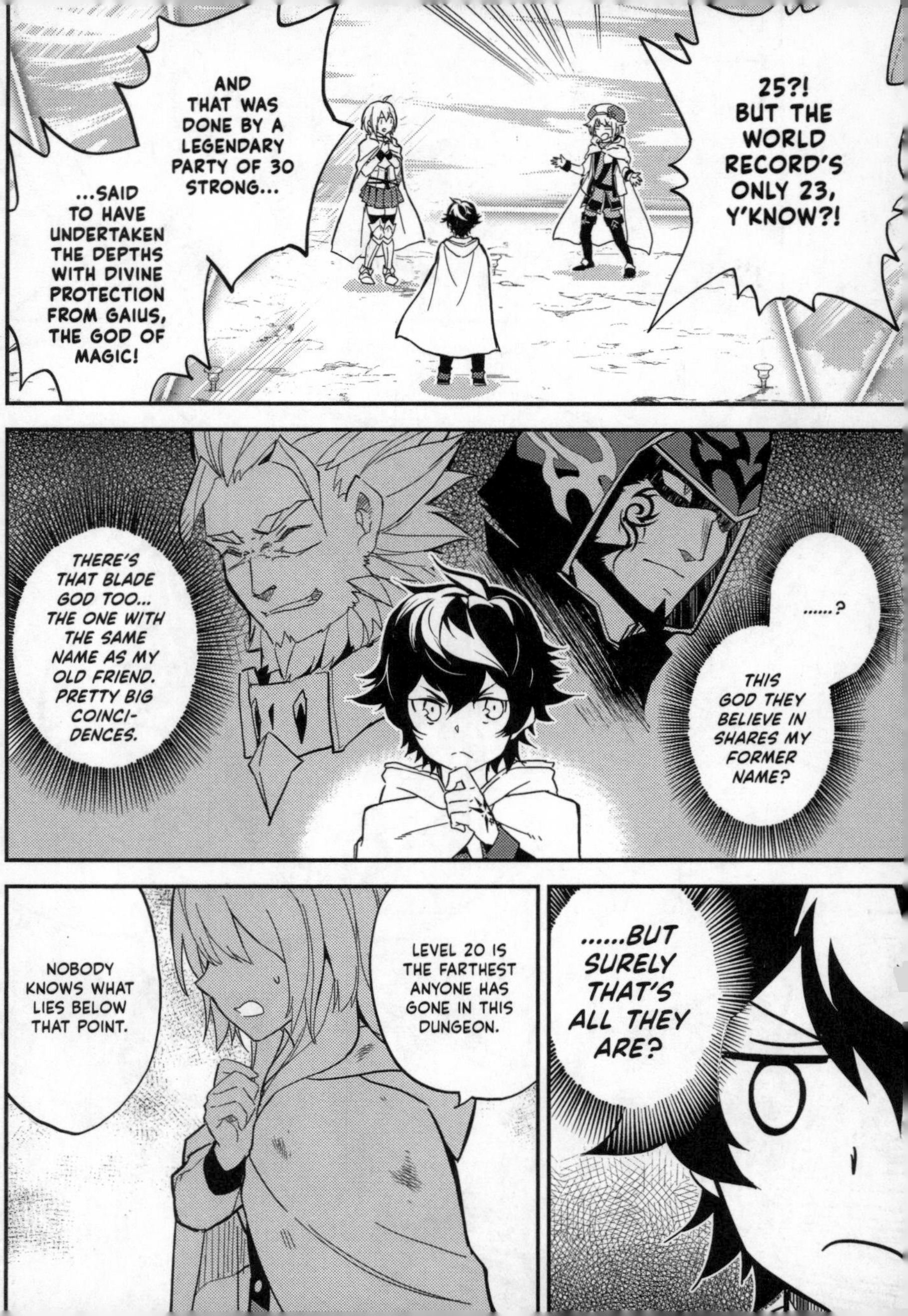
25?! BUT THE WORLD RECORD'S ONLY 23, Y'KNOW?!
AND THAT WAS DONE BY A LEGENDARY PARTY OF 30 STRONG...
...SAID TO HAVE UNDERTAKEN THE DEPTHS WITH DIVINE PROTECTION FROM GAIUS, THE GOD OF MAGIC!
......?
THIS GOD THEY BELIEVE IN SHARES MY FORMER NAME?
THERE'S THAT BLADE GOD TOO... THE ONE WITH THE SAME NAME AS MY OLD FRIEND. PRETTY BIG COINCI-DENCES.
......BUT SURELY THAT'S ALL THEY ARE?
LEVEL 20 IS THE FARTHEST ANYONE HAS GONE IN THIS DUNGEON.
NOBODY KNOWS WHAT LIES BELOW THAT POINT.

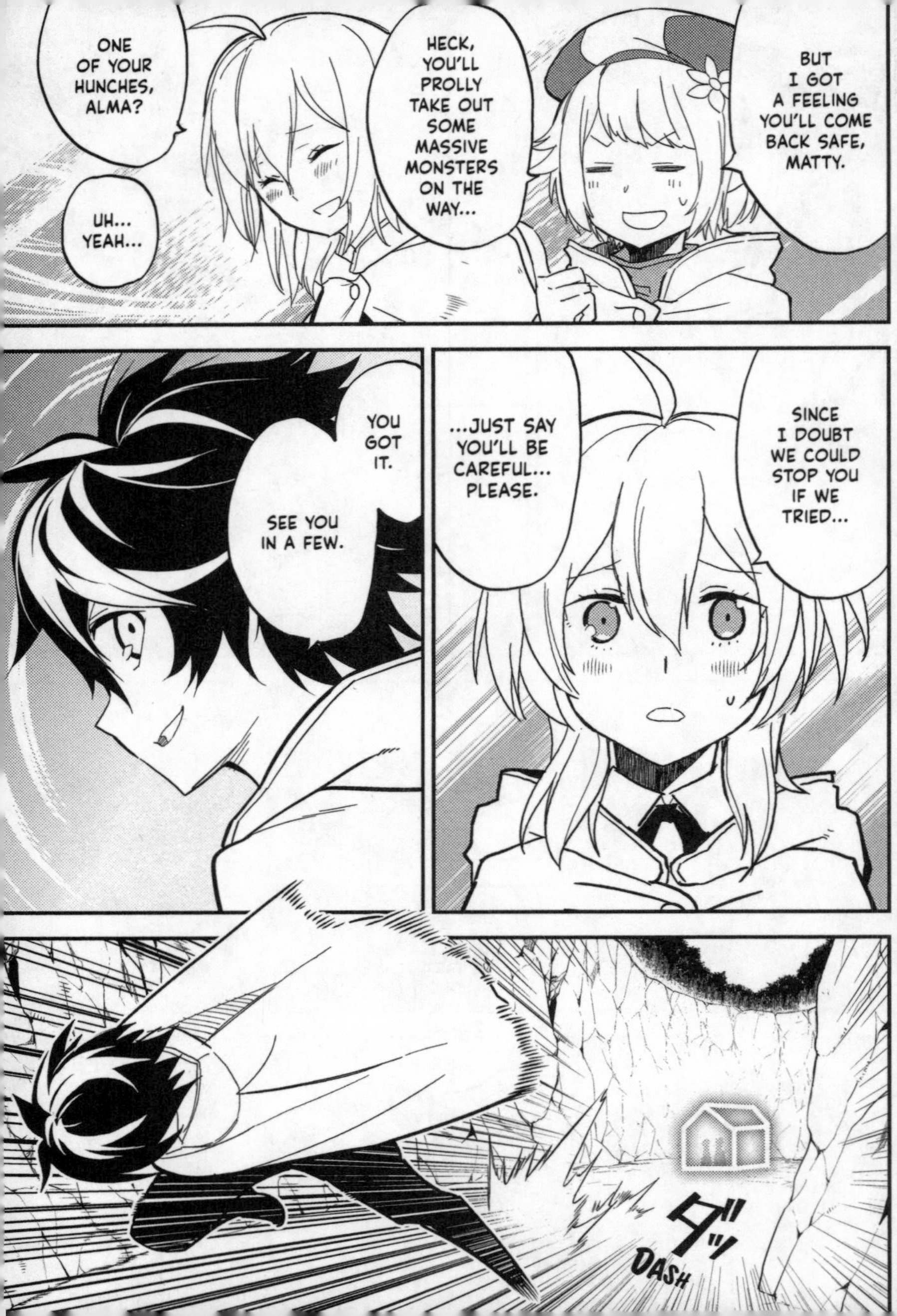
BUT I GOT A FEELING YOU'LL COME BACK SAFE, MATTY.
HECK, YOU'LL PROLLY TAKE OUT SOME MASSIVE MONSTERS ON THE WAY...
ONE OF YOUR HUNCHES, ALMA?
UH... YEAH...
SINCE I DOUBT WE COULD STOP YOU IF WE TRIED...
...JUST SAY YOU'LL BE CAREFUL... PLEASE.
YOU GOT IT.
SEE YOU IN A FEW.
ダッ
DASH

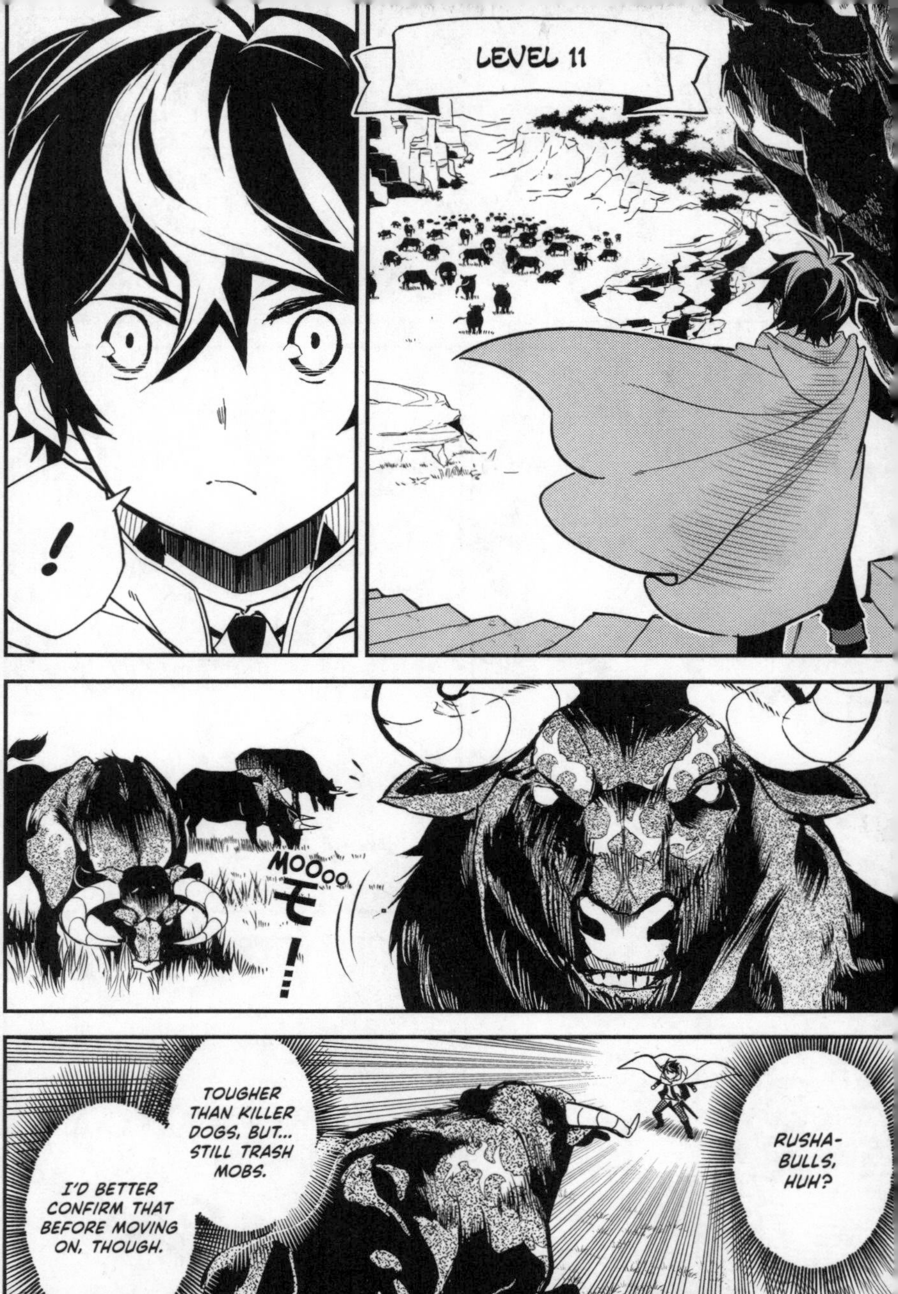
LEVEL 11
!
MOOOO
モ
!!!
RUSHA-BULLS, HUH?
TOUGHER THAN KILLER DOGS, BUT... STILL TRASH MOBS.
I'D BETTER CONFIRM THAT BEFORE MOVING ON, THOUGH.

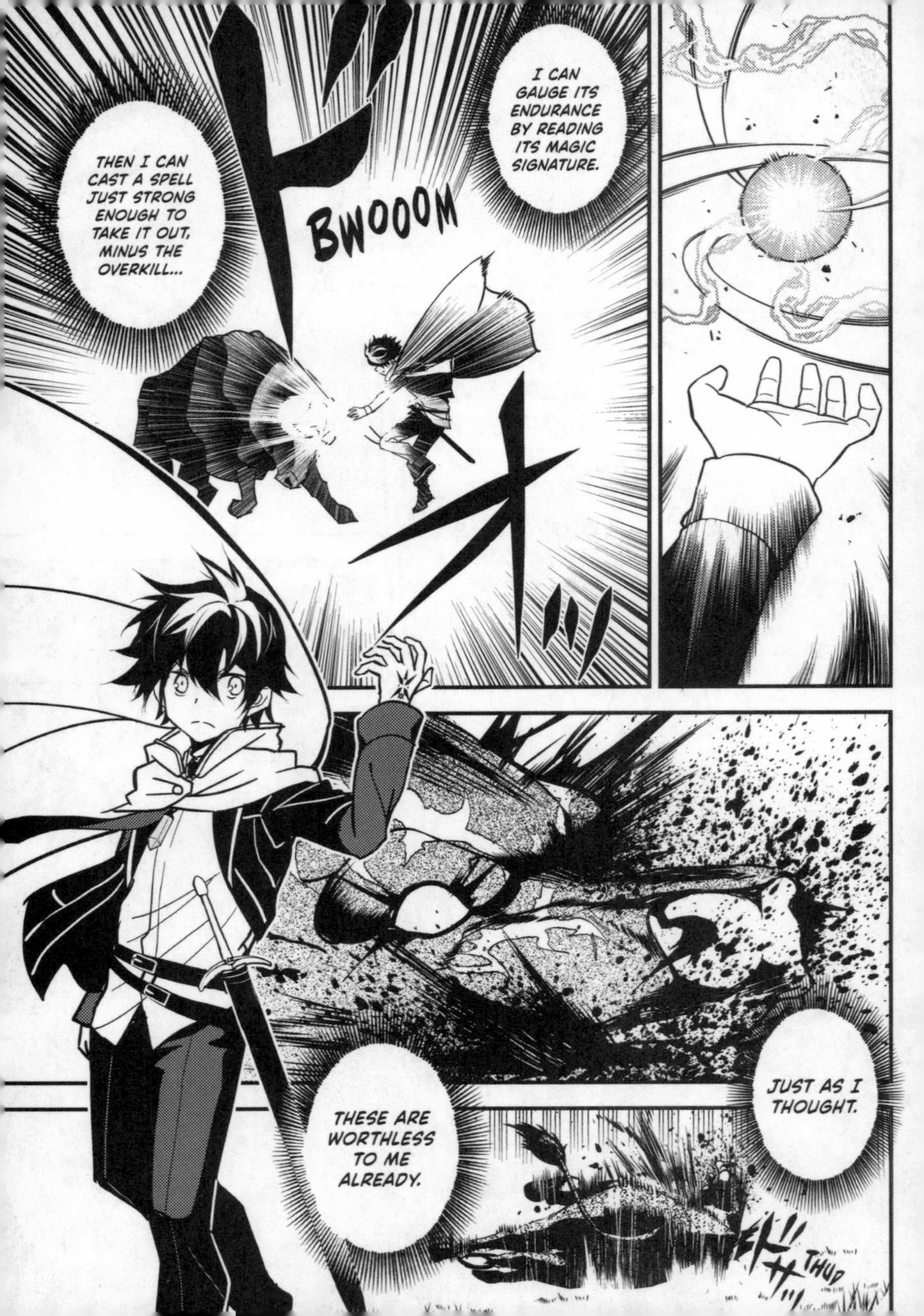

I CAN GAUGE ITS ENDURANCE BY READING ITS MAGIC SIGNATURE.
THEN I CAN CAST A SPELL JUST STRONG ENOUGH TO TAKE IT OUT, MINUS THE OVERKILL...
BWOOOM
JUST AS I THOUGHT.
THESE ARE WORTHLESS TO ME ALREADY.
THUD

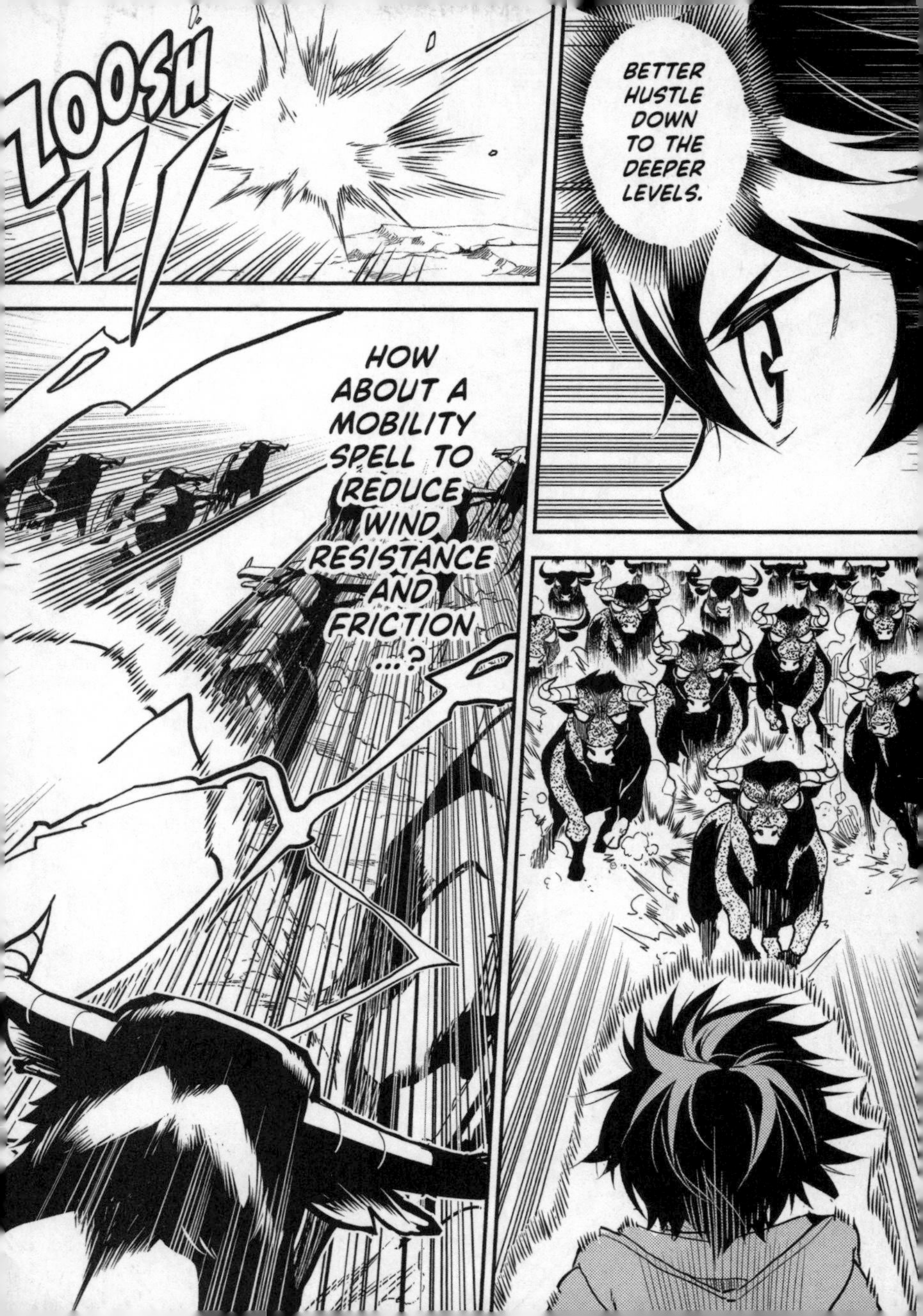
BETTER HUSTLE DOWN TO THE DEEPER LEVELS.
ZOOSH
HOW ABOUT A MOBILITY SPELL TO REDUCE WIND RESISTANCE AND FRICTION ...?

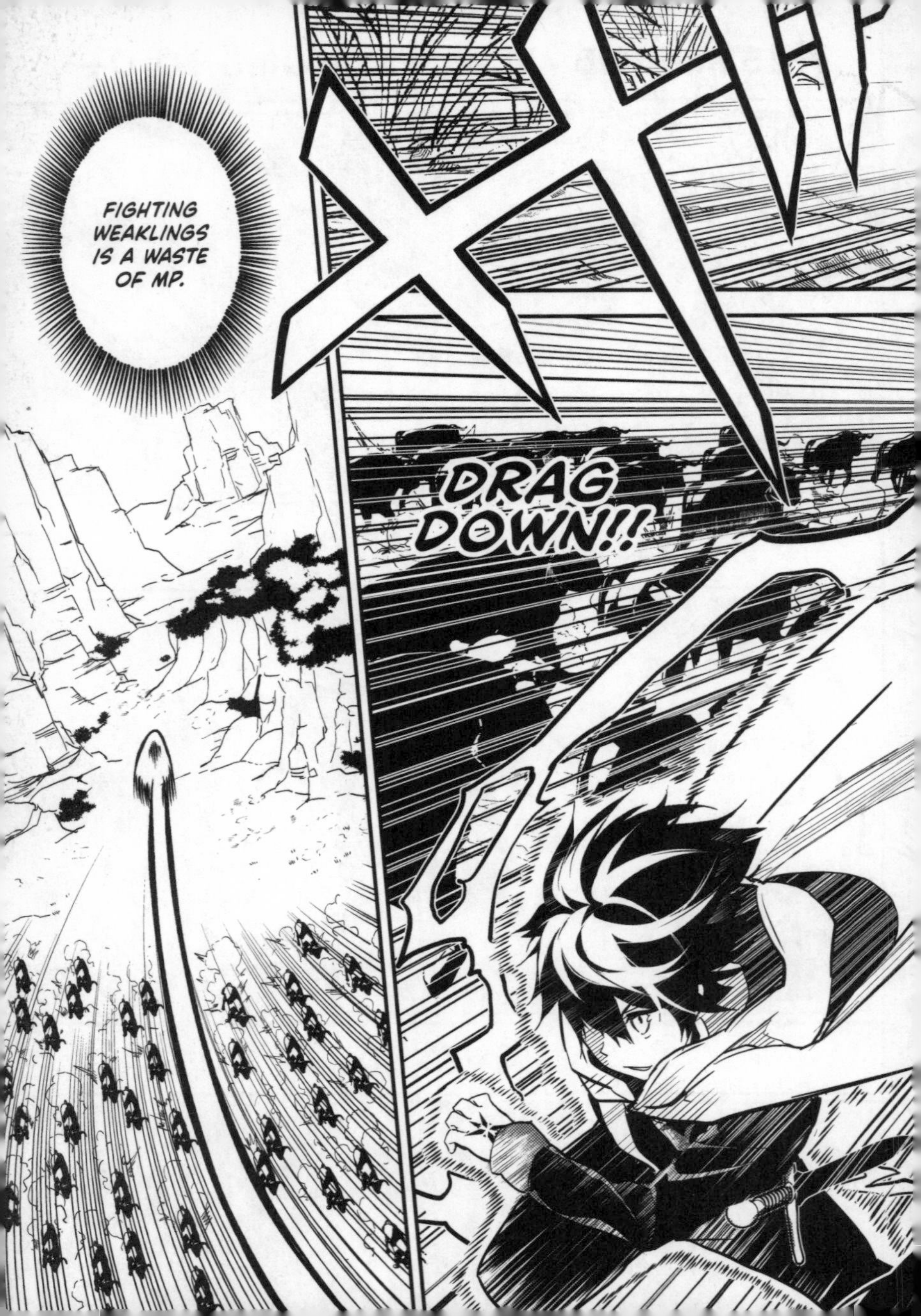
DRAG DOWN!!
FIGHTING WEAKLINGS IS A WASTE OF MP.

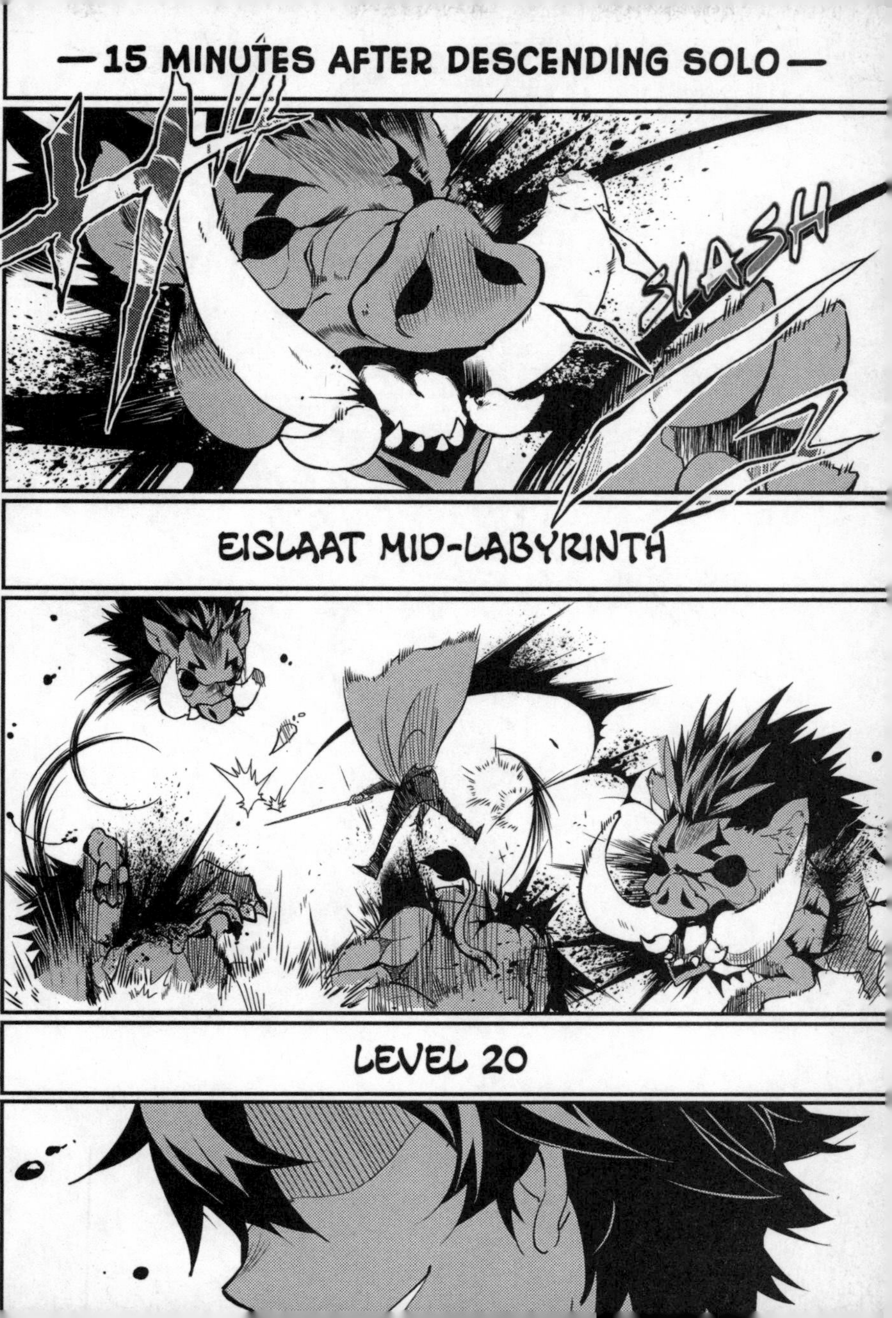
—15 MINUTES AFTER DESCENDING SOLO—
SLASH
EISLAAT MID-LABYRINTH
LEVEL 20

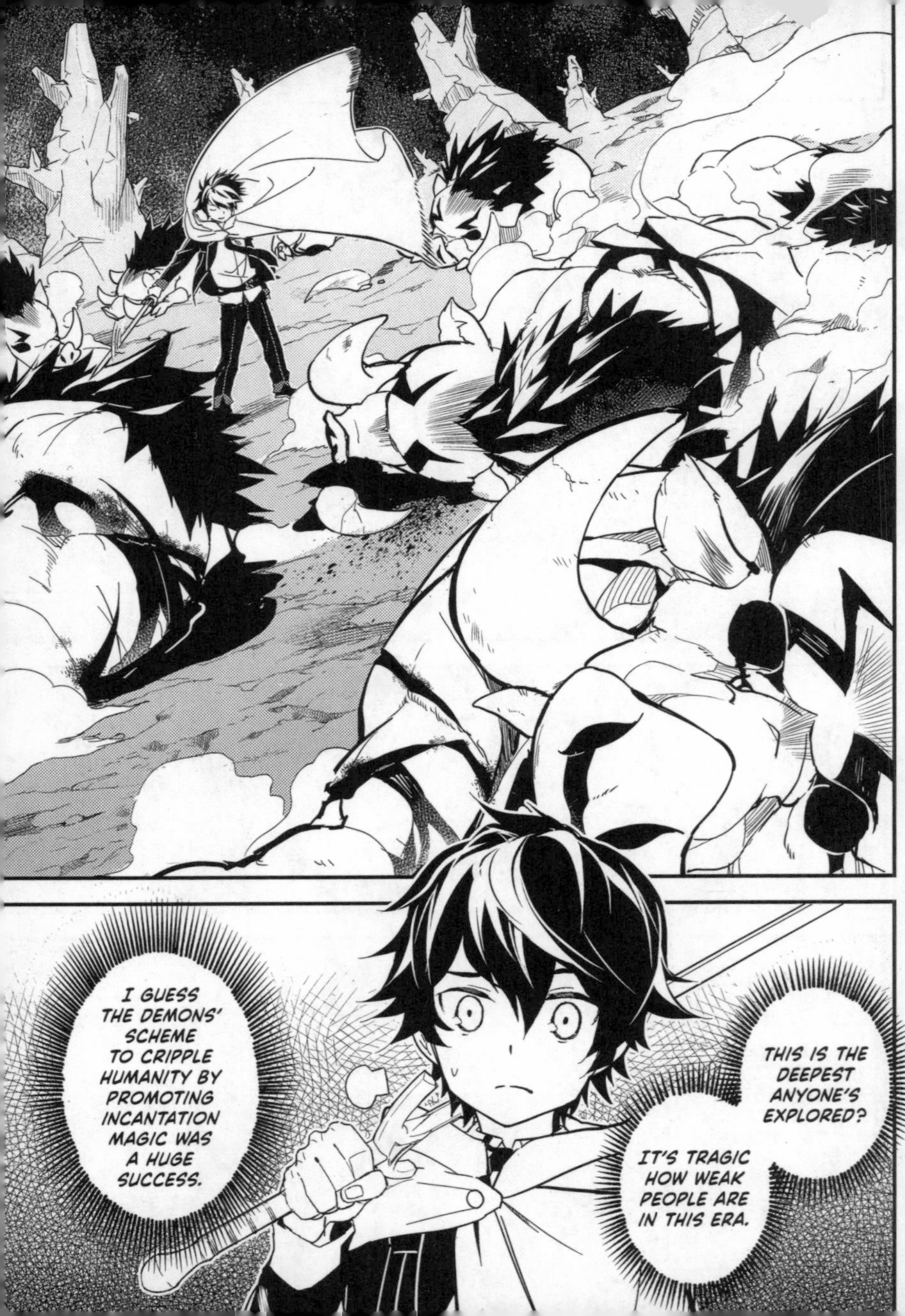
THIS IS THE DEEPEST ANYONE'S EXPLORED?
IT'S TRAGIC HOW WEAK PEOPLE ARE IN THIS ERA.
I GUESS THE DEMONS' SCHEME TO CRIPPLE HUMANITY BY PROMOTING INCANTATION MAGIC WAS A HUGE SUCCESS.

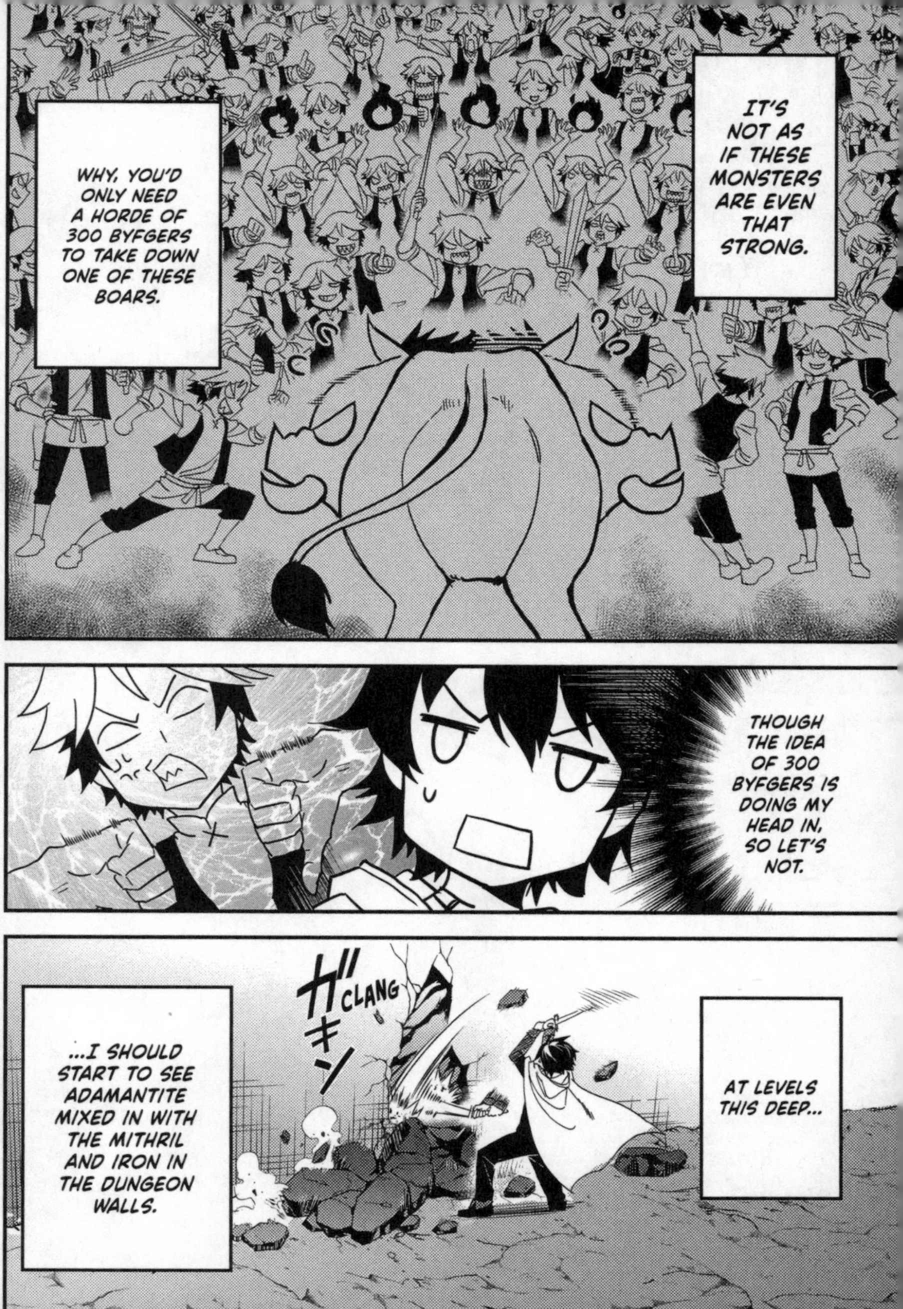
IT'S NOT AS IF THESE MONSTERS ARE EVEN THAT STRONG.
WHY, YOU'D ONLY NEED A HORDE OF 300 BYFGERS TO TAKE DOWN ONE OF THESE BOARS.
THOUGH THE IDEA OF 300 BYFGERS IS DOING MY HEAD IN, SO LET'S NOT.
AT LEVELS THIS DEEP...
ガキン
CLANG
...I SHOULD START TO SEE ADAMANTITE MIXED IN WITH THE MITHRIL AND IRON IN THE DUNGEON WALLS.

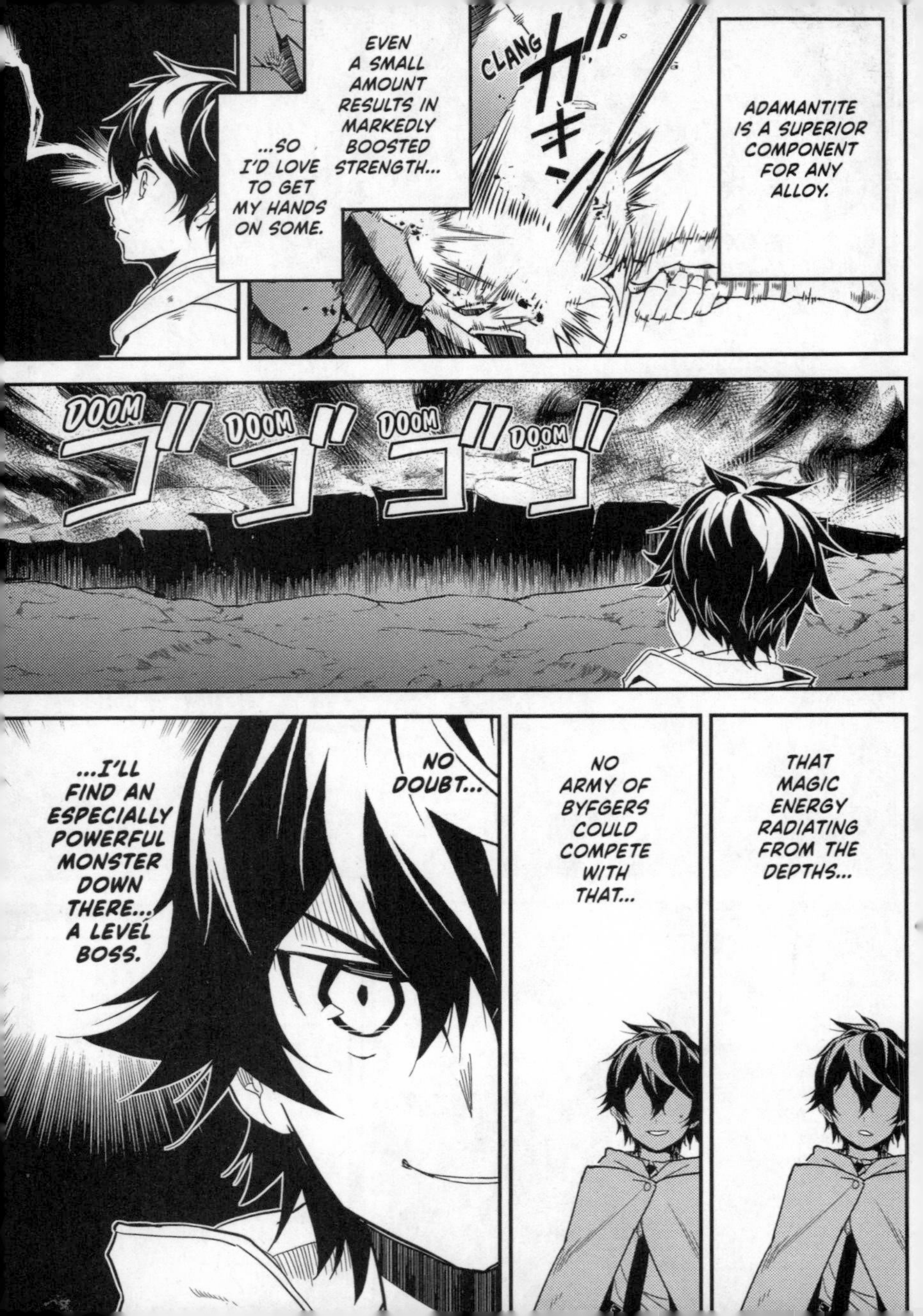
ADAMANTITE IS A SUPERIOR COMPONENT FOR ANY ALLOY.
CLANG
EVEN A SMALL AMOUNT RESULTS IN MARKEDLY BOOSTED STRENGTH...
...SO I'D LOVE TO GET MY HANDS ON SOME.
DOOM
DOOM
DOOM
DOOM
THAT MAGIC ENERGY RADIATING FROM THE DEPTHS...
NO ARMY OF BYFGERS COULD COMPETE WITH THAT...
NO DOUBT...
...I'LL FIND AN ESPECIALLY POWERFUL MONSTER DOWN THERE... A LEVEL BOSS.

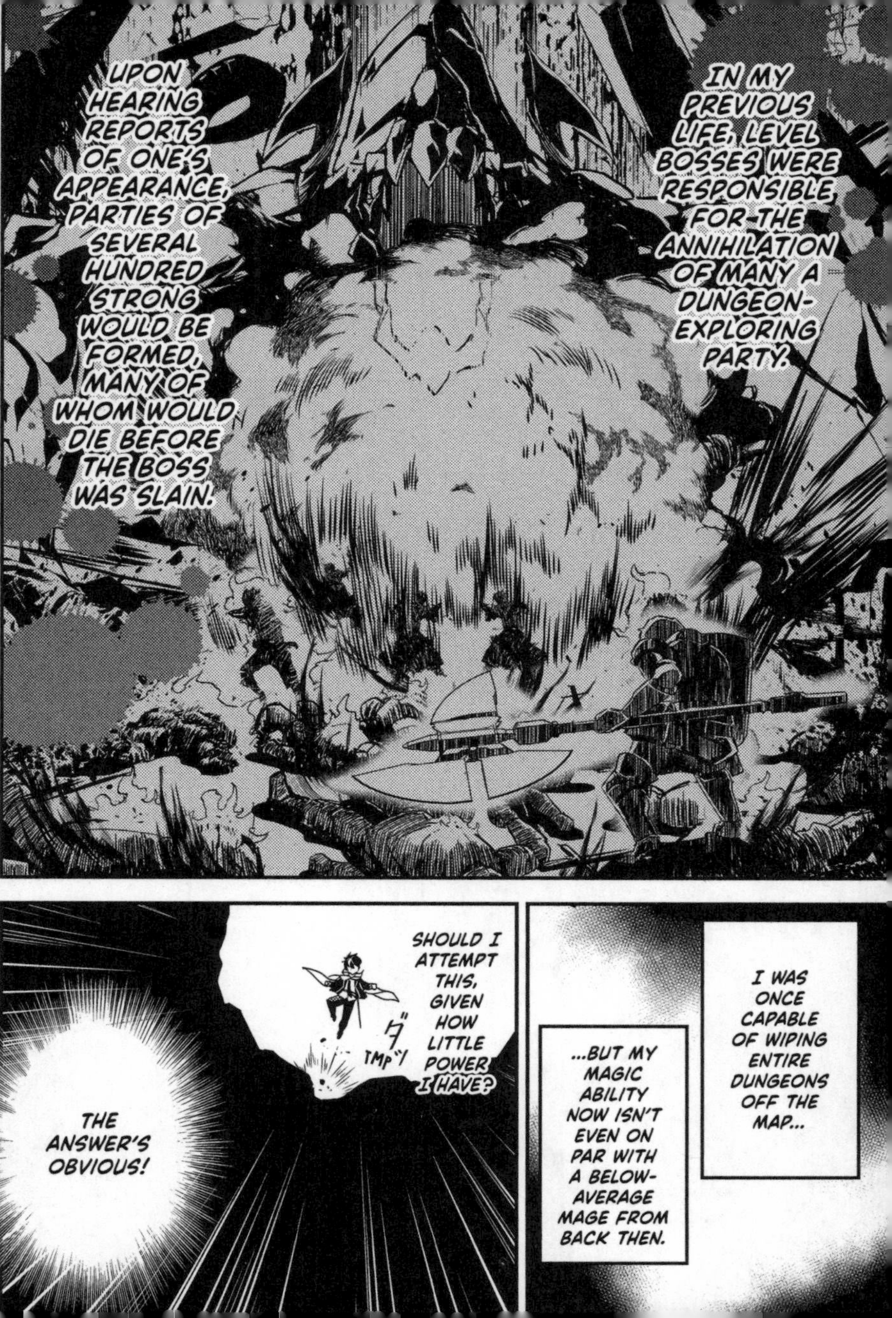
IN MY PREVIOUS LIFE, LEVEL BOSSES WERE RESPONSIBLE FOR THE ANNIHILATION OF MANY A DUNGEON-EXPLORING PARTY.
UPON HEARING REPORTS OF ONE'S APPEARANCE, PARTIES OF SEVERAL HUNDRED STRONG WOULD BE FORMED, MANY OF WHOM WOULD DIE BEFORE THE BOSS WAS SLAIN.
I WAS ONCE CAPABLE OF WIPING ENTIRE DUNGEONS OFF THE MAP...
...BUT MY MAGIC ABILITY NOW ISN'T EVEN ON PAR WITH A BELOW-AVERAGE MAGE FROM BACK THEN.
SHOULD I ATTEMPT THIS, GIVEN HOW LITTLE POWER I HAVE?
TMP
THE ANSWER'S OBVIOUS!

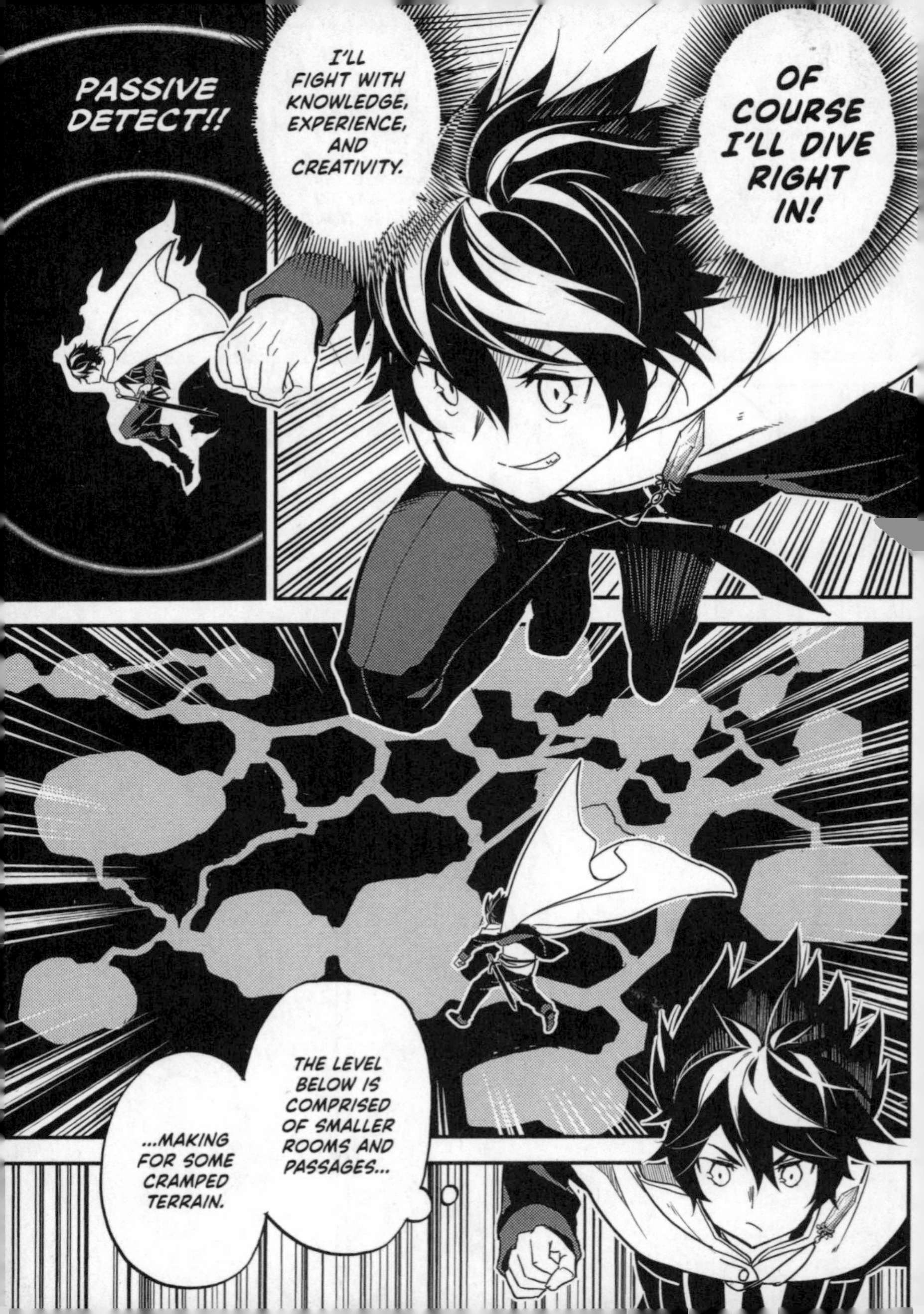
OF COURSE I'LL DIVE RIGHT IN!
I'LL FIGHT WITH KNOWLEDGE, EXPERIENCE, AND CREATIVITY.
PASSIVE DETECT!!
THE LEVEL BELOW IS COMPRISED OF SMALLER ROOMS AND PASSAGES...
...MAKING FOR SOME CRAMPED TERRAIN.

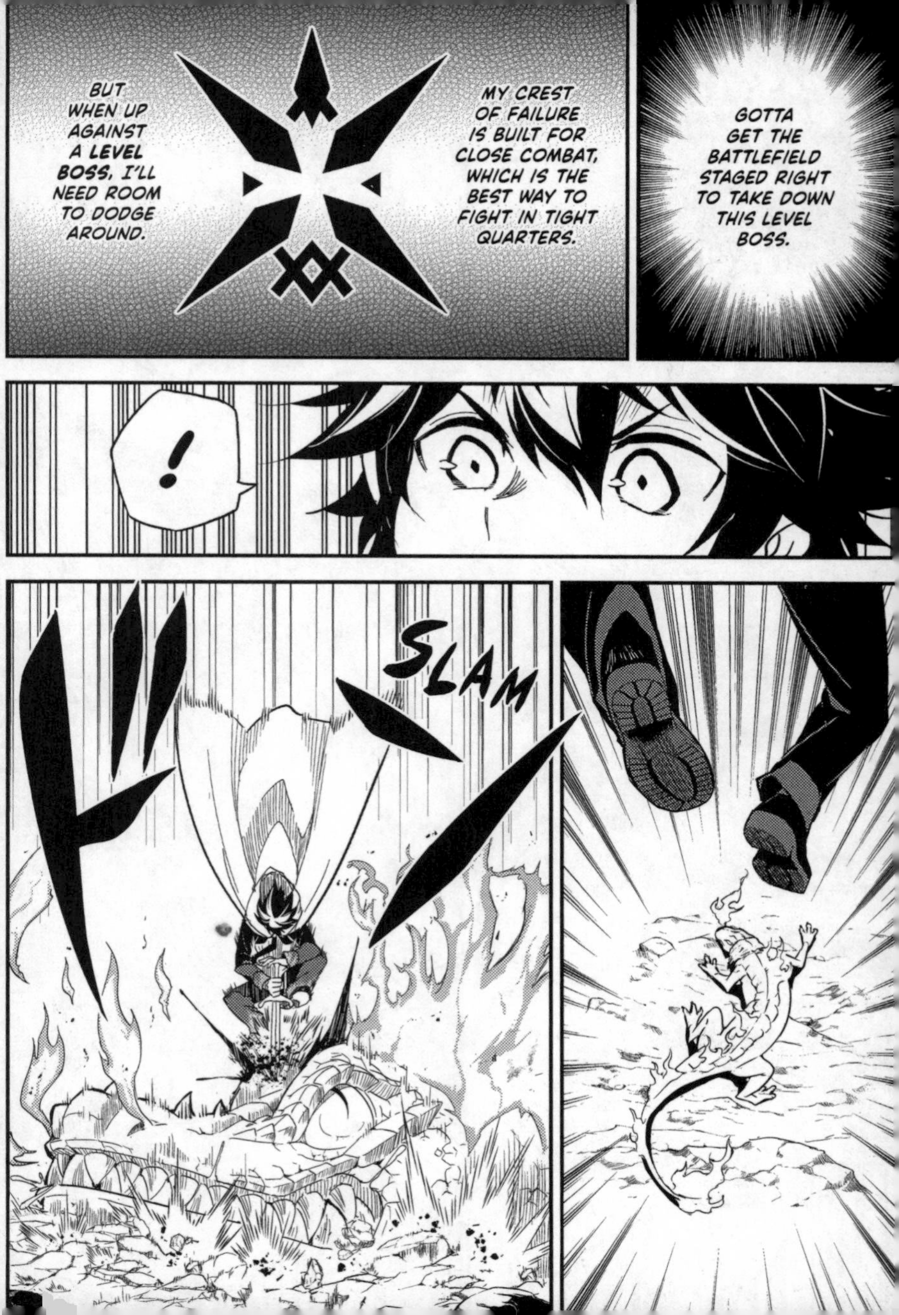
GOTTA GET THE BATTLEFIELD STAGED RIGHT TO TAKE DOWN THIS LEVEL BOSS.
MY CREST OF FAILURE IS BUILT FOR CLOSE COMBAT, WHICH IS THE BEST WAY TO FIGHT IN TIGHT QUARTERS.
BUT WHEN UP AGAINST A LEVEL BOSS, I'LL NEED ROOM TO DODGE AROUND.
!
SLAM

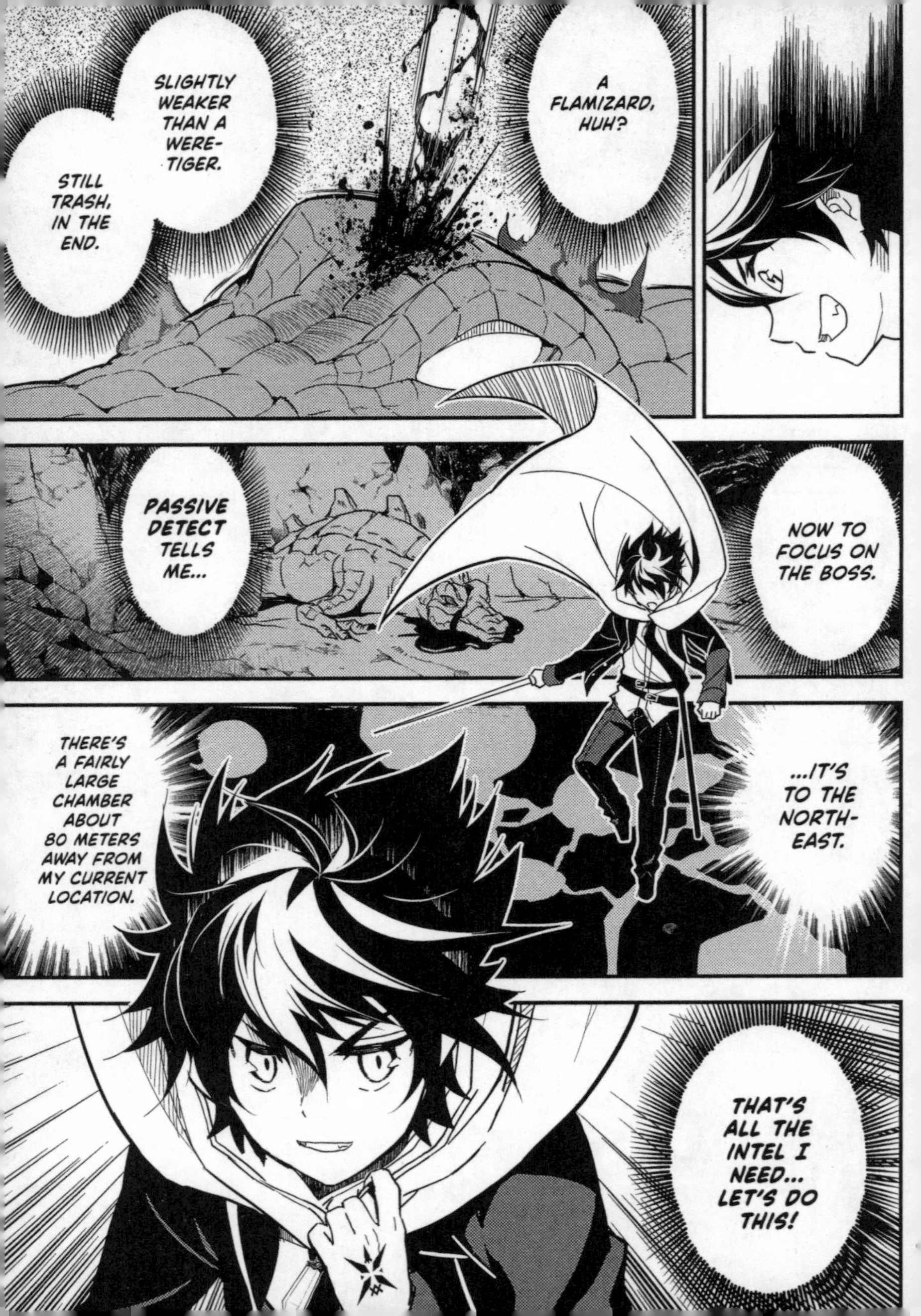
A FLAMIZARD, HUH?
SLIGHTLY WEAKER THAN A WERE-TIGER.
STILL TRASH, IN THE END.
NOW TO FOCUS ON THE BOSS.
PASSIVE DETECT TELLS ME...
...IT'S TO THE NORTH-EAST.
THERE'S A FAIRLY LARGE CHAMBER ABOUT 80 METERS AWAY FROM MY CURRENT LOCATION.
THAT'S ALL THE INTEL I NEED... LET'S DO THIS!

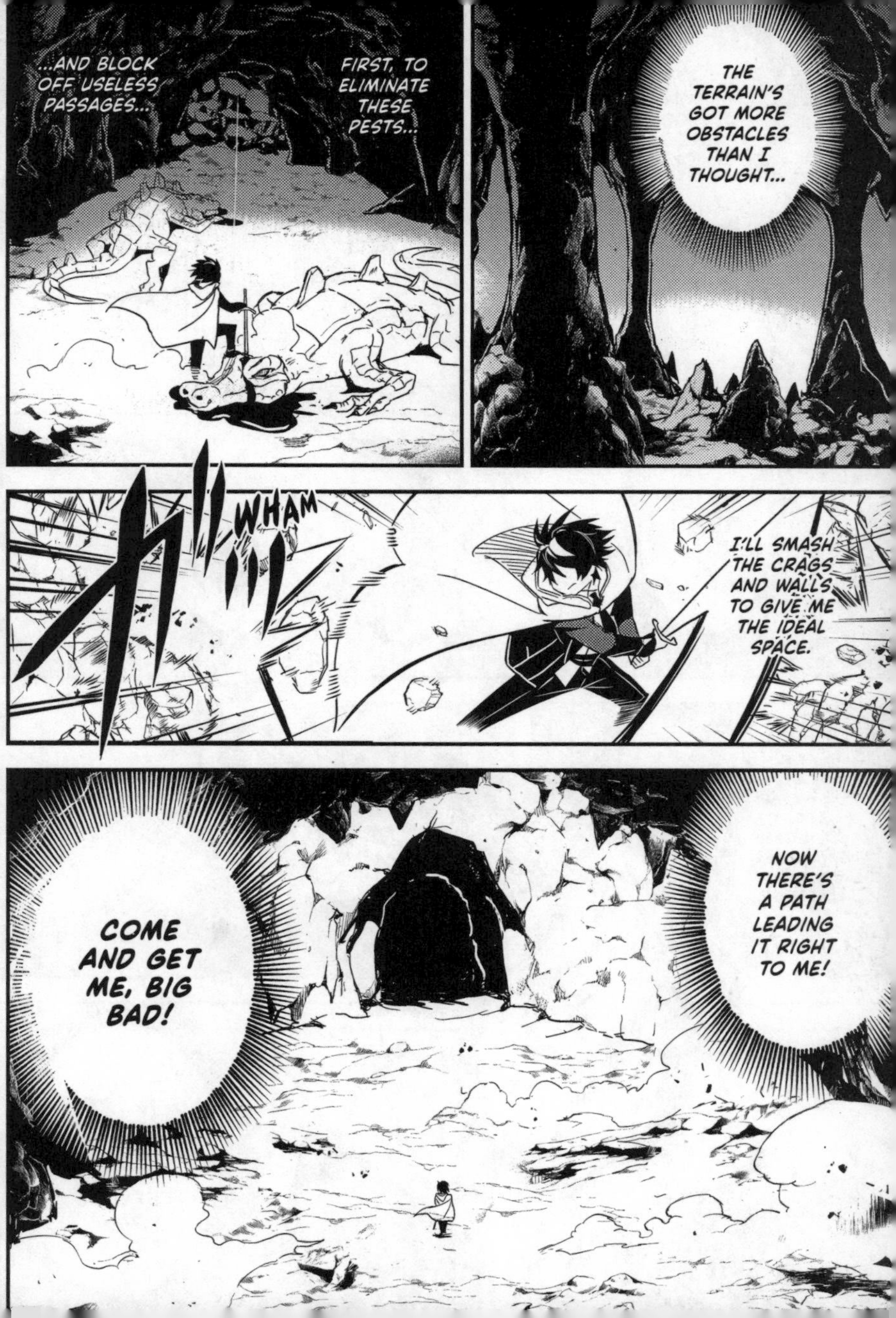
THE TERRAIN'S GOT MORE OBSTACLES THAN I THOUGHT...
FIRST, TO ELIMINATE THESE PESTS...
...AND BLOCK OFF USELESS PASSAGES...
I'LL SMASH THE CRAGS AND WALLS TO GIVE ME THE IDEAL SPACE.
WHAM
NOW THERE'S A PATH LEADING IT RIGHT TO ME!
COME AND GET ME, BIG BAD!

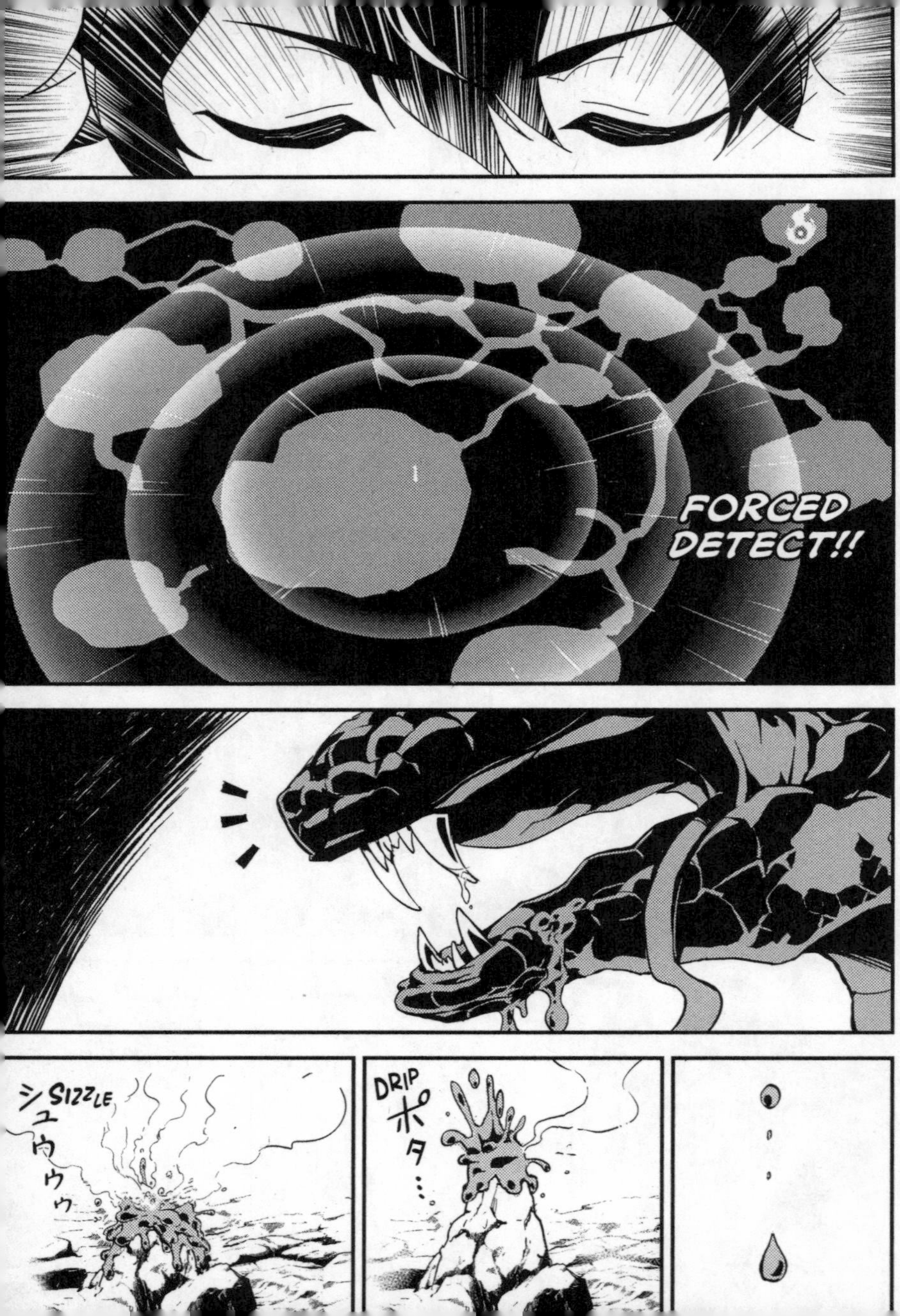
FORCED DETECT!!
DRIP
ポタ…
シュウウゥ
SIZZLE

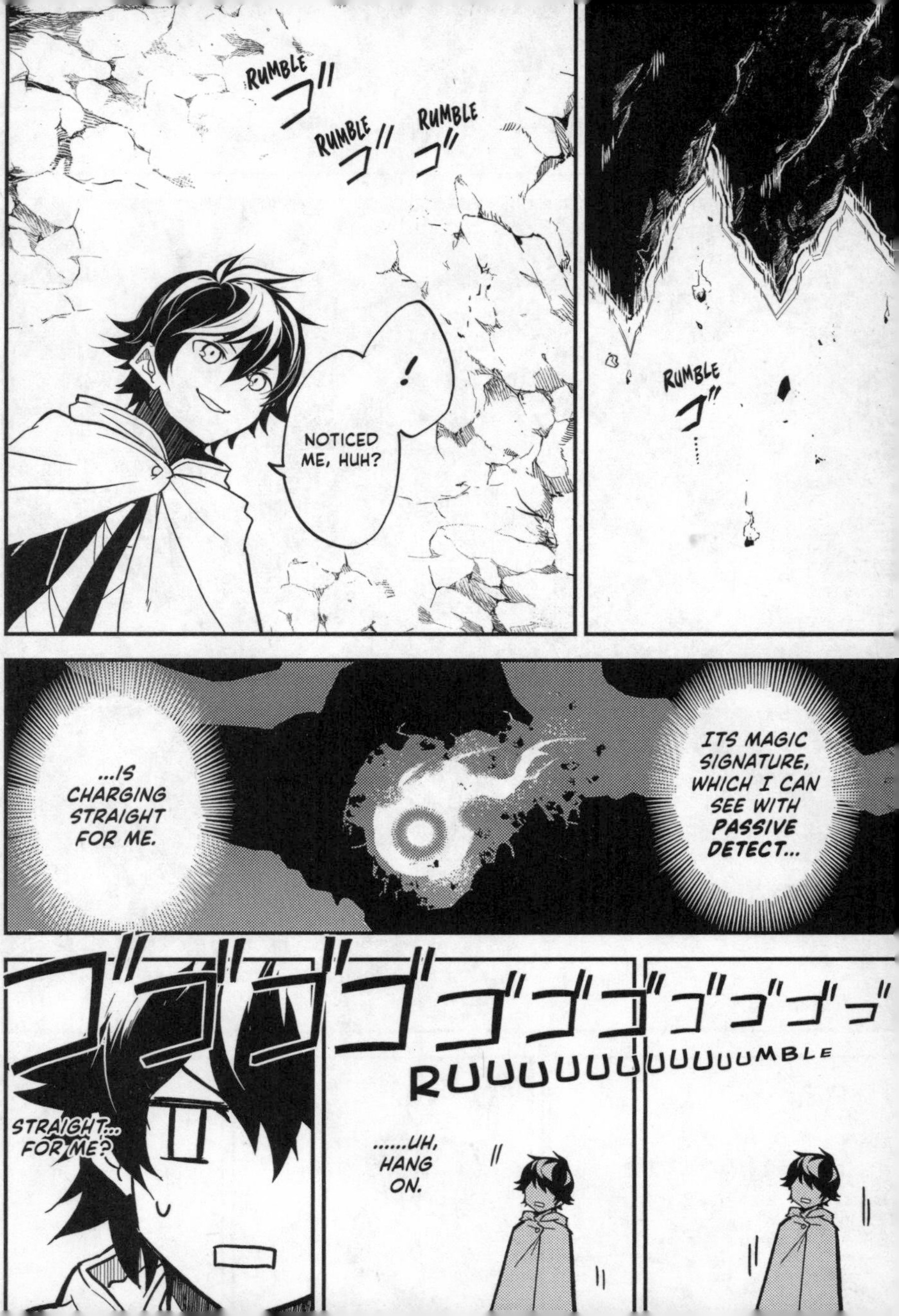
RUMBLE
ゴ
...
RUMBLE
ゴ
RUMBLE
ゴ
RUMBLE
ゴ
!
NOTICED ME, HUH?
ITS MAGIC SIGNATURE, WHICH I CAN SEE WITH PASSIVE DETECT...
...IS CHARGING STRAIGHT FOR ME.
ゴゴゴゴゴゴゴゴゴッ
RUUUUUUUUUUUUMBLE
......UH, HANG ON.
STRAIGHT... FOR ME?

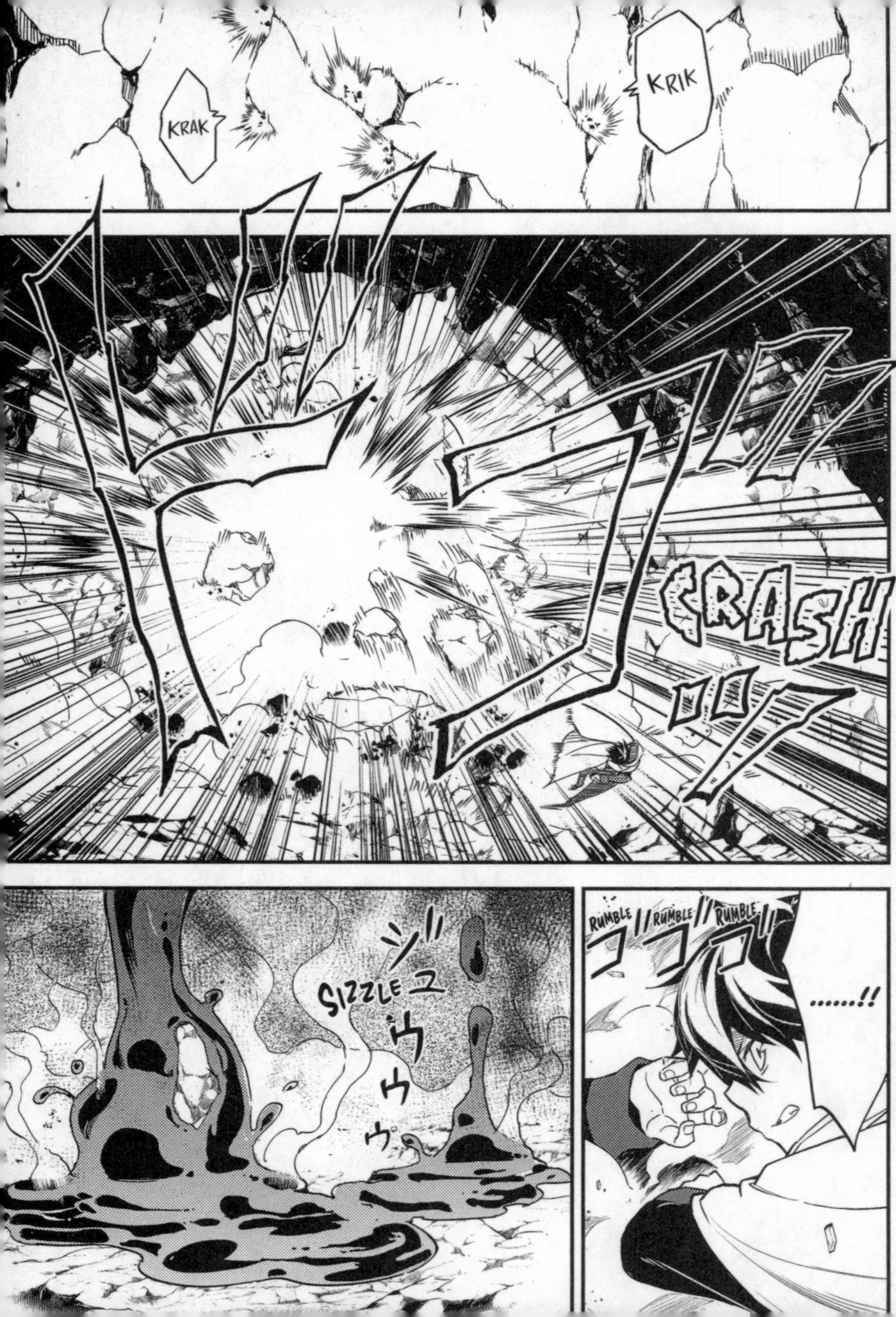
KRIK
KRAK
CRASH
RUMBLE RUMBLE RUMBLE
ゴゴゴ
......!!
SIZZLE
ジュウウ

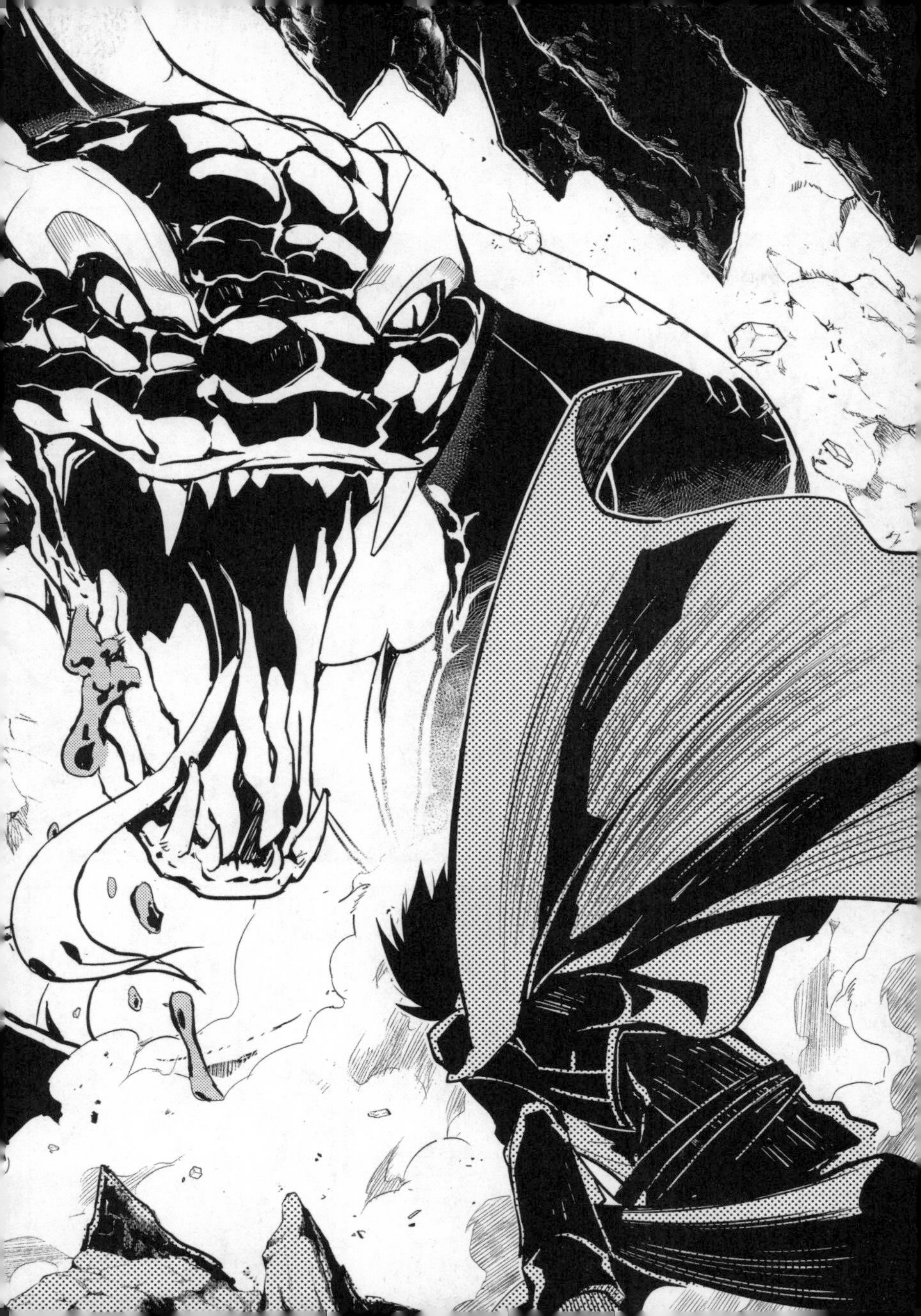

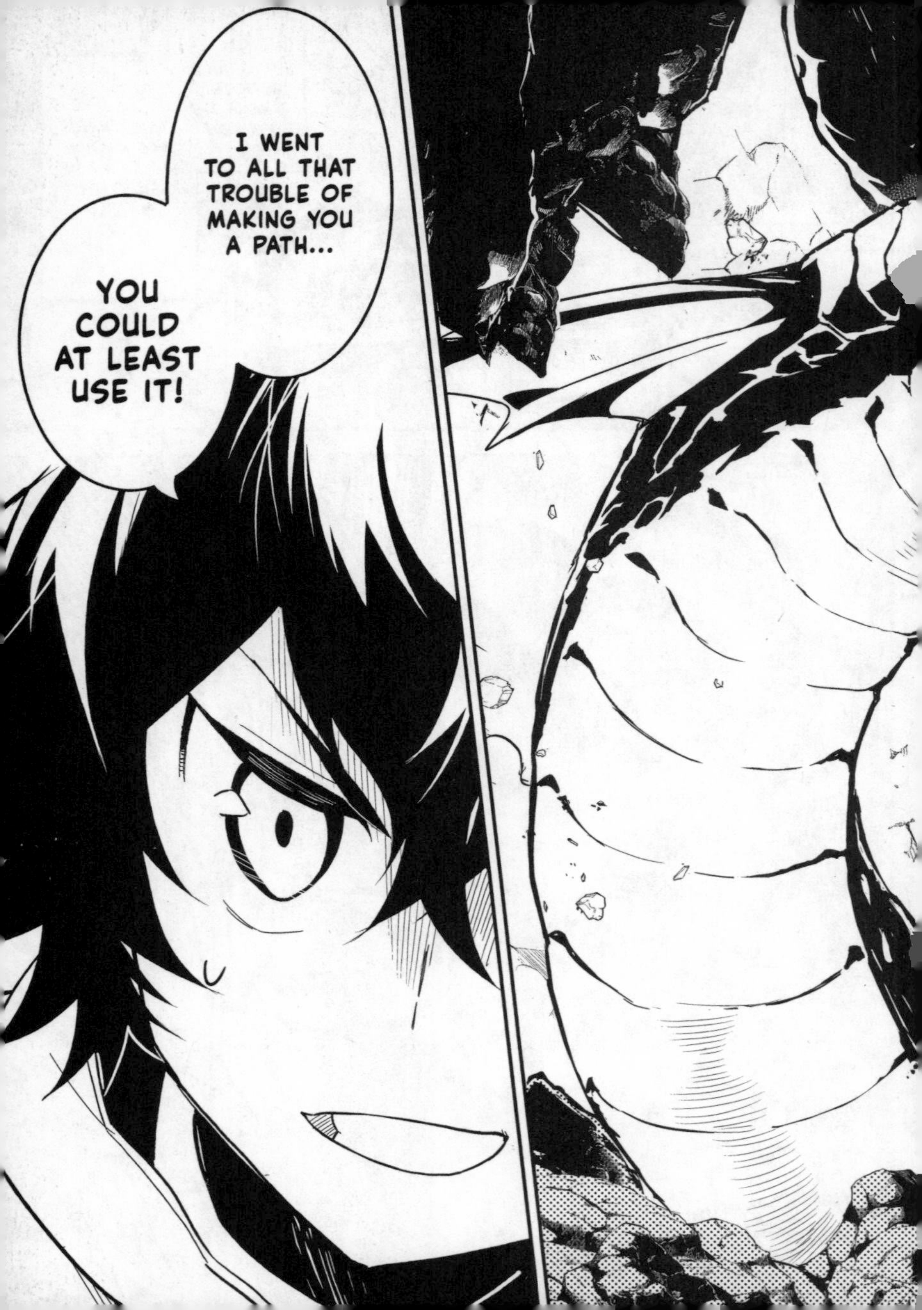
I WENT TO ALL THAT TROUBLE OF MAKING YOU A PATH...
YOU COULD AT LEAST USE IT!

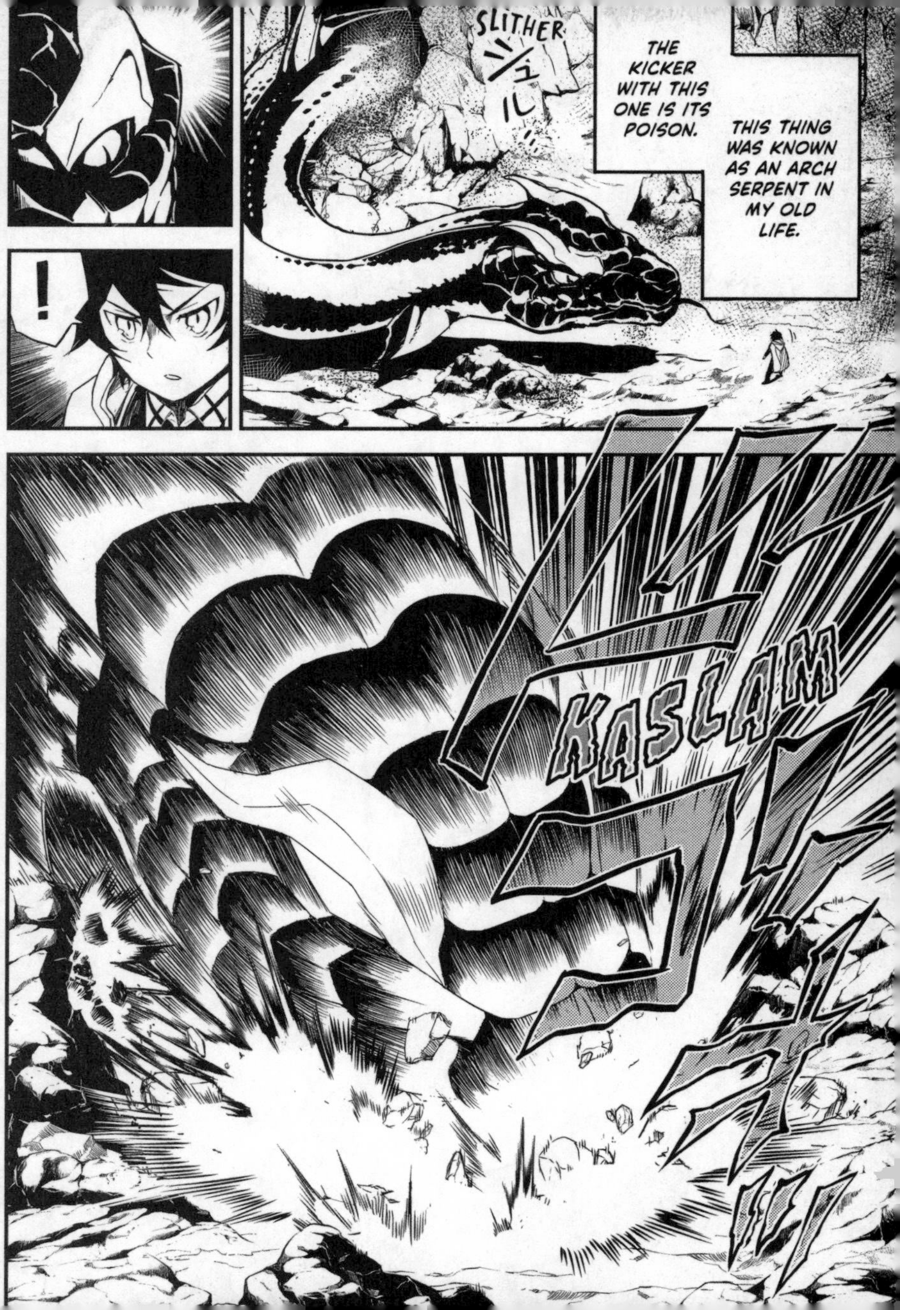
THE KICKER WITH THIS ONE IS ITS POISON.
THIS THING WAS KNOWN AS AN ARCH SERPENT IN MY OLD LIFE.
SLITHER
ジュル!!
!
KASLAM

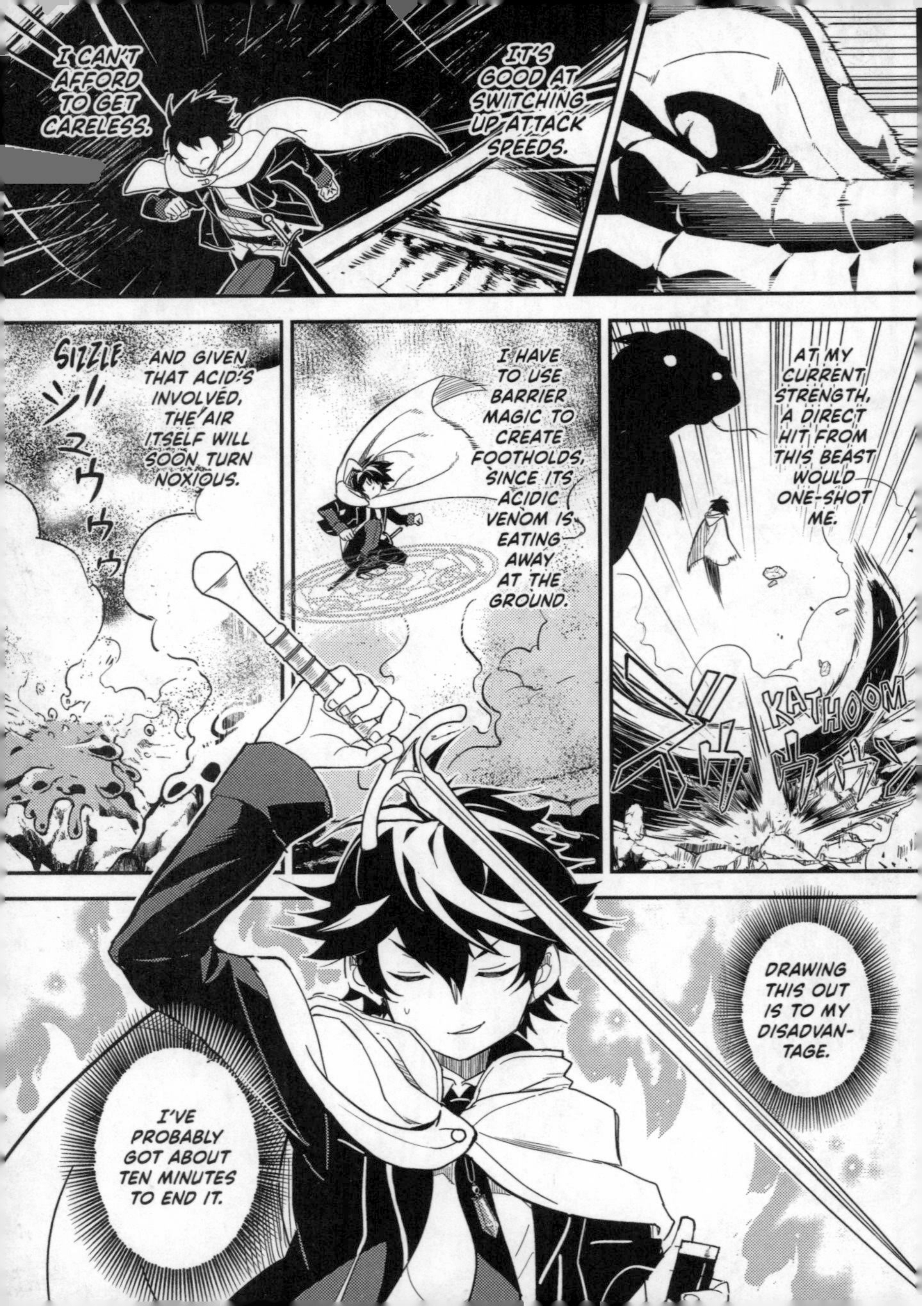
IT'S GOOD AT SWITCHING UP ATTACK SPEEDS.
I CAN'T AFFORD TO GET CARELESS.
AT MY CURRENT STRENGTH, A DIRECT HIT FROM THIS BEAST WOULD ONE-SHOT ME.
KATHOOM
I HAVE TO USE BARRIER MAGIC TO CREATE FOOTHOLDS, SINCE ITS ACIDIC VENOM IS EATING AWAY AT THE GROUND.
AND GIVEN THAT ACID'S INVOLVED, THE AIR ITSELF WILL SOON TURN NOXIOUS.
SIZZLE
DRAWING THIS OUT IS TO MY DISADVANTAGE.
I'VE PROBABLY GOT ABOUT TEN MINUTES TO END IT.

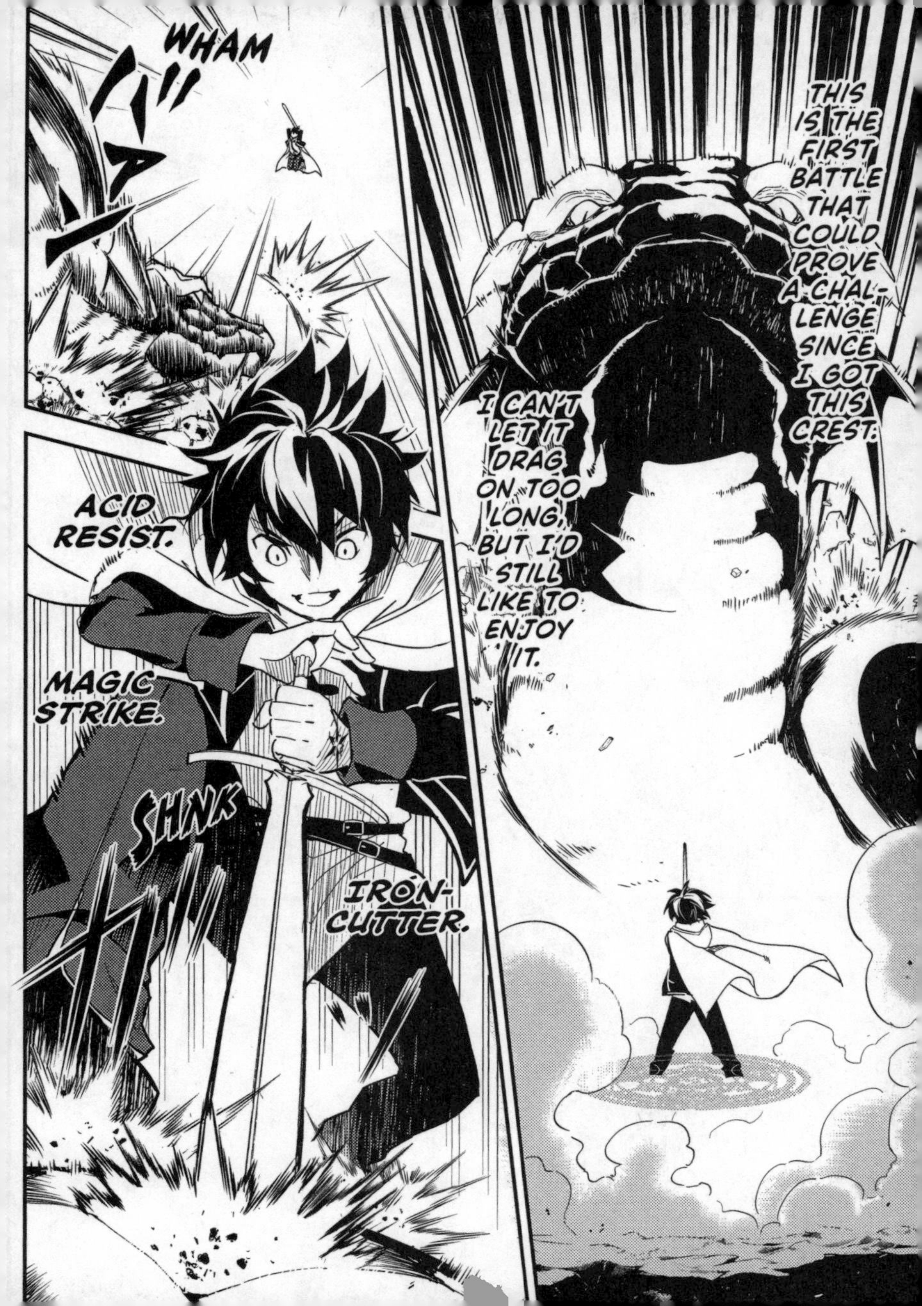
THIS IS THE FIRST BATTLE THAT COULD PROVE A CHAL-LENGE SINCE I GOT THIS CREST.
I CAN'T LET IT DRAG ON TOO LONG, BUT I'D STILL LIKE TO ENJOY IT.
WHAM
ACID RESIST.
MAGIC STRIKE.
SHNK
IRON-CUTTER.

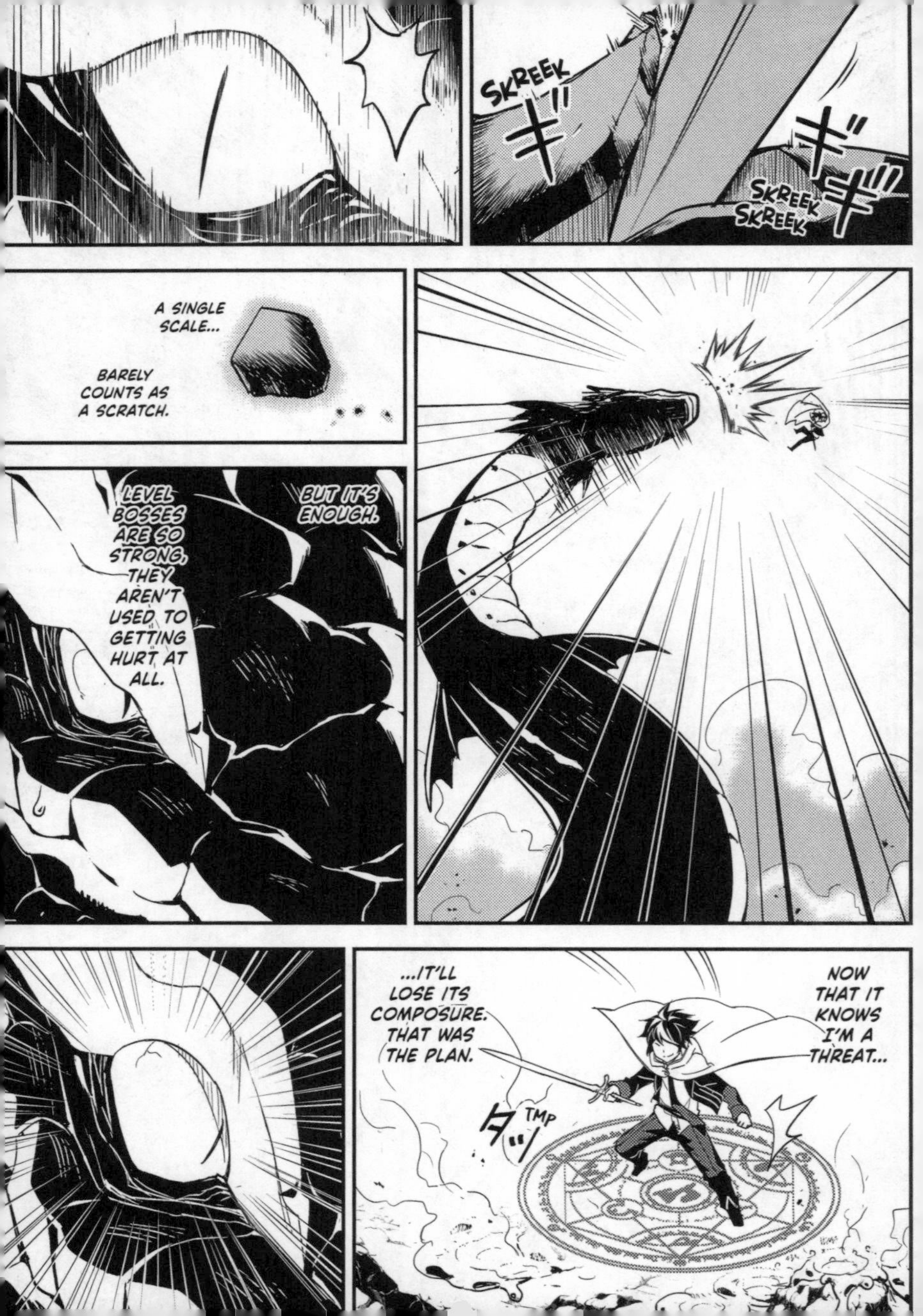
SKREEK
ギッ
ギギッ
SKREEK SKREEK
A SINGLE SCALE...
BARELY COUNTS AS A SCRATCH.
BUT IT'S ENOUGH.
LEVEL BOSSES ARE SO STRONG, THEY AREN'T USED TO GETTING HURT AT ALL.
NOW THAT IT KNOWS I'M A THREAT...
...IT'LL LOSE ITS COMPOSURE. THAT WAS THE PLAN.
タッ
TMP

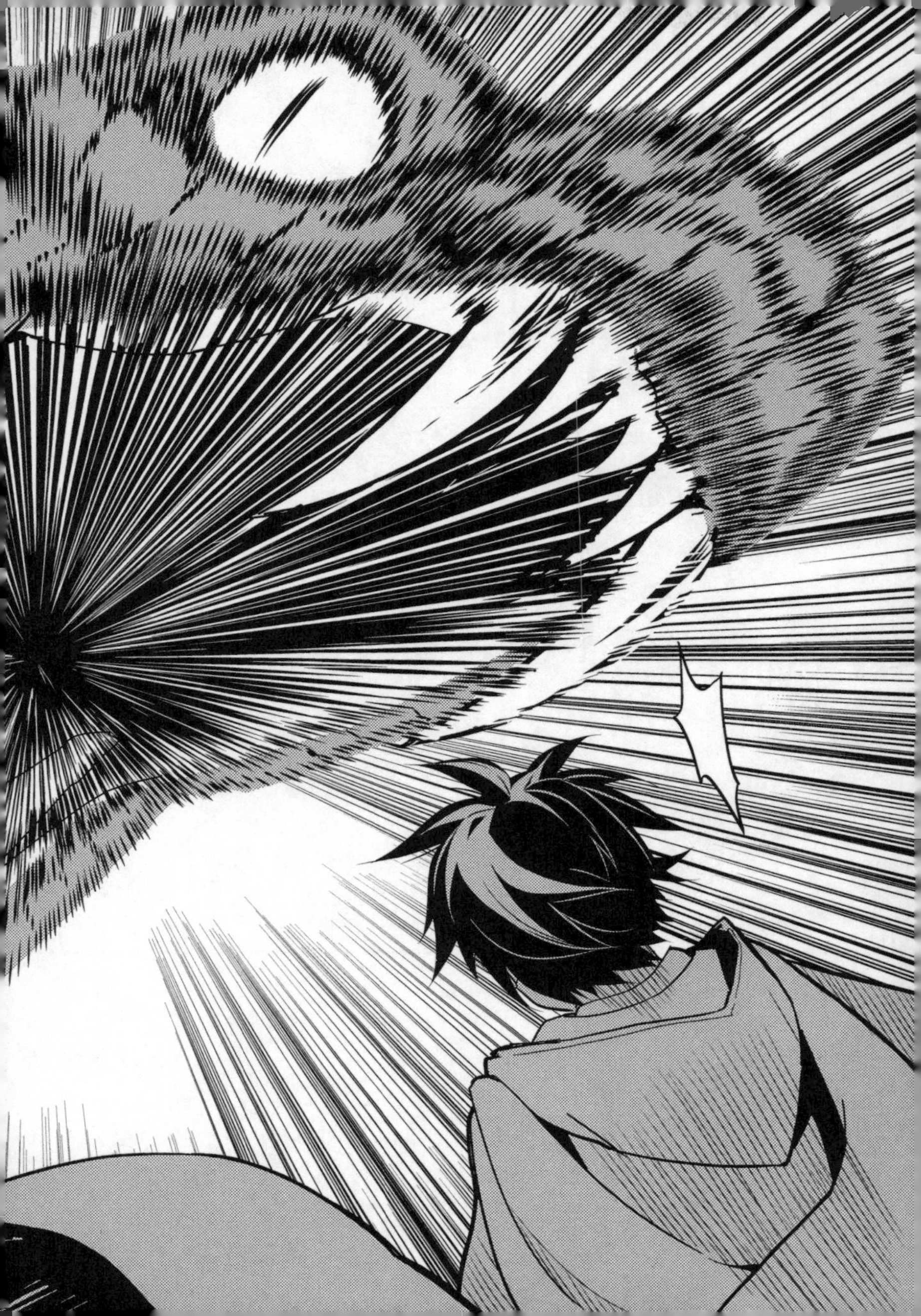

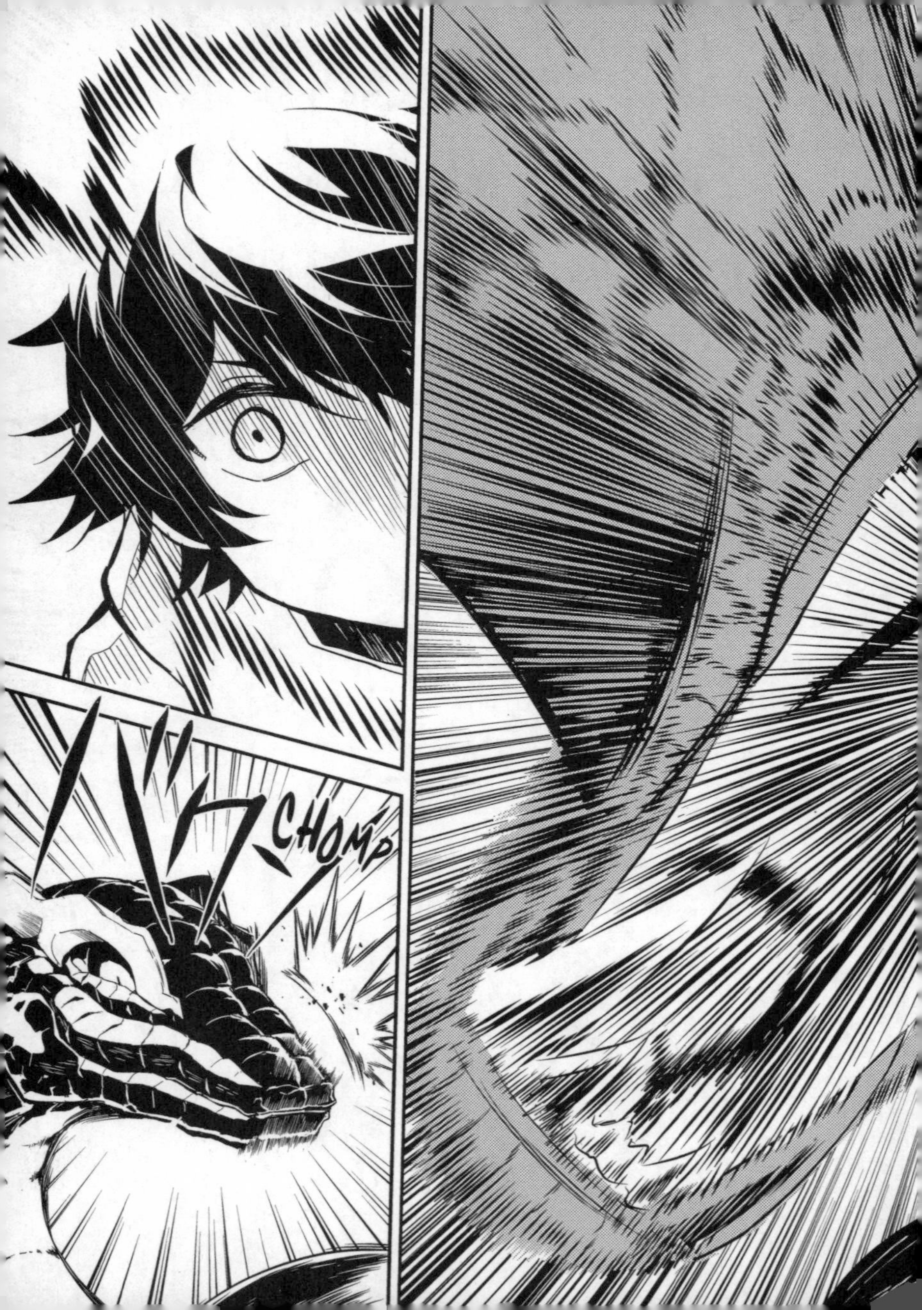
CHOMP

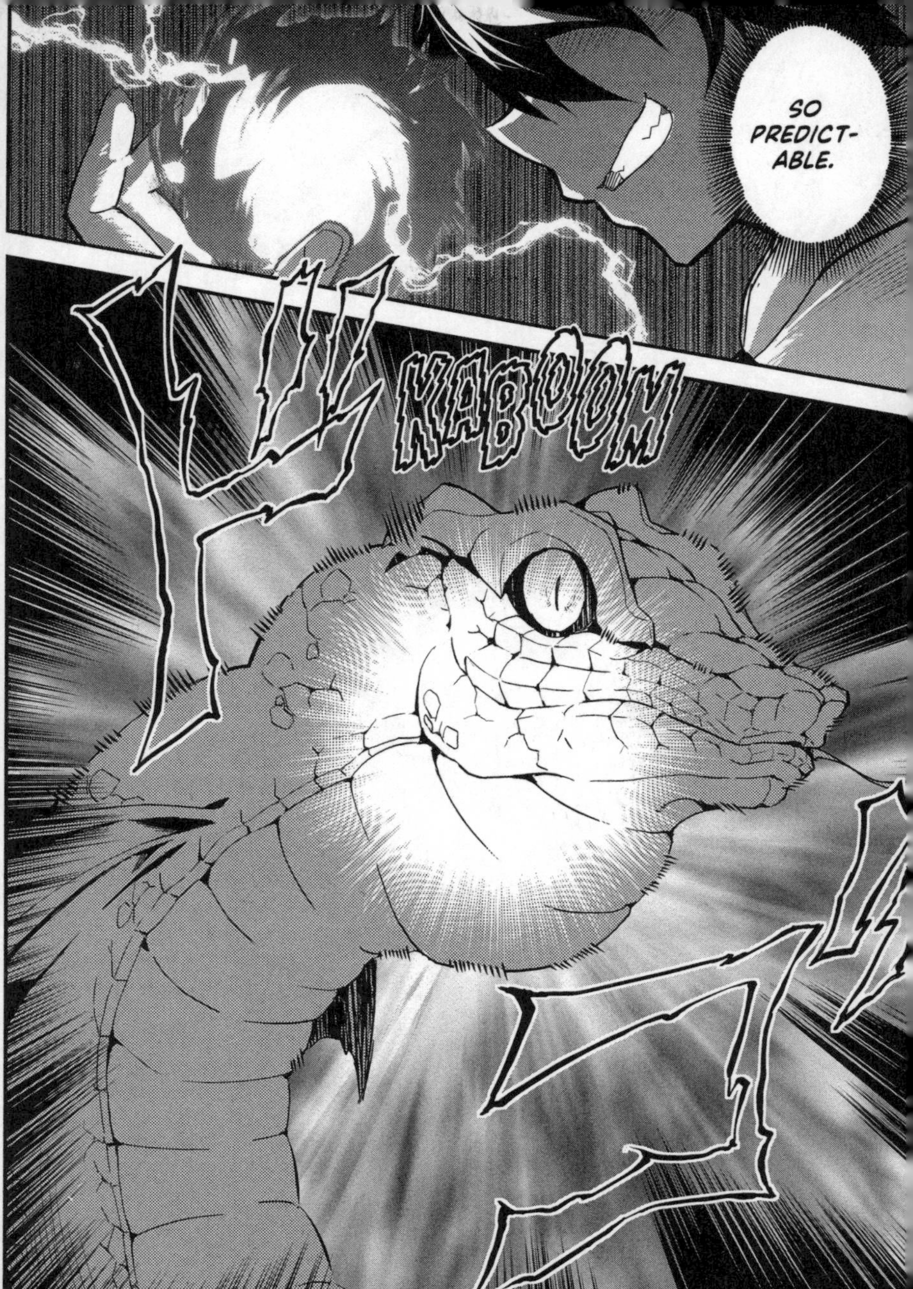
SO PREDICT-ABLE.
KABOOM

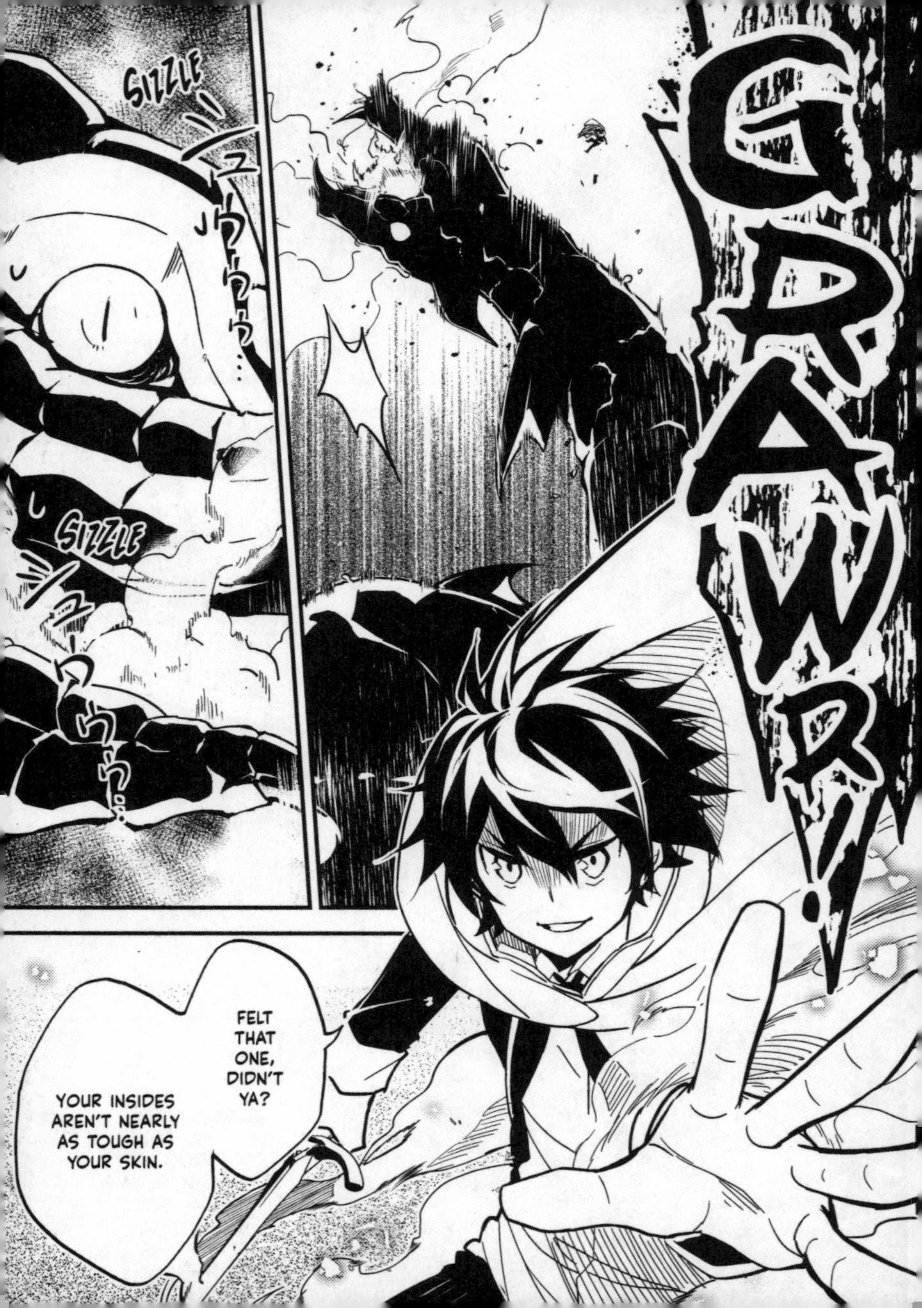
GRAWR!!
SIZZLE
SIZZLE
FELT THAT ONE, DIDN'T YA?
YOUR INSIDES AREN'T NEARLY AS TOUGH AS YOUR SKIN.

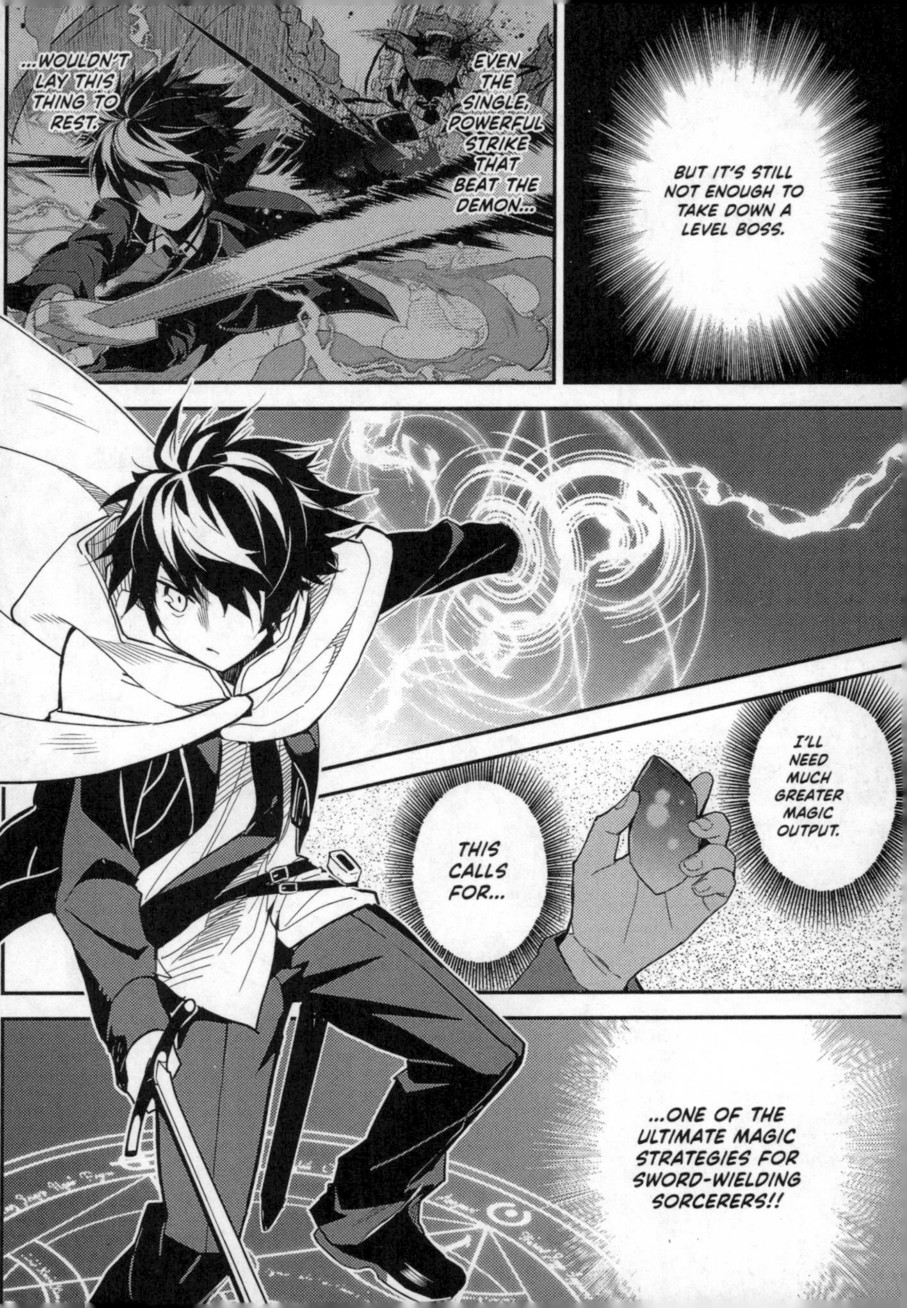
BUT IT'S STILL NOT ENOUGH TO TAKE DOWN A LEVEL BOSS.
EVEN THE SINGLE, POWERFUL STRIKE THAT BEAT THE DEMON...
...WOULDN'T LAY THIS THING TO REST.
I'LL NEED MUCH GREATER MAGIC OUTPUT.
THIS CALLS FOR...
...ONE OF THE ULTIMATE MAGIC STRATEGIES FOR SWORD-WIELDING SORCERERS!!

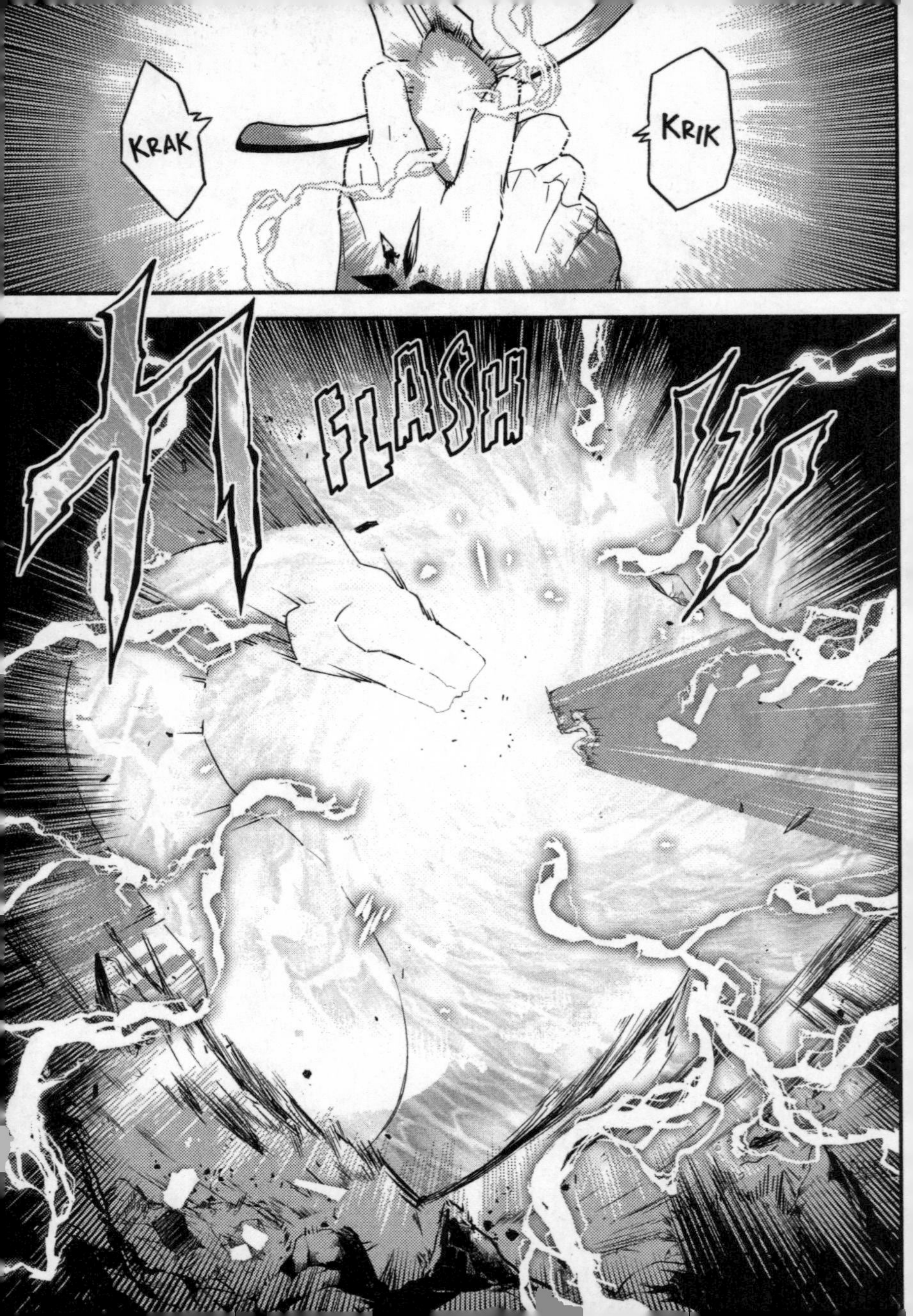
KRIK
KRAK
FLASH

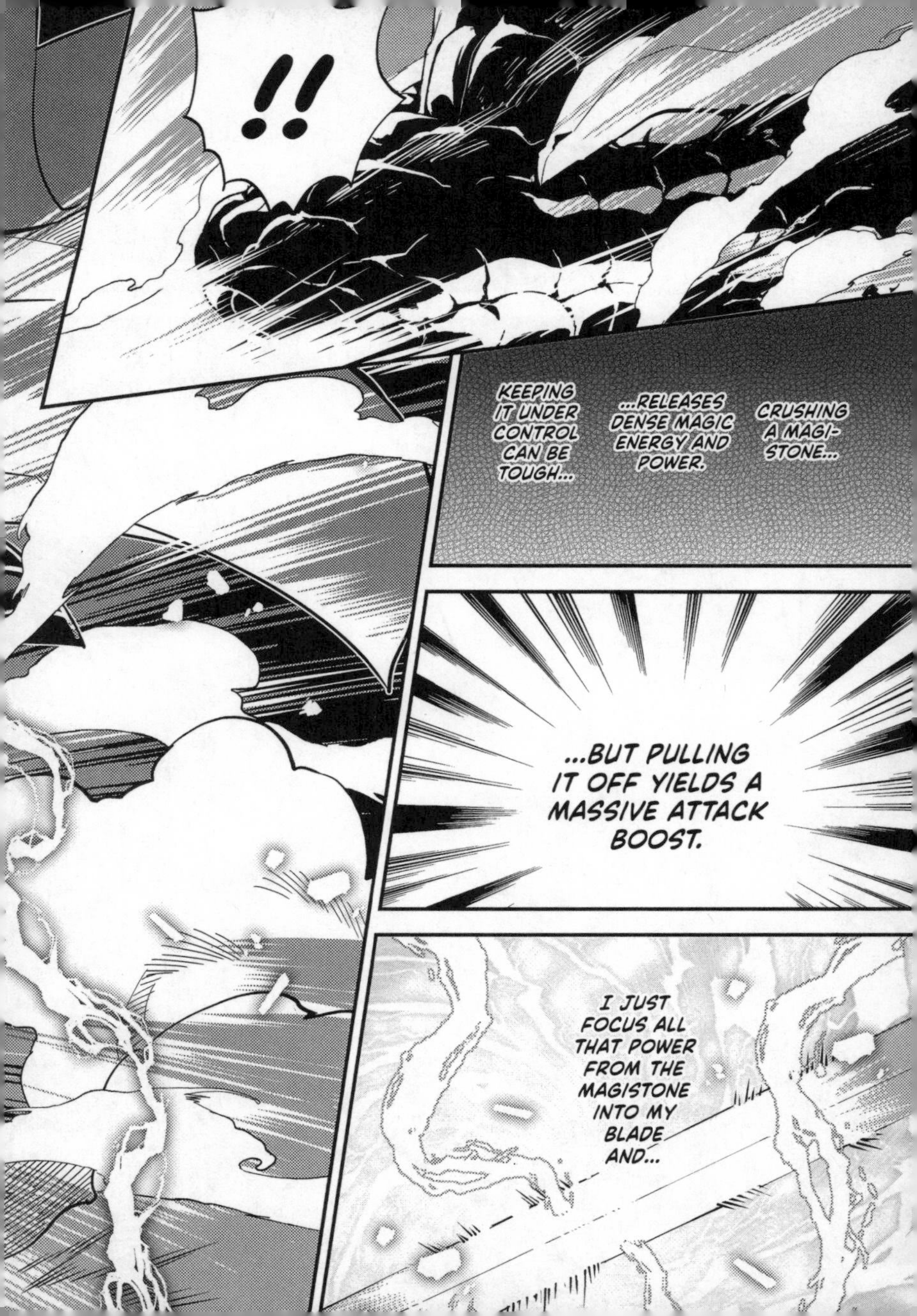
!!
CRUSHING A MAGI-STONE...
...RELEASES DENSE MAGIC ENERGY AND POWER.
KEEPING IT UNDER CONTROL CAN BE TOUGH...
...BUT PULLING IT OFF YIELDS A MASSIVE ATTACK BOOST.
I JUST FOCUS ALL THAT POWER FROM THE MAGISTONE INTO MY BLADE AND...

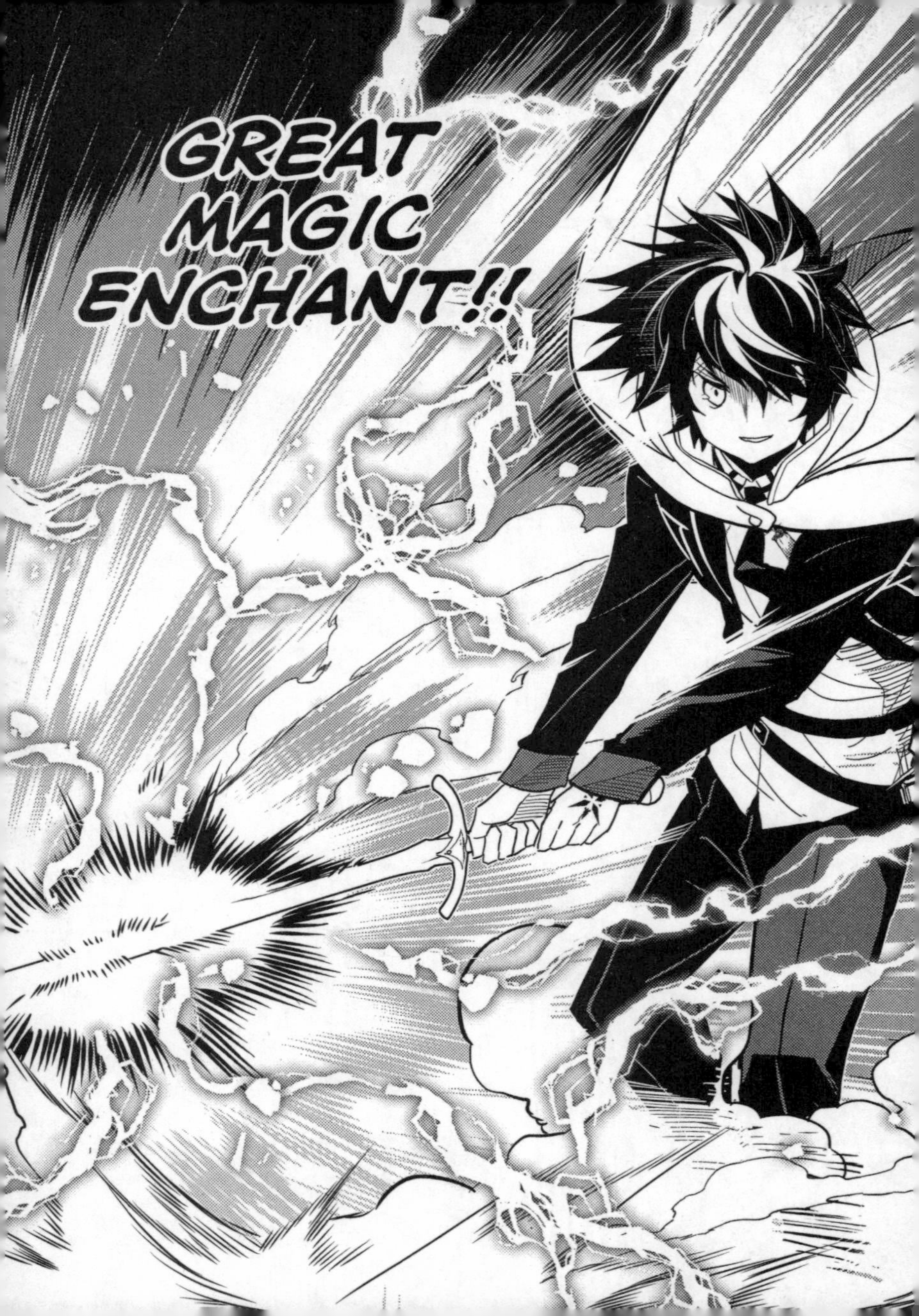
GREAT MAGIC ENCHANT!!

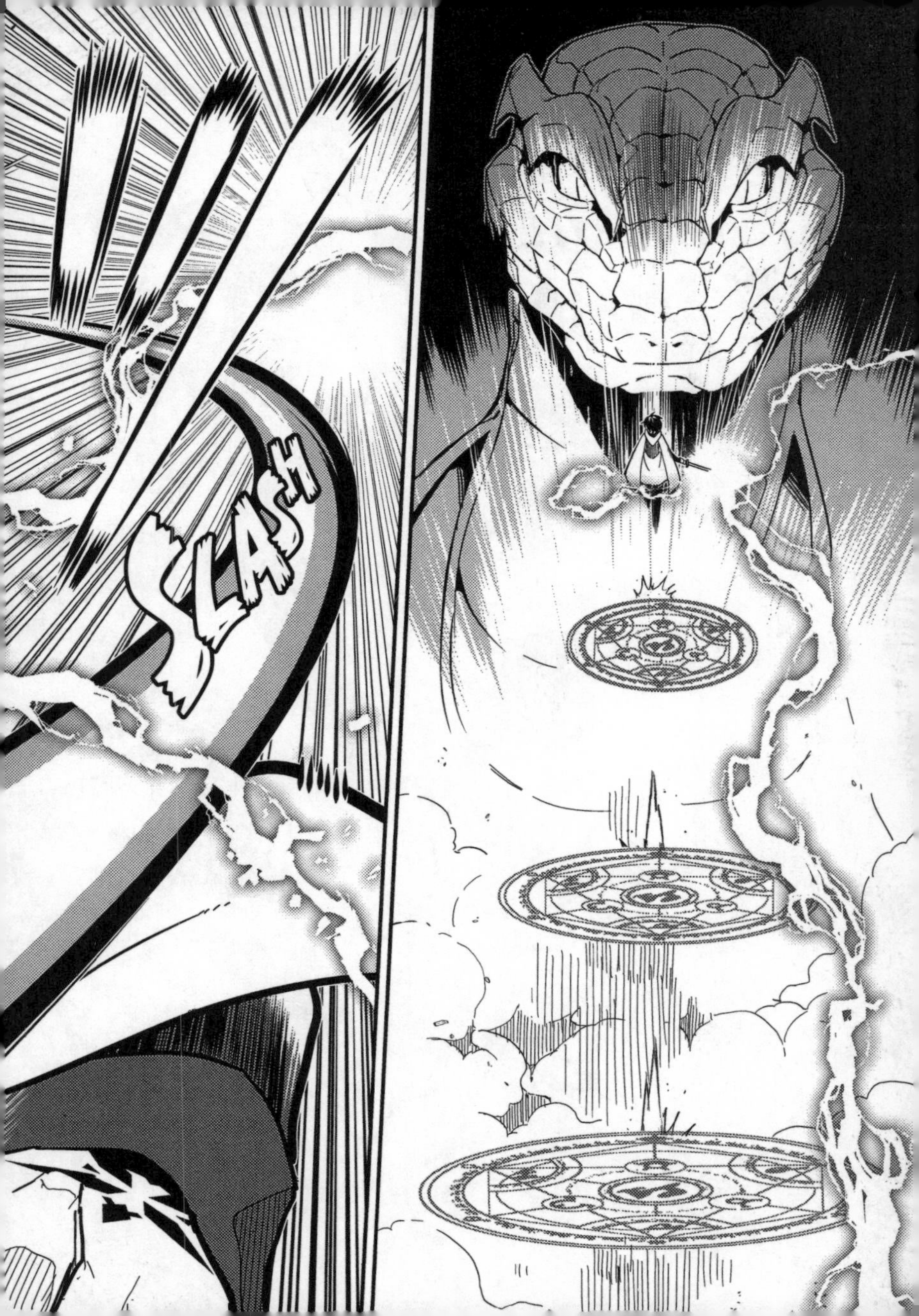
SLASH

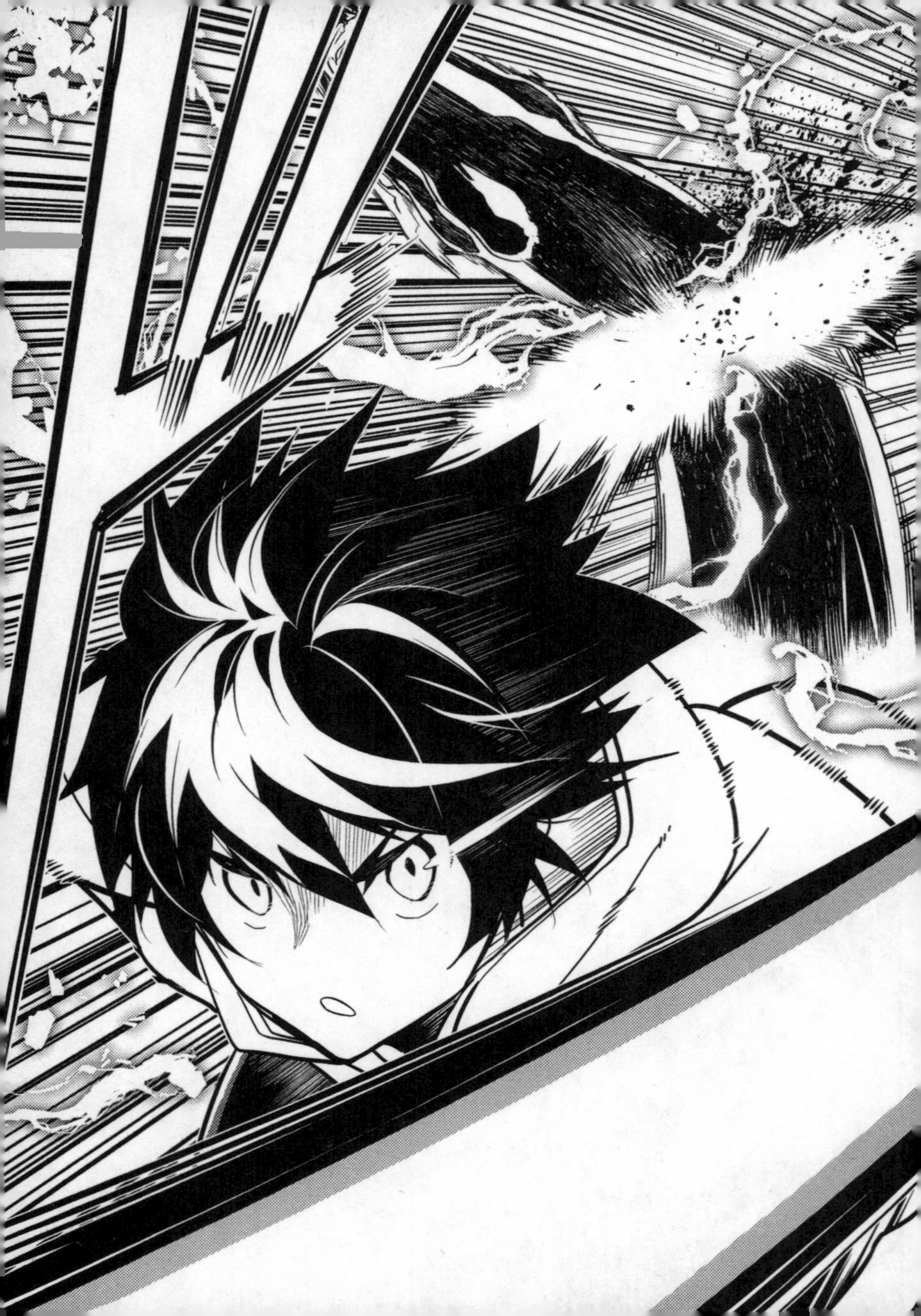

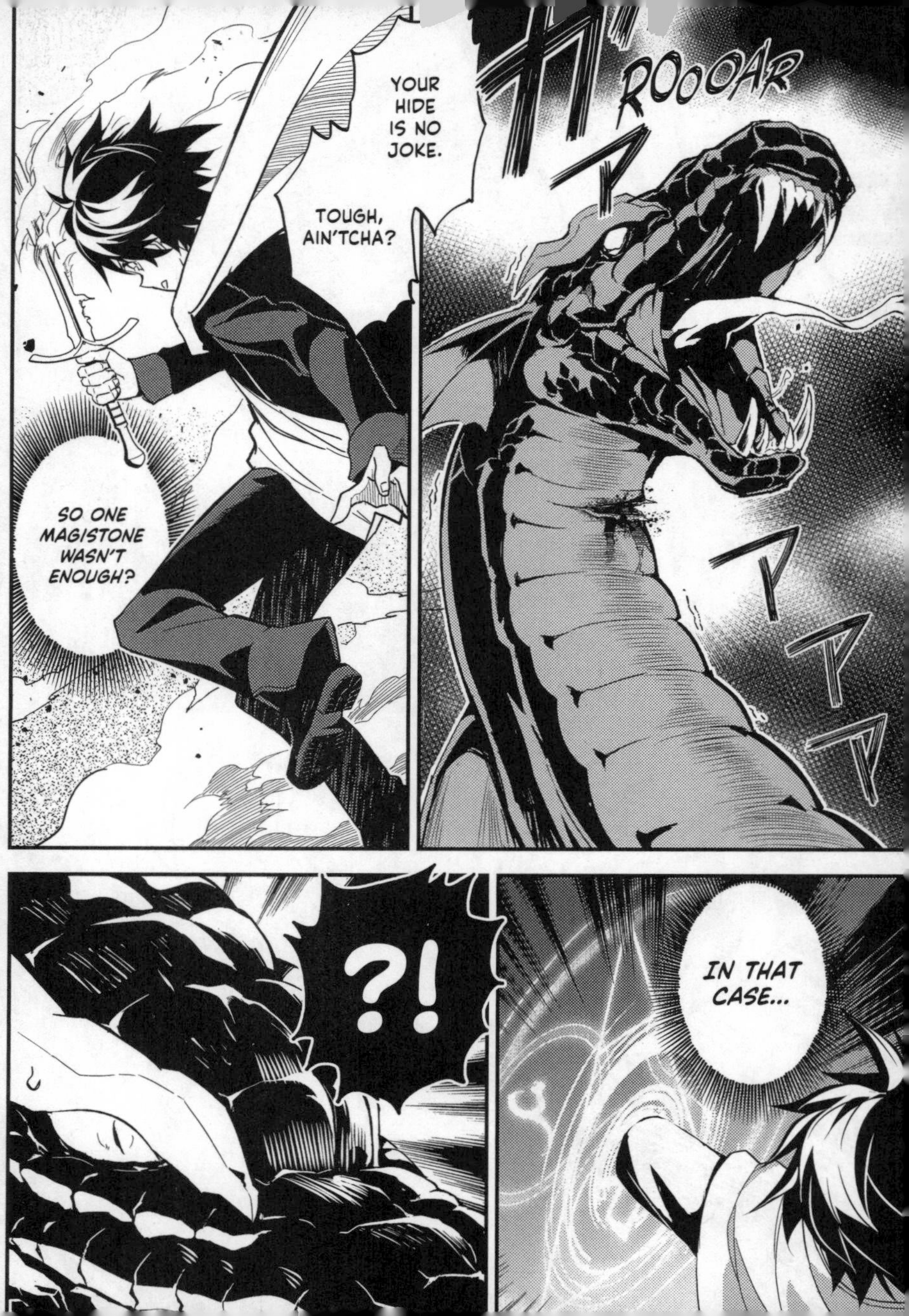
ROOOAR
YOUR HIDE IS NO JOKE.
TOUGH, AIN'TCHA?
SO ONE MAGISTONE WASN'T ENOUGH?
IN THAT CASE...
?!

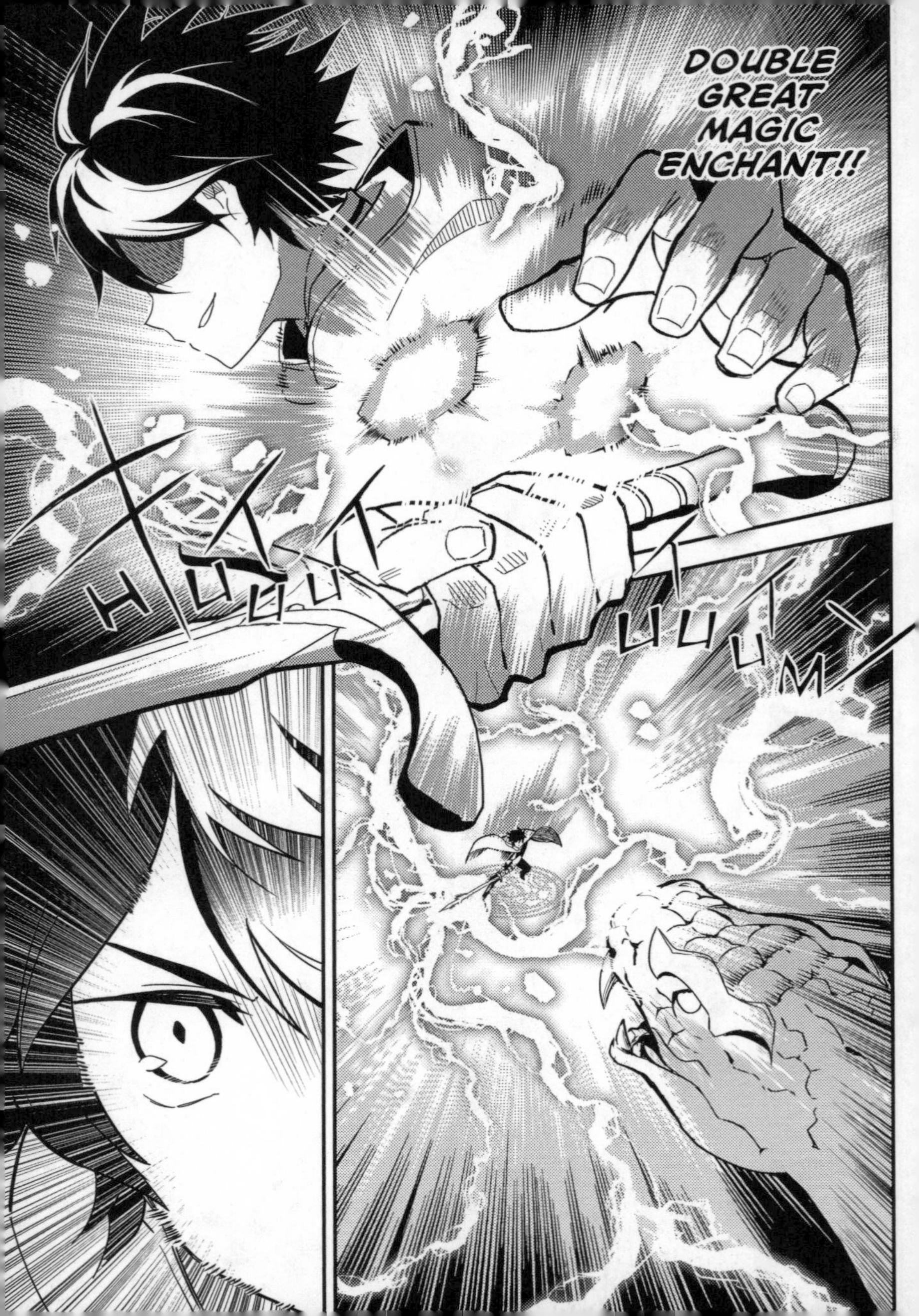
DOUBLE GREAT MAGIC ENCHANT!!
HUUUUUUUUM

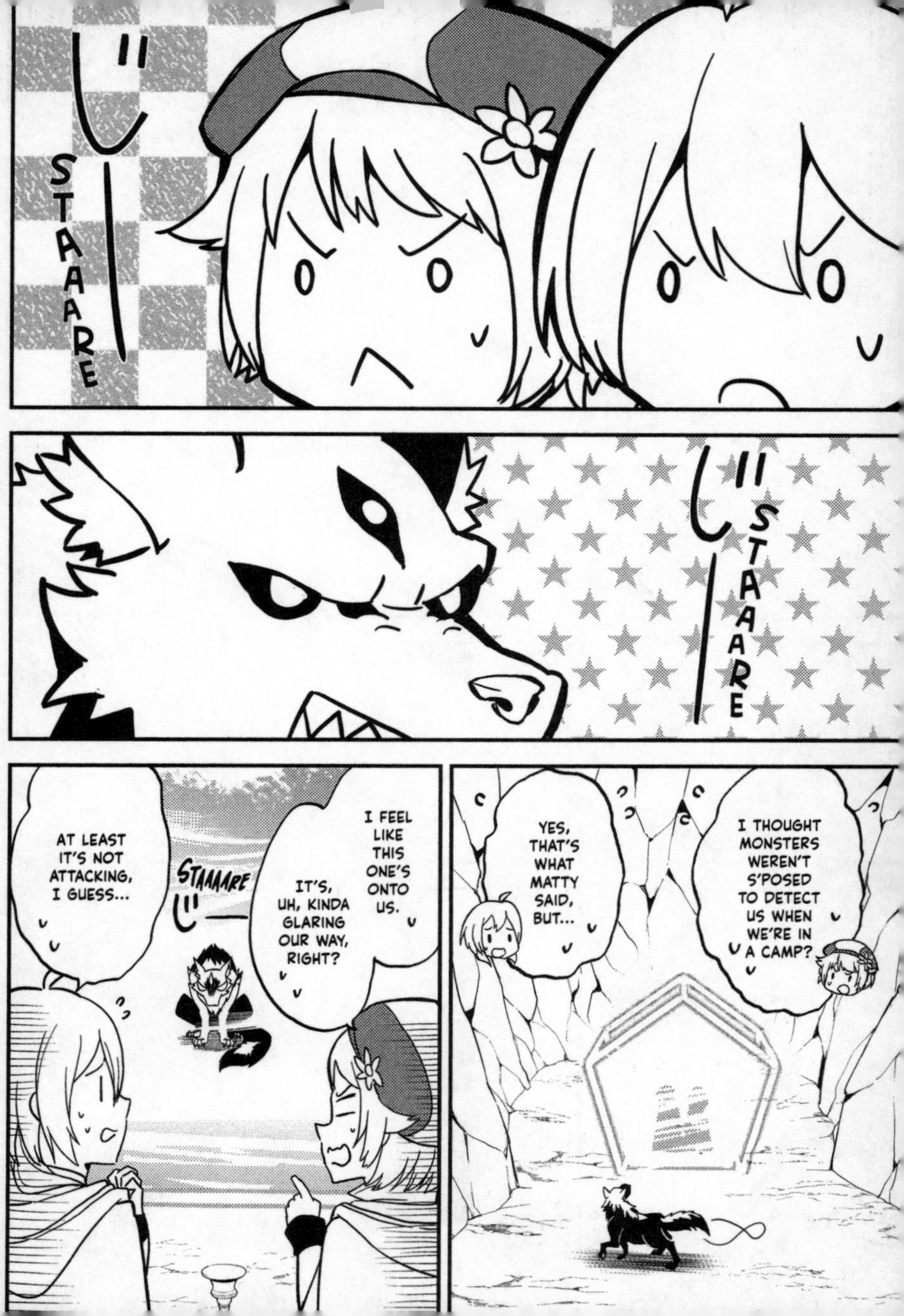
じー
STAAARE
じー
STAAARE
I THOUGHT MONSTERS WEREN'T S'POSED TO DETECT US WHEN WE'RE IN A CAMP?
YES, THAT'S WHAT MATTY SAID, BUT...
I FEEL LIKE THIS ONE'S ONTO US.
IT'S, UH, KINDA GLARING OUR WAY, RIGHT?
STAAAARE
じー
AT LEAST IT'S NOT ATTACKING, I GUESS...

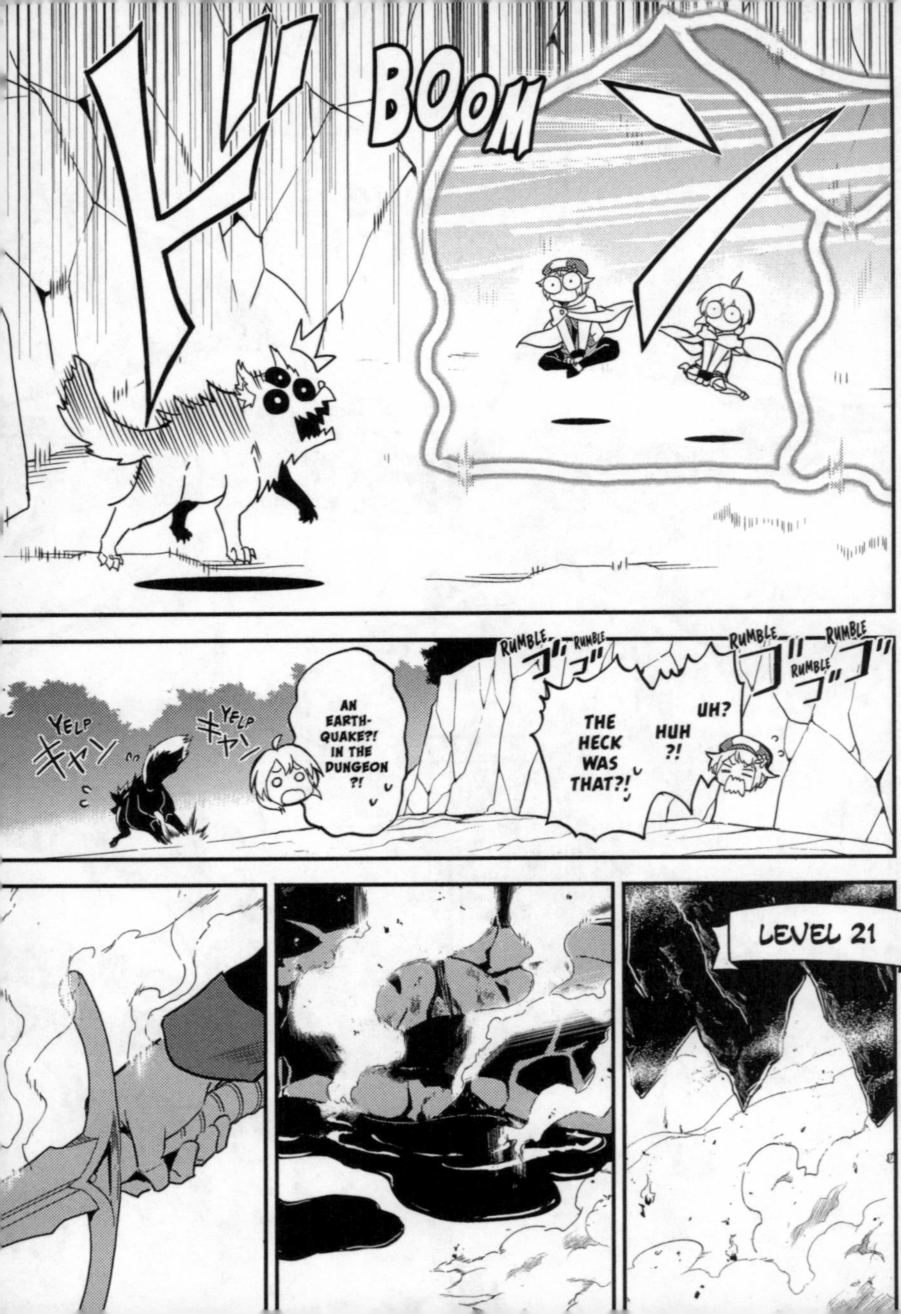

BOOM
RUMBLE RUMBLE RUMBLE ゴゴゴ
RUMBLE RUMBLE ゴゴ
UH?
HUH?!
THE HECK WAS THAT?!
AN EARTHQUAKE?! IN THE DUNGEON?!
YELP キャン
YELP キャン
LEVEL 21

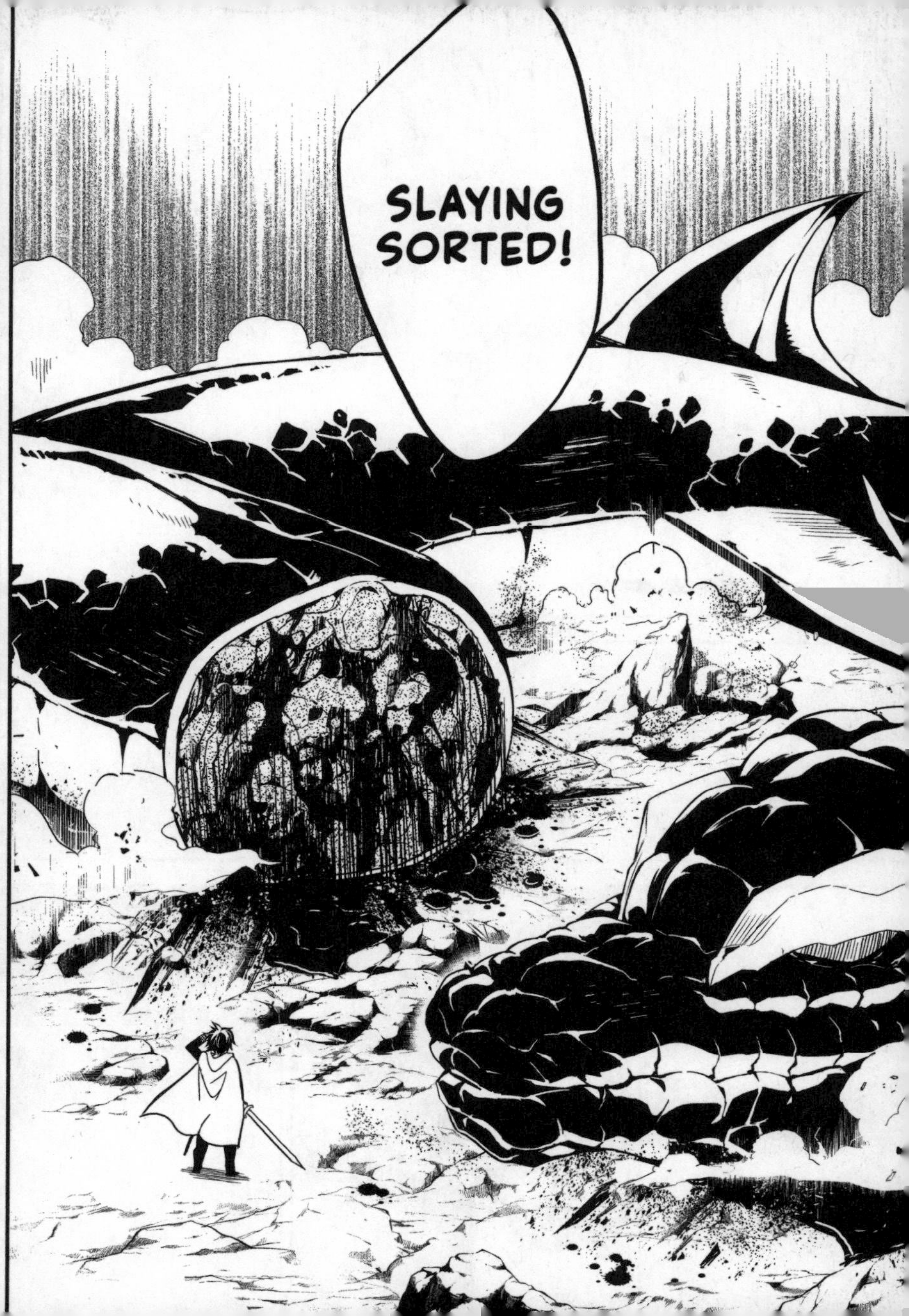
SLAYING SORTED!

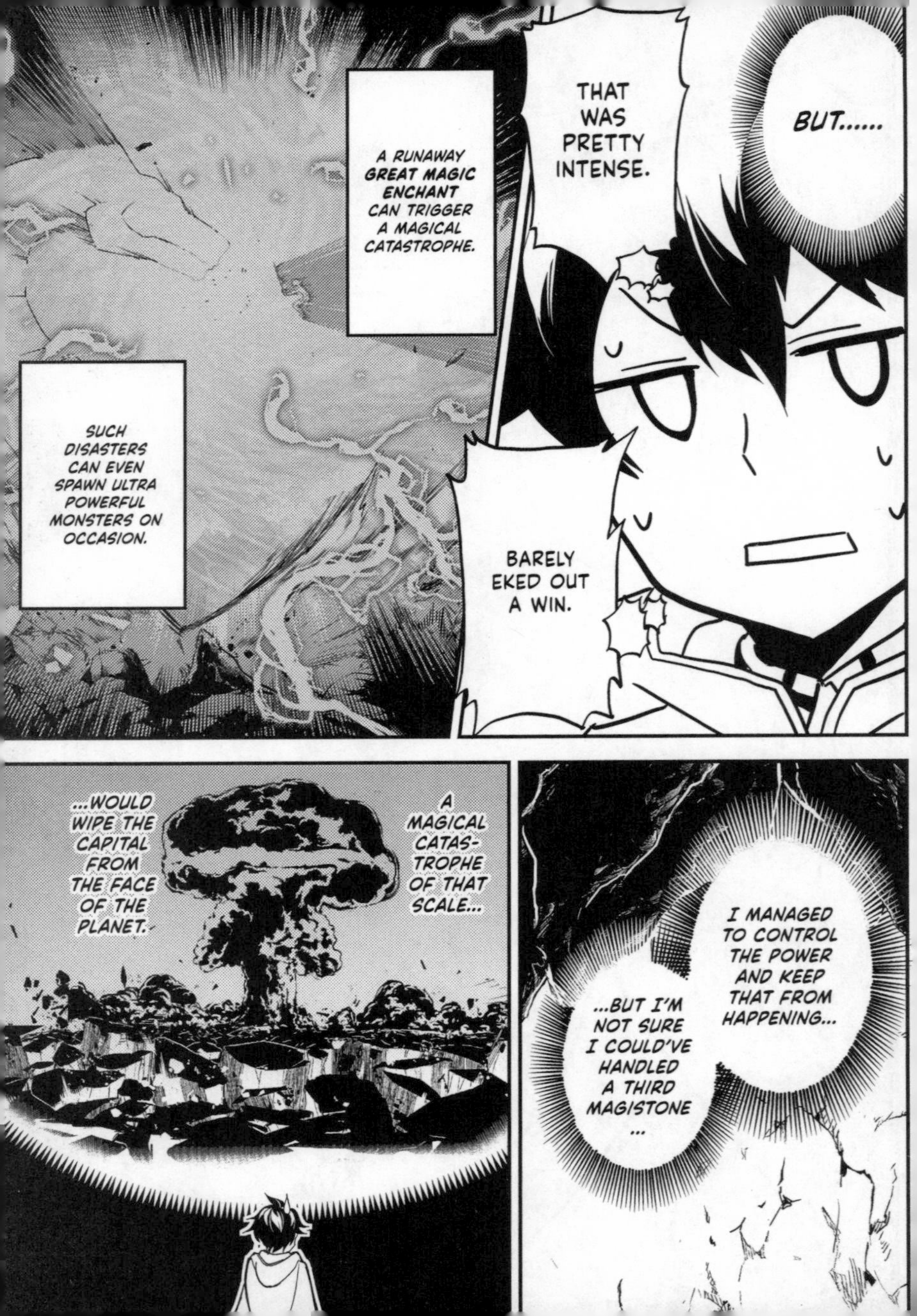
BUT......
THAT WAS PRETTY INTENSE.
BARELY EKED OUT A WIN.
A RUNAWAY GREAT MAGIC ENCHANT CAN TRIGGER A MAGICAL CATASTROPHE.
SUCH DISASTERS CAN EVEN SPAWN ULTRA POWERFUL MONSTERS ON OCCASION.
I MANAGED TO CONTROL THE POWER AND KEEP THAT FROM HAPPENING...
...BUT I'M NOT SURE I COULD'VE HANDLED A THIRD MAGISTONE ...
A MAGICAL CATAS-TROPHE OF THAT SCALE...
...WOULD WIPE THE CAPITAL FROM THE FACE OF THE PLANET.

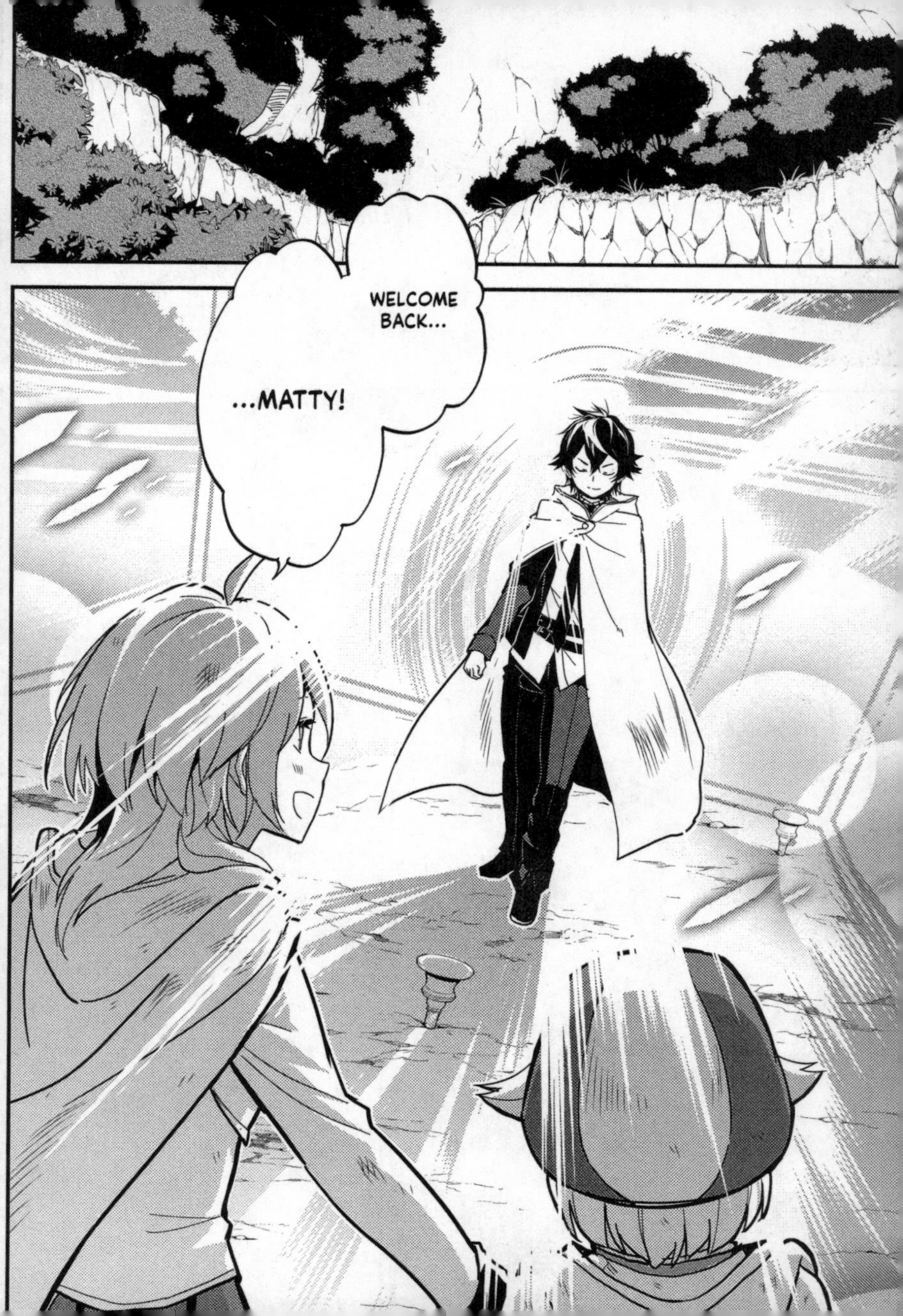
WELCOME BACK...
...MATTY!

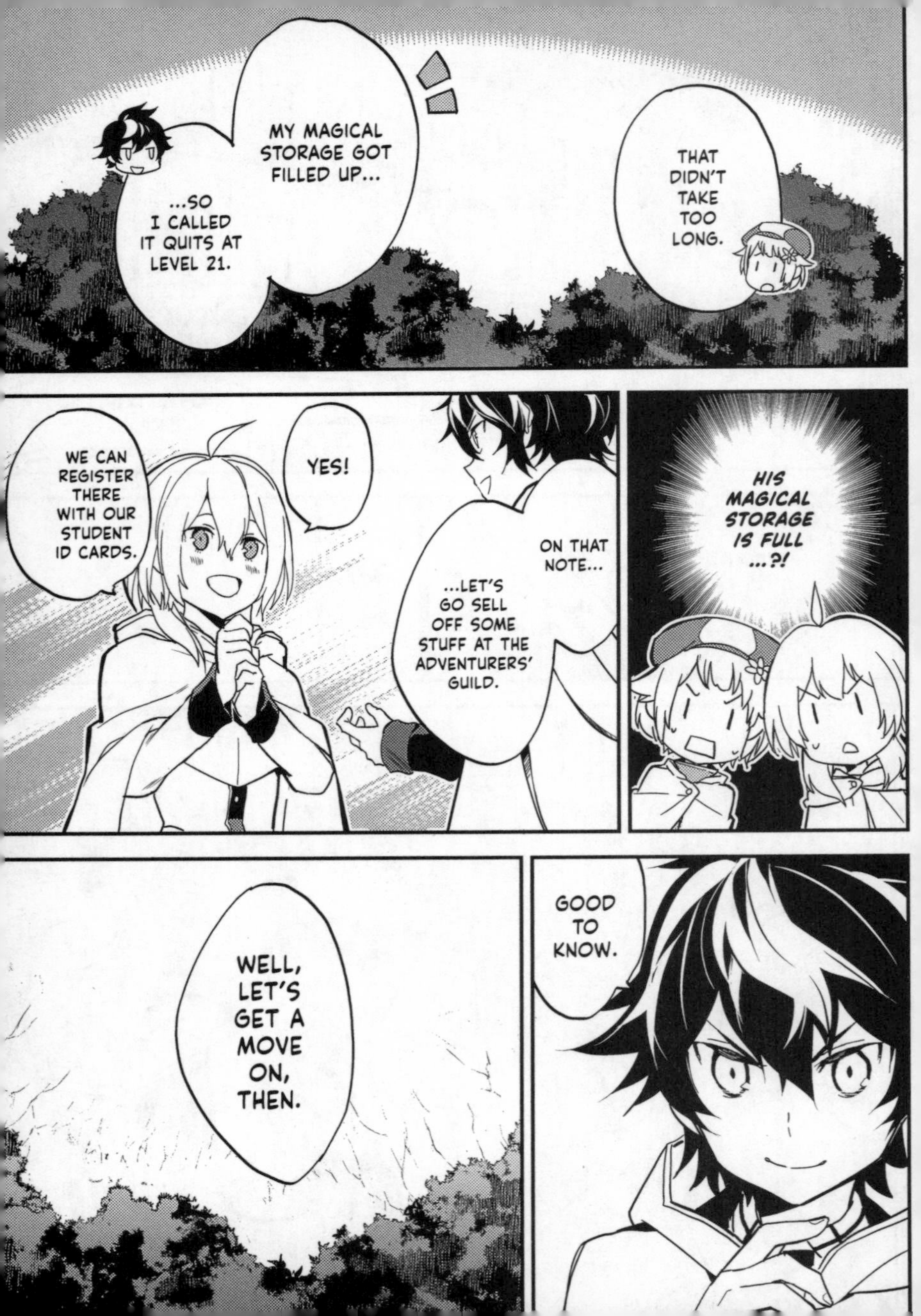
THAT DIDN'T TAKE TOO LONG.
MY MAGICAL STORAGE GOT FILLED UP...
...SO I CALLED IT QUITS AT LEVEL 21.
HIS MAGICAL STORAGE IS FULL ...?!
ON THAT NOTE...
...LET'S GO SELL OFF SOME STUFF AT THE ADVENTURERS' GUILD.
YES!
WE CAN REGISTER THERE WITH OUR STUDENT ID CARDS.
GOOD TO KNOW.
WELL, LET'S GET A MOVE ON, THEN.

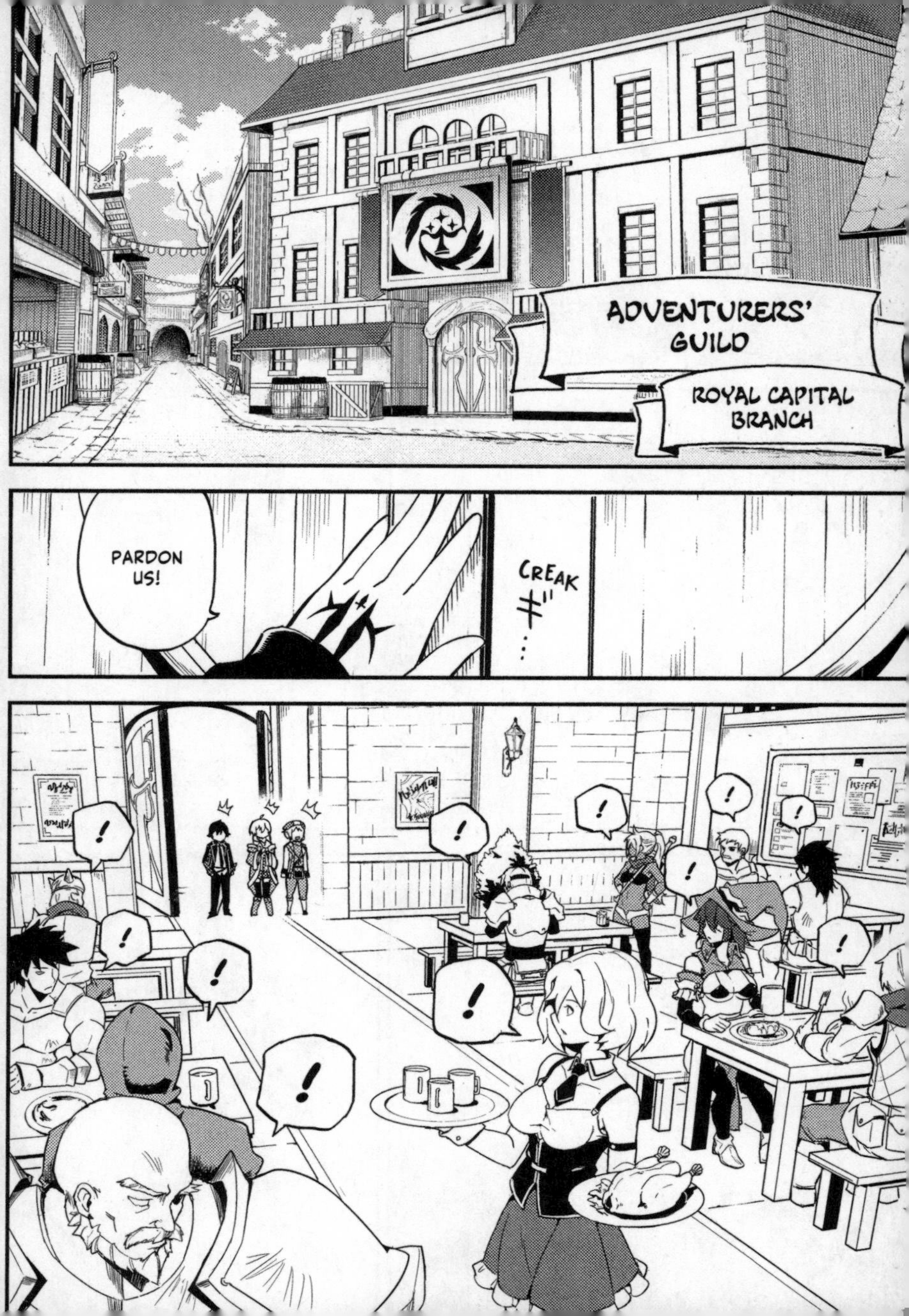
ADVENTURERS' GUILD
ROYAL CAPITAL BRANCH
CREAK
ギ
PARDON US!
!
!
!
!
!
!
!
!
!
!
!
!

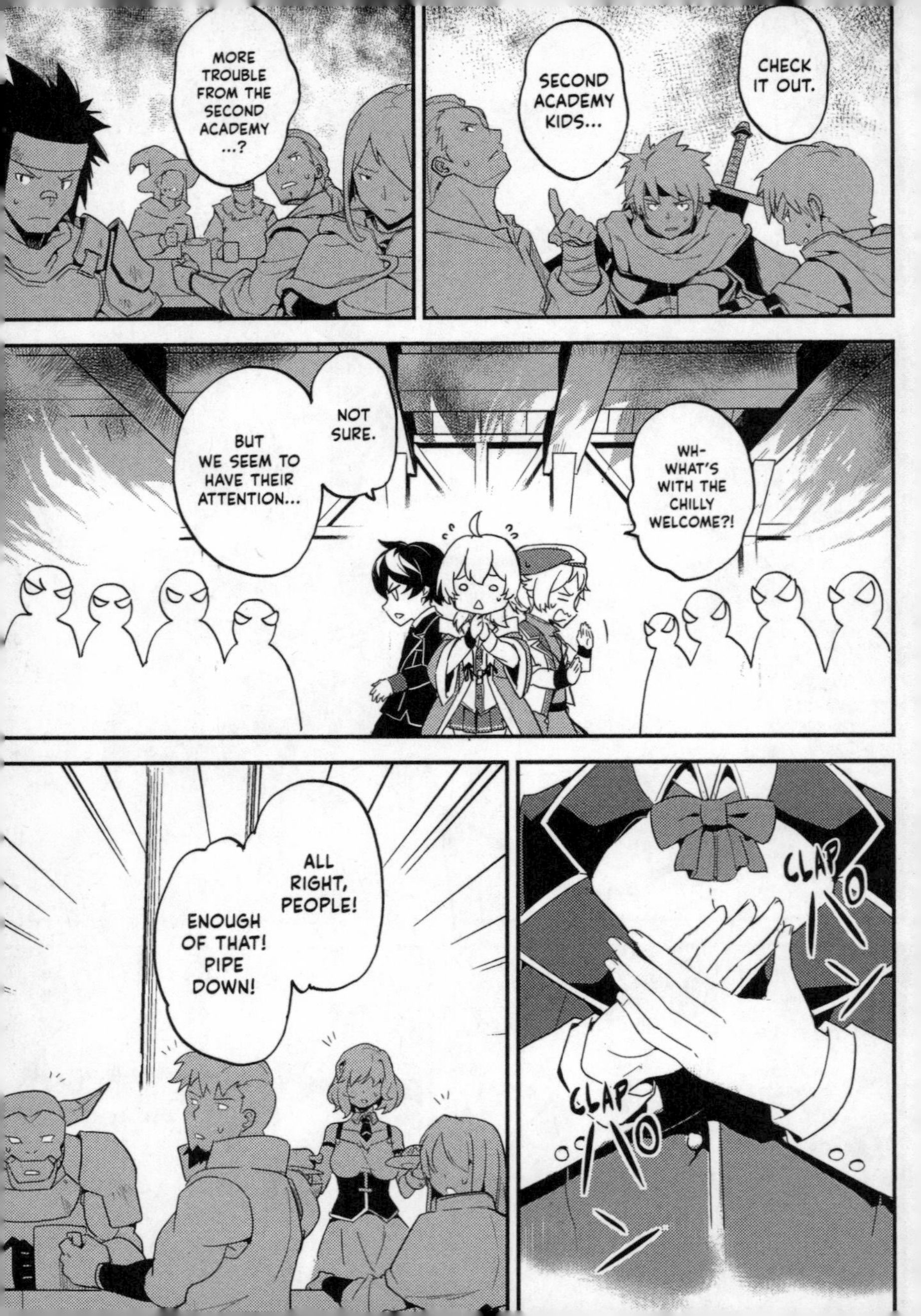
CHECK IT OUT.
SECOND ACADEMY KIDS...
MORE TROUBLE FROM THE SECOND ACADEMY ...?
WH-WHAT'S WITH THE CHILLY WELCOME?!
NOT SURE.
BUT WE SEEM TO HAVE THEIR ATTENTION...
CLAP
CLAP
ALL RIGHT, PEOPLE!
ENOUGH OF THAT! PIPE DOWN!

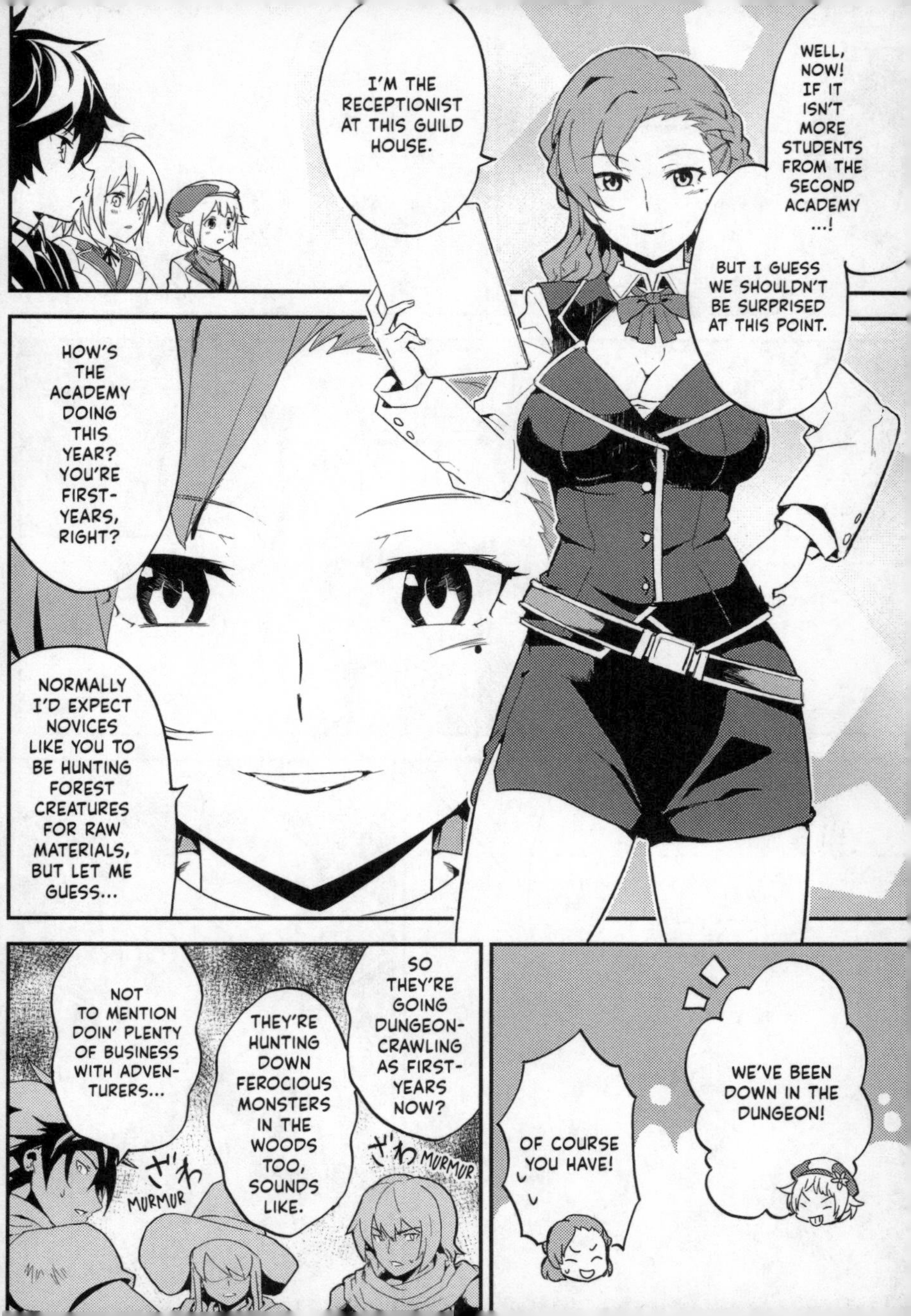
WELL, NOW! IF IT ISN'T MORE STUDENTS FROM THE SECOND ACADEMY ...!
BUT I GUESS WE SHOULDN'T BE SURPRISED AT THIS POINT.
I'M THE RECEPTIONIST AT THIS GUILD HOUSE.
HOW'S THE ACADEMY DOING THIS YEAR? YOU'RE FIRST-YEARS, RIGHT?
NORMALLY I'D EXPECT NOVICES LIKE YOU TO BE HUNTING FOREST CREATURES FOR RAW MATERIALS, BUT LET ME GUESS...
WE'VE BEEN DOWN IN THE DUNGEON!
OF COURSE YOU HAVE!
SO THEY'RE GOING DUNGEON-CRAWLING AS FIRST-YEARS NOW?
ざわ MURMUR
THEY'RE HUNTING DOWN FEROCIOUS MONSTERS IN THE WOODS TOO, SOUNDS LIKE.
NOT TO MENTION DOIN' PLENTY OF BUSINESS WITH ADVEN-TURERS...
ざわ MURMUR

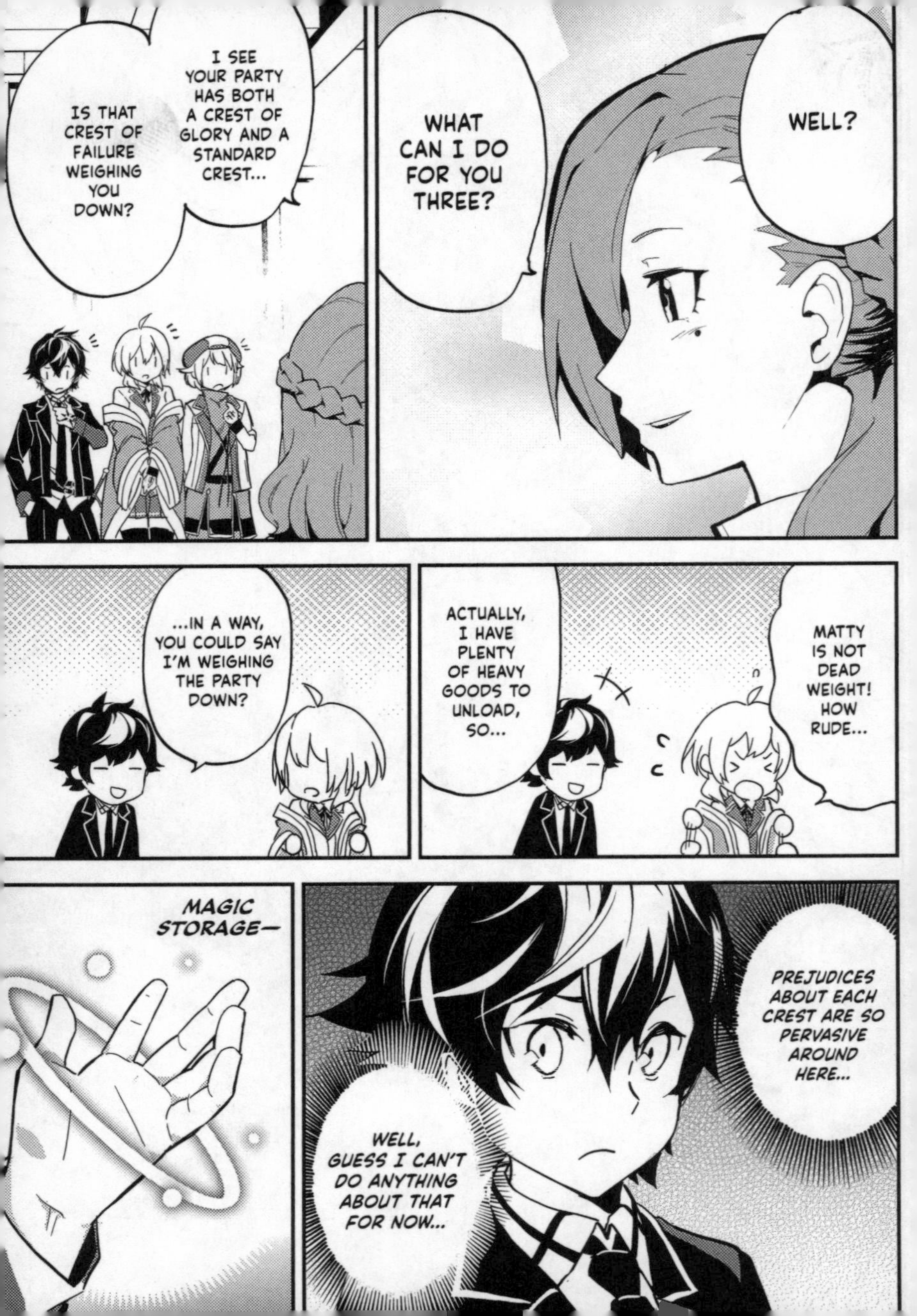
WELL?
WHAT CAN I DO FOR YOU THREE?
I SEE YOUR PARTY HAS BOTH A CREST OF GLORY AND A STANDARD CREST...
IS THAT CREST OF FAILURE WEIGHING YOU DOWN?
MATTY IS NOT DEAD WEIGHT! HOW RUDE...
ACTUALLY, I HAVE PLENTY OF HEAVY GOODS TO UNLOAD, SO...
...IN A WAY, YOU COULD SAY I'M WEIGHING THE PARTY DOWN?
PREJUDICES ABOUT EACH CREST ARE SO PERVASIVE AROUND HERE...
WELL, GUESS I CAN'T DO ANYTHING ABOUT THAT FOR NOW...
MAGIC STORAGE—

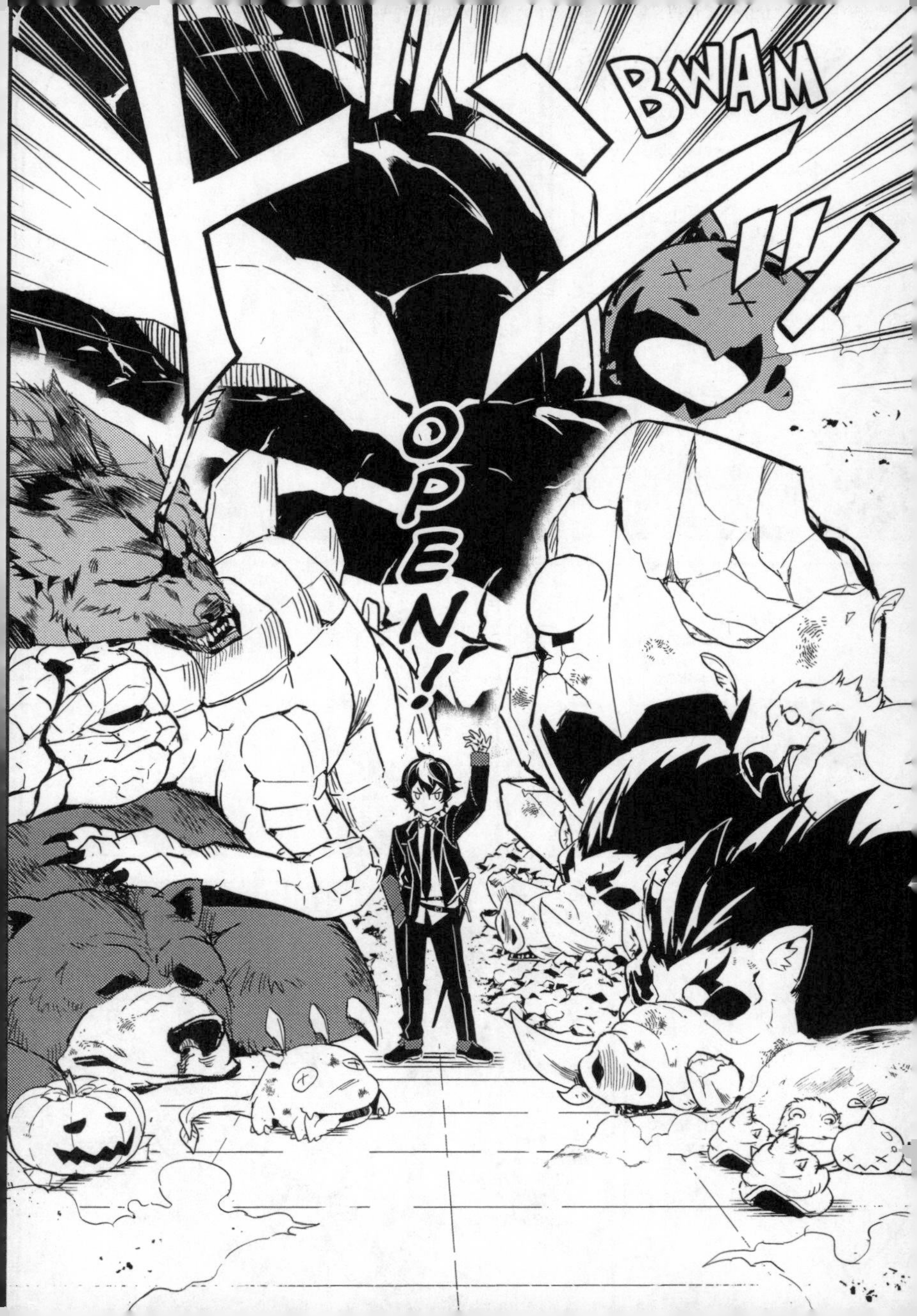
BWAM
OPEN!

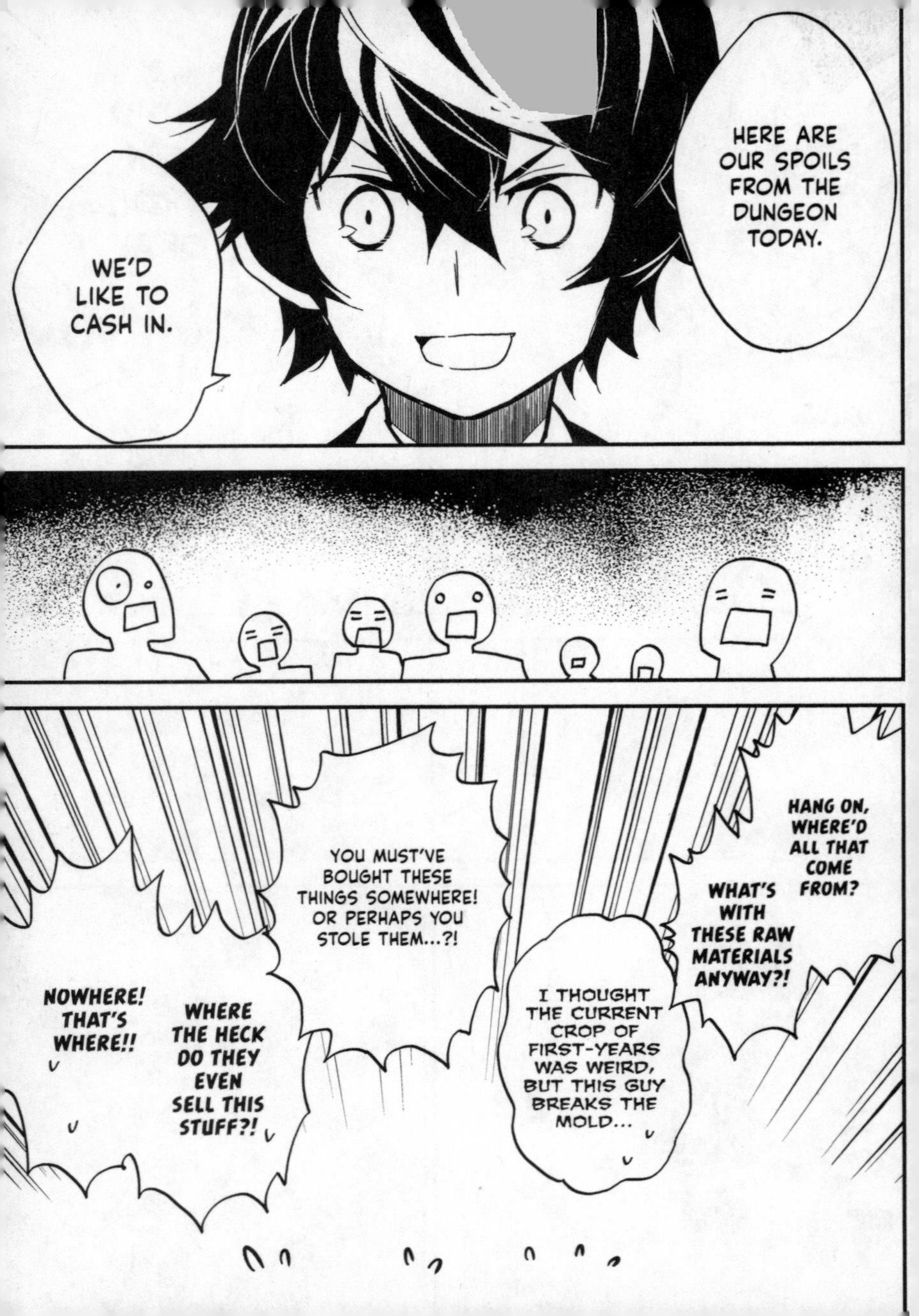
HERE ARE OUR SPOILS FROM THE DUNGEON TODAY.
WE'D LIKE TO CASH IN.
HANG ON, WHERE'D ALL THAT COME FROM?
WHAT'S WITH THESE RAW MATERIALS ANYWAY?!
I THOUGHT THE CURRENT CROP OF FIRST-YEARS WAS WEIRD, BUT THIS GUY BREAKS THE MOLD...
YOU MUST'VE BOUGHT THESE THINGS SOMEWHERE! OR PERHAPS YOU STOLE THEM...?!
WHERE THE HECK DO THEY EVEN SELL THIS STUFF?!
NOWHERE! THAT'S WHERE!!

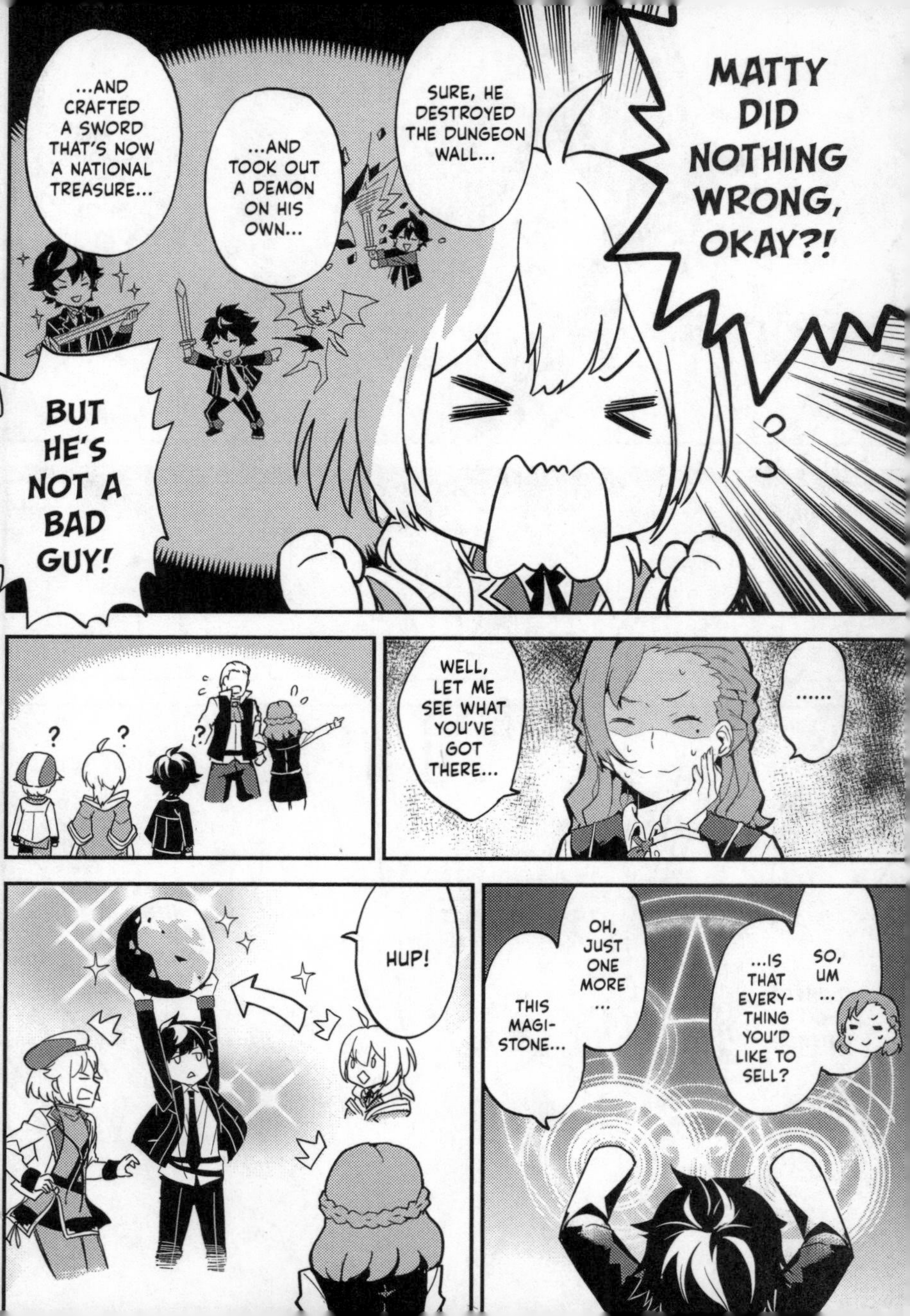
SURE, HE DESTROYED THE DUNGEON WALL...
...AND TOOK OUT A DEMON ON HIS OWN...
...AND CRAFTED A SWORD THAT'S NOW A NATIONAL TREASURE...
BUT HE'S NOT A BAD GUY!
MATTY DID NOTHING WRONG, OKAY?!
......
WELL, LET ME SEE WHAT YOU'VE GOT THERE...
?
?
?
SO, UM...
...IS THAT EVERY-THING YOU'D LIKE TO SELL?
OH, JUST ONE MORE...
THIS MAGI-STONE...
HUP!

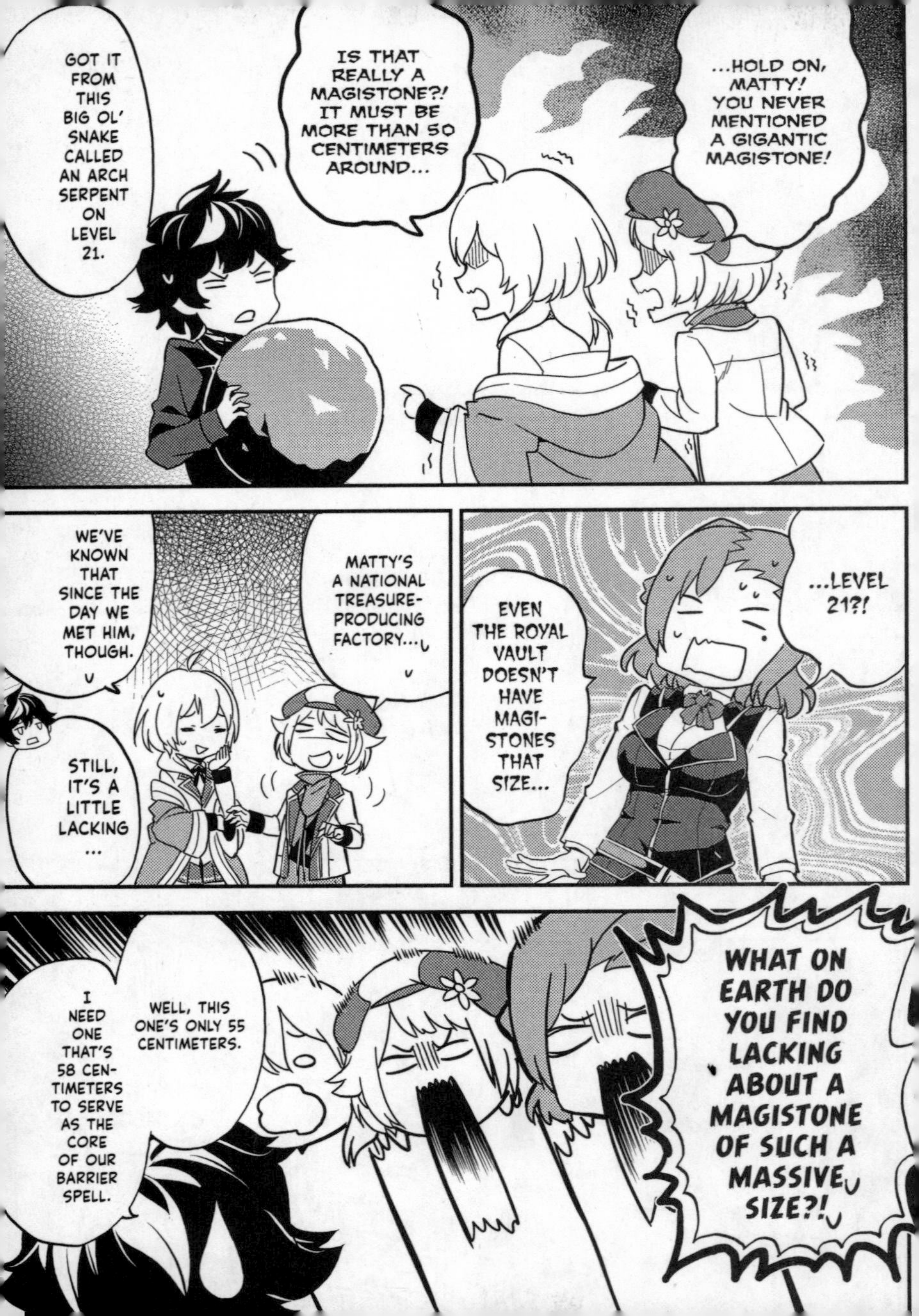
...HOLD ON, MATTY! YOU NEVER MENTIONED A GIGANTIC MAGISTONE!
IS THAT REALLY A MAGISTONE?! IT MUST BE MORE THAN 50 CENTIMETERS AROUND...
GOT IT FROM THIS BIG OL' SNAKE CALLED AN ARCH SERPENT ON LEVEL 21.
...LEVEL 21?!
EVEN THE ROYAL VAULT DOESN'T HAVE MAGISTONES THAT SIZE...
MATTY'S A NATIONAL TREASURE-PRODUCING FACTORY...
WE'VE KNOWN THAT SINCE THE DAY WE MET HIM, THOUGH.
STILL, IT'S A LITTLE LACKING...
WHAT ON EARTH DO YOU FIND LACKING ABOUT A MAGISTONE OF SUCH A MASSIVE SIZE?!
WELL, THIS ONE'S ONLY 55 CENTIMETERS.
I NEED ONE THAT'S 58 CENTIMETERS TO SERVE AS THE CORE OF OUR BARRIER SPELL.

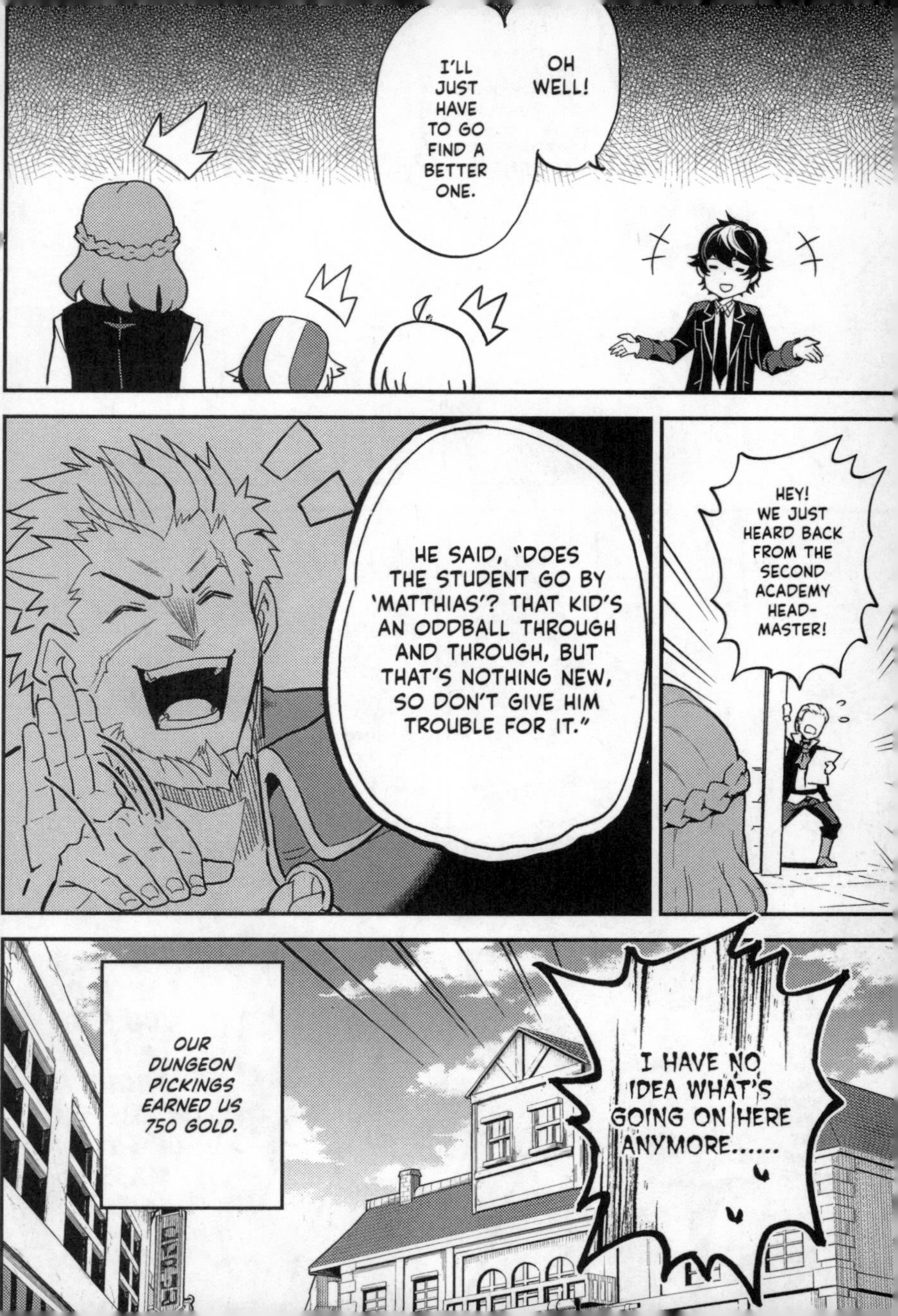
OH WELL!
I'LL JUST HAVE TO GO FIND A BETTER ONE.
HEY! WE JUST HEARD BACK FROM THE SECOND ACADEMY HEAD-MASTER!
HE SAID, "DOES THE STUDENT GO BY 'MATTHIAS'? THAT KID'S AN ODDBALL THROUGH AND THROUGH, BUT THAT'S NOTHING NEW, SO DON'T GIVE HIM TROUBLE FOR IT."
I HAVE NO IDEA WHAT'S GOING ON HERE ANYMORE......
OUR DUNGEON PICKINGS EARNED US 750 GOLD.

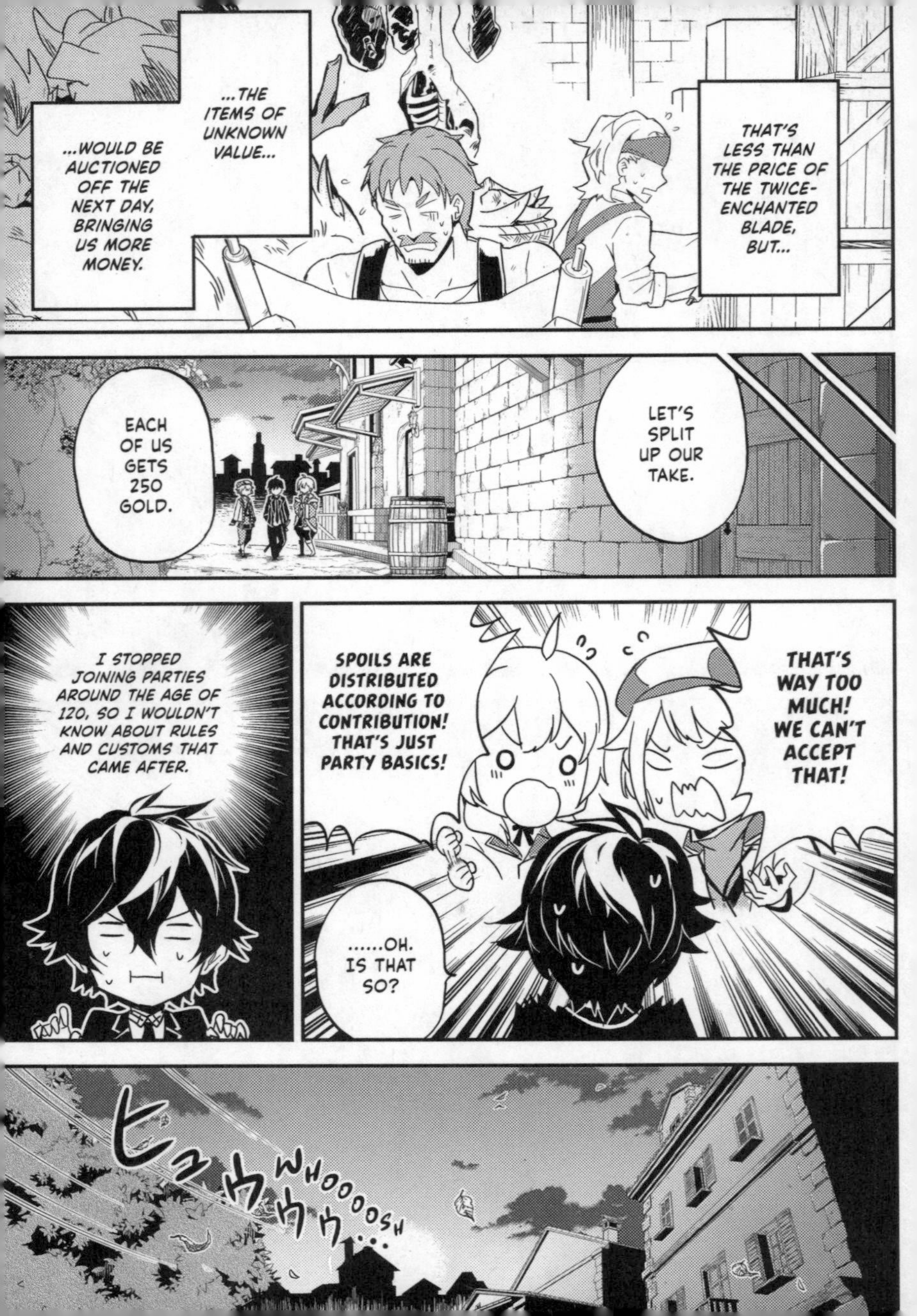
THAT'S LESS THAN THE PRICE OF THE TWICE-ENCHANTED BLADE, BUT...
...THE ITEMS OF UNKNOWN VALUE...
...WOULD BE AUCTIONED OFF THE NEXT DAY, BRINGING US MORE MONEY.
LET'S SPLIT UP OUR TAKE.
EACH OF US GETS 250 GOLD.
THAT'S WAY TOO MUCH! WE CAN'T ACCEPT THAT!
SPOILS ARE DISTRIBUTED ACCORDING TO CONTRIBUTION! THAT'S JUST PARTY BASICS!
......OH. IS THAT SO?
I STOPPED JOINING PARTIES AROUND THE AGE OF 120, SO I WOULDN'T KNOW ABOUT RULES AND CUSTOMS THAT CAME AFTER.
ヒュウウウ...
WHOOOOSH...

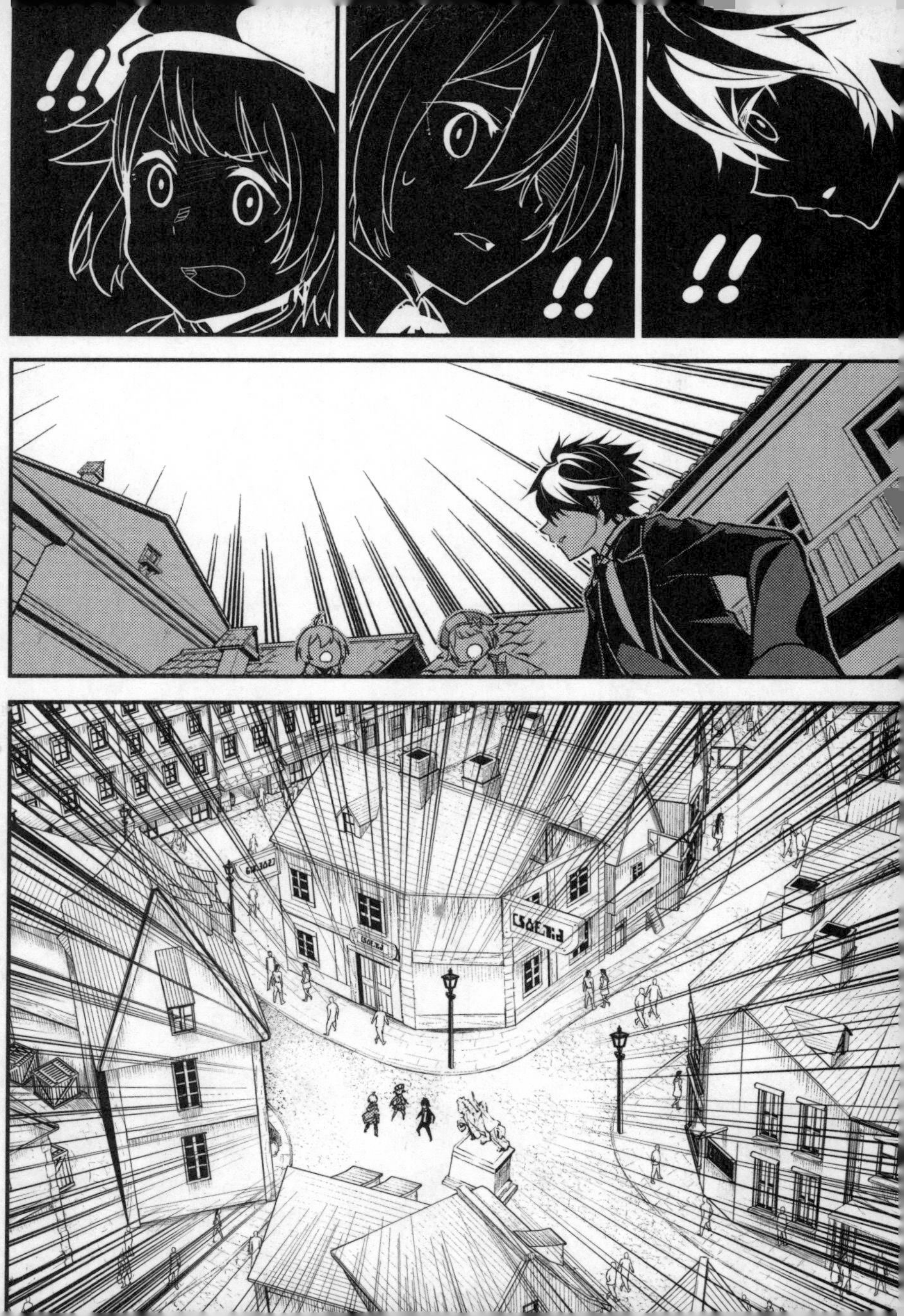
!!
!!
!!

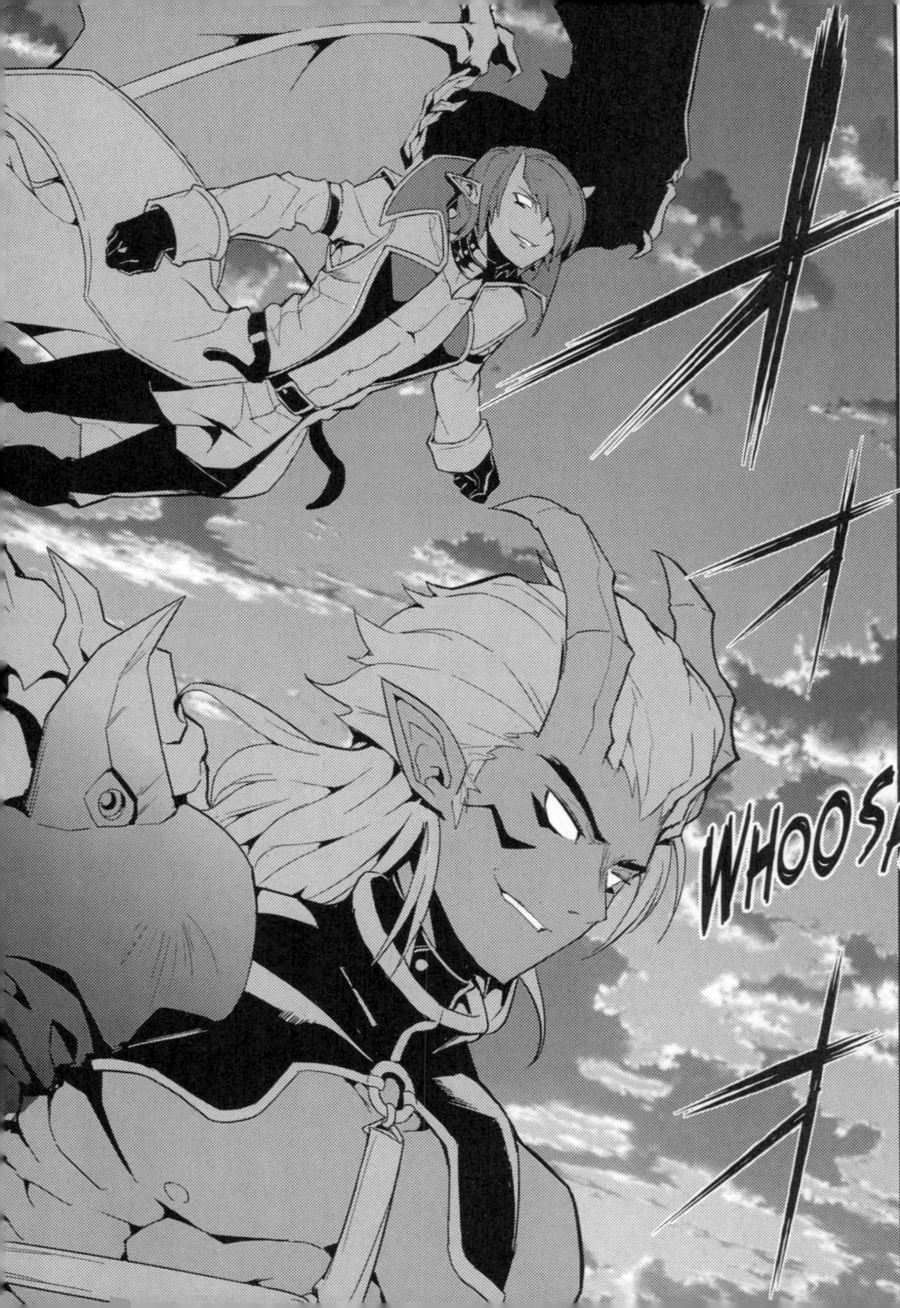
WHOOSH

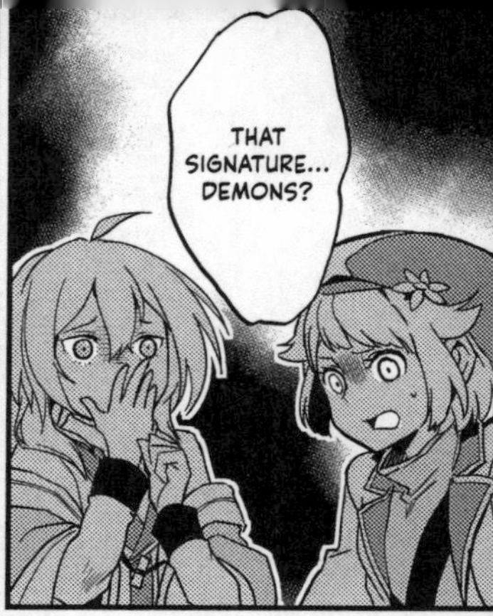
THAT SIGNATURE... DEMONS?

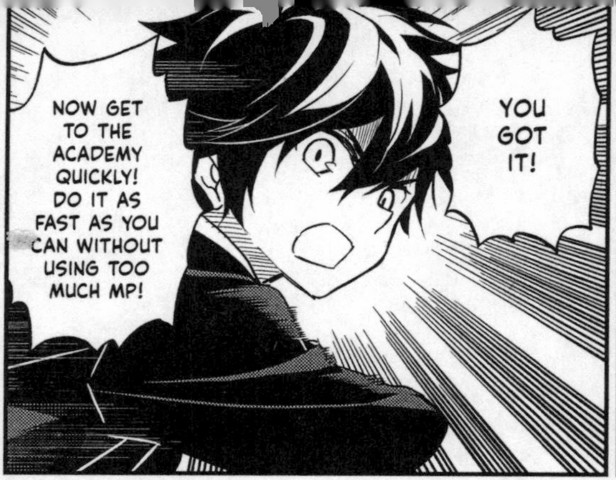
YOU GOT IT!
NOW GET TO THE ACADEMY QUICKLY! DO IT AS FAST AS YOU CAN WITHOUT USING TOO MUCH MP!

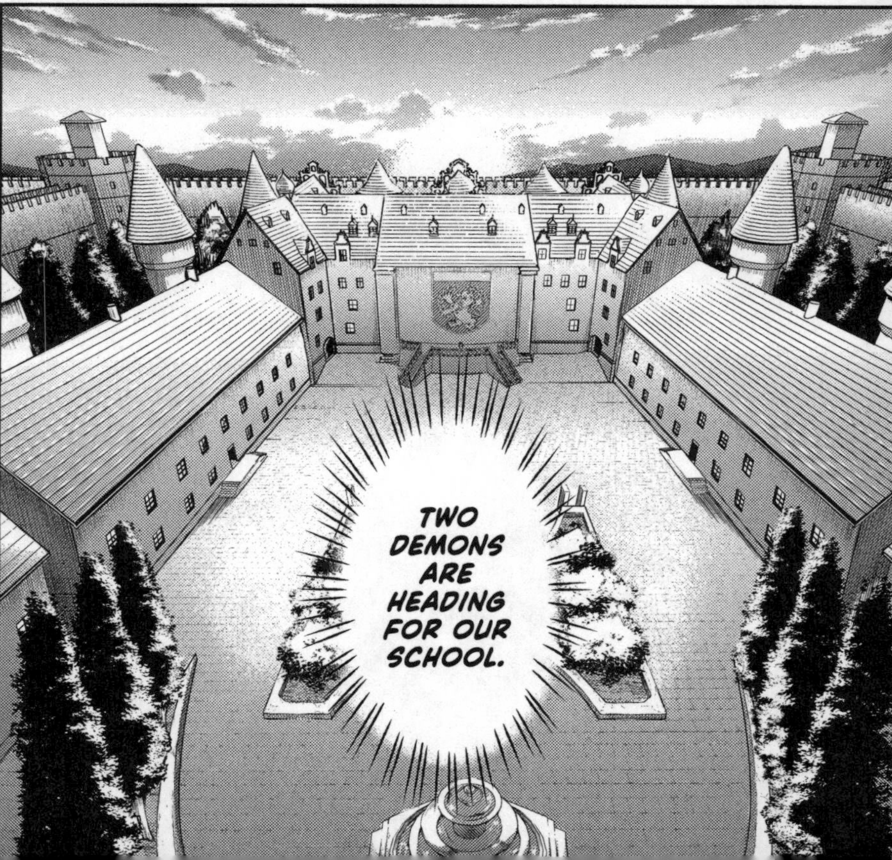
TWO DEMONS ARE HEADING FOR OUR SCHOOL.

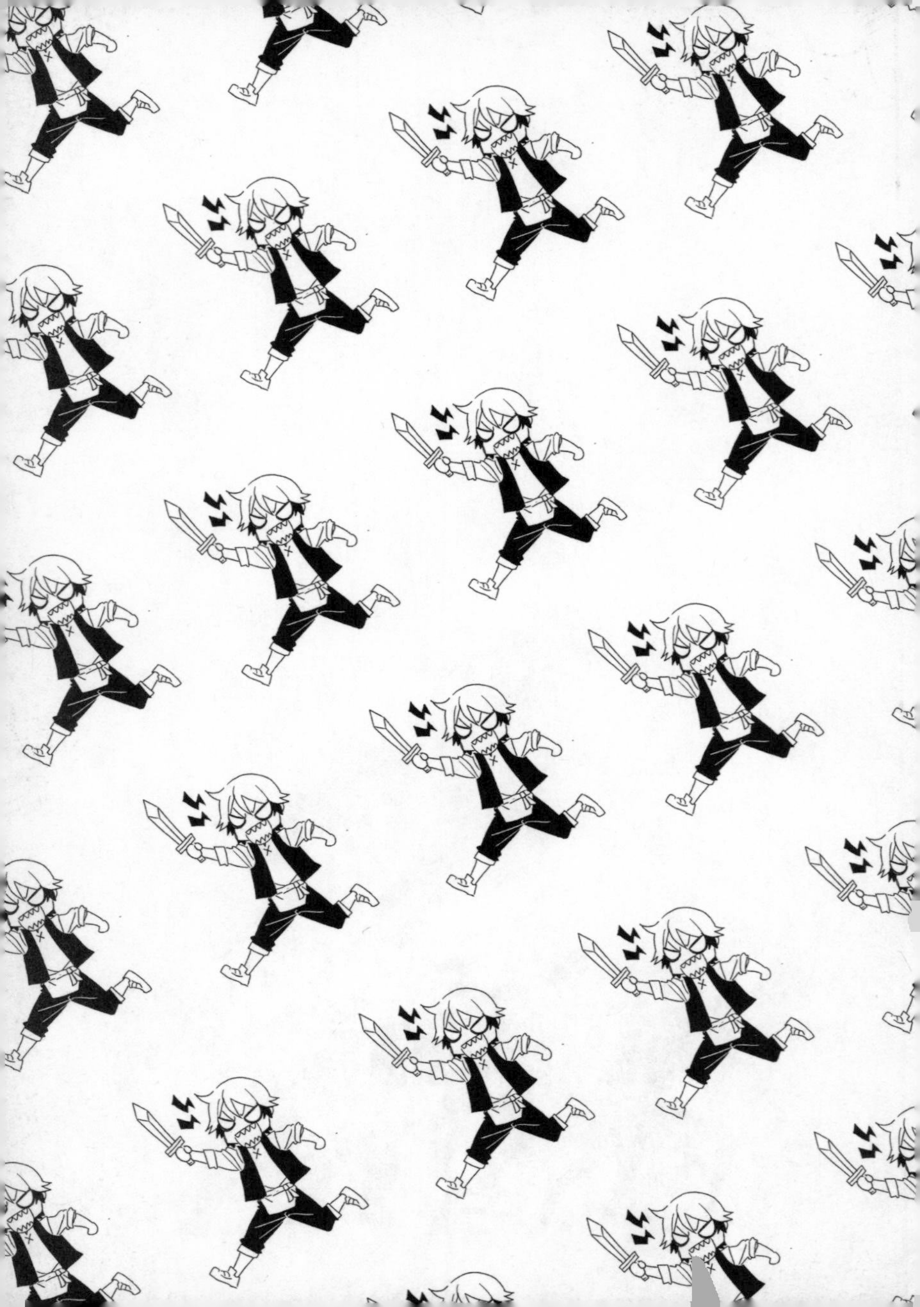

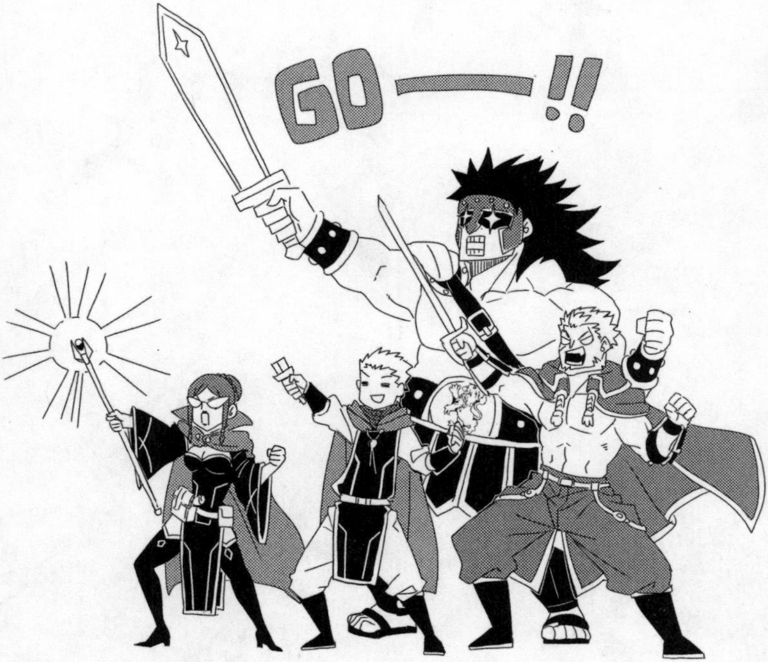
GO——!!

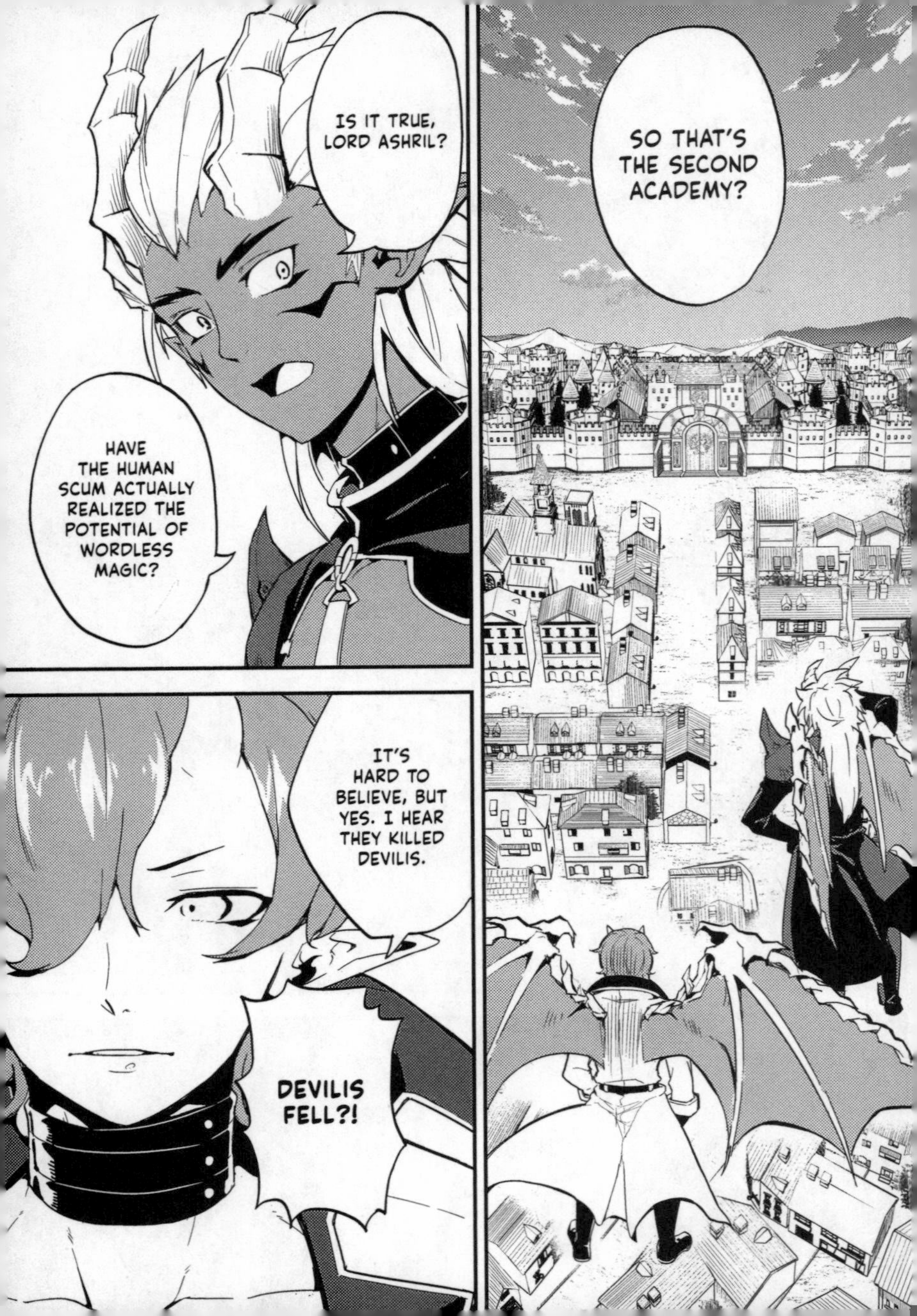
SO THAT'S THE SECOND ACADEMY?
IS IT TRUE, LORD ASHRIL?
HAVE THE HUMAN SCUM ACTUALLY REALIZED THE POTENTIAL OF WORDLESS MAGIC?
IT'S HARD TO BELIEVE, BUT YES. I HEAR THEY KILLED DEVILIS.
DEVILIS FELL?!

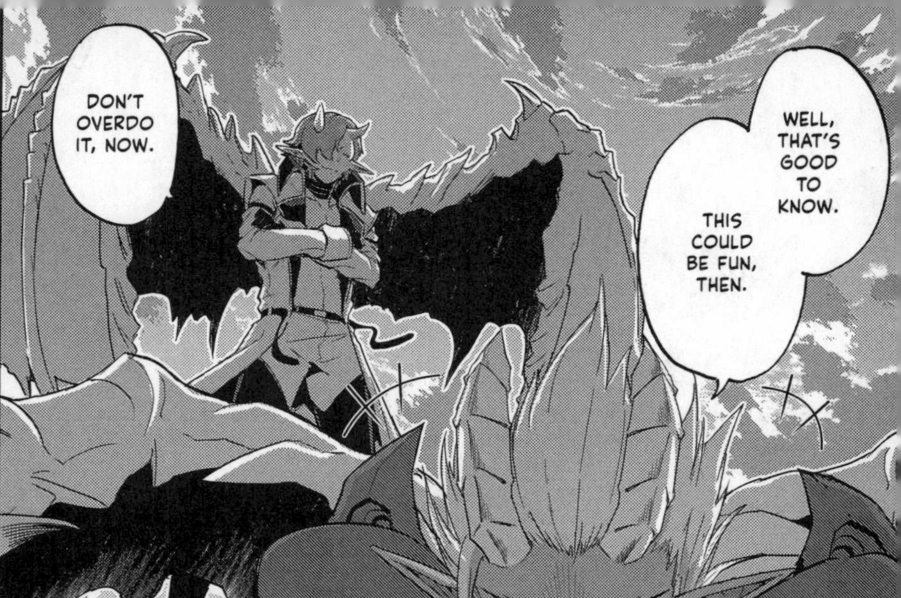
WELL, THAT'S GOOD TO KNOW.
THIS COULD BE FUN, THEN.
DON'T OVERDO IT, NOW.
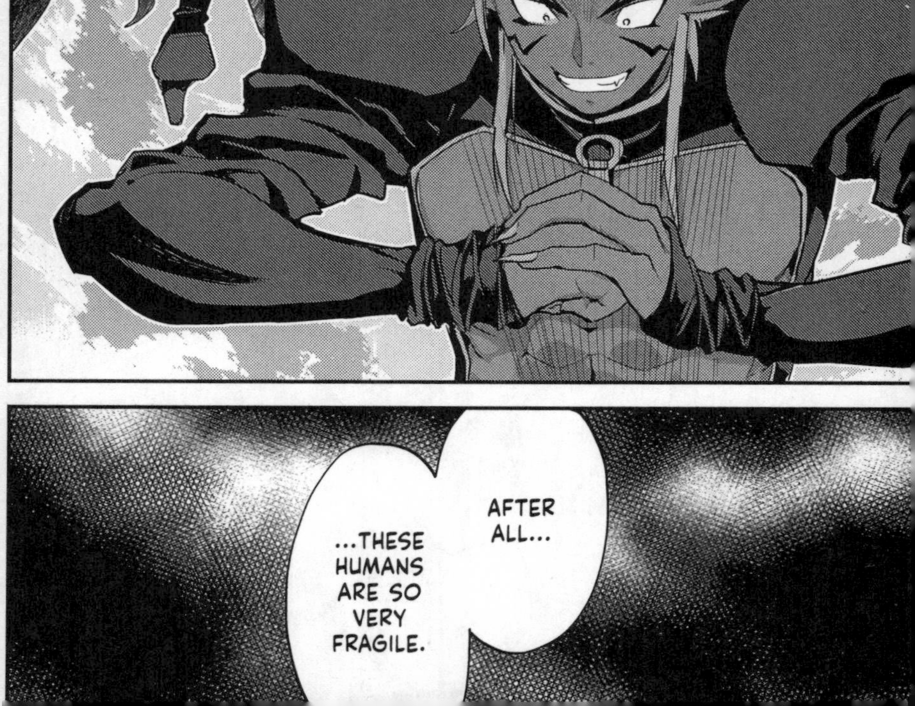
AFTER ALL...
...THESE HUMANS ARE SO VERY FRAGILE.

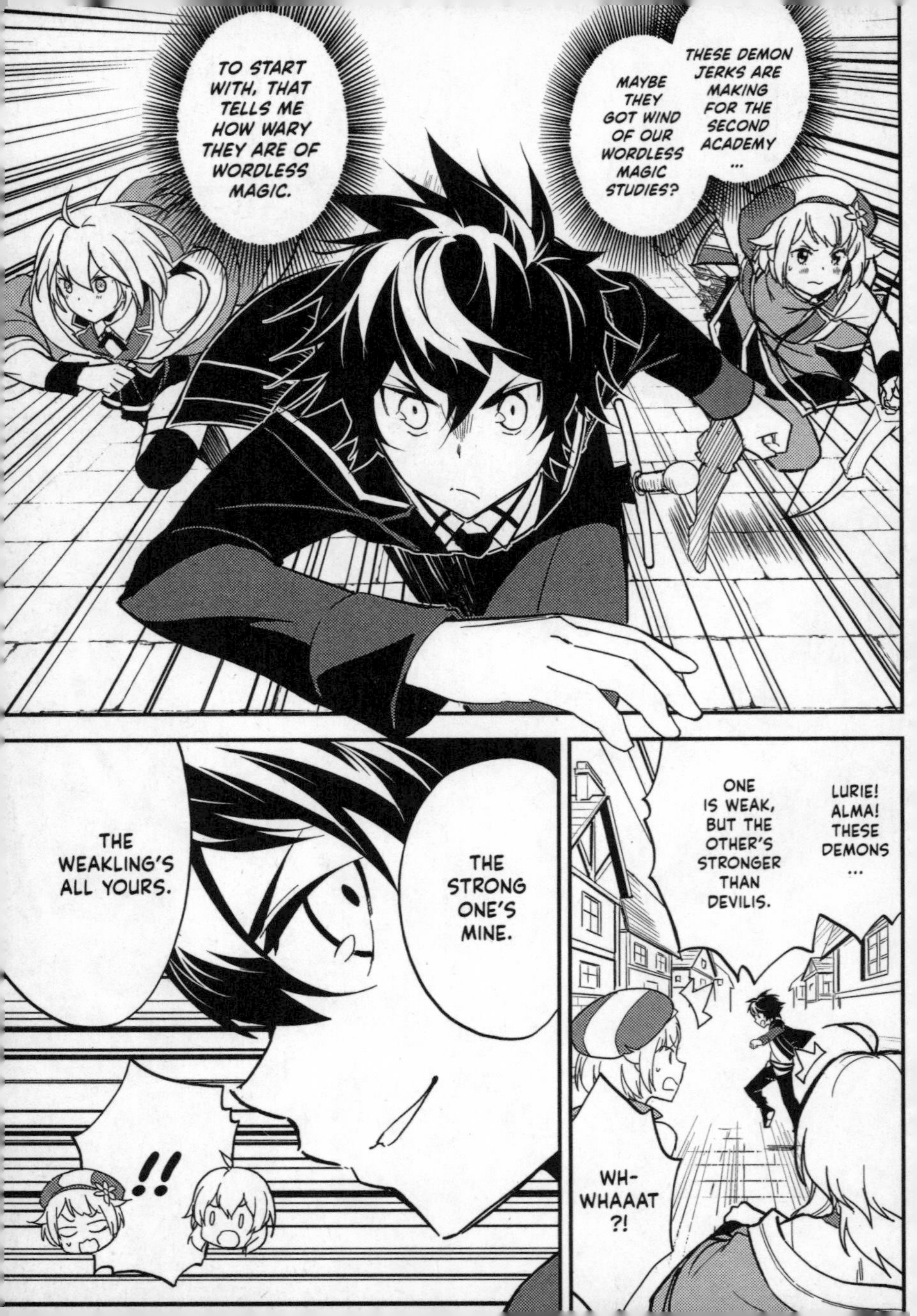
THESE DEMON JERKS ARE MAKING FOR THE SECOND ACADEMY ...
MAYBE THEY GOT WIND OF OUR WORDLESS MAGIC STUDIES?
TO START WITH, THAT TELLS ME HOW WARY THEY ARE OF WORDLESS MAGIC.
LURIE! ALMA! THESE DEMONS ...
ONE IS WEAK, BUT THE OTHER'S STRONGER THAN DEVILIS.
WH-WHAAAT ?!
THE STRONG ONE'S MINE.
THE WEAKLING'S ALL YOURS.
!!

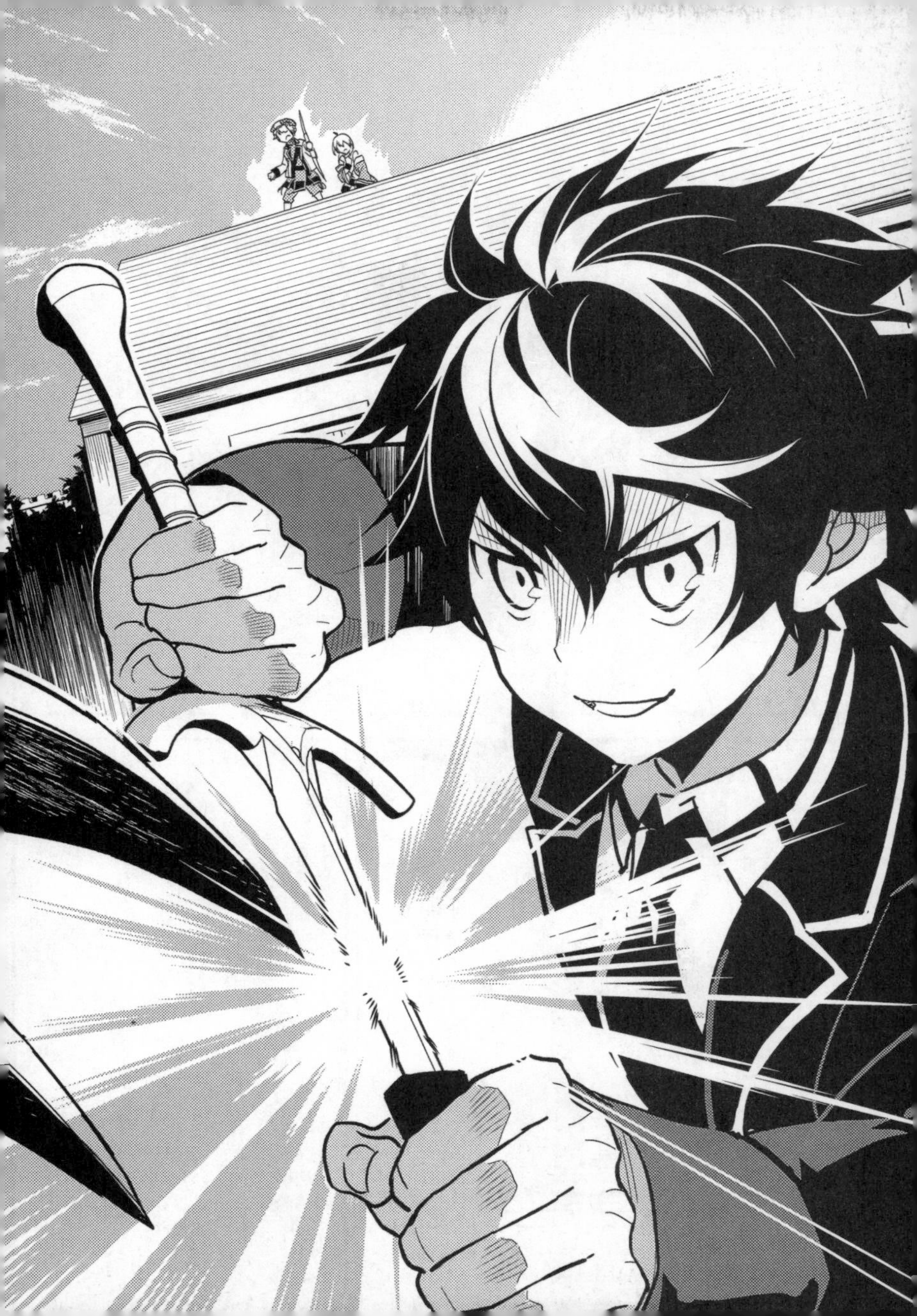

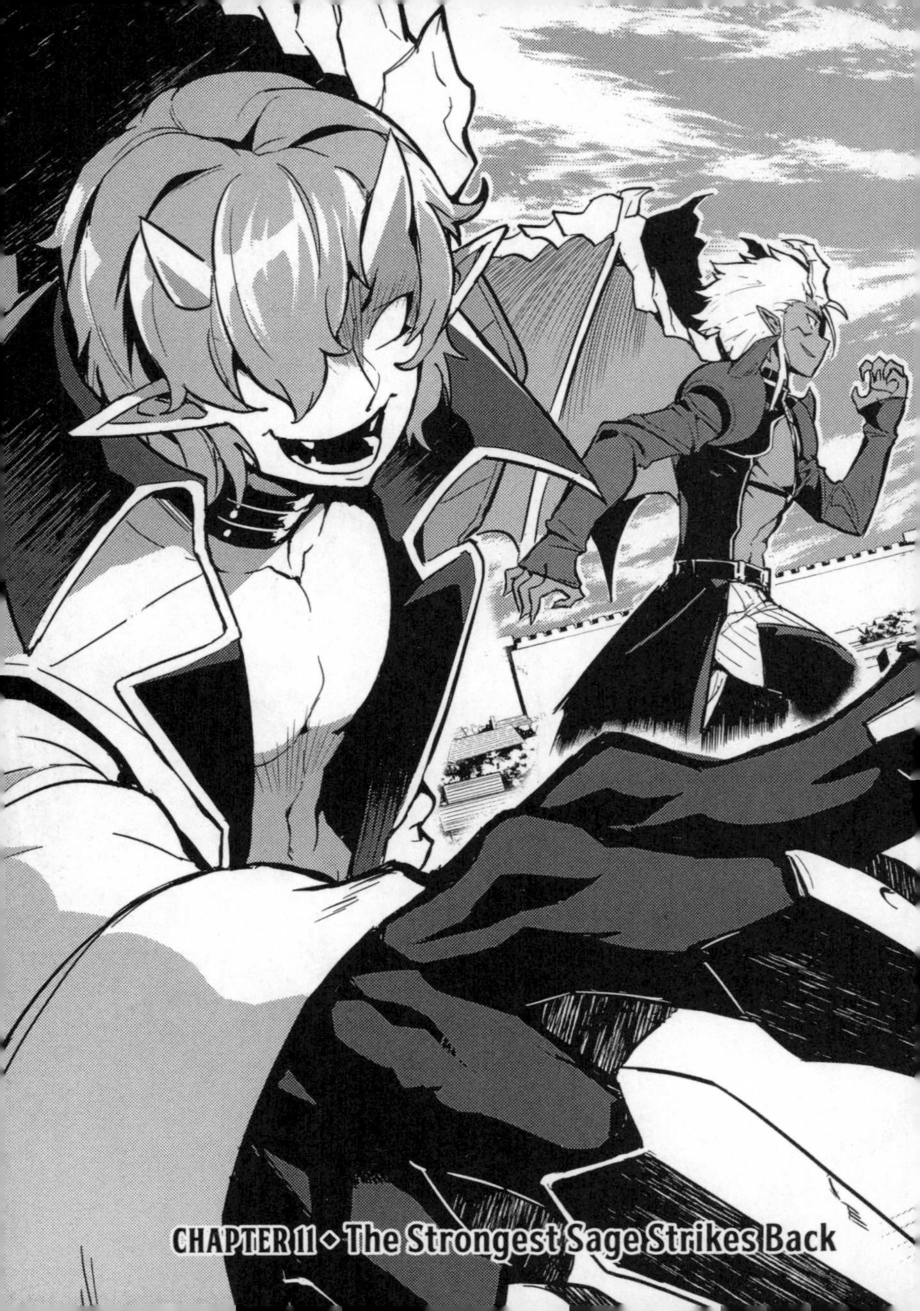

CHAPTER 11 ◆ The Strongest Sage Strikes Back

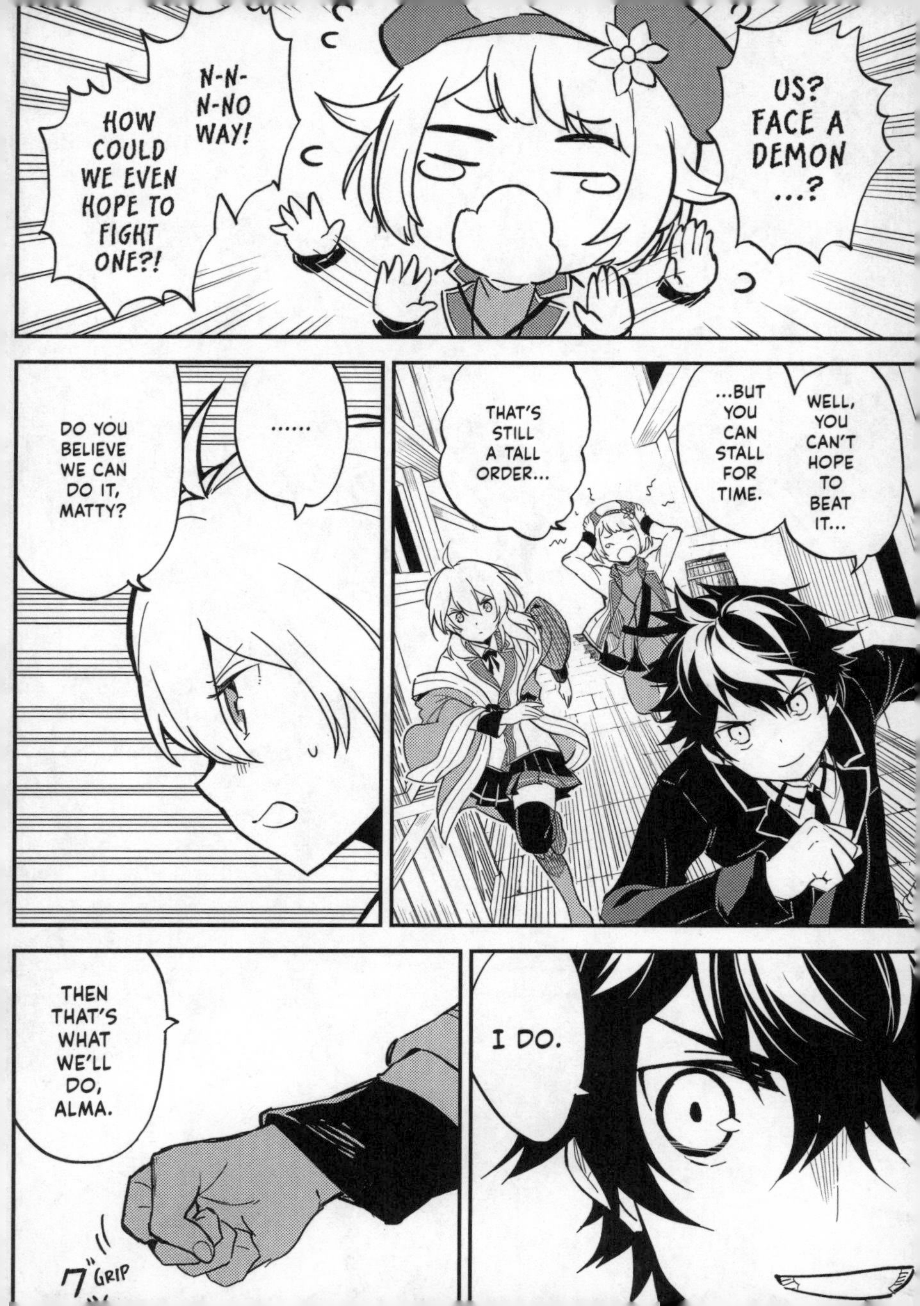
US? FACE A DEMON ...?
N-N-N-NO WAY!
HOW COULD WE EVEN HOPE TO FIGHT ONE?!
WELL, YOU CAN'T HOPE TO BEAT IT...
...BUT YOU CAN STALL FOR TIME.
THAT'S STILL A TALL ORDER...
......
DO YOU BELIEVE WE CAN DO IT, MATTY?
I DO.
THEN THAT'S WHAT WE'LL DO, ALMA.
GRIP

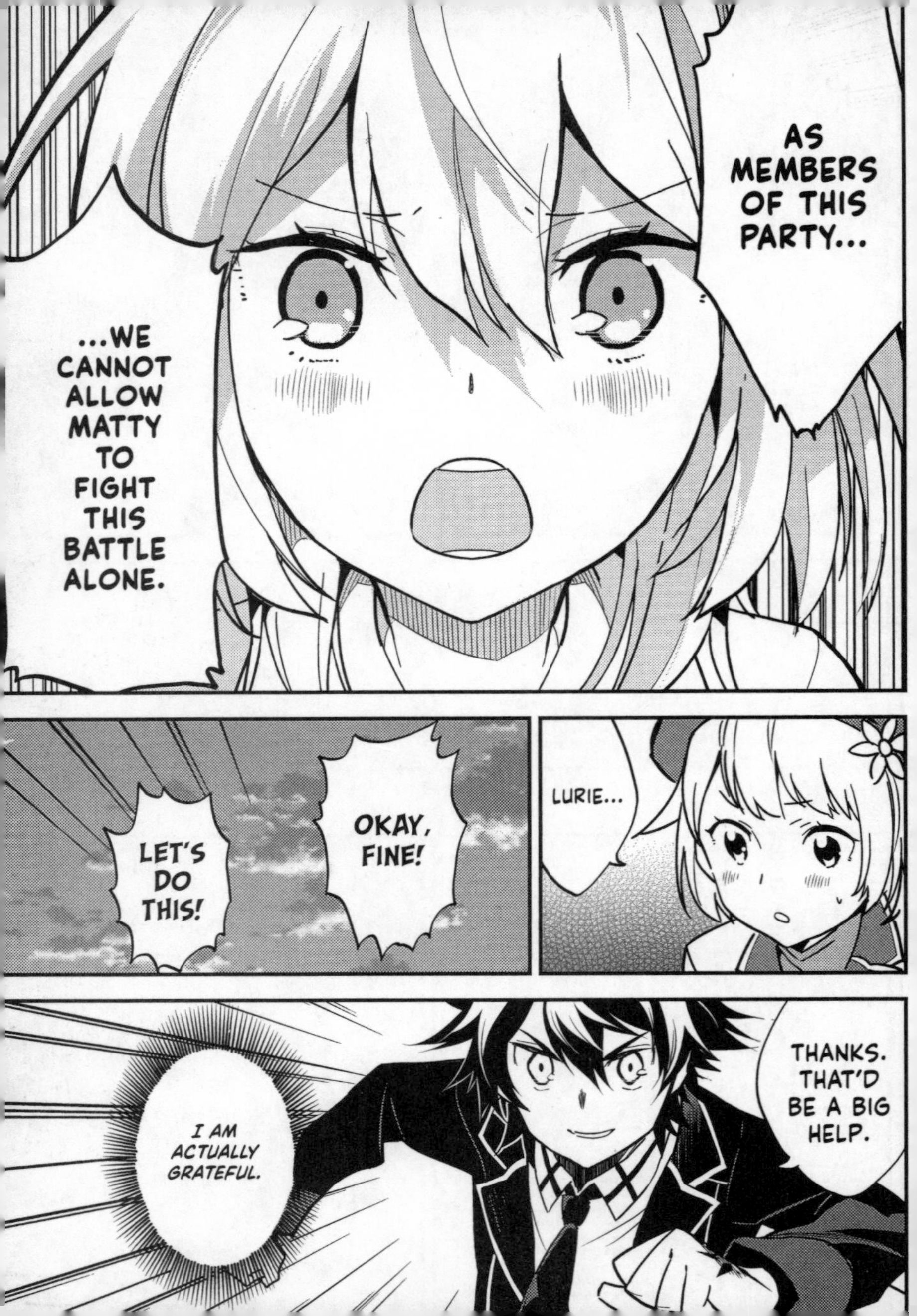
AS MEMBERS OF THIS PARTY...
...WE CANNOT ALLOW MATTY TO FIGHT THIS BATTLE ALONE.
LURIE...
OKAY, FINE!
LET'S DO THIS!
THANKS. THAT'D BE A BIG HELP.
I AM ACTUALLY GRATEFUL.

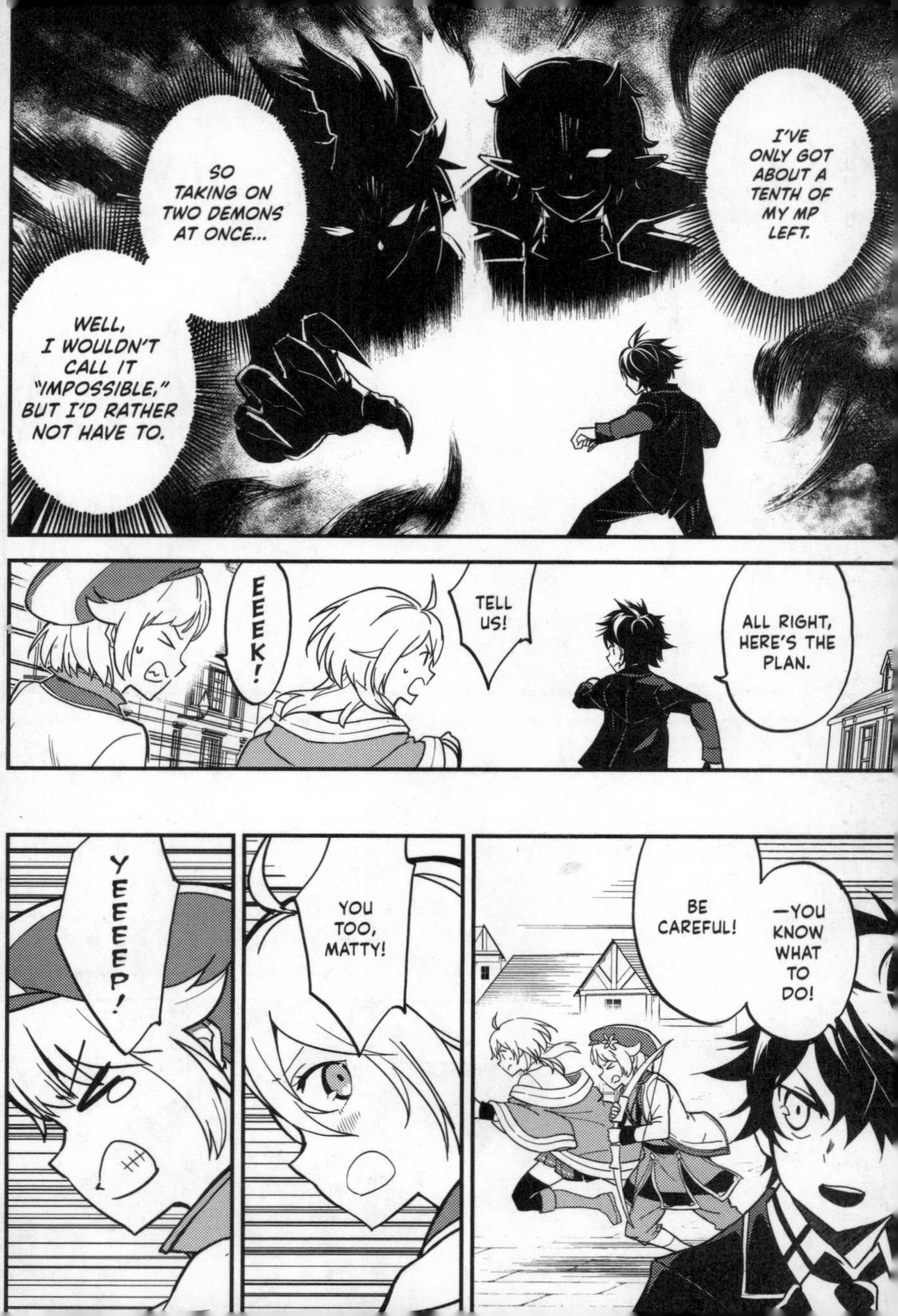
I'VE ONLY GOT ABOUT A TENTH OF MY MP LEFT.
SO TAKING ON TWO DEMONS AT ONCE...
WELL, I WOULDN'T CALL IT "IMPOSSIBLE," BUT I'D RATHER NOT HAVE TO.
ALL RIGHT, HERE'S THE PLAN.
TELL US!
EEEK!
—YOU KNOW WHAT TO DO!
BE CAREFUL!
YOU TOO, MATTY!
YEEEEP!

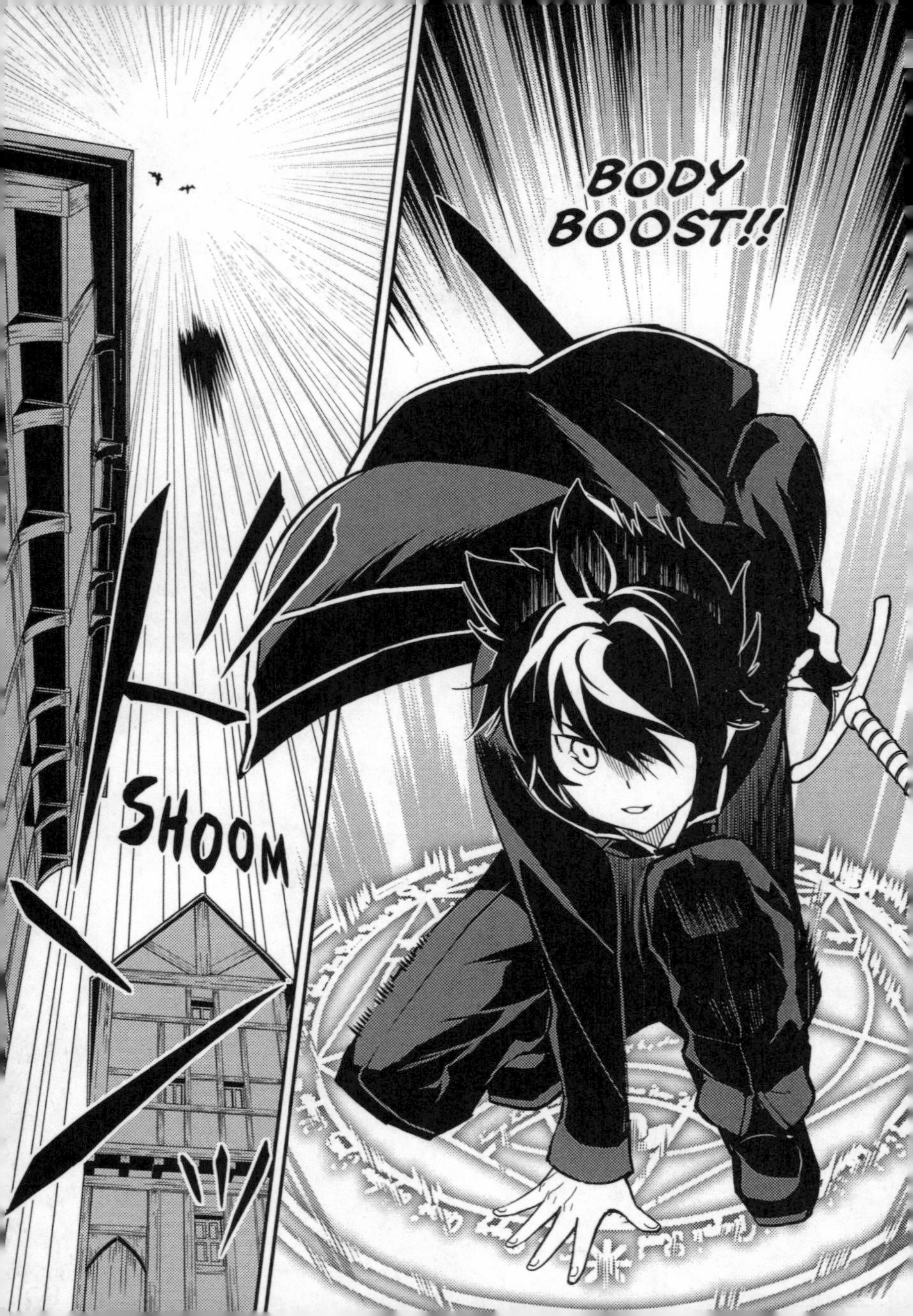
BODY BOOST!!
SHOOM

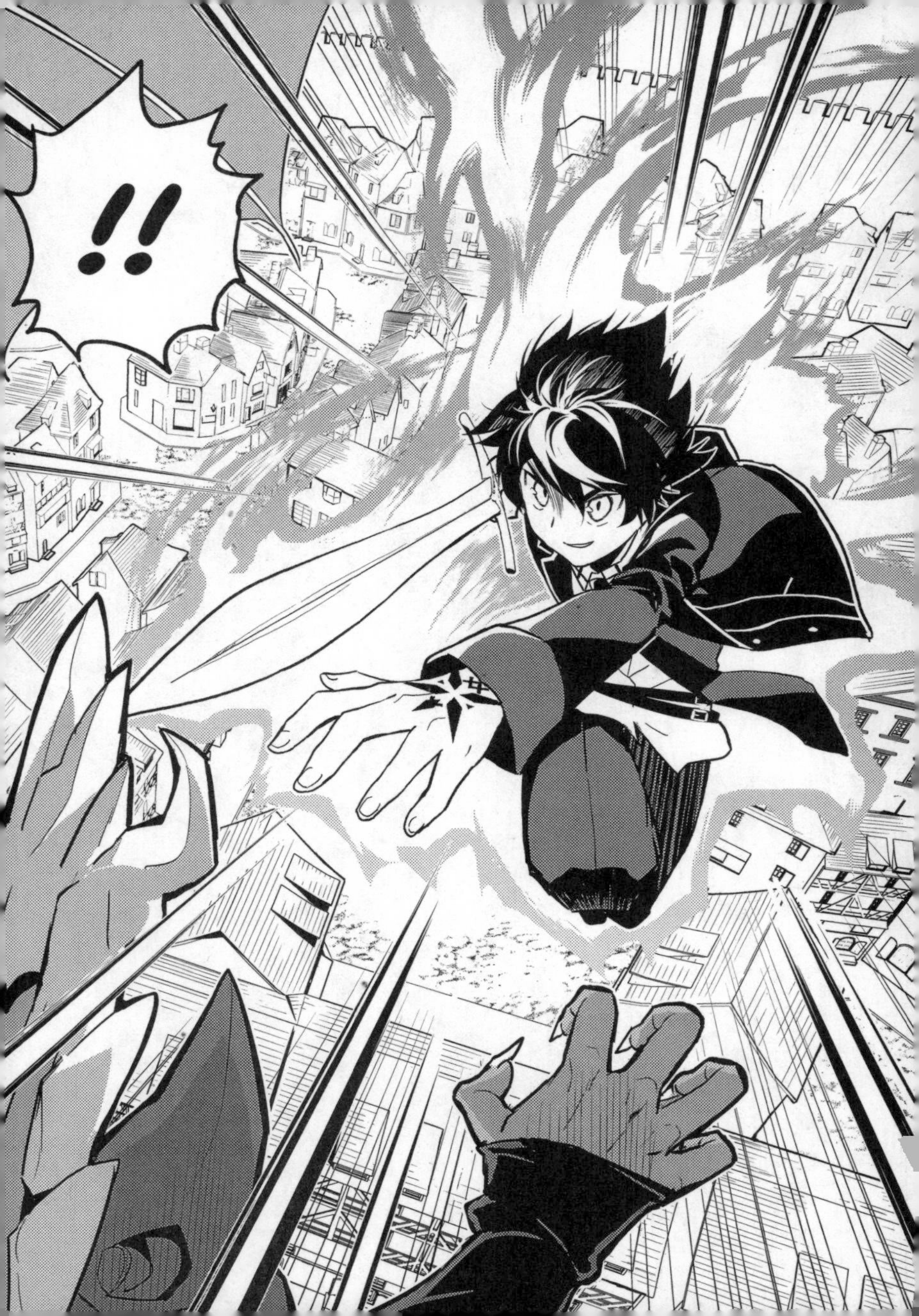
!!

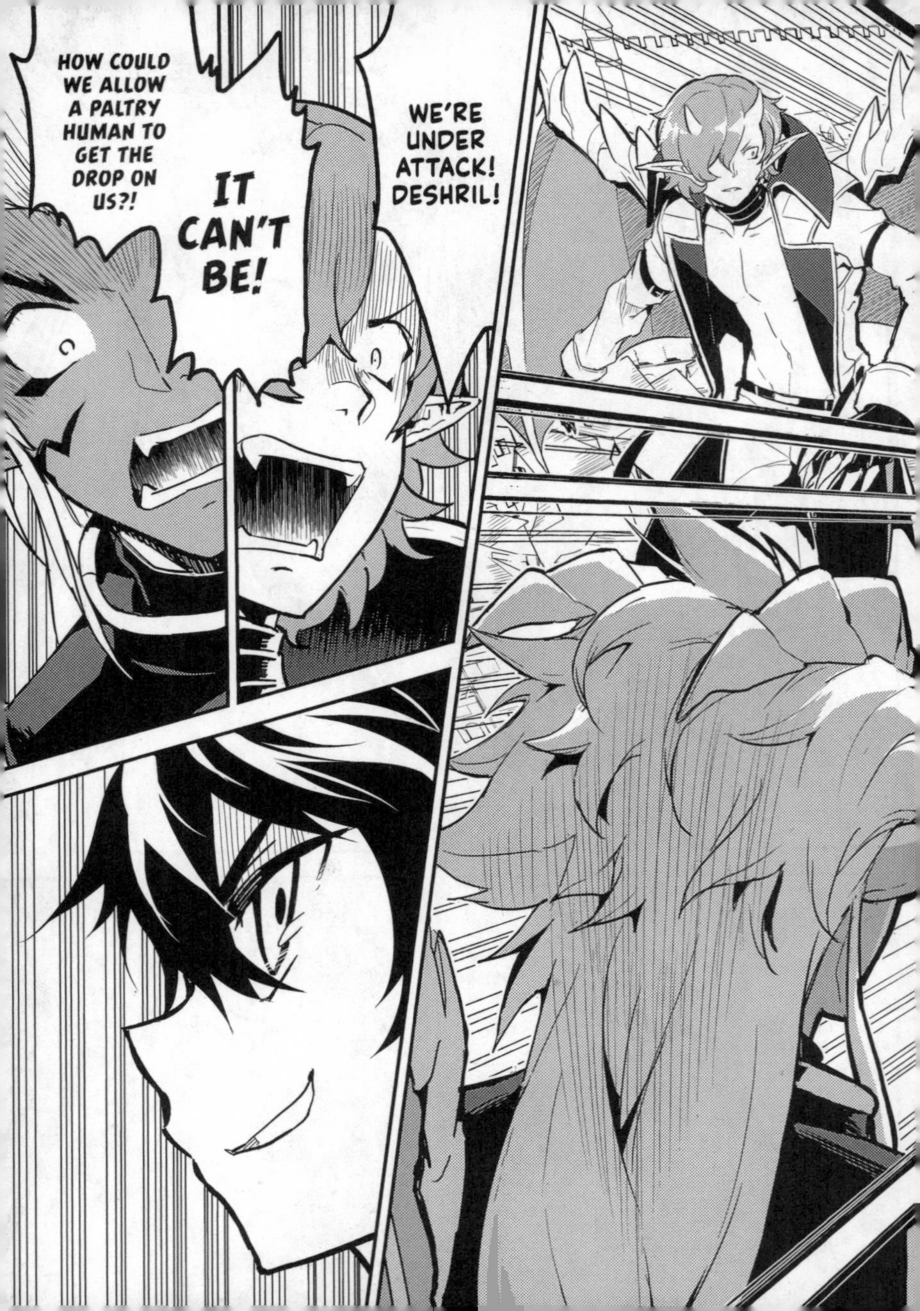
WE'RE UNDER ATTACK! DESHRIL!
IT CAN'T BE!
HOW COULD WE ALLOW A PALTRY HUMAN TO GET THE DROP ON US?!

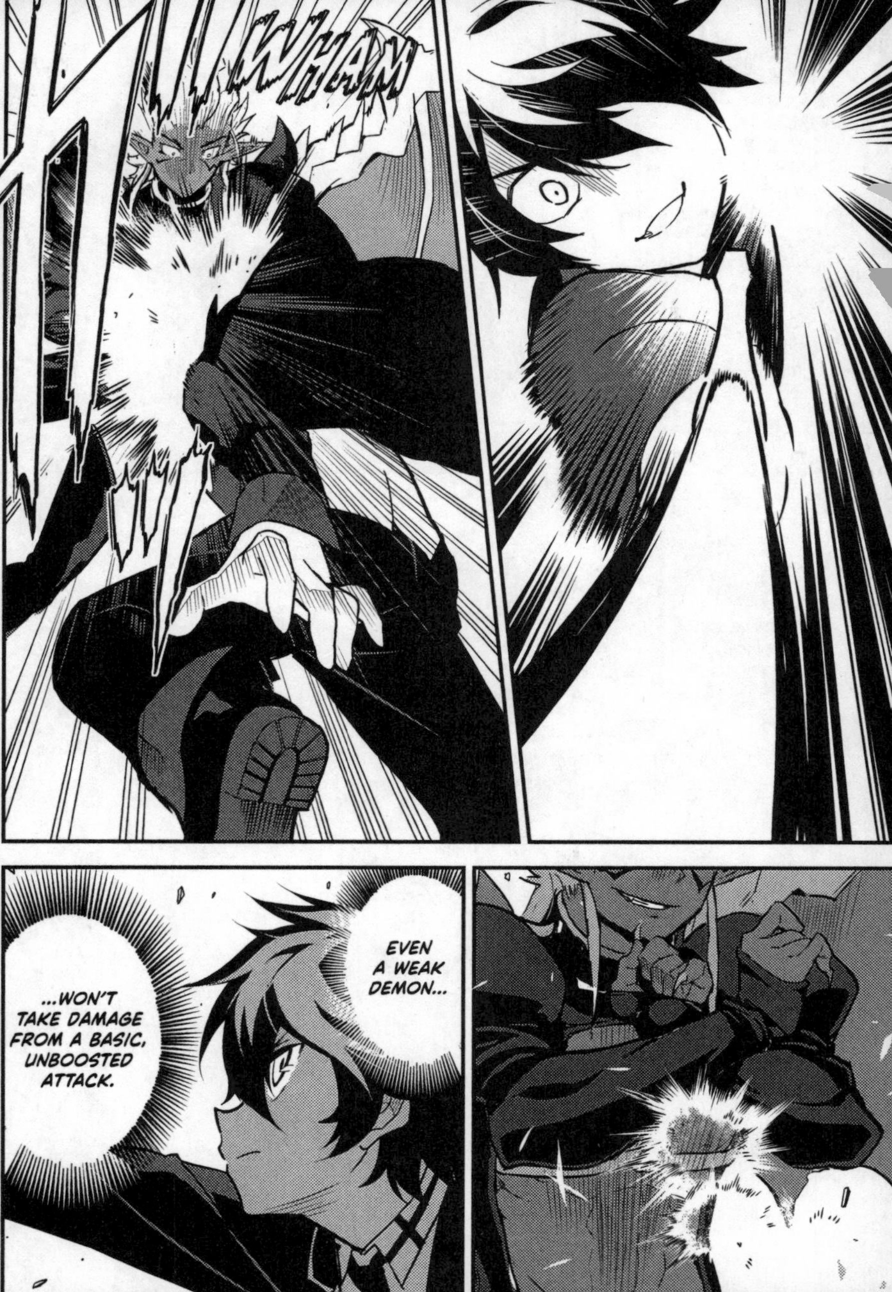
EVEN A WEAK DEMON...
...WON'T TAKE DAMAGE FROM A BASIC, UNBOOSTED ATTACK.

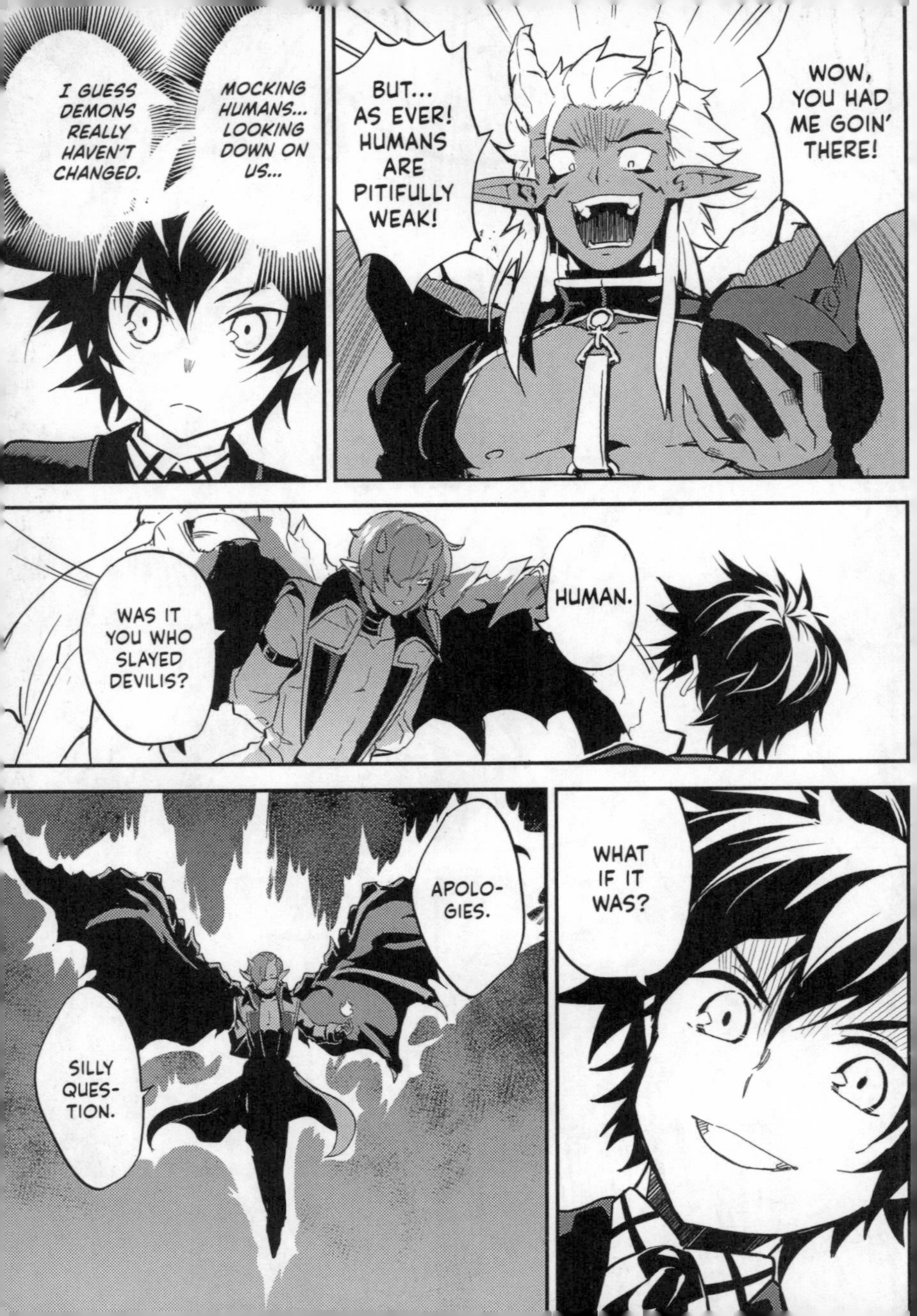
WOW, YOU HAD ME GOIN' THERE!
BUT... AS EVER! HUMANS ARE PITIFULLY WEAK!
MOCKING HUMANS... LOOKING DOWN ON US...
I GUESS DEMONS REALLY HAVEN'T CHANGED.
HUMAN.
WAS IT YOU WHO SLAYED DEVILIS?
WHAT IF IT WAS?
APOLOGIES.
SILLY QUESTION.

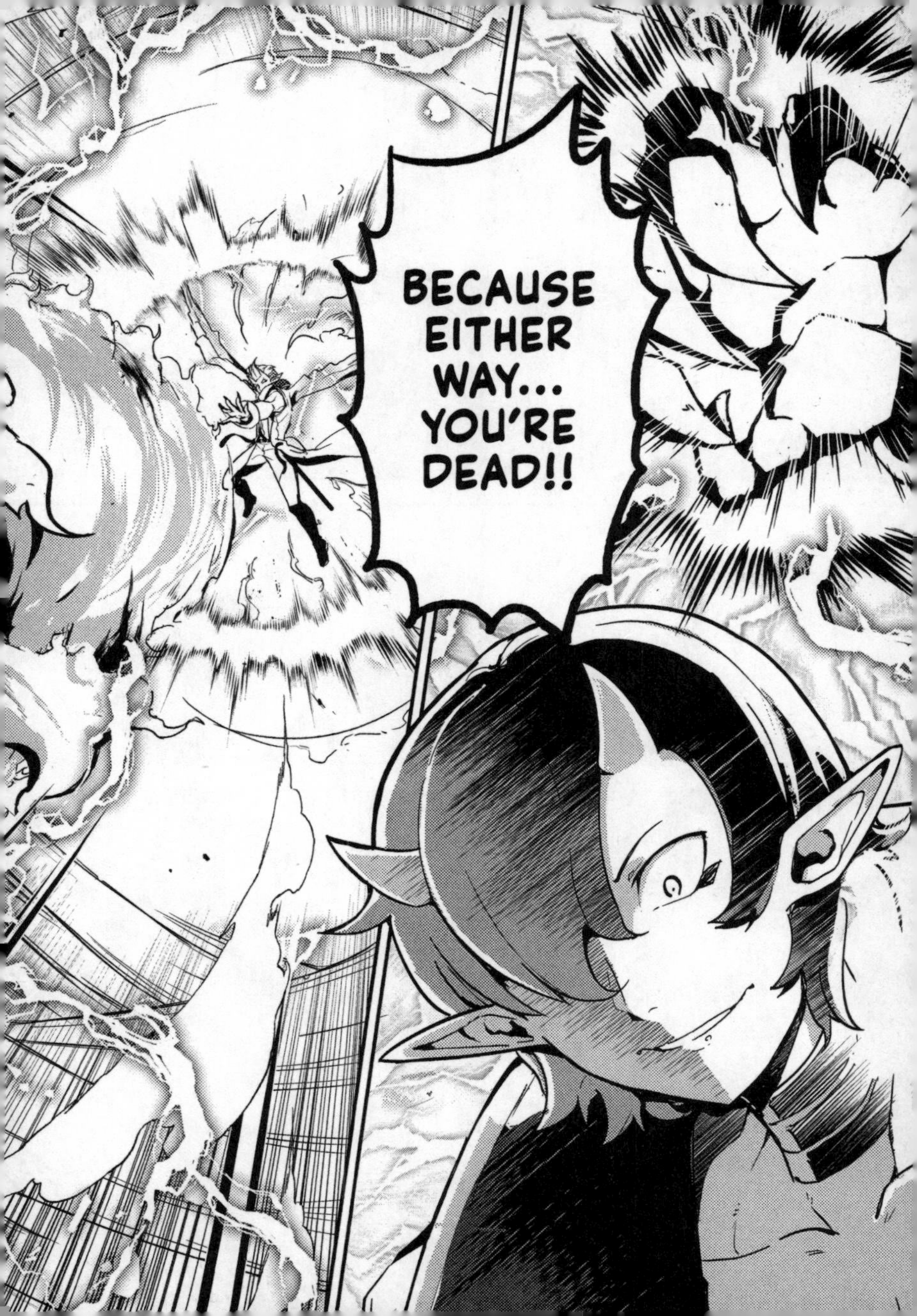
BECAUSE EITHER WAY... YOU'RE DEAD!!

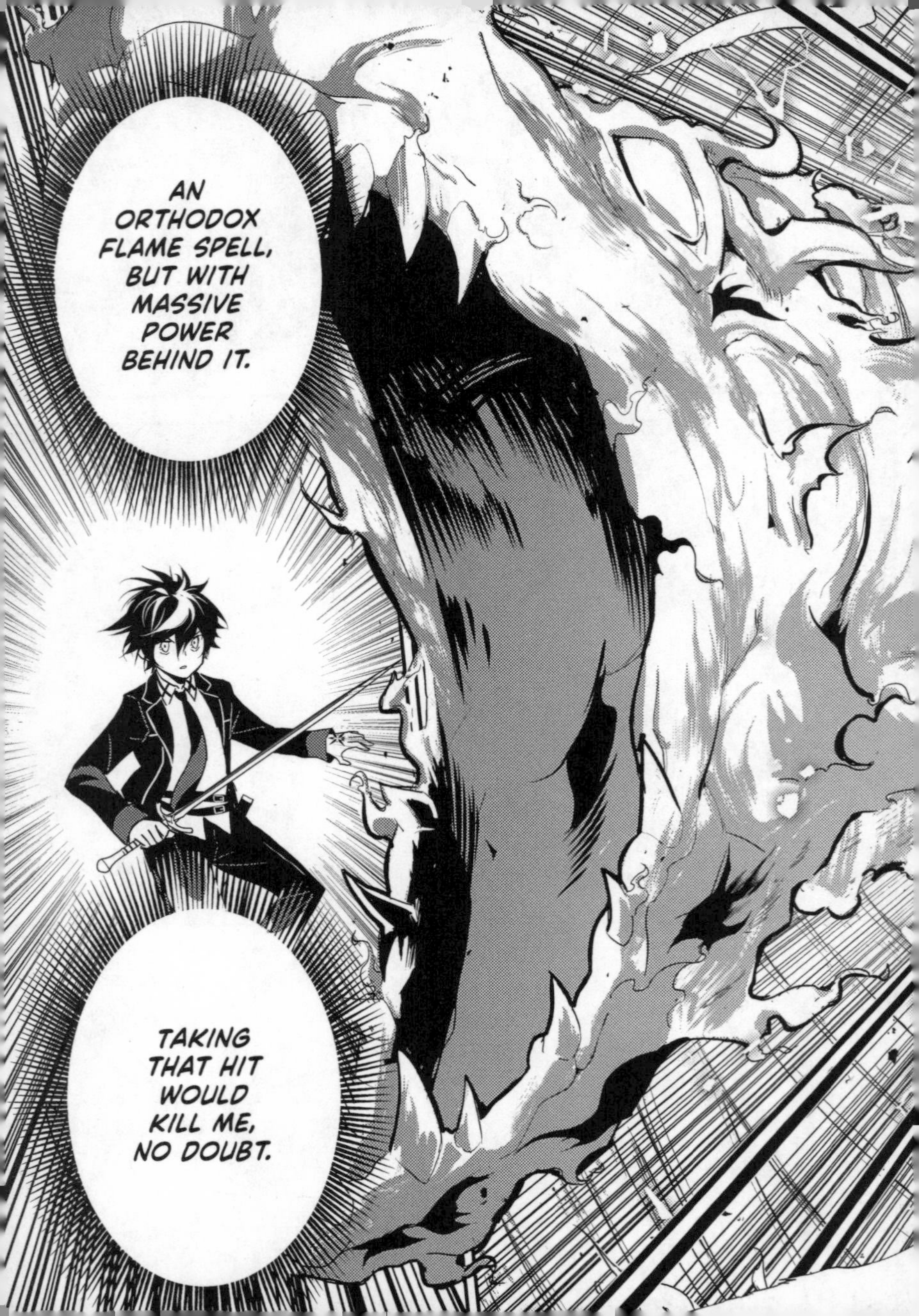
AN ORTHODOX FLAME SPELL, BUT WITH MASSIVE POWER BEHIND IT.
TAKING THAT HIT WOULD KILL ME, NO DOUBT.

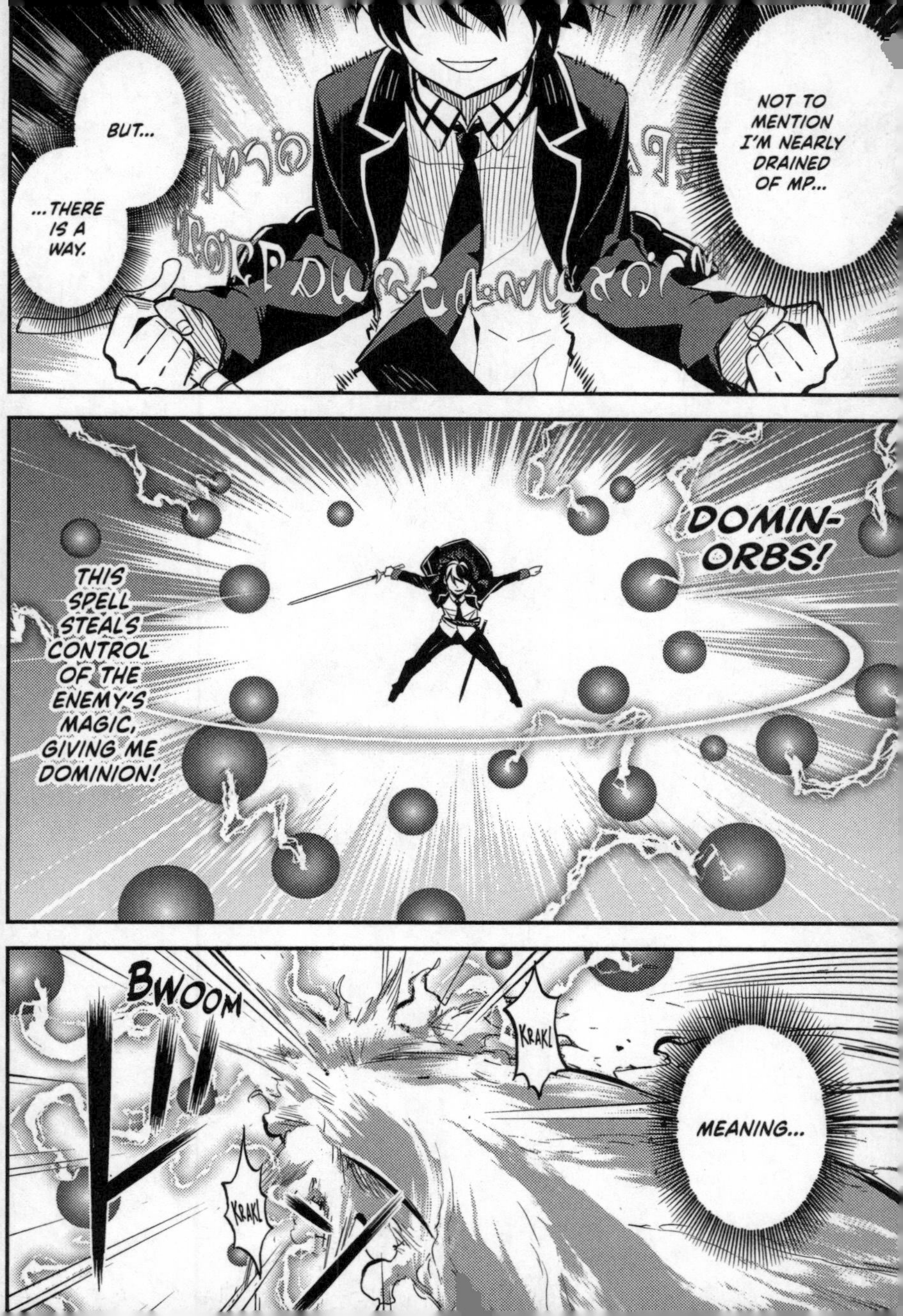
NOT TO MENTION I'M NEARLY DRAINED OF MP...
BUT...
...THERE IS A WAY.
DOMIN-ORBS!
THIS SPELL STEALS CONTROL OF THE ENEMY'S MAGIC, GIVING ME DOMINION!
MEANING...
KRAK!
BWOOM
KRAK!

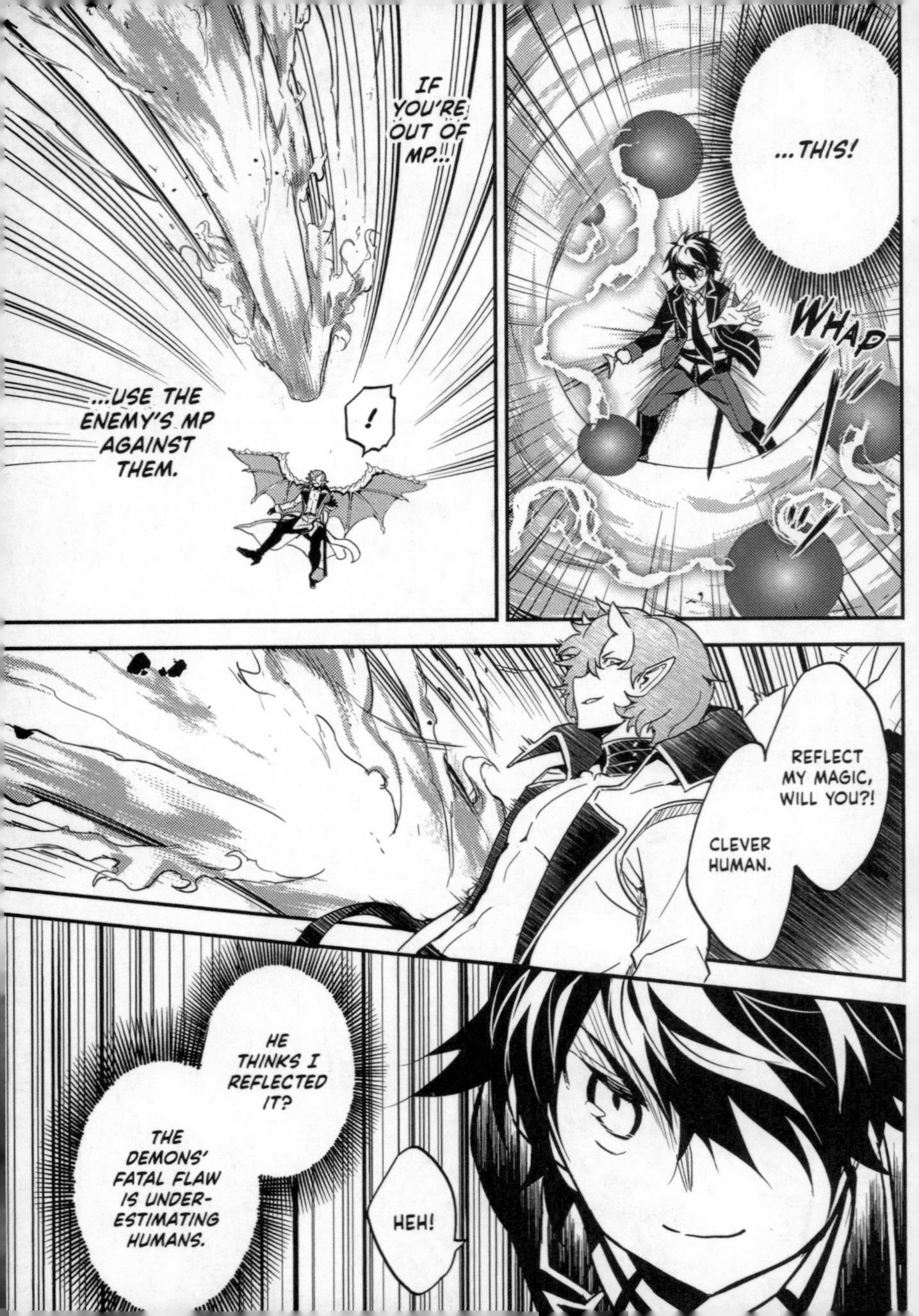
...THIS!
WHAP
IF YOU'RE OUT OF MP...!
...USE THE ENEMY'S MP AGAINST THEM.
!
REFLECT MY MAGIC, WILL YOU?!
CLEVER HUMAN.
HE THINKS I REFLECTED IT?
THE DEMONS' FATAL FLAW IS UNDER-ESTIMATING HUMANS.
HEH!

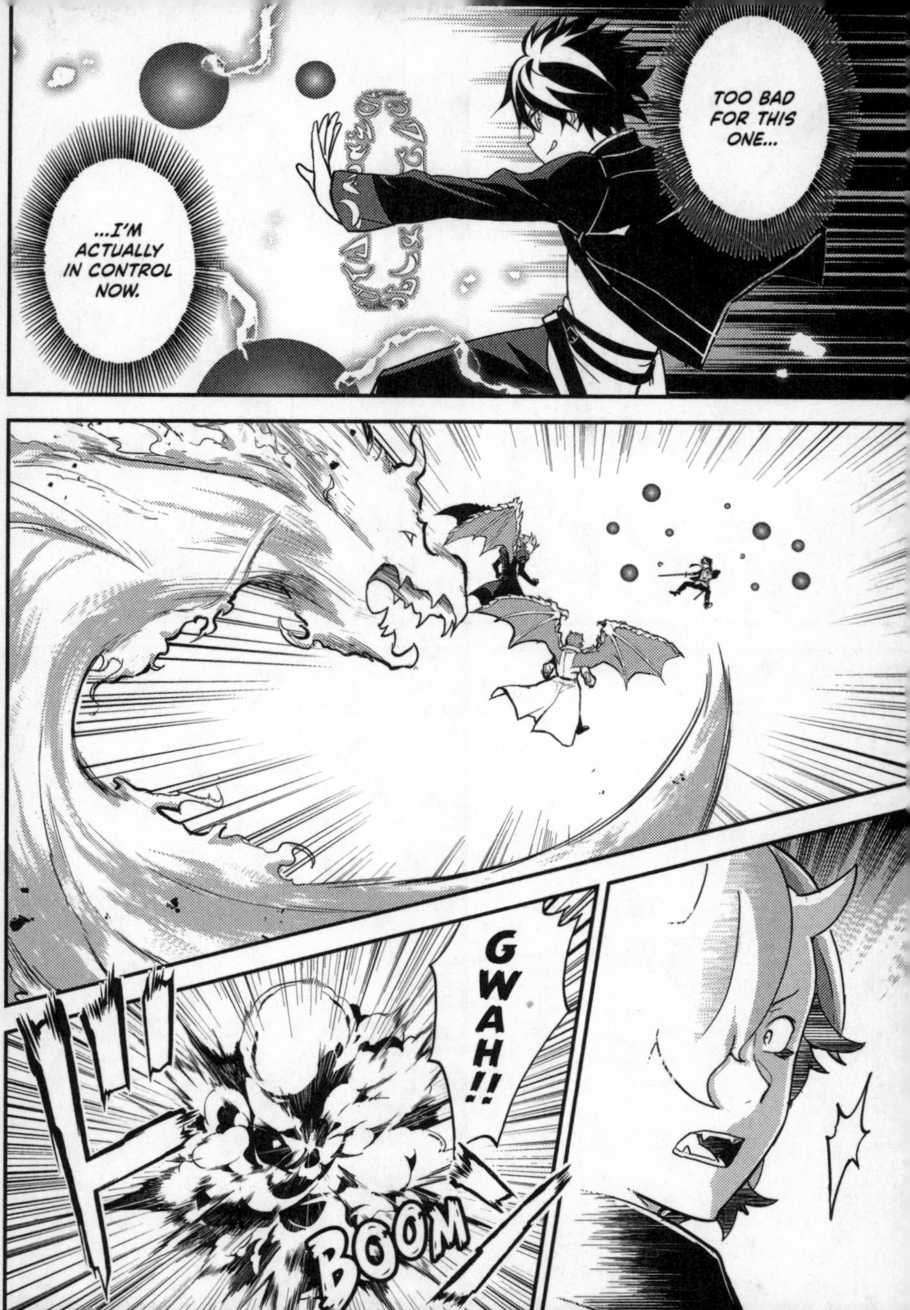
TOO BAD FOR THIS ONE...
...I'M ACTUALLY IN CONTROL NOW.
GWAH!!
BOOM

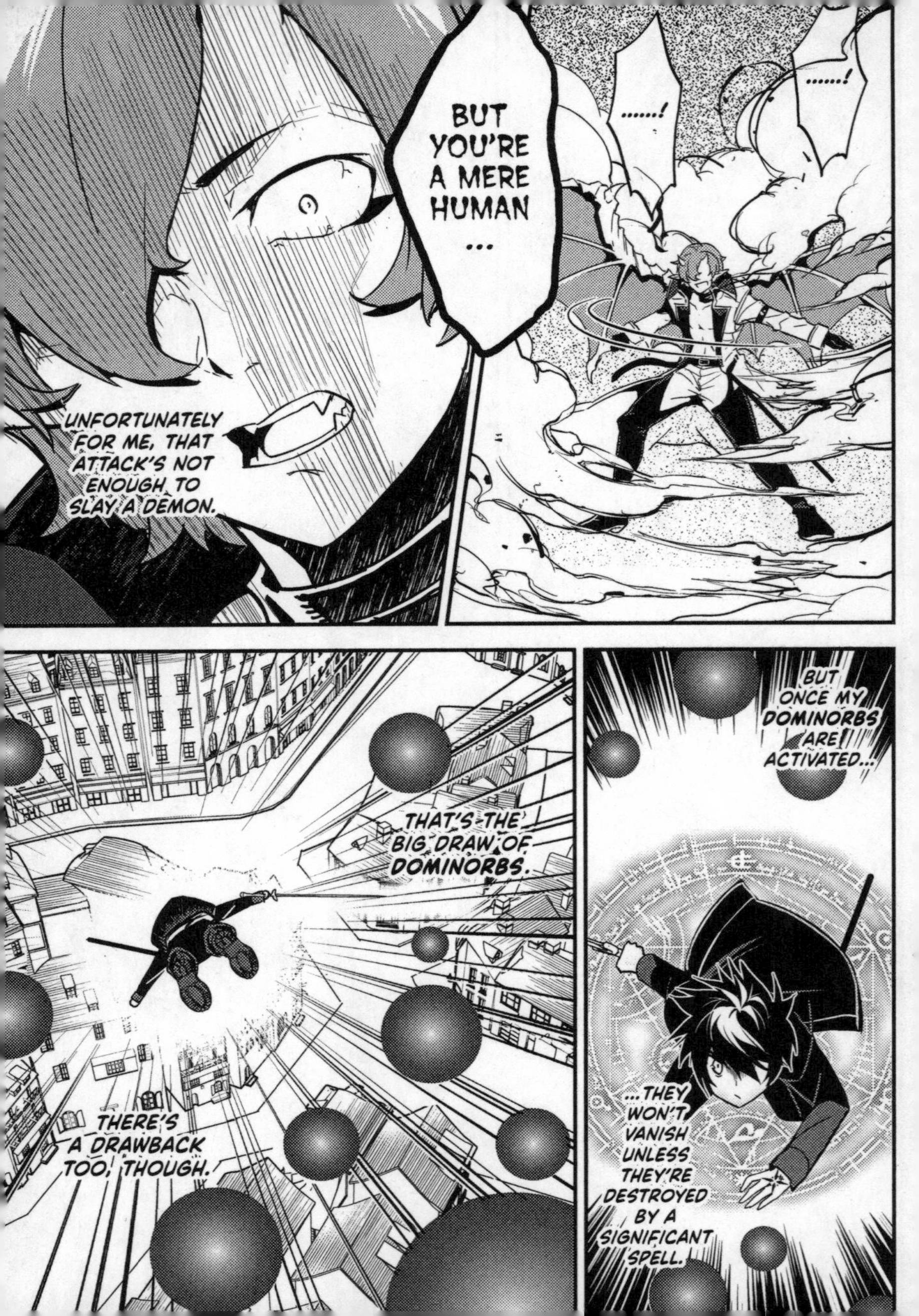
......!
......!
BUT YOU'RE A MERE HUMAN...
UNFORTUNATELY FOR ME, THAT ATTACK'S NOT ENOUGH TO SLAY A DEMON.
BUT ONCE MY DOMINORBS ARE ACTIVATED...
...THEY WON'T VANISH UNLESS THEY'RE DESTROYED BY A SIGNIFICANT SPELL.
THAT'S THE BIG DRAW OF DOMINORBS.
THERE'S A DRAWBACK TOO, THOUGH.

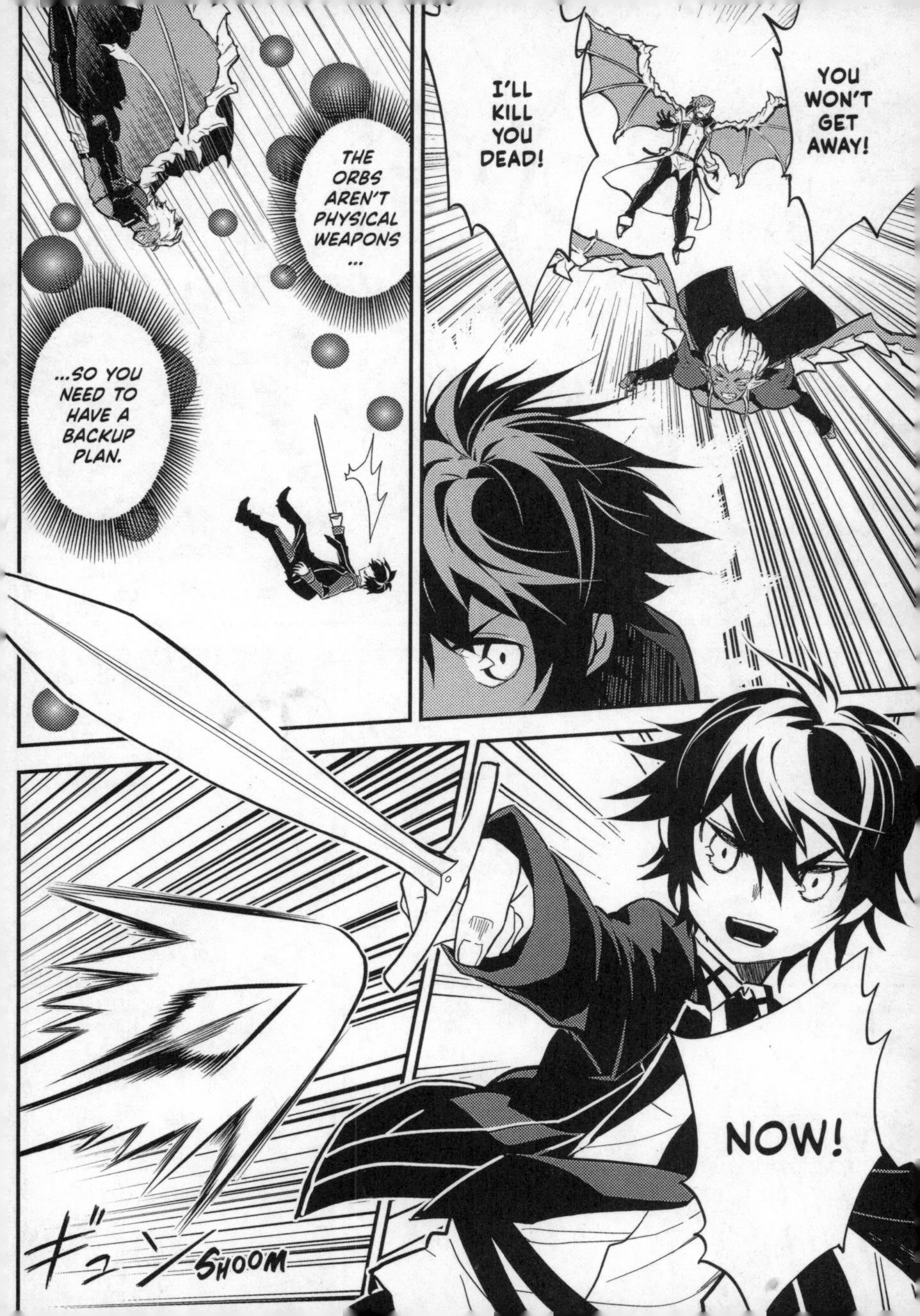
YOU WON'T GET AWAY!
I'LL KILL YOU DEAD!
THE ORBS AREN'T PHYSICAL WEAPONS...
...SO YOU NEED TO HAVE A BACKUP PLAN.
NOW!
ギュン
SHOOM

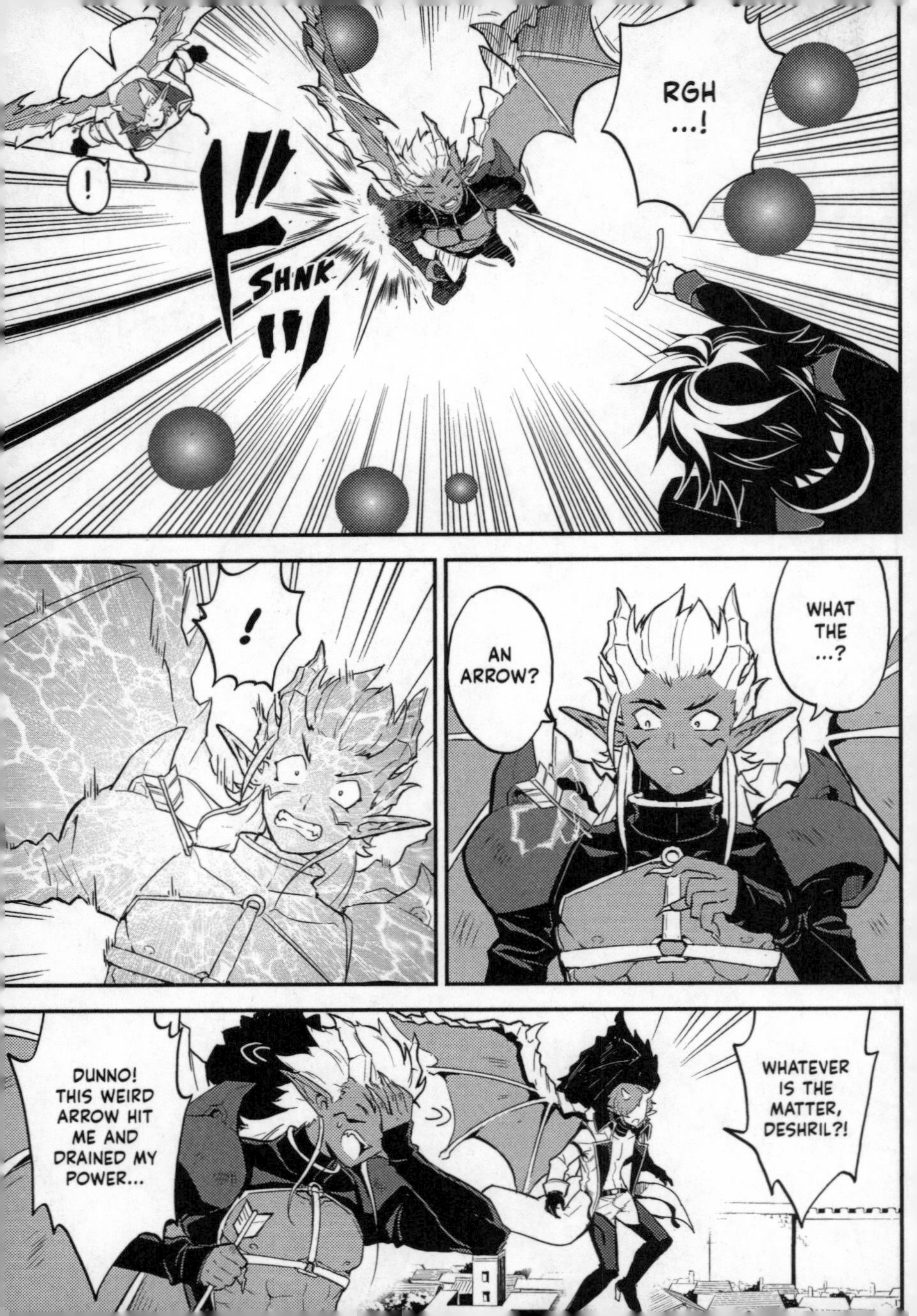
RGH ...!
ド
SHNK
!
WHAT THE ...?
AN ARROW?
!
WHATEVER IS THE MATTER, DESHRIL?!
DUNNO! THIS WEIRD ARROW HIT ME AND DRAINED MY POWER...

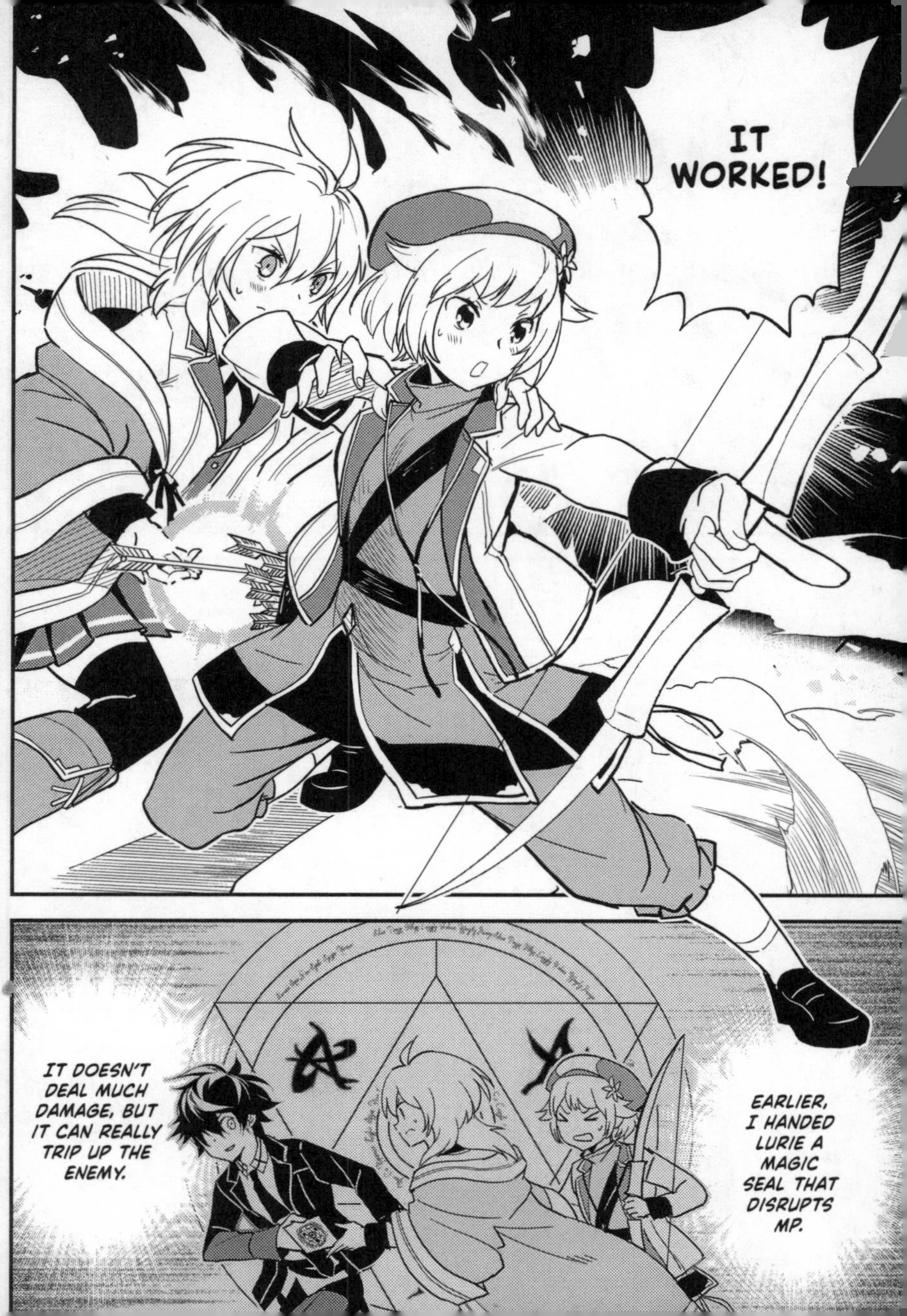
IT WORKED!
EARLIER, I HANDED LURIE A MAGIC SEAL THAT DISRUPTS MP.
IT DOESN'T DEAL MUCH DAMAGE, BUT IT CAN REALLY TRIP UP THE ENEMY.

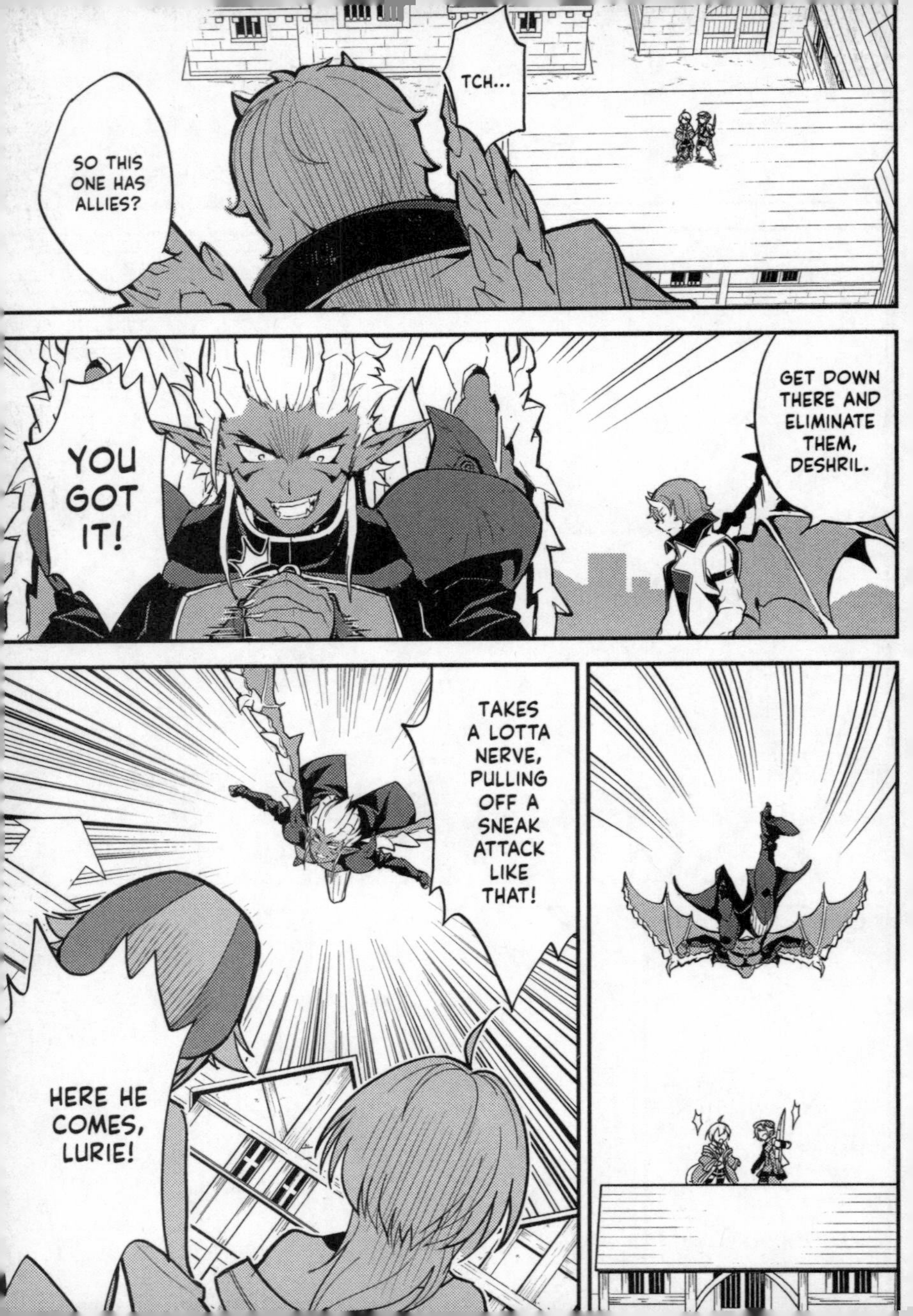
TCH...
SO THIS ONE HAS ALLIES?
GET DOWN THERE AND ELIMINATE THEM, DESHRIL.
YOU GOT IT!
TAKES A LOTTA NERVE, PULLING OFF A SNEAK ATTACK LIKE THAT!
HERE HE COMES, LURIE!

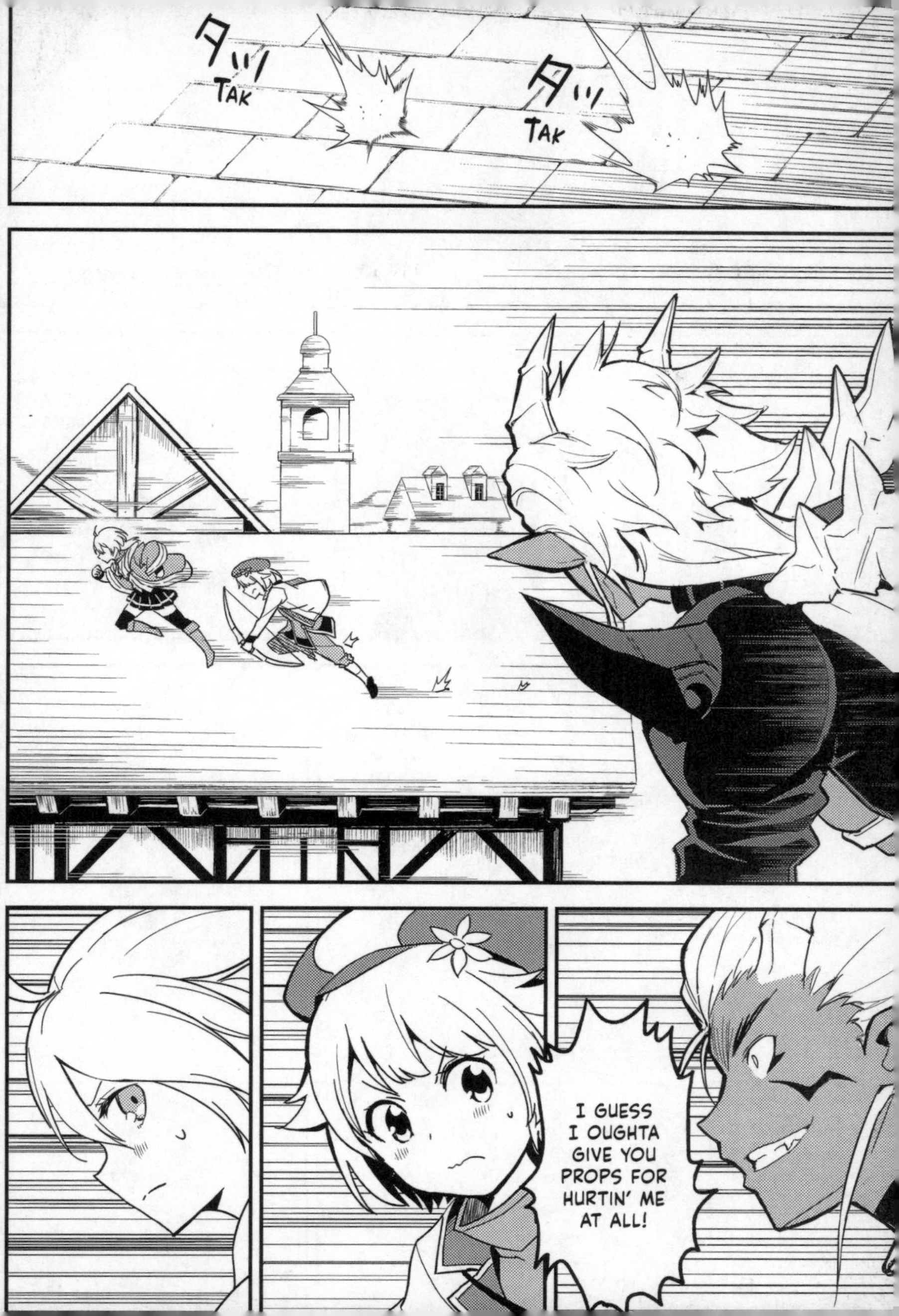
タッ
TAK
タッ
TAK
I GUESS I OUGHTA GIVE YOU PROPS FOR HURTIN' ME AT ALL!

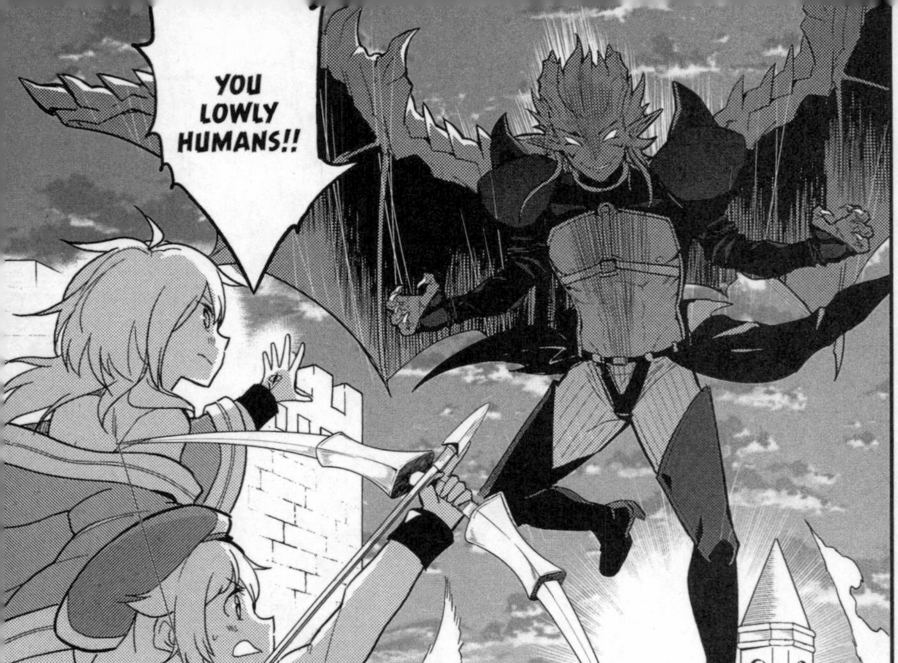
YOU LOWLY HUMANS!!

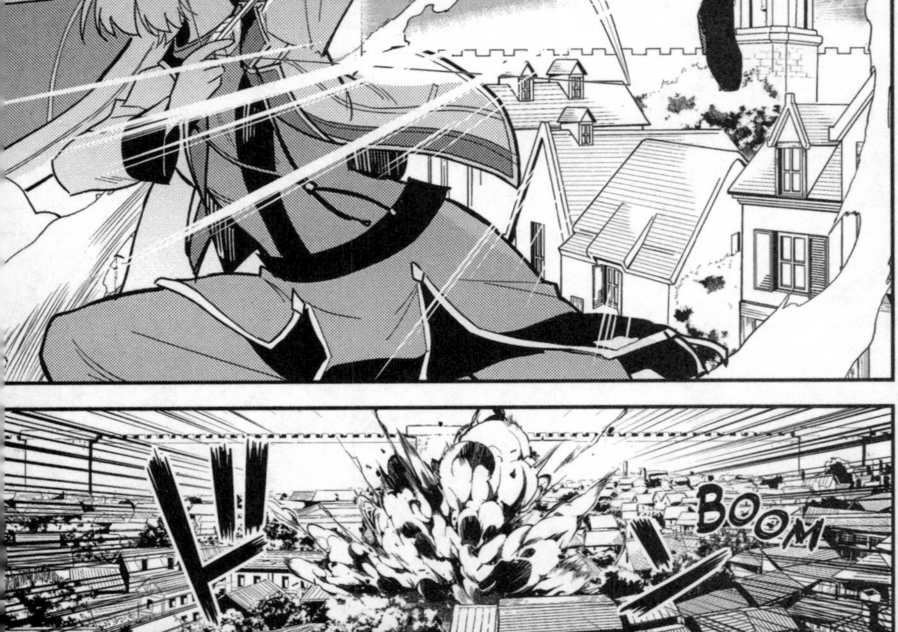
BOOM

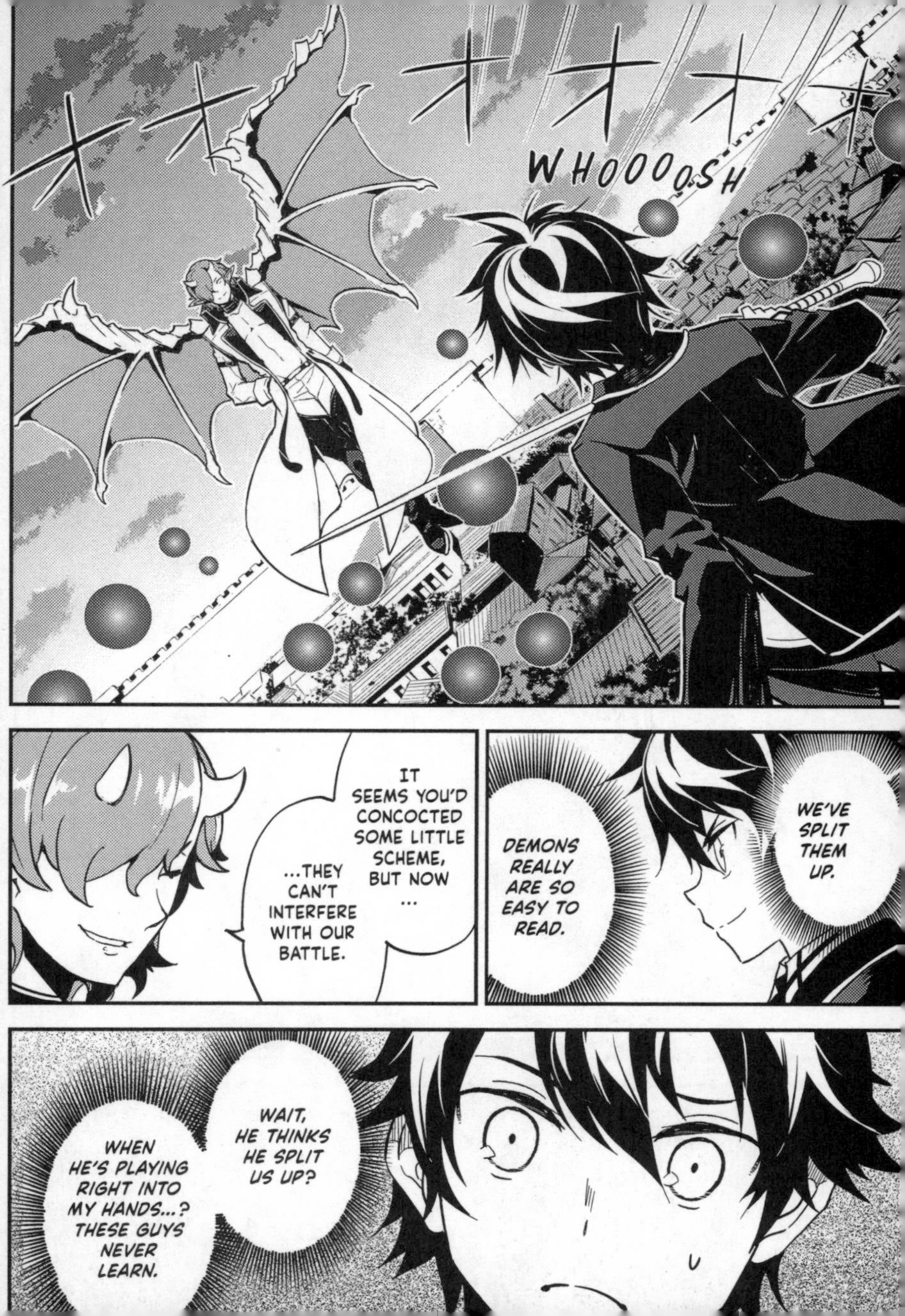
WHOOOOSH
WE'VE SPLIT THEM UP.
DEMONS REALLY ARE SO EASY TO READ.
IT SEEMS YOU'D CONCOCTED SOME LITTLE SCHEME, BUT NOW ...
...THEY CAN'T INTERFERE WITH OUR BATTLE.
WAIT, HE THINKS HE SPLIT US UP?
WHEN HE'S PLAYING RIGHT INTO MY HANDS...? THESE GUYS NEVER LEARN.

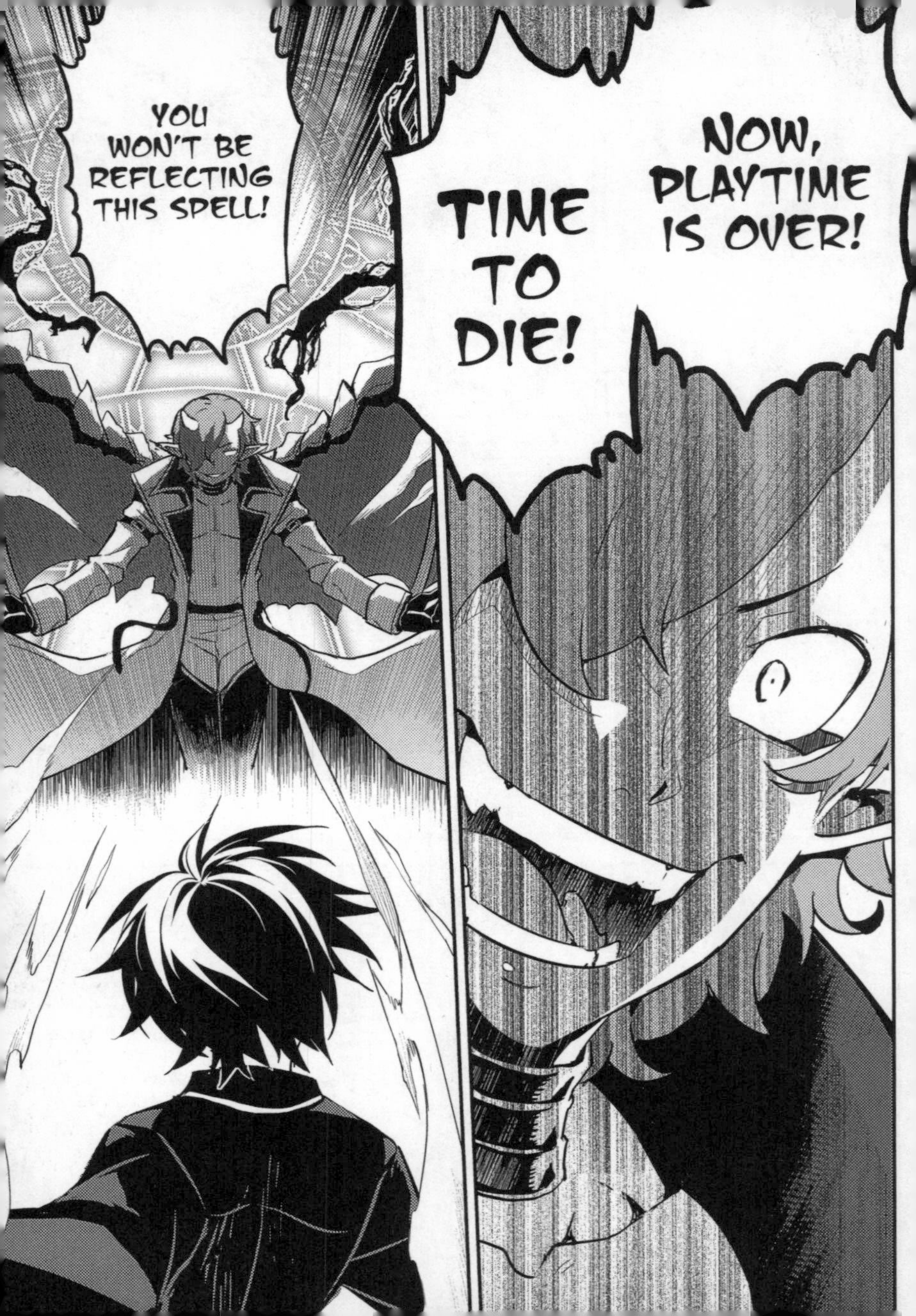
NOW, PLAYTIME IS OVER!
TIME TO DIE!
YOU WON'T BE REFLECTING THIS SPELL!

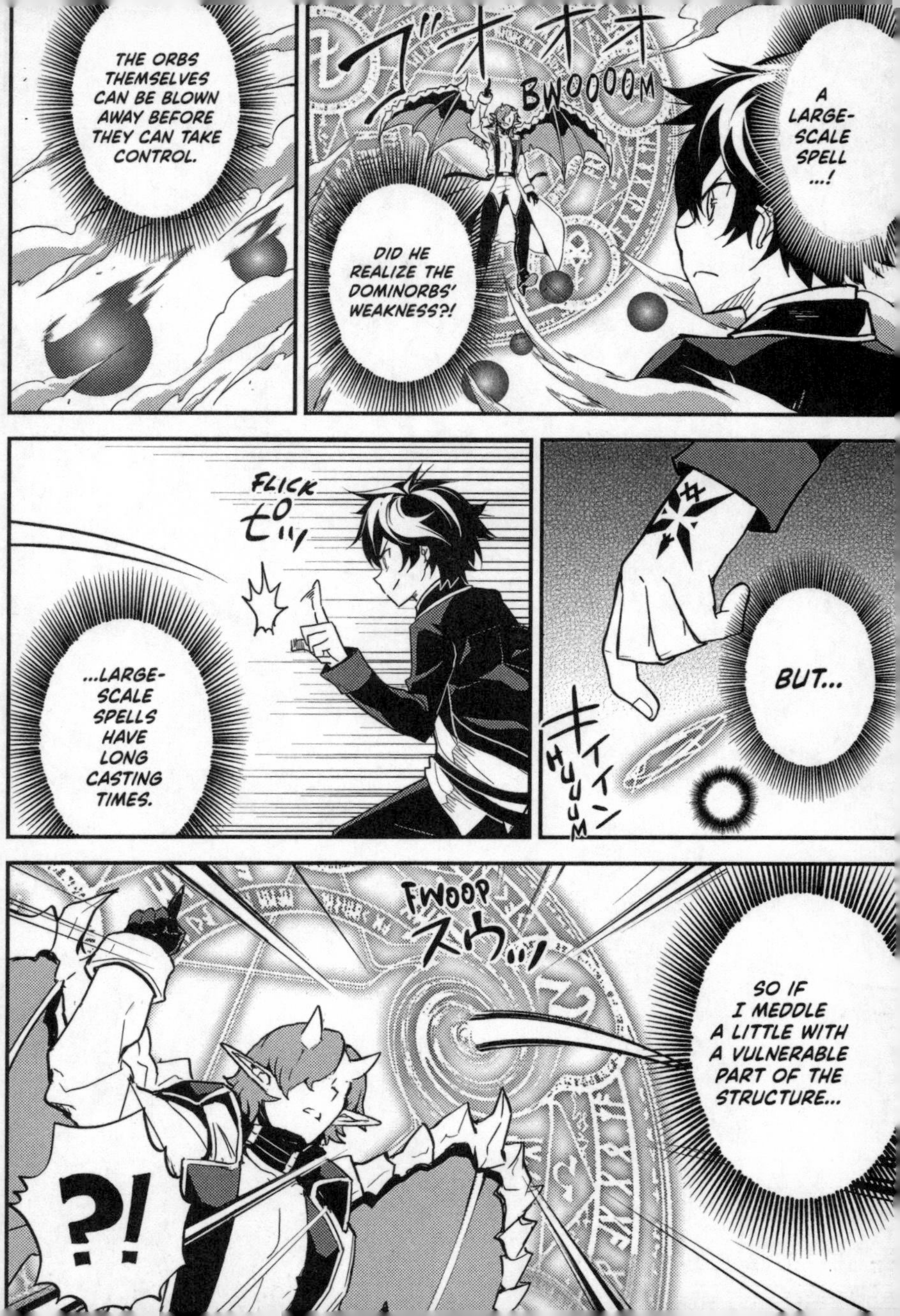
A LARGE-SCALE SPELL ...!
BWOOOOM
DID HE REALIZE THE DOMINORBS' WEAKNESS?!
THE ORBS THEMSELVES CAN BE BLOWN AWAY BEFORE THEY CAN TAKE CONTROL.
HUUUUM
キイイン
BUT...
FLICK
ピッ
...LARGE-SCALE SPELLS HAVE LONG CASTING TIMES.
FWOOP
スゥッ
SO IF I MEDDLE A LITTLE WITH A VULNERABLE PART OF THE STRUCTURE...
?!

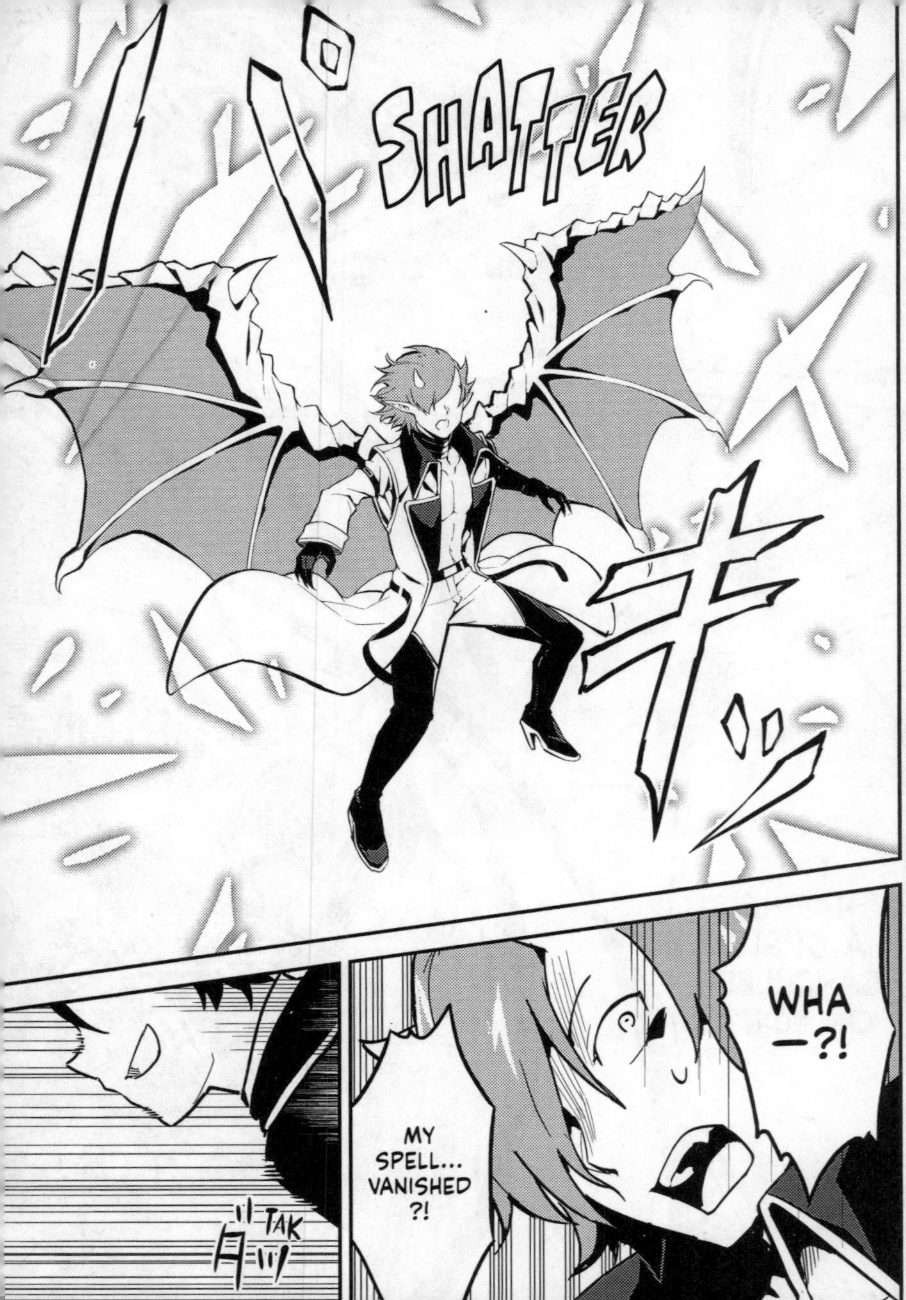
SHATTER
WHA—?!
MY SPELL... VANISHED?!
TAK

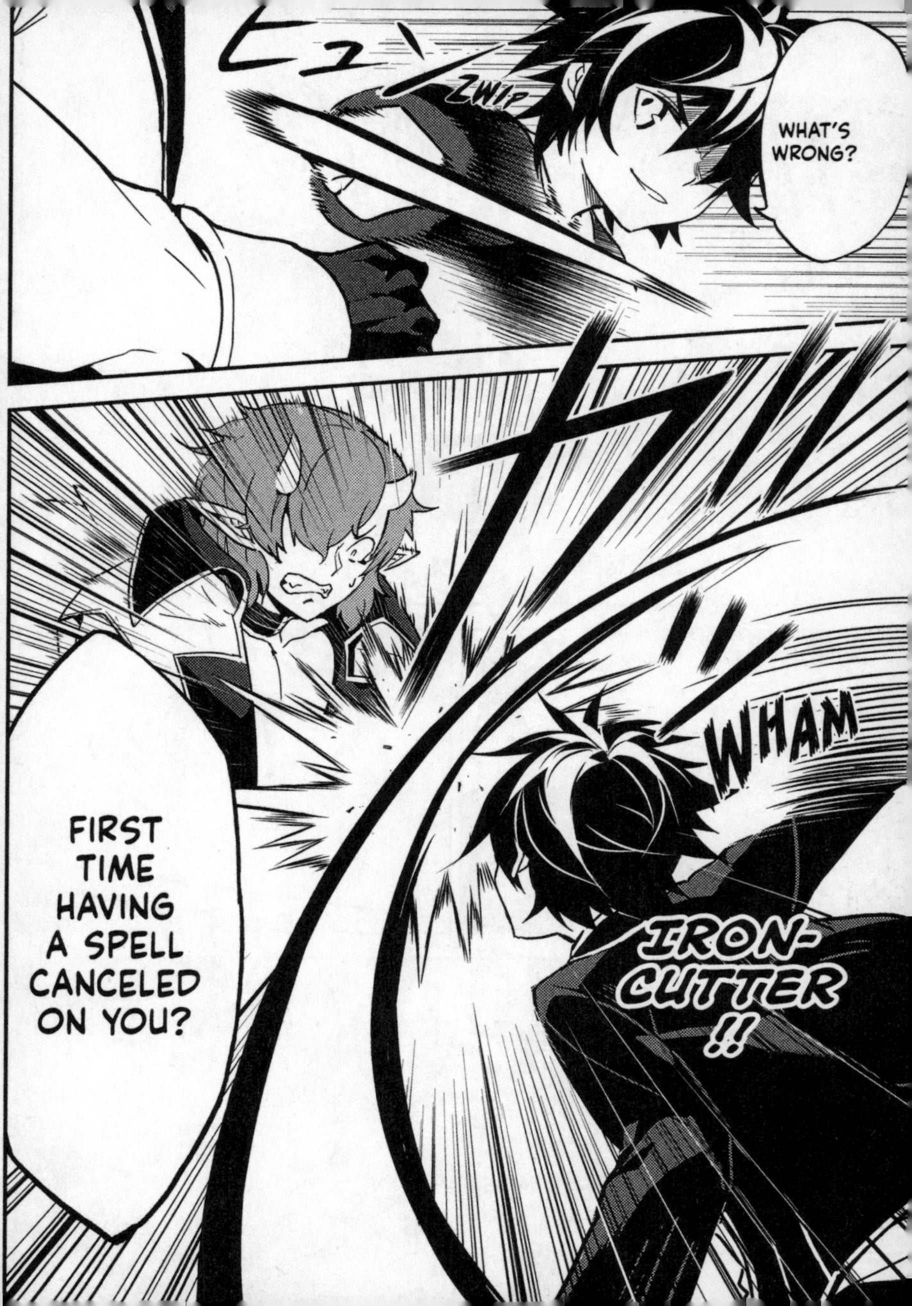

ヒュ
ZWIP
WHAT'S WRONG?
WHAM
IRON-CUTTER!!
FIRST TIME HAVING A SPELL CANCELED ON YOU?

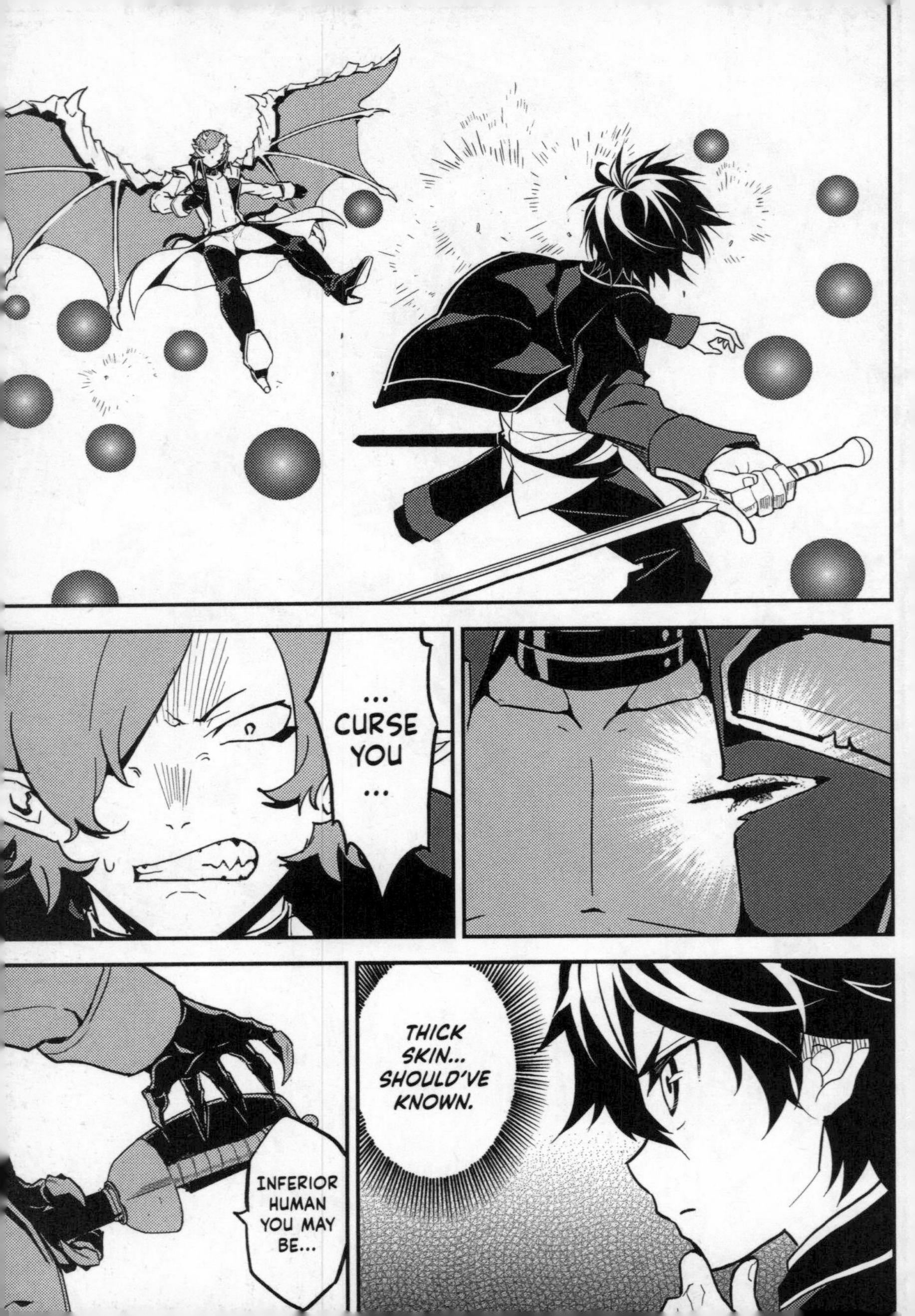
...CURSE YOU...
THICK SKIN... SHOULD'VE KNOWN.
INFERIOR HUMAN YOU MAY BE...

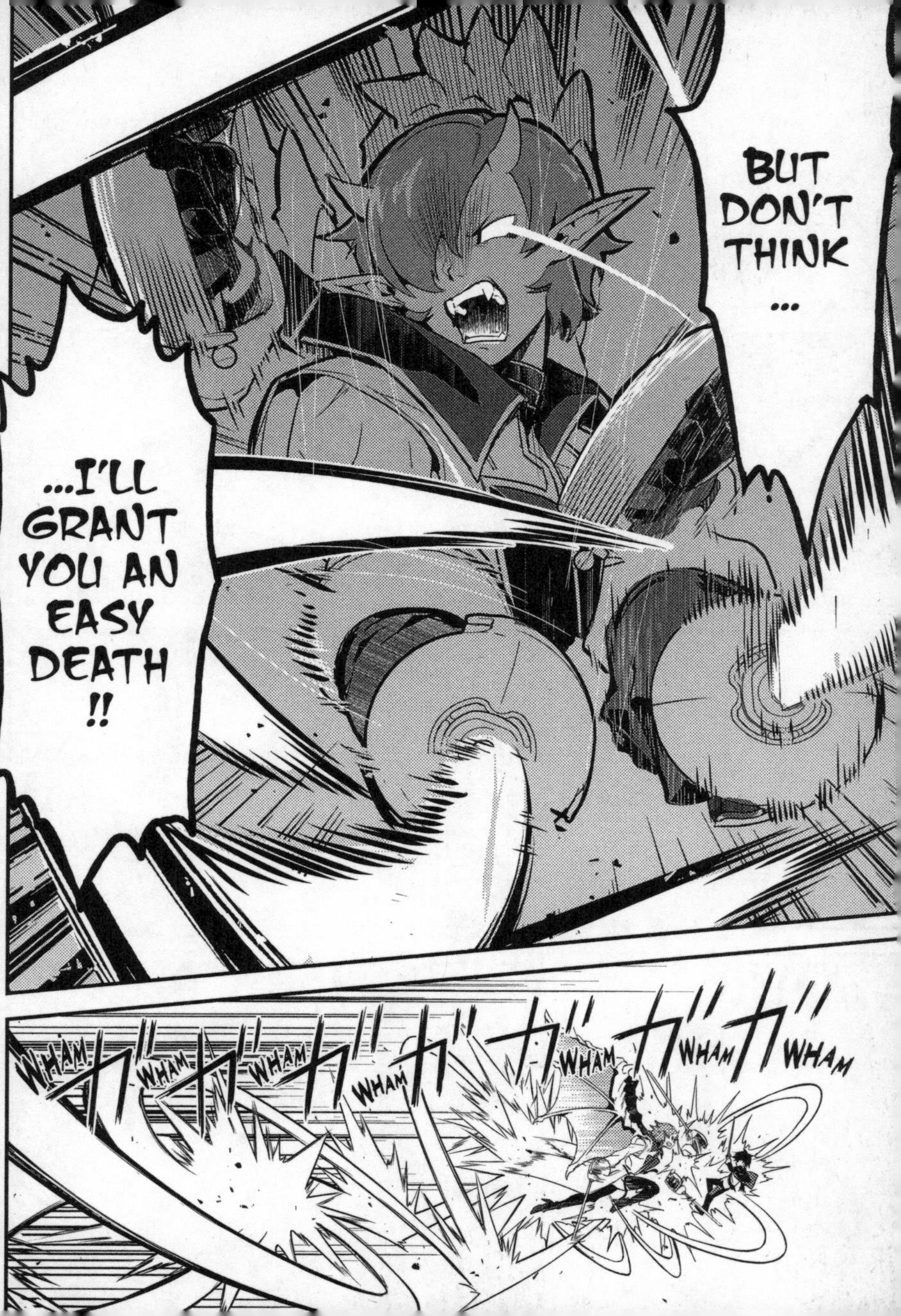
BUT DON'T THINK ...
...I'LL GRANT YOU AN EASY DEATH !!
WHAM
ガ
WHAM
ガ
WHAM
ガ
WHAM
ガ
WHAM
ガ
WHAM
ガ
WHAM

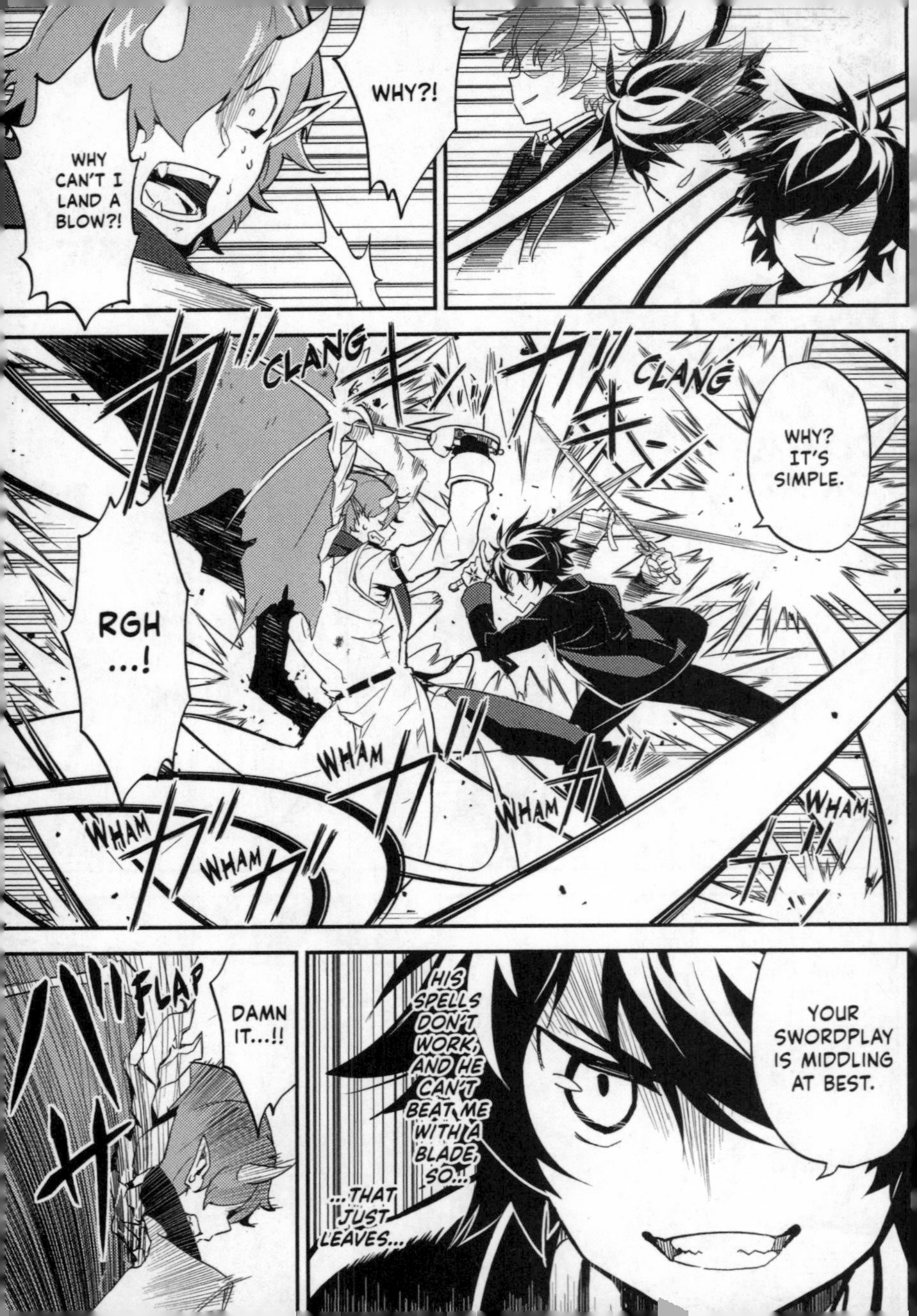
WHY?!
WHY CAN'T I LAND A BLOW?!
WHY? IT'S SIMPLE.
CLANG
CLANG
RGH ...!
WHAM
WHAM
WHAM
WHAM
WHAM
YOUR SWORDPLAY IS MIDDLING AT BEST.
HIS SPELLS DON'T WORK, AND HE CAN'T BEAT ME WITH A BLADE, SO...
...THAT JUST LEAVES...
DAMN IT...!!
FLAP

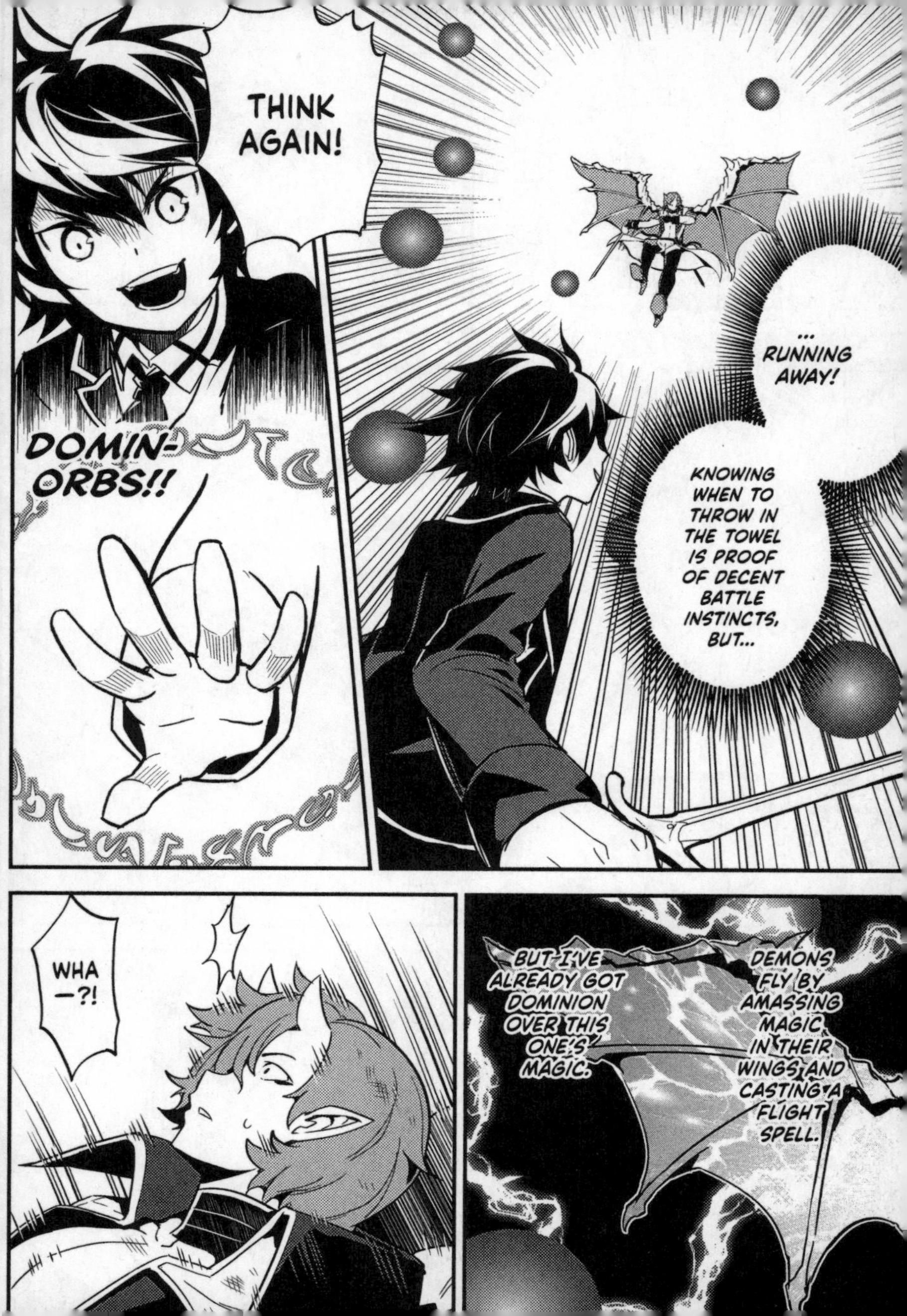
... RUNNING AWAY!
KNOWING WHEN TO THROW IN THE TOWEL IS PROOF OF DECENT BATTLE INSTINCTS, BUT...
THINK AGAIN!
DOMIN-ORBS!!
DEMONS FLY BY AMASSING MAGIC IN THEIR WINGS AND CASTING A FLIGHT SPELL.
BUT I'VE ALREADY GOT DOMINION OVER THIS ONE'S MAGIC.
WHA—?!

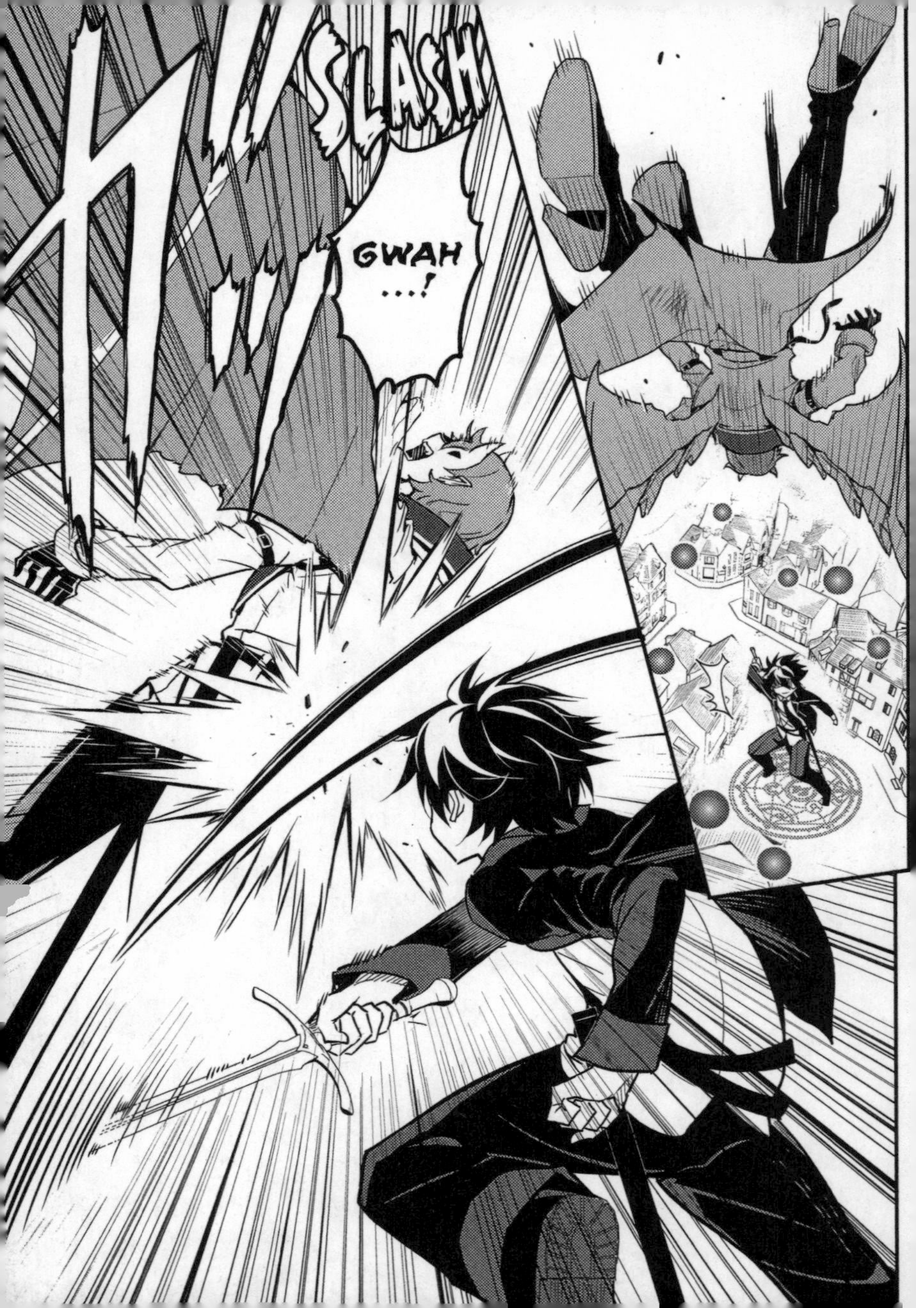
SLASH
GWAH ...!

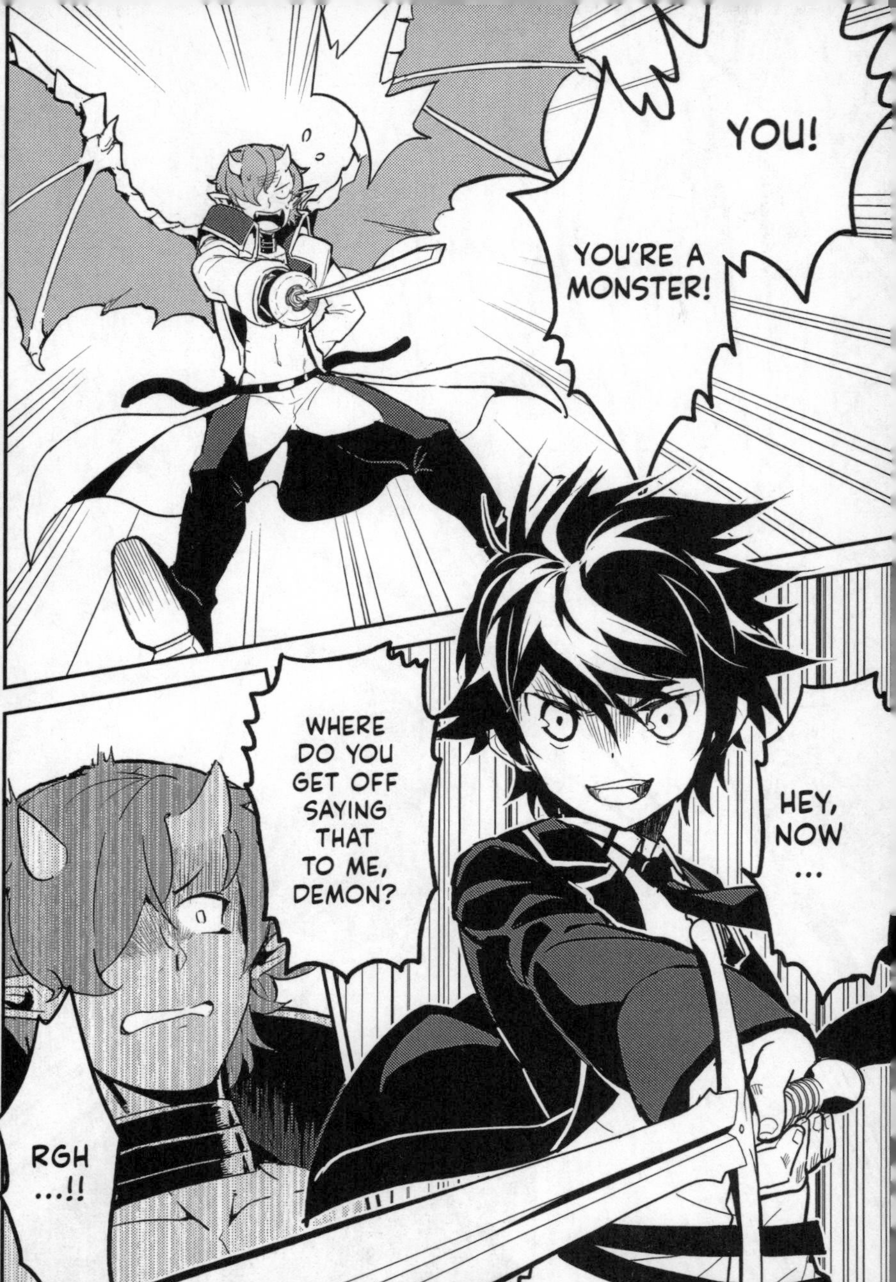
YOU!
YOU'RE A MONSTER!
HEY, NOW ...
WHERE DO YOU GET OFF SAYING THAT TO ME, DEMON?
RGH ...!!

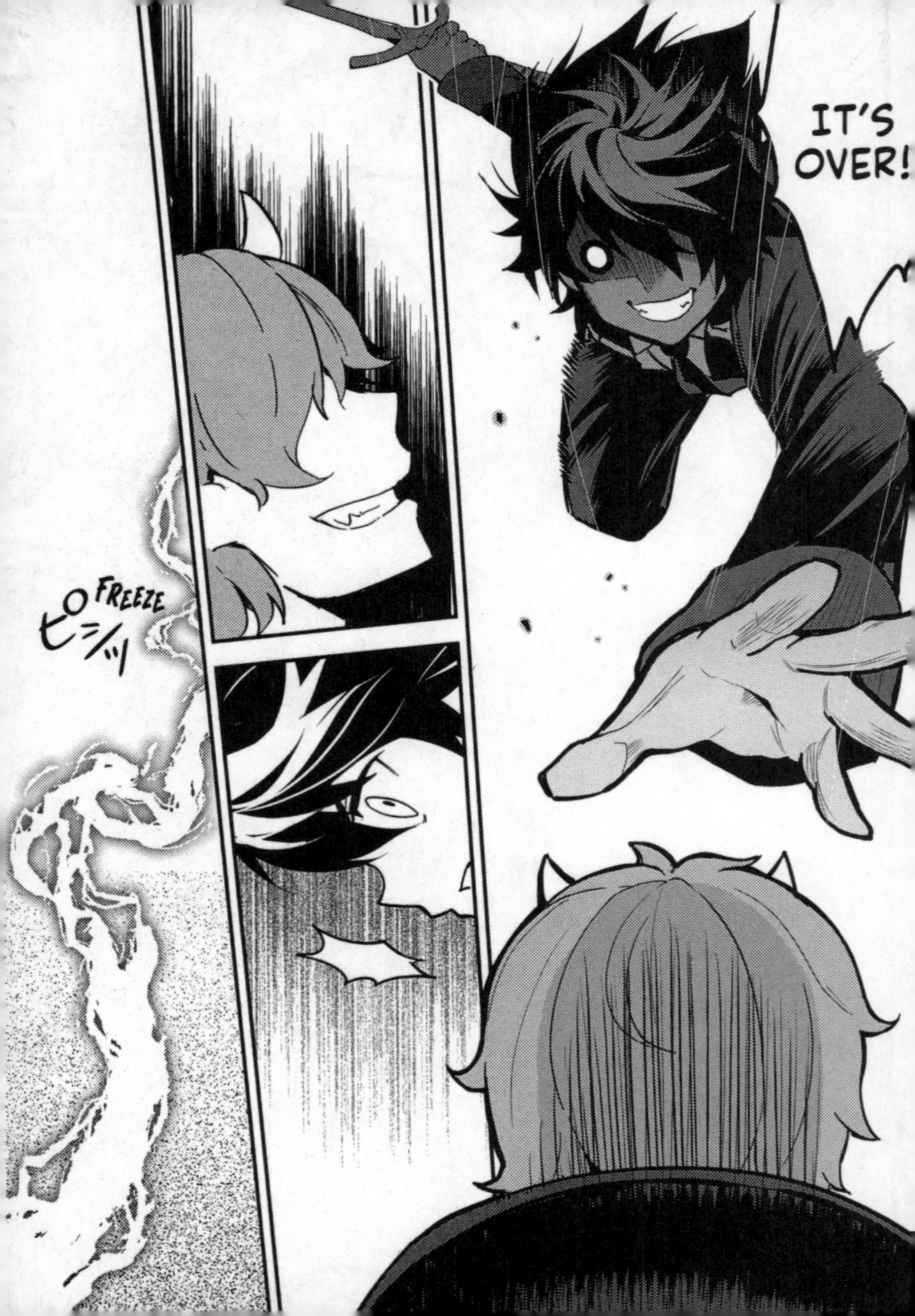
IT'S OVER!
FREEZE
ピシッ

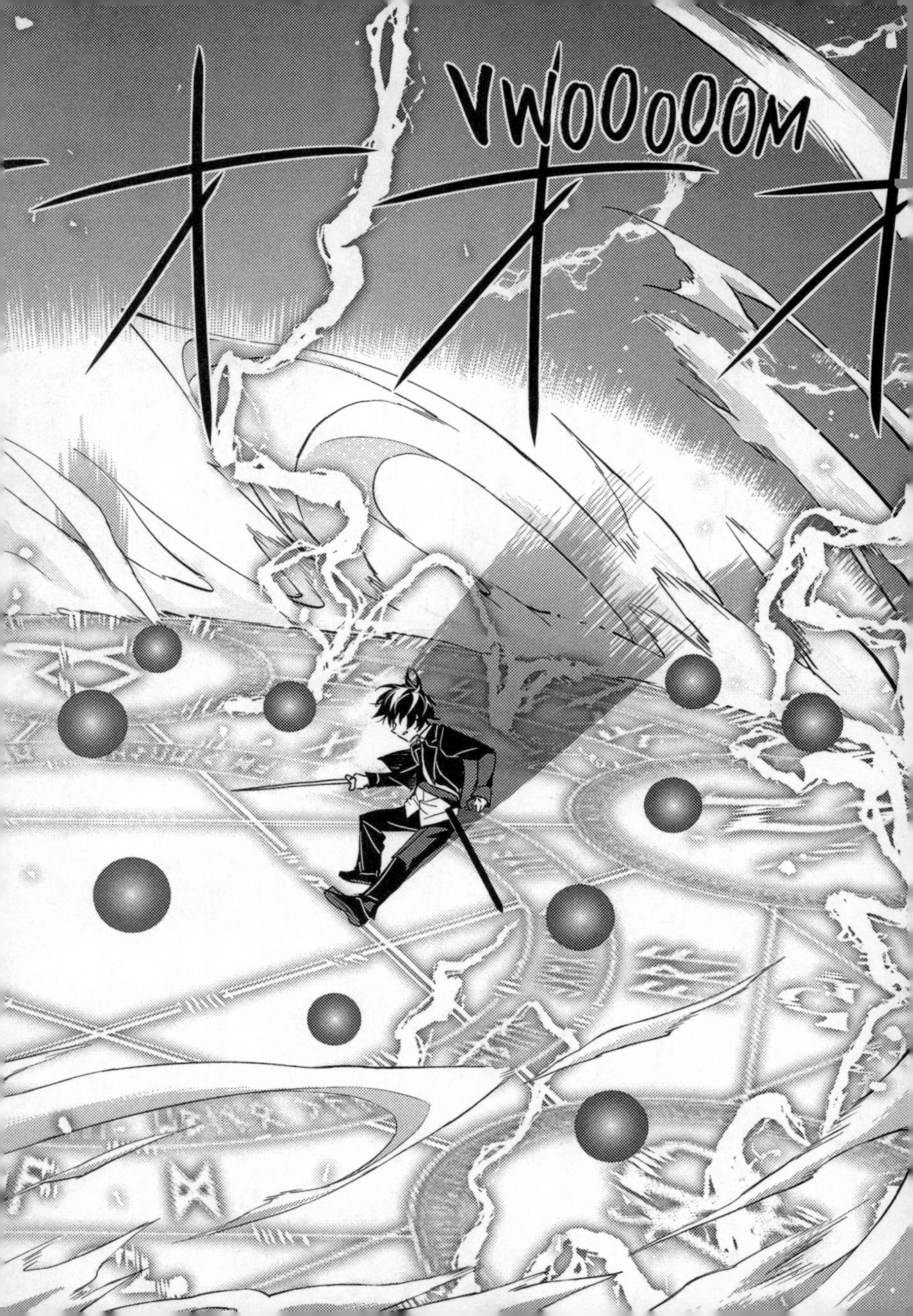
VWOOOOOOM
オオオオ

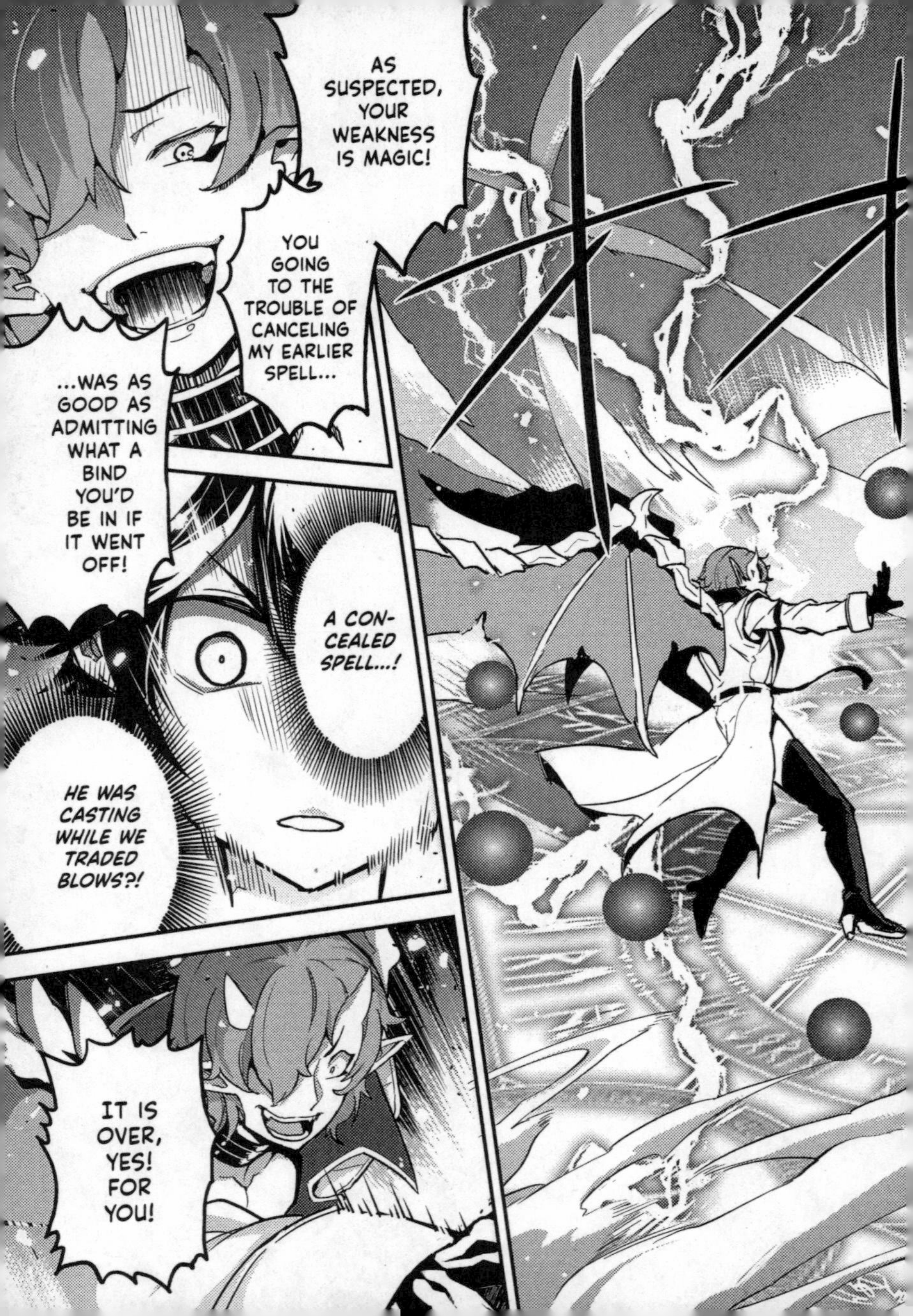
AS SUSPECTED, YOUR WEAKNESS IS MAGIC!
YOU GOING TO THE TROUBLE OF CANCELING MY EARLIER SPELL...
...WAS AS GOOD AS ADMITTING WHAT A BIND YOU'D BE IN IF IT WENT OFF!
A CON-CEALED SPELL...!
HE WAS CASTING WHILE WE TRADED BLOWS?!
IT IS OVER, YES! FOR YOU!

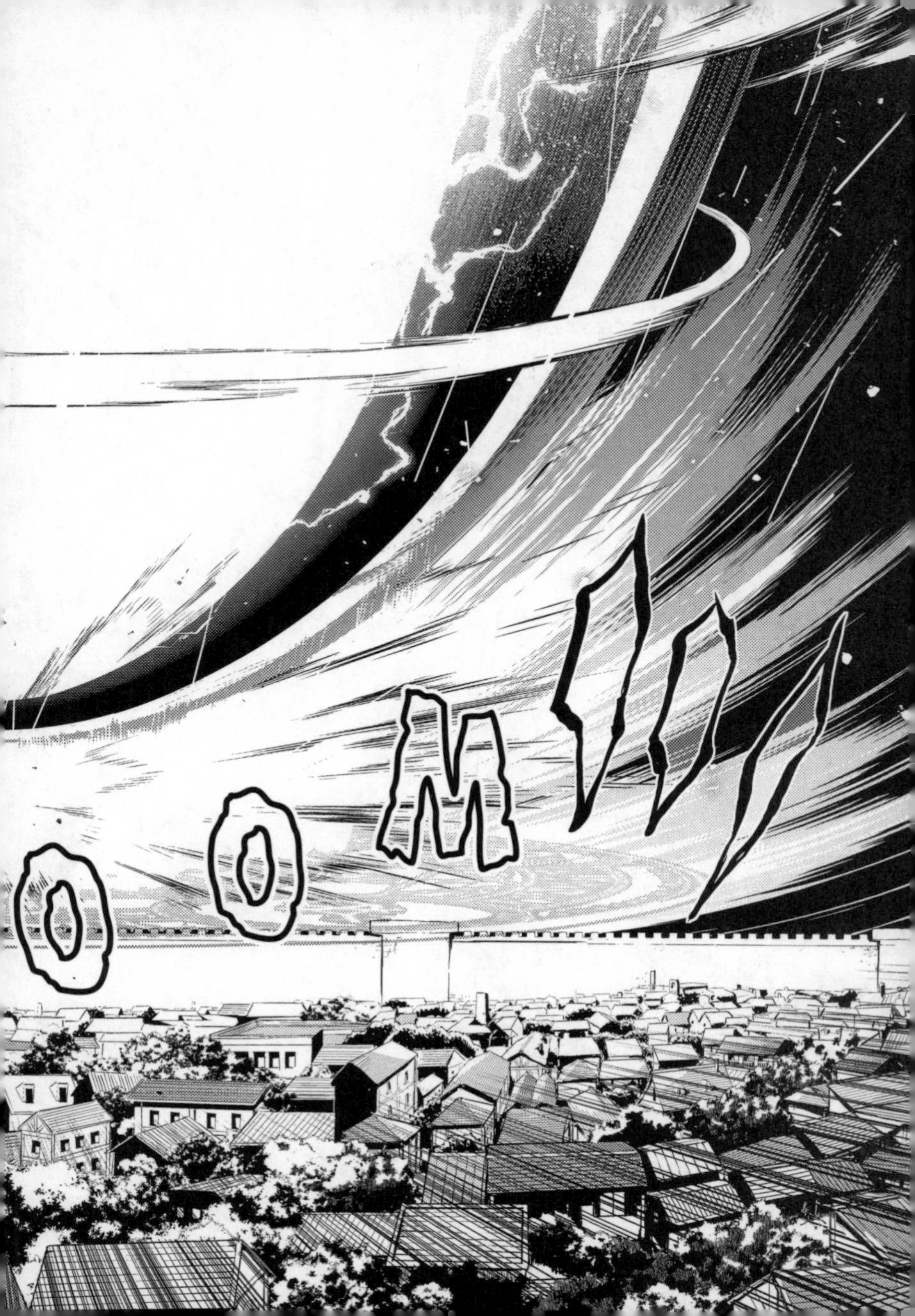
OOMWV

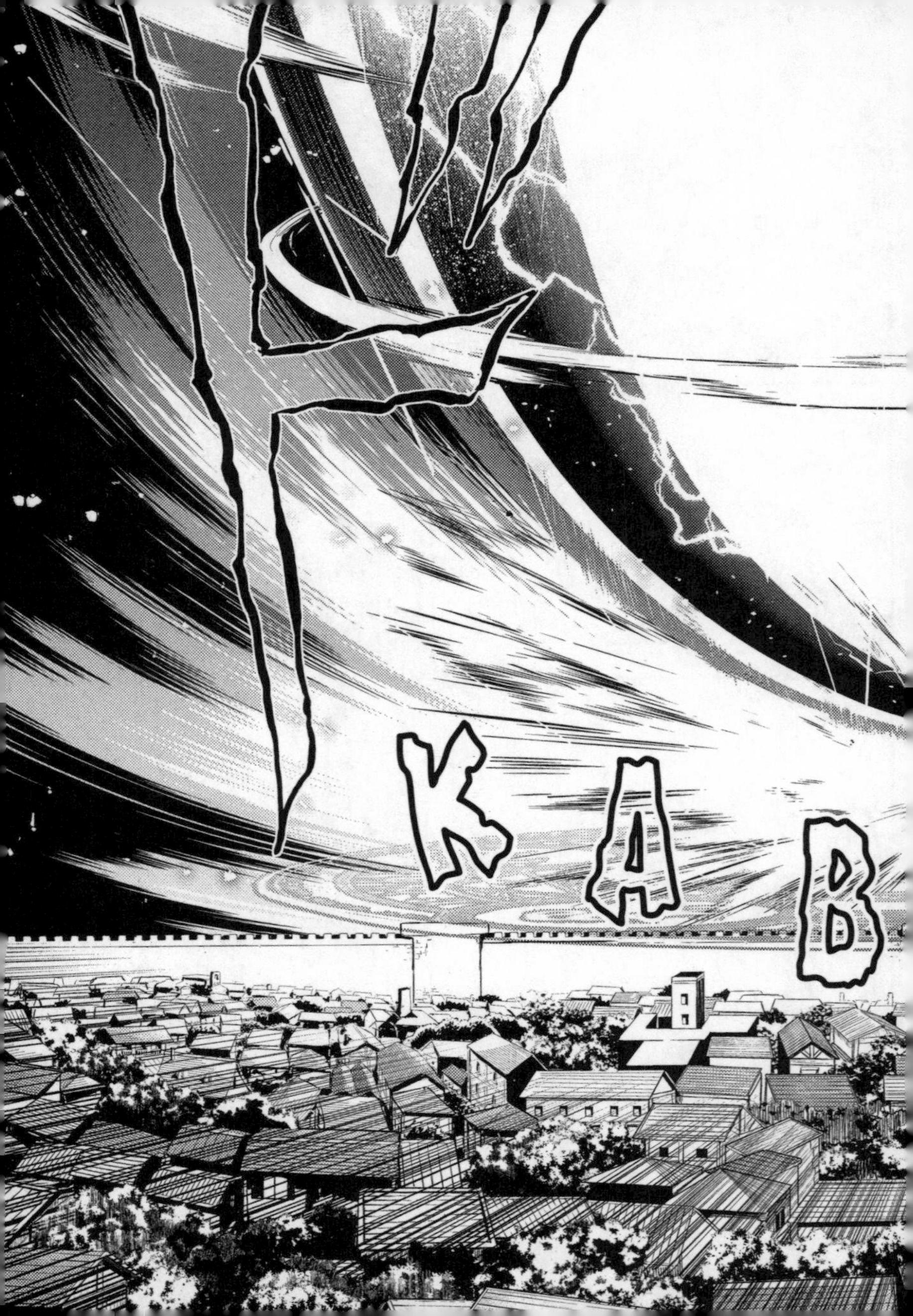
KAB

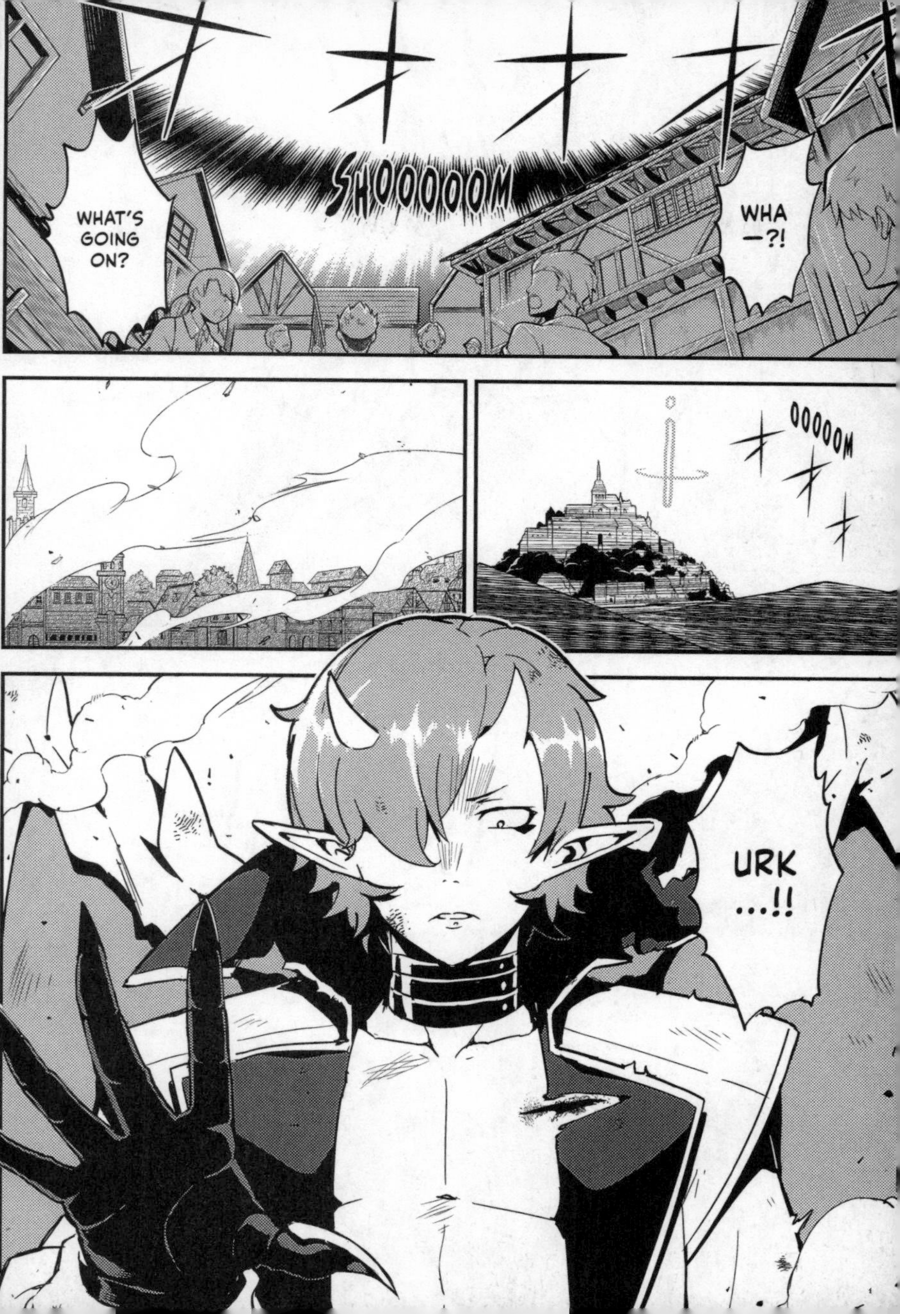
WHA —?!
SHOOOOOM
WHAT'S GOING ON?
OOOOOM
URK ...!!

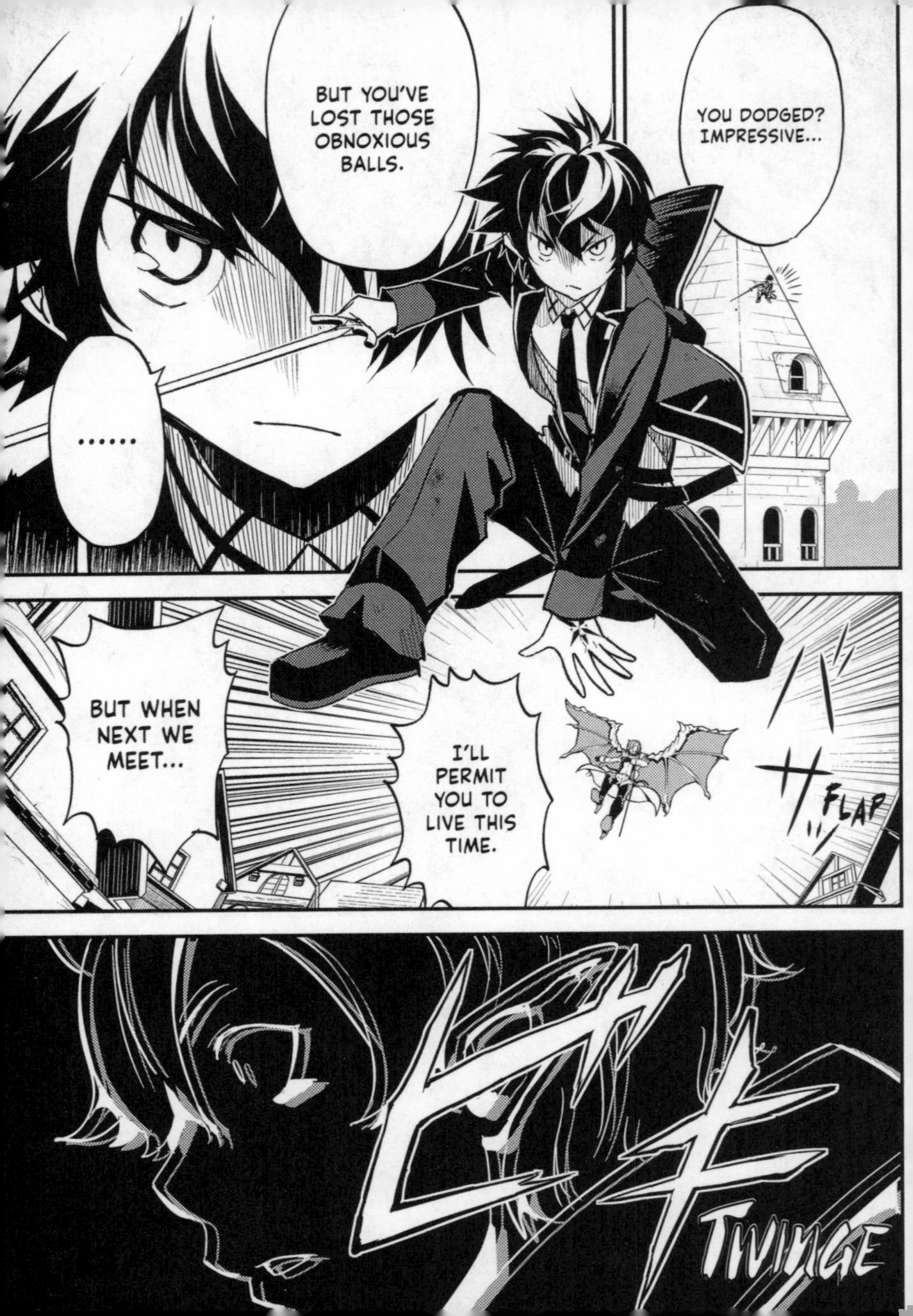
YOU DODGED? IMPRESSIVE...
BUT YOU'VE LOST THOSE OBNOXIOUS BALLS.
......
FLAP
I'LL PERMIT YOU TO LIVE THIS TIME.
BUT WHEN NEXT WE MEET...
TWINGE

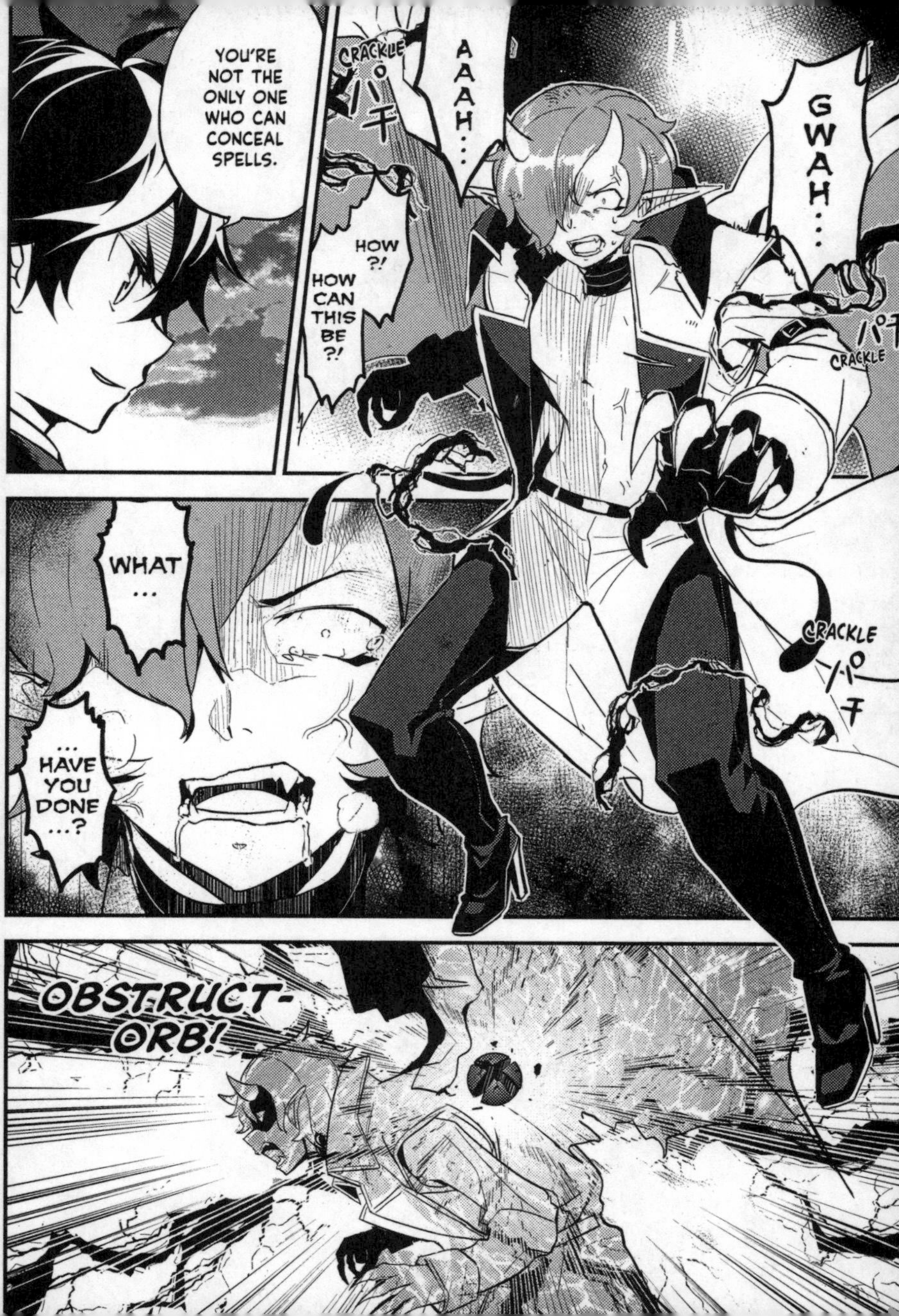
GWAH...
パチ
CRACKLE
AAAH...
CRACKLE
パチ
HOW?!
HOW CAN THIS BE?!
YOU'RE NOT THE ONLY ONE WHO CAN CONCEAL SPELLS.
CRACKLE
パチ
WHAT...
...HAVE YOU DONE...?
OBSTRUCT-ORB!

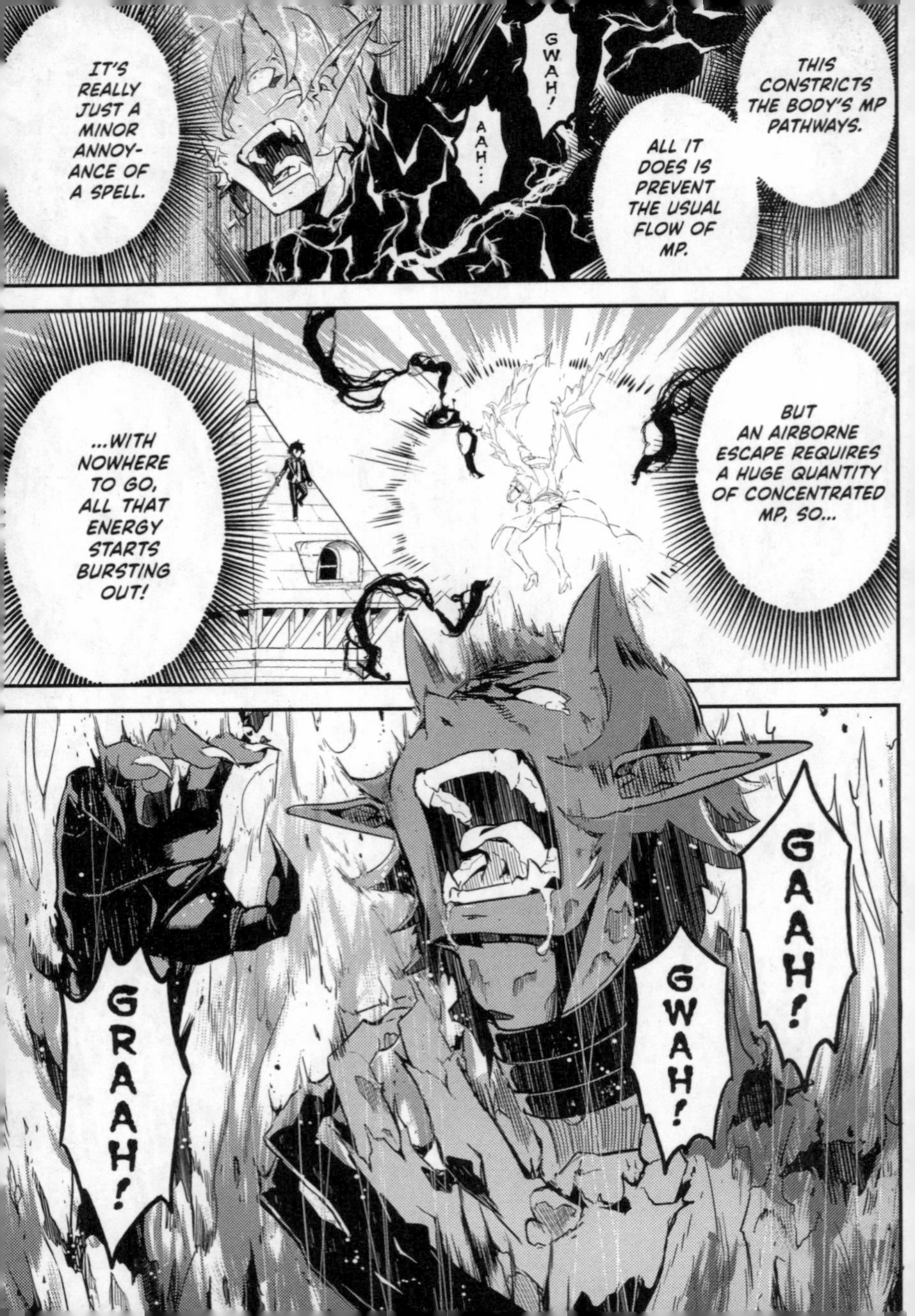
THIS CONSTRICTS THE BODY'S MP PATHWAYS.
ALL IT DOES IS PREVENT THE USUAL FLOW OF MP.
GWAH!
AAH...
IT'S REALLY JUST A MINOR ANNOY-ANCE OF A SPELL.
BUT AN AIRBORNE ESCAPE REQUIRES A HUGE QUANTITY OF CONCENTRATED MP, SO...
...WITH NOWHERE TO GO, ALL THAT ENERGY STARTS BURSTING OUT!
GAAH!
GWAH!
GRAAH!

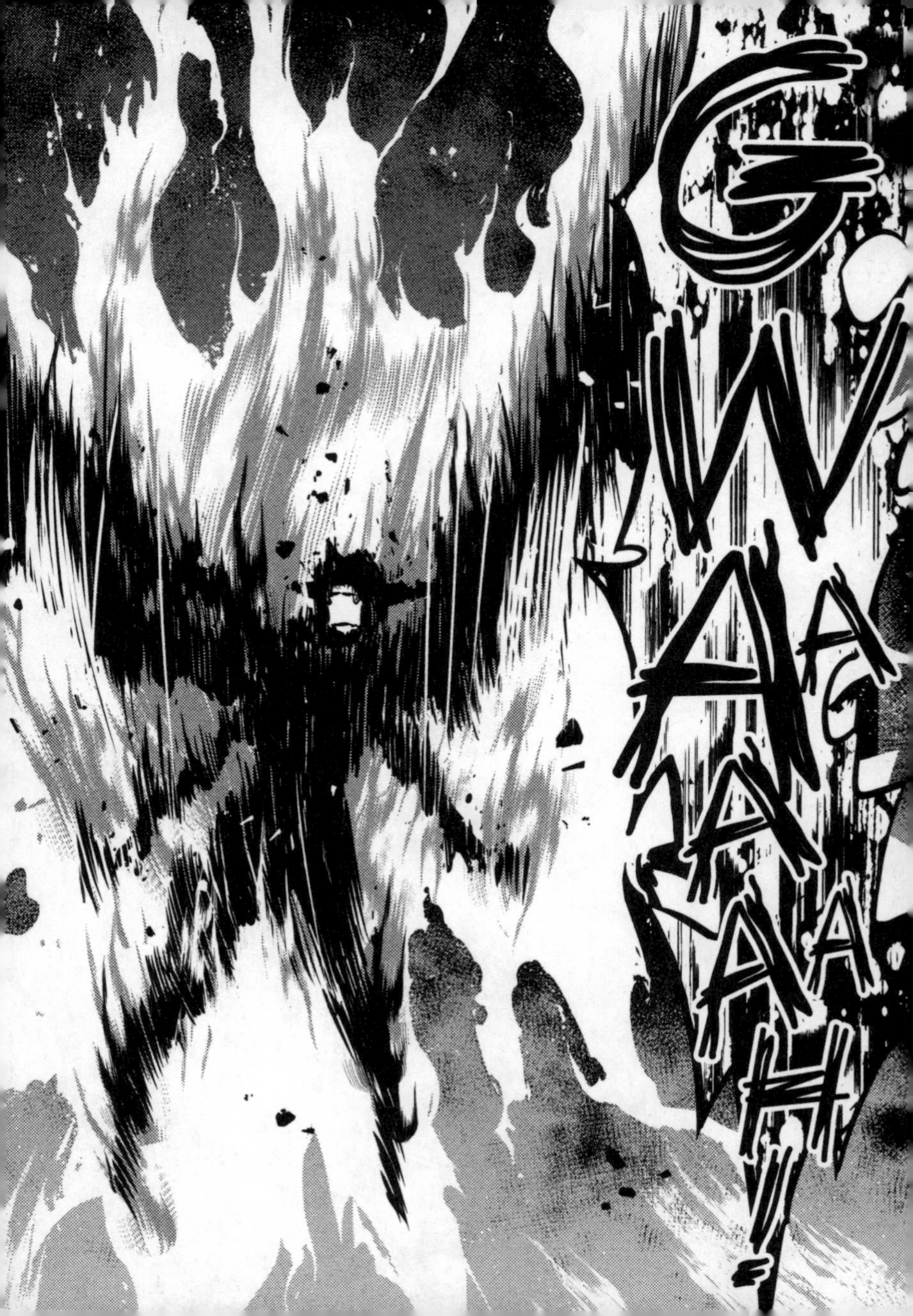
GWAAAAAH!

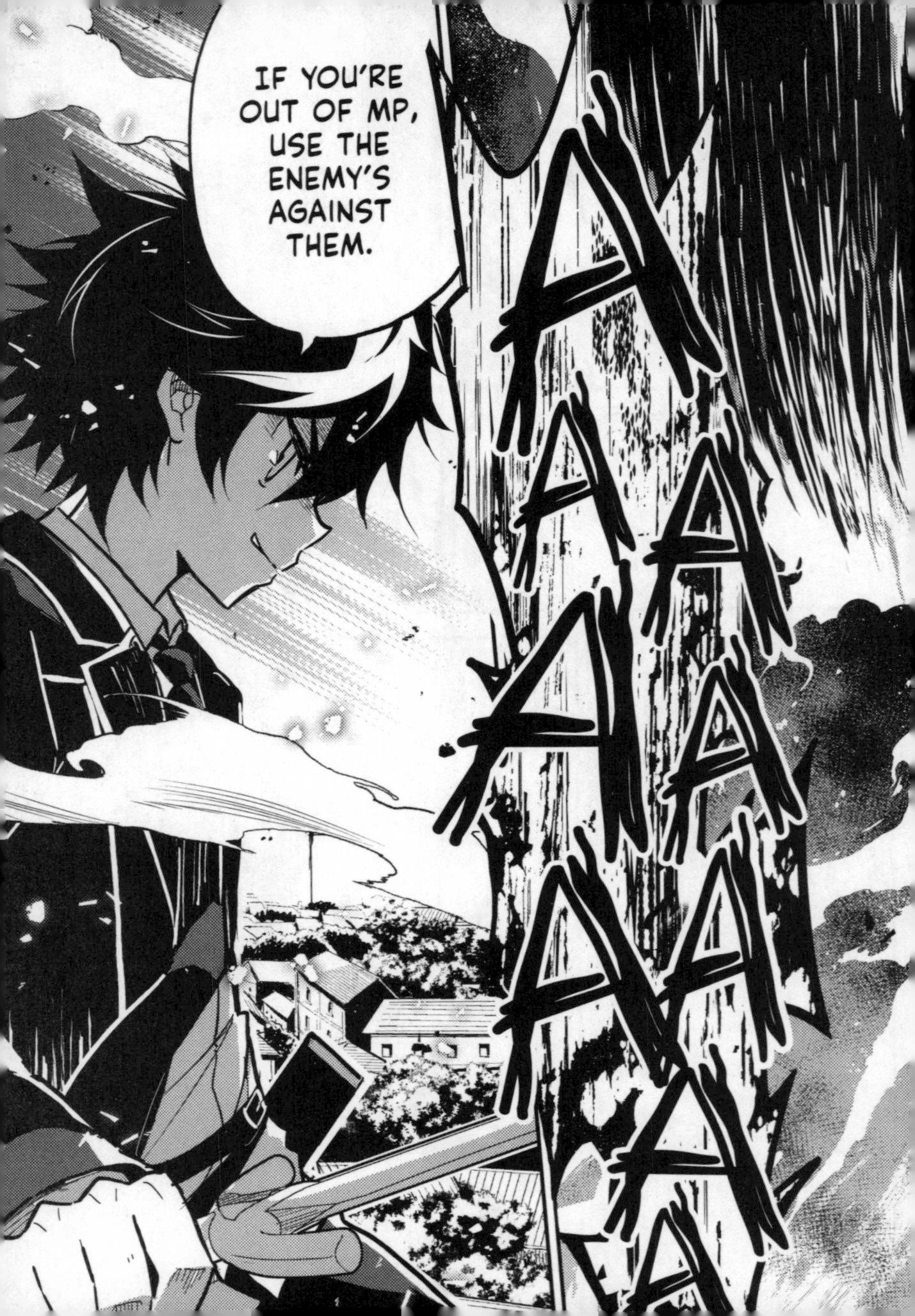
IF YOU'RE OUT OF MP, USE THE ENEMY'S AGAINST THEM.
AAAAAAAAA

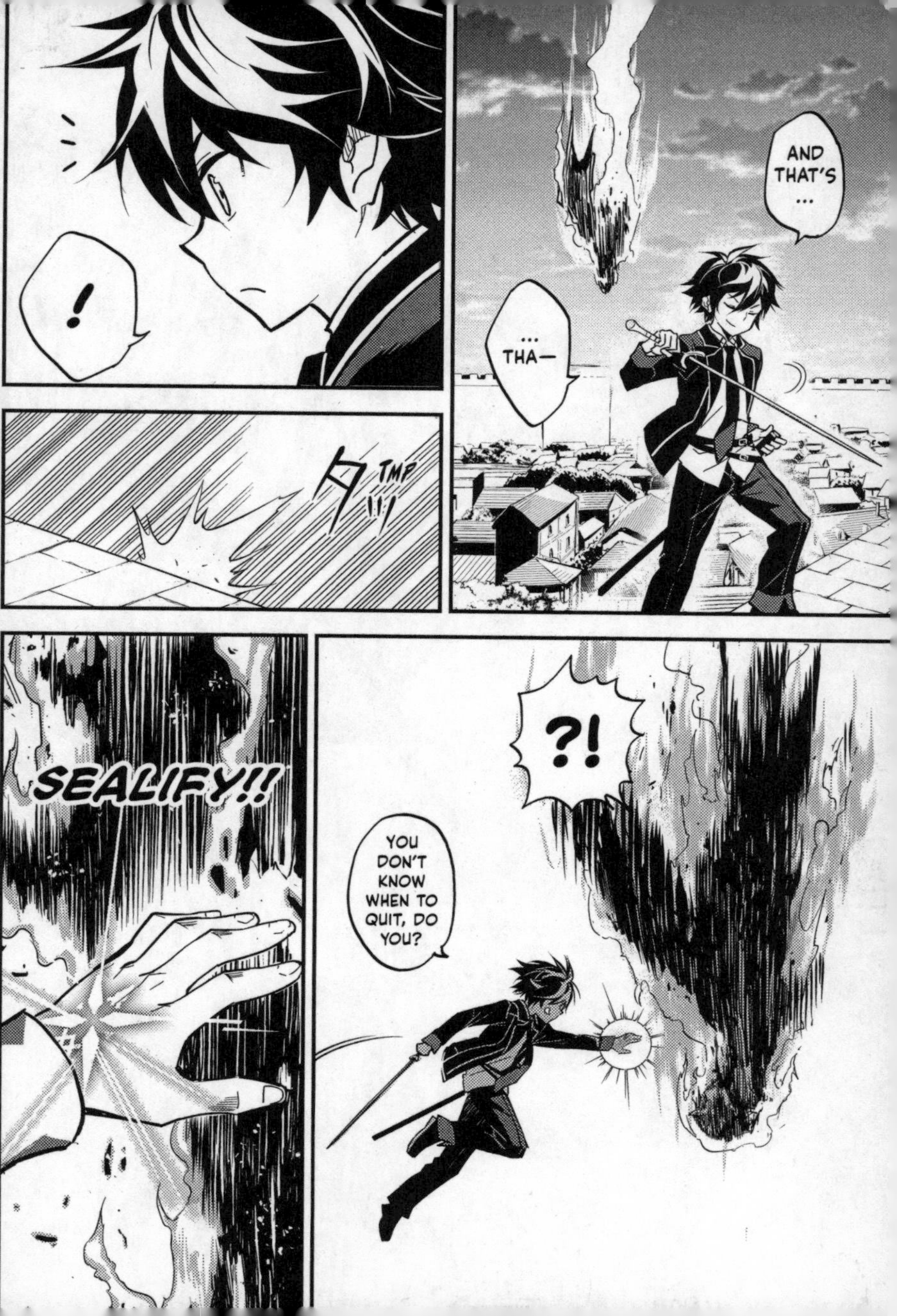
AND THAT'S ...
... THA—
!
TMP
?!
YOU DON'T KNOW WHEN TO QUIT, DO YOU?
SEALIFY!!

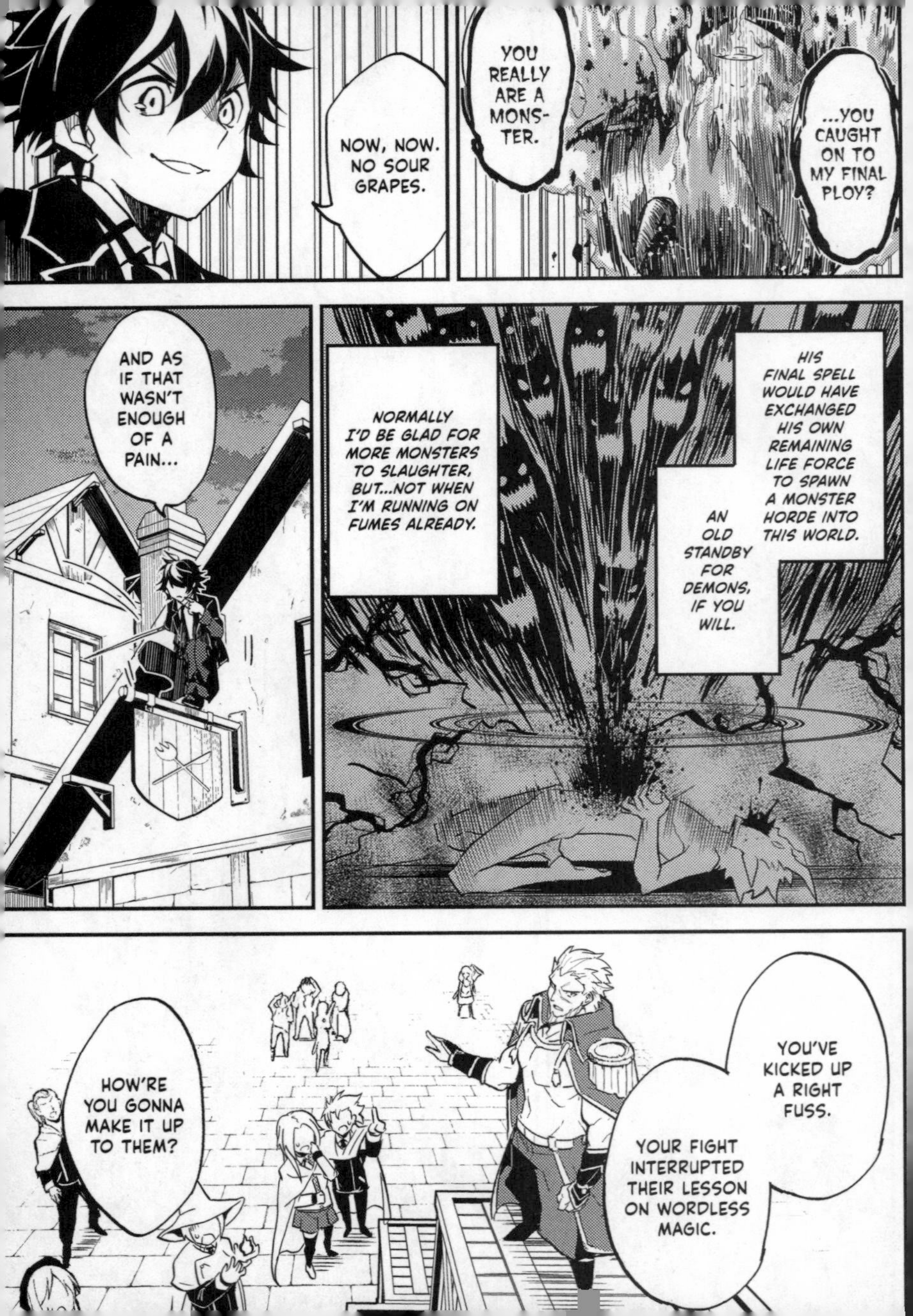
...YOU CAUGHT ON TO MY FINAL PLOY?
YOU REALLY ARE A MONS-TER.
NOW, NOW. NO SOUR GRAPES.
HIS FINAL SPELL WOULD HAVE EXCHANGED HIS OWN REMAINING LIFE FORCE TO SPAWN A MONSTER HORDE INTO THIS WORLD.
AN OLD STANDBY FOR DEMONS, IF YOU WILL.
NORMALLY I'D BE GLAD FOR MORE MONSTERS TO SLAUGHTER, BUT...NOT WHEN I'M RUNNING ON FUMES ALREADY.
AND AS IF THAT WASN'T ENOUGH OF A PAIN...
YOU'VE KICKED UP A RIGHT FUSS.
YOUR FIGHT INTERRUPTED THEIR LESSON ON WORDLESS MAGIC.
HOW'RE YOU GONNA MAKE IT UP TO THEM?

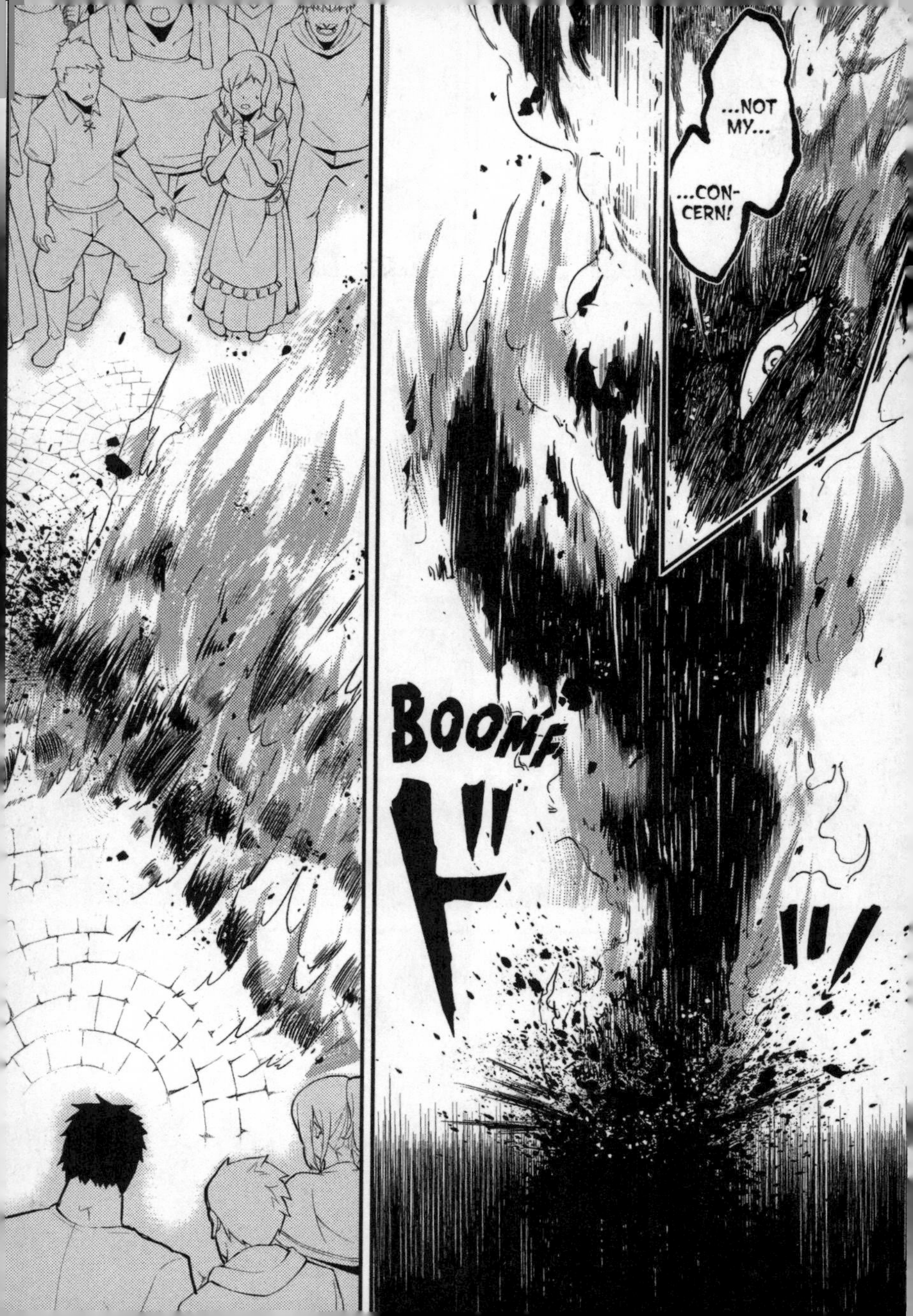
...NOT MY...
...CON-CERN!
BOOMF

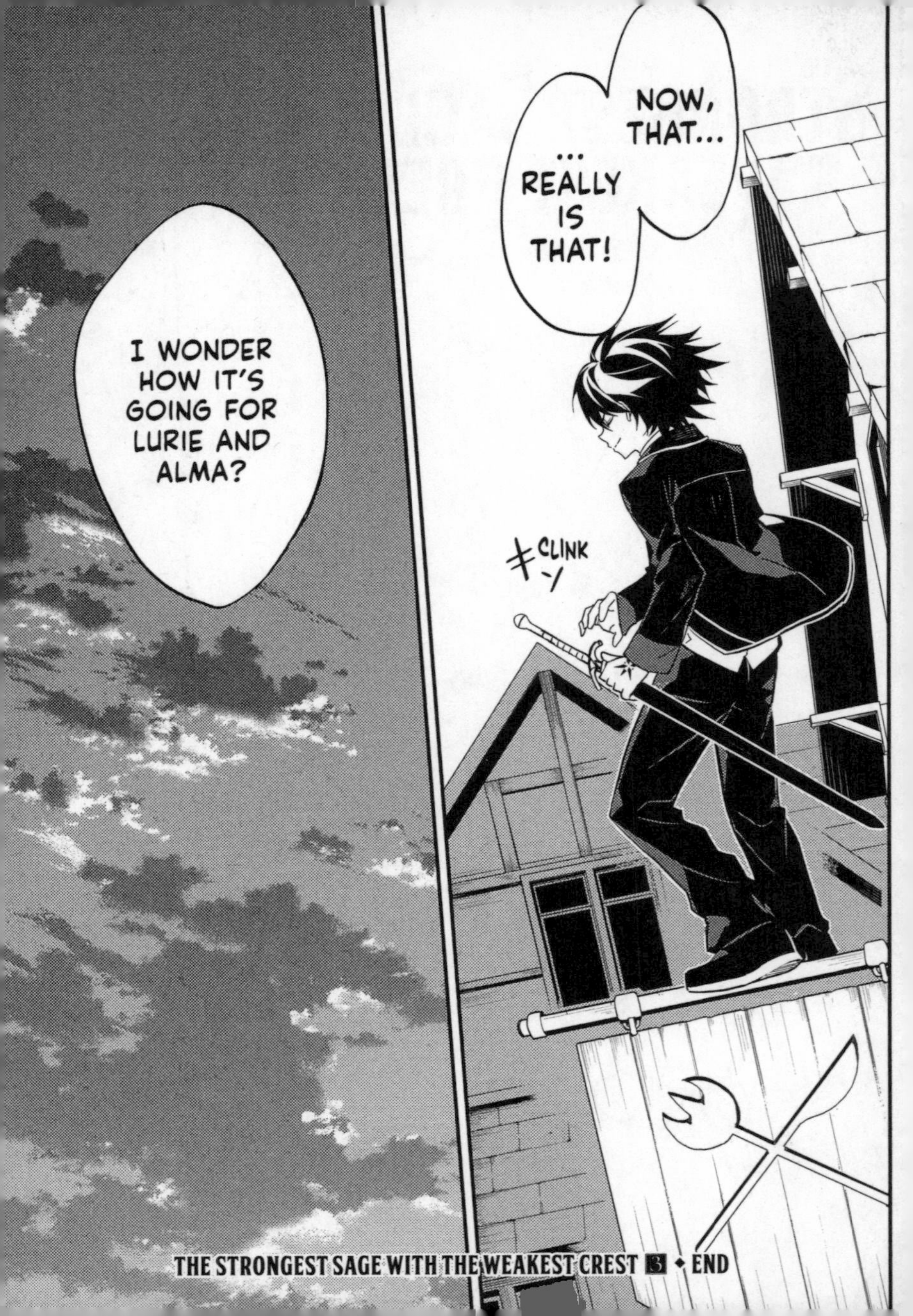
NOW, THAT...
...REALLY IS THAT!
CLINK
I WONDER HOW IT'S GOING FOR LURIE AND ALMA?

THE STRONGEST SAGE WITH THE WEAKEST CREST 3 ◆ END

THE STRONGEST SAGE WITH THE WEAKEST CREST

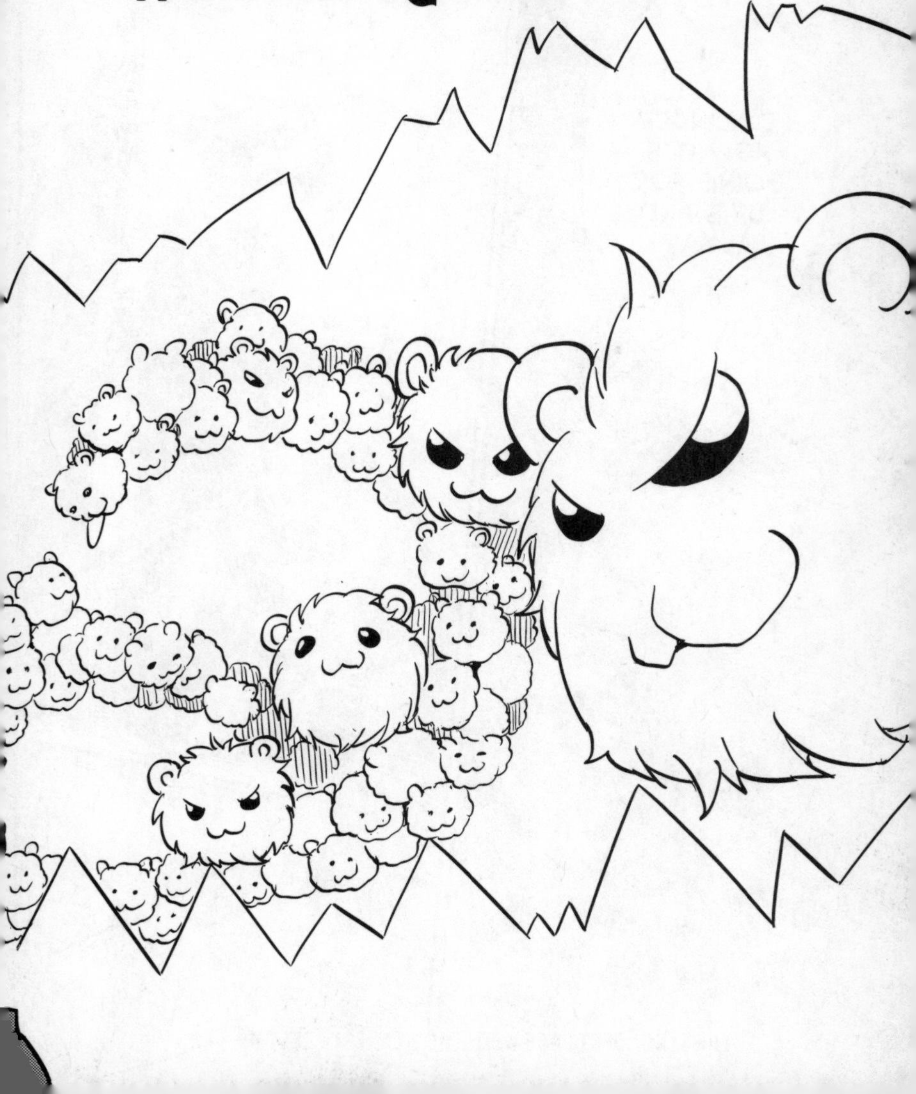

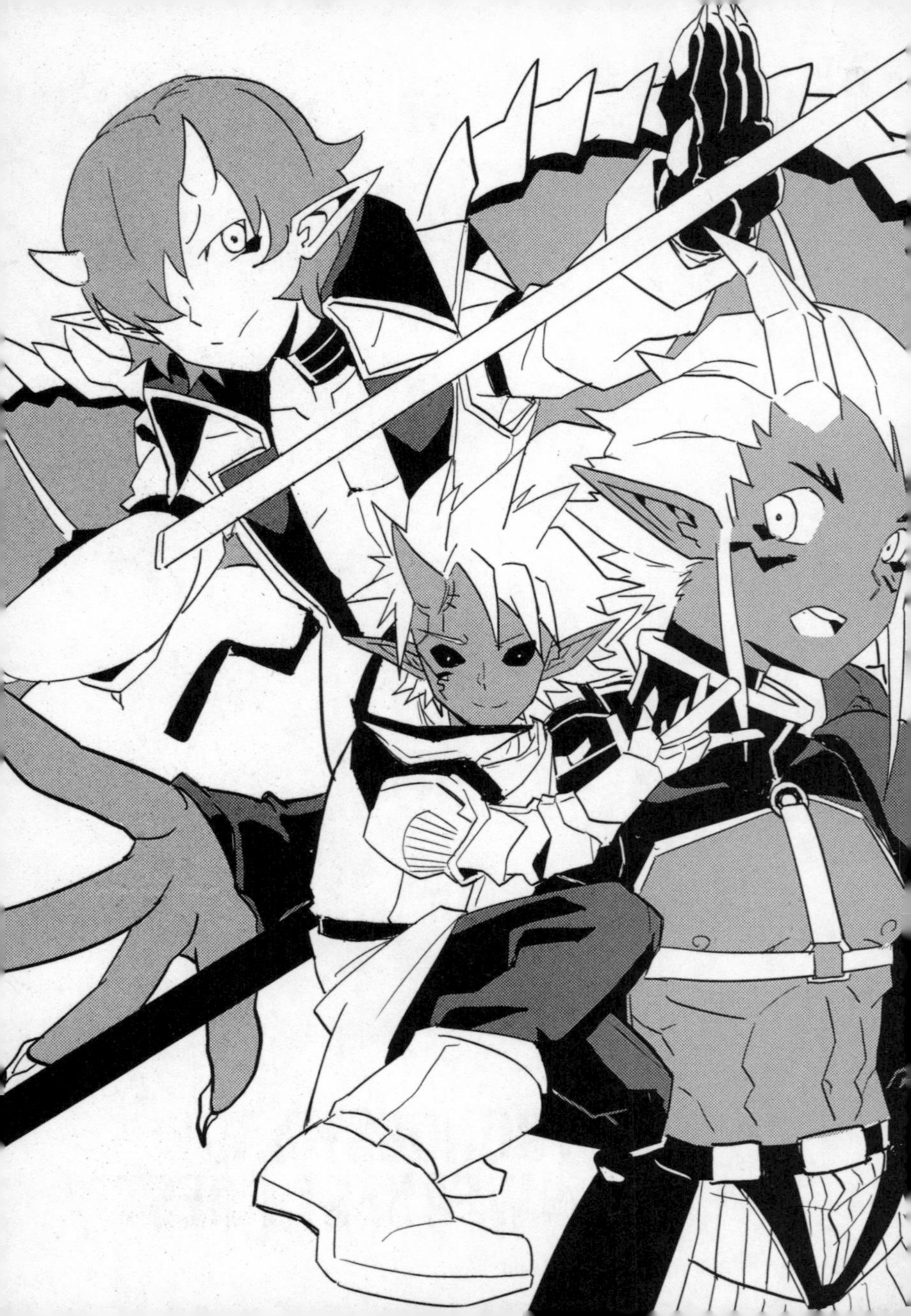

THE STRONGEST SAGE
with the WEAKEST CREST

To read a brand-new short story by Shinkoshoto, the author of *The Strongest Sage with the Weakest Crest*, please turn to page 172 of this book, where you'll find the story presented in left-to-right reading order!!

THE STRONGEST SAGE WITH THE WEAKEST CREST

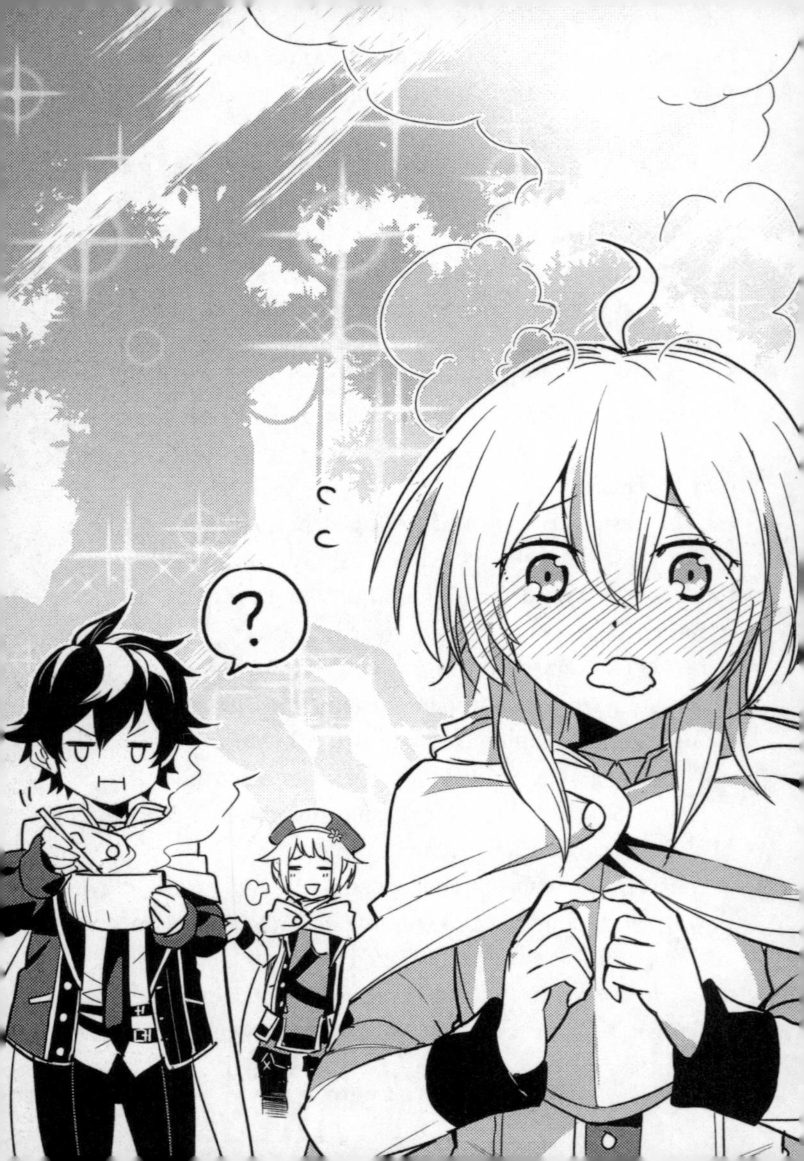
?

item's output. I didn't remember her packing it or the pot for this expedition, so she must have crafted both on the spot. From what I could tell, her ingredients were already poison-free and safe to eat.

Five minutes after we got there, Lurie's meal was ready to serve. It looked like a simple meat-based soup. What it was called, I couldn't say.

"Bon appétit, everyone!" said Lurie.

She refashioned the cooking pot into bowls with a crafting spell and doled out our portions. I took a taste.

"Delicious…" I mumbled.

"He ain't wrong! How the heck didja make something so tasty from the crap in this dungeon?" said Alma, heaping on the praise.

The dish was polished enough that I never would've guessed it involved any so-called "shortcuts." One wouldn't think soup would be filling, but the savory meat gave it unexpected volume. In a word…perfect. I could only remember a scant handful of people from my previous life who could whip up proper dungeon fare so quickly. As I thought on this while savoring my meal, Alma spoke up.

"You're gonna make a killer wife someday, Lurie!"

"Ah! A wife? Me? I couldn't possibly…" murmured Lurie, shooting a furtive glance at me.

Lurie thought she couldn't possibly be a wife? Oh, maybe she'd rather spend her time honing her magic item crafting.

We chatted some more, finished our meal, and got back to dungeon-crawling. But not before I thought I noticed Alma looking a bit fed up with me. Was it just my imagination?

THE END

"It might look tricky, but give it a try and you'll see it's no big deal. So collect some ingredients, get the hang of the detox process, and get cooking."

"No prob!"

"Very well!"

With that, Alma and Lurie went off to find food, but not ten minutes had passed when I heard a distant blast. A quick scan of magic signatures told me it was at Alma's location.

"Are you okay?! What happened?" I asked when I reached her.

With an awkward smile on her face, Alma held up a burnt husk of what I assumed started out as meat. She wasn't in any danger, but the crispy black lump no longer belonged in the category of "food."

"Um... So I tried purifying the meat with some MP, but then it decided to blow up in my face..." Alma explained.

An explosion? From a simple detox spell? Surely this girl was cursed by the culinary gods.

"All right, Alma. No more detox for you... Hang on to this for emergencies," I said, handing her a magic item made just for neutralizing poisons.

"Thanks," she said, stowing it in her pouch. "Though I hope it never comes to that."

She'd have to find herself in a real pinch to warrant using it, I thought, as we both made for Lurie's position. When we found her, Lurie was tossing ingredients into a pot and heating it with a magical item of her own. We were only fifteen minutes into the exercise, and she was nearly done cooking her meal.

"Since we're in a dungeon, I'm taking some shortcuts in the interest of time!" said Lurie as she boosted the heating

 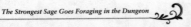

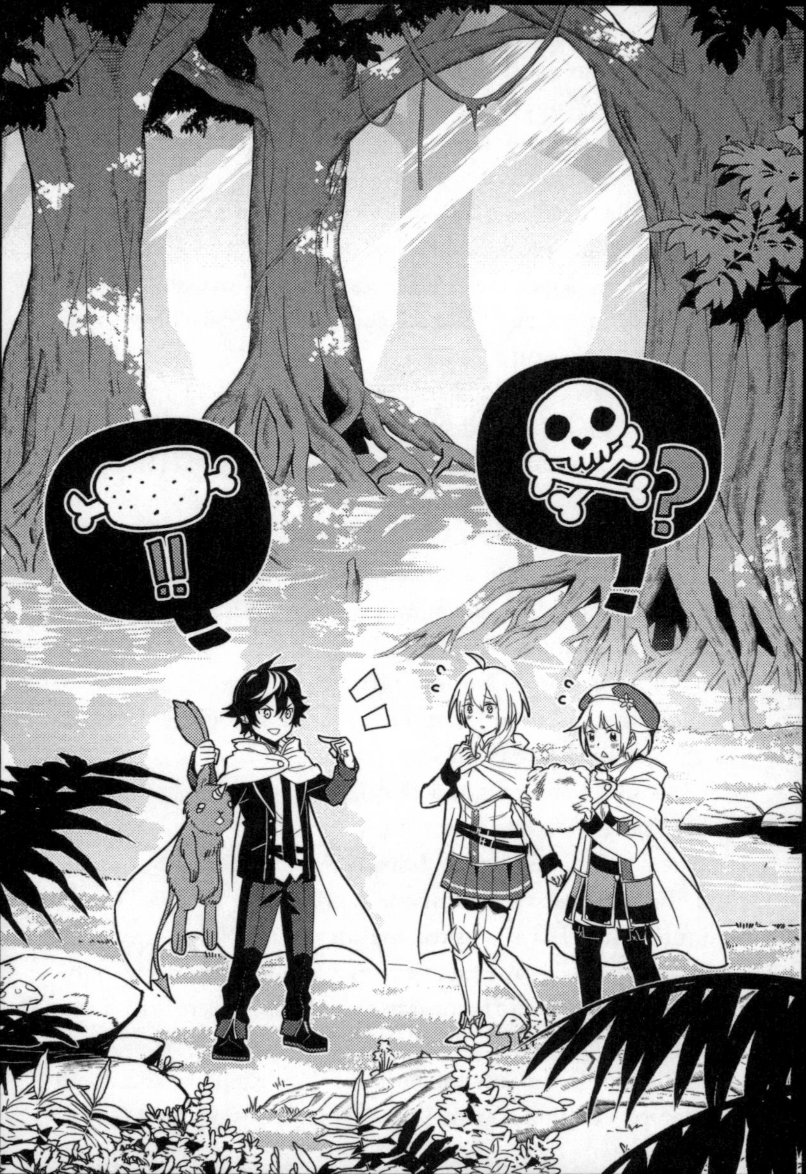

As suspected, people in this era knew little about keeping themselves fed inside a dungeon. Lurie wasn't entirely wrong, though—you can't just slay a monster and start chowing down, and about 90 percent of dungeon-dwelling plants are indeed poisonous. While three days is enough for the toxins to fade on their own, that strategy is only effective when you're doing your thing up on the surface; it won't cut it if you're down in the dungeon and need food in a hurry.

"Yeah, most stuff here is toxic, but there are two main ways to deal with it," I said.

"Two ways…?" said Lurie.

"Yep. Option one: Use a magic item to detox immediately after ingestion. I wouldn't recommend it myself. Stronger poisons can paralyze you before you can take the antidote."

"Yikes…" said Alma.

"Yes, let's not resort to that…" agreed Lurie. Both girls grimaced. I couldn't blame them.

"So we'll go with option two," I said. "Dungeon foodstuffs are only poisonous because of the corrupted magic energy that pervades such places. So we just have to clean up that energy with some of our own…"

As I spoke, I retrieved a chunk of monster meat from an earlier kill and began pumping some MP into it. The meat began to take on a somewhat more edible color.

"There," I said, "Poison neutralized."

"It's that simple?!" asked both girls in unison.

"Yep. No reason we can't cook this up for a feast."

I summoned an appropriately sized flame spell to roast the meat and popped a charred piece into my mouth. It tasted odd, to say the least, but that was nothing a little seasoning couldn't fix.

 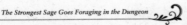

THE STRONGEST SAGE GOES FORAGING IN THE DUNGEON

by **Shinkoshoto**

"I think it's feeding time," I said, mid-dungeon crawl.

"Does that mean we're out of your gray emergency ration sticks?" asked Alma.

"No, I've still got a few of those, but I'm getting sick of them," I said.

"Sick of them? Really...?"

"It's not just that, though," I explained. "Knowing how to find food in the dungeon itself is the hallmark of a good adventurer."

There are a few tricks to foraging in a dungeon, so I figured they might as well get the knack sooner than later. Besides, none of the monsters on this level of the dungeon posed a threat to my two party members.

"Food in the dungeon, though...?" said Alma. "You mean there's grub just lyin' around?"

"I suppose there are plants and the monsters themselves," said Lurie. "But those are poisonous, and I've heard it takes up to three days for the toxins to be neutralized..."

THE STRONGEST SAGE WITH THE WEAKEST CREST

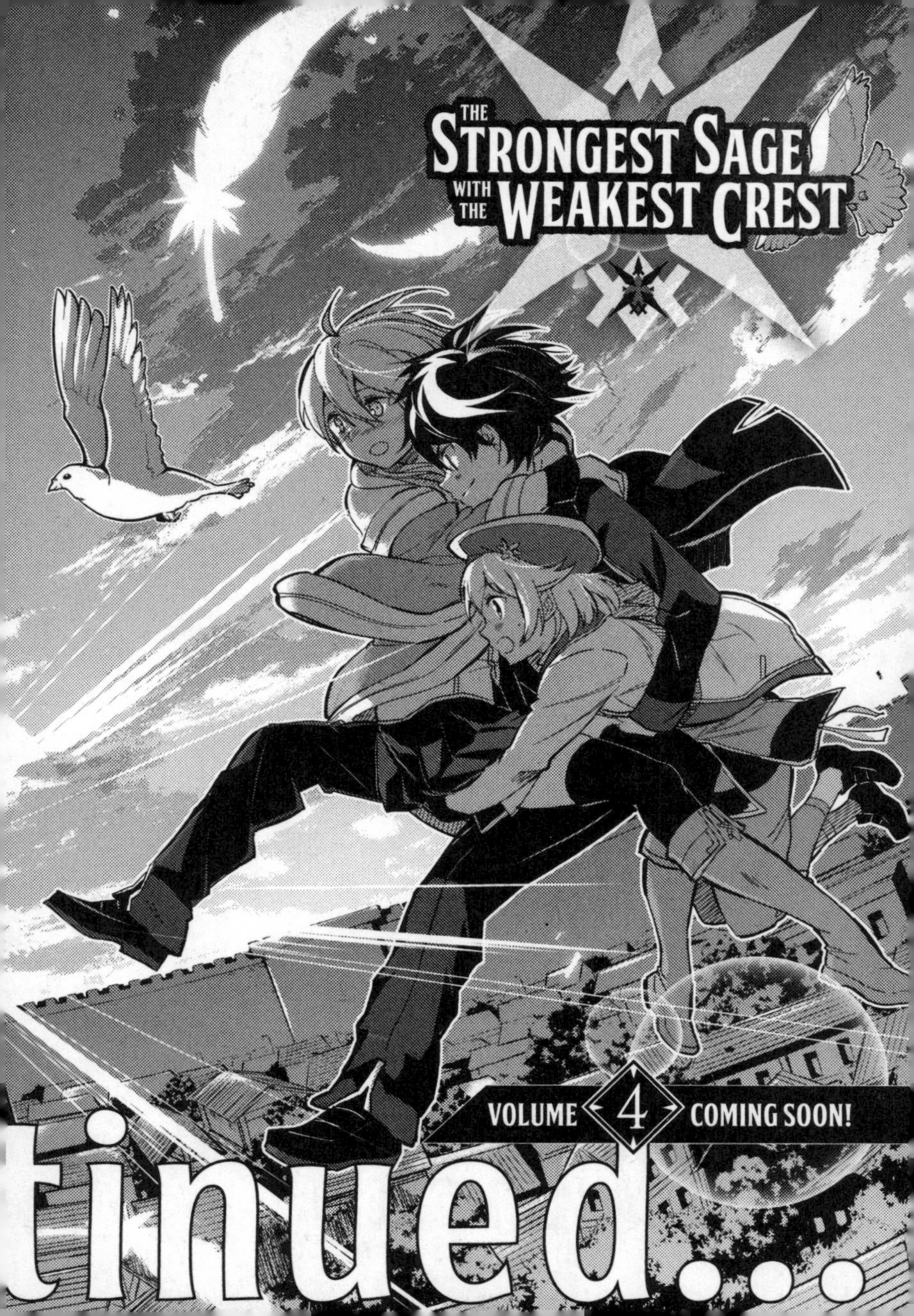
THE STRONGEST SAGE WITH THE WEAKEST CREST
VOLUME 4 COMING SOON!
tinued...